T0181431

Security Compliance in Model-driven Development of Software Systems in Presence of Long-Term Evolution and Variants

Sven Matthias Peldszus

Security Compliance in Model-driven Development of Software Systems in Presence of Long-Term Evolution and Variants

 Springer Vieweg

Sven Matthias Peldszus
Koblenz, Germany

Approved Dissertation thesis for the partial fulfillment of the requirements for a Doctor of Natural Sciences (Dr. rer. Nat.) at the Fachbereich 4: Informatik of the Universität Koblenz-Landau in Koblenz.
Chair of PhD Board: Prof. Dr. Ralf Lämmel
Chair of PhD Commission: Prof. Dr. Patrick Delfmann
Examiner and Supervisor: Prof. Dr. Jan Jürjens
Further Examiners: Prof. Dr. Malte Lochau, Dr. Daniel Strüber
Co-Supervisor: Dr. Amir Shayan Ahmadian
Date of the doctoral viva: December 10, 2021

ISBN 978-3-658-37664-2   ISBN 978-3-658-37665-9   (eBook)
https://doi.org/10.1007/978-3-658-37665-9

Planung/Lektorat: Stefanie Eggert
This Springer Vieweg imprint is published by the registered company Springer Fachmedien Wiesbaden GmbH part of Springer Nature.
The registered company address is: Abraham-Lincoln-Str. 46, 65189 Wiesbaden, Germany

"Science is fun. Science is curiosity. We all have natural curiosity. Science is a process of investigating. It's posing questions and coming up with a method. It's delving in."

—Sally Ride

Acknowledgements

First of all, I want to thank my supervisor Jan Jürjens for his support and feedback. It was a pleasure to work with you and being part of your group. During this time, you gave me the support for freely researching an interesting topic and finding my own research direction. You have always been there when I had questions or needed feedback.

I thank Malte Lochau and Daniel Strüber for immediately agreeing to function as second and third referees when I asked them. Thank you for spending your time reading this thesis. Also, many thanks got to the Ph.D. committee.

Thinking back to my time as Bachelor's and Master's student in Darmstadt, I would like to thank Malte Lochau, Géza Kulcsár, and Andy Schürr from the Real-Time Systems Lab at TU Darmstadt, and Sandro Schulze from the University of Magdeburg for introducing me to science. Without you, I would never have started writing this thesis. The interesting topics we have been working on, directly lead to this thesis. Also, our movie nights are unforgettable.

Many thanks go to Daniel Strüber for always giving me feedback and inspiring me in our joint research to do better research, independently of our joint time in Koblenz or your time in Gothenburg or Nijmegen. I am also grateful that you warmly welcomed me at my research visits to Gothenburg and Nijmegen.

Furthermore, I thank Shayan Ahmadian for not only co-supervising me but also being a friend. Most likely, you are the one who read this thesis the most times. Also, I will never forget our running sessions and game nights. I enjoyed working with you in the past five years.

The same applies to my current and former colleagues in Koblenz. Thank you very much for the good times we had. Special thanks go to Katharina GroßŸer, Marco Konersmann, Matthias Lohr, Qusai Ramadan, and Volker Riediger for proofreading this thesis.

Furthermore, many thanks to my other co-authors and project partners whom I have not yet mentioned by name. Also, to all students that directly or indirectly contributed to the research presented in this thesis. I enjoyed working with all of you. I want to thank the eMoflon team for supporting me whenever I faced issues with the technology used in this thesis.

I would like to thank my family, my parents Elke and Rüdiger, and my brother Tobias for always supporting me. Without your support, I would never have accomplished it. Finally, I would like to thank Andrea for always being there, supporting me, and reminding me of taking breaks from work when I forgot the world around me.

Koblenz
July 2021

Abstract

Many software systems tend to be used on a long-term basis, are highly intercon-
nected, share many common parts, and often process security-critical data. Due
to these trends, it is vital to keep up with ever-changing security precautions,
attacks, and mitigations for preserving a software system's security. Model-based
system development enables us to address security issues in the early phases of
the software design, e.g., using UMLsec in UML models or using SecDFDs.
Unfortunately, such design-time models are often inconsistent with the implementation or even among themselves. This inconsistency might cause security
violations. The main reason for this is continuous changes in the security assumptions and the design of software systems, for instance, due to structural decay. To
prevent such inconsistencies, all changes have to be reflected in both the design-
time models of the software system and the software system's implementation.
The detection of where which changes have to be applied has currently to be
performed manually by developers. As this task requires considering many and
often indiscernible dependencies, manual changes often give rise to new inconsistencies that are likely to lead to security violations. An additional burden to
detecting security violations and preserving a software system's maintainability
is potential reuse among different variants of an individual software system.

In this thesis, we present the GRaViTY approach for continuously supporting
developers with an automated propagation of changes on a single representation
of a software system to all other representations for avoiding inconsistencies. Our
synchronization is based on Triple Graph Grammars as supported by the eMoflon
transformation tool and currently supports bidirectional synchronization between
Java source code and UML class diagrams. Based on this synchronization, security experts can specify security requirements on the most suitable software
system representation using the UMLsec or SecDFD approach. For example,

domain models can be suitable for the classification of sensitive information of the domain and implementation models for tailoring encryption according to the planned deployment. We reuse these security requirements for the verification and enforcement of them on all representations of the software system using automated security checks. This allows us to verify whether the implementation is compliant with the specified security requirements, as needed in certifications. To preserve this compliance when restructuring the software system, we provide support for semantics preserving refactorings that are enriched with security preserving constraints. Here, we leverage the formalism of algebraic graph transformation rules for the specification and implemented these using the transformation tool Henshin. For both security checks and refactorings, we show how these can be applied to variant-rich software systems, also known as software product lines. For this purpose, we leverage an interpretation of OCL constraints on product lines and extend the Henshin tool to support variability. To allow the application of the approach to legacy systems, we show how variability-aware UML models can be reverse-engineered from an existing software product line using Antenna preprocessor statements and how existing early SecDFD design models can be semi-automatically mapped to the implementation. In addition to an evaluation of the single parts of the approach, the overall approach is demonstrated in two real-world case studies, the iTrust electronics health records system and the Eclipse Secure Storage.

Sven Matthias Peldszus
University of Koblenz-Landau
Koblenz, Germany

Zusammenfassung

Moderne Softwaresysteme werden über immer längere Zeiträume eingesetzt, stärker vernetzt, haben eine steigende Wiederverwertung und verarbeiten mehr sicherheitskritische Daten. Um die Sicherheit eines Softwaresysteme zu gewährleisten, ist es wichtig, mit sich ständig ändernden Sicherheitsvorkehrungen, Angriffen und Abwehrmaßnahmen Schritt zu halten. Die modellbasierte Entwicklung ermöglicht es, Sicherheitsprobleme bereits in frühen Softwareentwurfsphasen, z. B. mittels UMLsec auf UML-Modellen oder mittels SecDFDs, zu adressieren. Leider sind diese Entwurfsmodelle oft mit ihrer Implementierung oder sogar untereinander inkonsistent. Der Hauptgrund ist die kontinuierliche Veränderung von Sicherheitsannahmen und des Softwaresystemdesigns, z. B. aufgrund von strukturellem Verfall. Um solche Inkonsistenzen zu vermeiden, müssen alle Änderungen sowohl in den Entwurfsmodellen als auch in der Implementierung angewendet werden. Wo welche Änderungen angewendet werden müssen, muss derzeit manuell von den Entwicklern bestimmt werden. Da bei dieser Aufgabe viele und oft nicht erkennbare Abhängigkeiten berücksichtigt werden müssen, führen manuelle Änderungen häufig zu neuen Inkonsistenzen, die zu Sicherheitsproblemen führen können. Die hohe Wiederverwendung zwischen verschiedenen Varianten eines einzelnen Systems ist eine zusätzliche Belastung beim Erkennen von Sicherheitsproblemen und dem Wartbarhalten des Systems.

Zur Vermeidung von Inkonsistenzen stellt diese Dissertation einen Ansatz zur Unterstützung von Entwicklern basierend auf einer kontinuierlichen, automatisierten Änderungspropagation zwischen allen Systemrepräsentationen vor. Diese Änderungspropagation basiert auf einer Tripel-Graph-Grammatik, wie sie in eMoflon spezifiziert werden kann. Dabei unterstützen wir bidirektionale Änderungspropagationen zwischen Java Programmen und UML Klassendiagrammen. Durch diese Änderungspropagation wird Sicherheitsexperten ermöglicht,

Sicherheitseigenschaften mittels UMLsec oder SecDFD auf der am besten geeigneten Systemrepräsentation zu spezifizieren, z. B. Domänenmodelle zur Klassifizierung vertraulicher Informationen oder Implementierungsmodelle für Verschlüsselungen. Diese Sicherheitsspezifikationen werden automatisiert auf allen Systemrepräsentationen geprüft. Auf diese Weise kann nachgewiesen werden, dass die Implementierung der geplanten Sicherheitsspezifikation entspricht. Um diese Compliance bei einer Umstrukturierung zu erhalten, werden semantikerhaltende Refactorings, angereichert um sicherheitserhaltende Bedingungen, eingeführt. Diese Refactorings basieren auf algebraischen Graphtransformationen, die mittels Henshin spezifiziert werden. Sowohl für die Sicherheitsüberprüfungen als auch für die Refactorings zeigen wir deren Anwendung auf Softwareproduktlinien. Dafür verwenden wir eine Interpretation von OCL Constraints und haben das Transformationstool Henshin um eine Unterstützung von Variabilität erweitert. Um die Anwendung des Ansatzes auf Bestandssysteme zu unterstützen, zeigen wir, wie UML-Modelle, inklusive der Spezifikation von Varianten aus einer bestehenden Softwareproduktlinie, basierend auf Antenna Präprozessoranweisungen erstellt werden können und wie bestehende SecDFD Modelle halbautomatisch auf die Implementierung abgebildet werden können. Neben einer Evaluation der einzelnen Teile des Ansatzes wird der Gesamtansatz in zwei Open Source Fallstudien, dem elektronischen Patientenaktensystem iTrust und dem Eclipse Secure Storage, demonstriert.

Sven Matthias Peldszus
University of Koblenz-Landau
Koblenz, Germany

Contents

Part IV   Maintenance

Part V Variants

Abbreviations

AGT	Algebraic Graph Transformation
API	Application Programming Interface
ARTE	Automated Refactoring Test Environment
AST	Abstract Syntax Tree
BPMN	Business Process Model and Notation
CC	Common Criteria
CFG	Control Flow Graph
CIA	Confidentiality, Integrity, and Availability
CRA	Class Responsibility Assignment
CSC	Create SuperClass Refactoring
CVE	Common Vulnerability Enumeration
CVSS	Common Vulnerability Scoring System
CWE	Common Weakness Enumeration
DFD	Data Flow Diagram
DSL	Domain Specific Language
EA	Enterprise Architect
EU	European Union
EMF	Eclipse Modeling Framework
FF	Fully Flattened
FN	False Negative
FP	False Positive
GC	Garbage Collection
GDPR	General Data Protection Regulation
GSM	Global System for Mobile Communications
HCP	Health Care Personnel
HCS	Health Care System

HTML	HyerText Markup Language
HTTP	HyerText Transfer Protocol
ID	IDentifier
IDE	Integrated Development Environment
IEC	International Electrotechnical Commission
ISO	International Organization for Standardization
JDK	Java Development Kit
JVM	Java Virtual Machine
JSP	Java Server Page
JSSE	Java Secure Socket Extension
LAN	Local Area Network
LHCP	Licensed Health Care Professional
LHS	Left Hand Side
LLOC	Logical Lines of Code
LOC	Lines of Code
MBSD	Model-based Software Development
MDD	Model-driven Software Development
MID	Medical IDentification name
NAC	Negative Application Condition
OCL	Object Constraint Language
OMG	Object Management Group
OO	Object-Orientation
OOP	Object-Oriented Programming
PF	Partially Flattened
PM	Program Model
PUM	Pull-Up Method Refactoring
RHS	Right Hand Side
RQ	Research Question
SAR	Security Assurance Requirement
SAT	Boolean Satisfiability Problem
SFR	Security Functional Requirement
SPL	Software Product Line
SQL	Structured Query Language
TGG	Triple Graph Grammar
TN	True Negative
TP	True Positive
UML	Unified Modeling Language

UMLsec	UML for Secure Systems Development
VB	Variability-based
VisiOn	Visual Privacy Management in User Centric Open Environments
XML	Extensible Markup Language

List of Figures

List of Tables

Listings

Part I
Opening Chapters

Introduction 1

Software has become a considerable part of today's life and is present everywhere around us. Nearly every device, including smartphones, TVs, fridges, and many more, is connected as part of the internet of things, and we rely on them to be safe, secure, and respect our privacy. The same trends are also entering more critical domains such as health care. For example, modern medical imaging devices such as computer tomography scanners or ultrasound machines come with a network connection and a software application that allows storing and managing the images centrally and specialists to access these from anywhere. Furthermore, modern software systems tend to be used on a long-term basis in environments prone to changes, and at the same time successors of a software system are developed rapidly. Here, a successor is often a variant of the previous system as significant parts are reused. Besides, multiple variants of a software system can exist at the same time, e.g., computer tomography scanners supporting a different number of acquired slices. In all cases, all changes, e.g., due to maintenance or extension, have to be continuously reflected in the whole software system, including all variants. These trends result in significant challenges regarding the correctness changes and the security of evolving software systems or their variants.

Traditionally, manufacturers of devices ensure their products' security by providing legal certifications. However, concerning today's short product cycles and the vast amount of product versions, certifying each product manually is impossible. For achieving a certification, it is necessary to consider all security-relevant aspects of the software system, which requires a substantial manual effort and is error-prone. Due to these circumstances, a product is certified quite often after its successor on the market has already replaced it. An example of this is smartphones certified for use in critical positions. The SiMKo 3 high-security cell phone, which was certified in September 2013 for usage by the German government [1], was based on a Samsung Galaxy S3 that was released in May 2012 and replaced by the Galaxy

S. M. Peldszus, *Security Compliance in Model-driven Development of Software Systems in Presence of Long-Term Evolution and Variants*, https://doi.org/10.1007/978-3-658-37665-9_1

S4 in March 2013. Also, even minor bug fixes are often not allowed without losing the certification of a product. One missing key to improve security is integrated tool support covering all software development phases. Tool support can reduce the manual effort required for certification and avoid mistakes during the certification. Furthermore, tool support can already support avoiding security violations during implementation. Nonetheless, the discussed trends continue to complicate keeping up with the ever-changing security precautions, attacks, and mitigations that are vital for preserving a software system's security. Therefore, it seems reasonable why a recent developer study pinpoints security as the number-one concern to be addressed by future software analysis tools [2].

A widely accepted approach for the successful development of software systems is *Model-Driven Development* (MDD) [3, 4]. MMD allows planning a software system's design upfront on an abstract level before implementing the software system. This development approach allows developing a well-structured software system, that can include systematic variation points for future extensions or variants of the software system. Furthermore, it enables us to address security issues in the early phases of the software design, such as in models specified at design time using the Unified Modeling Language (UML) [5, 6]. In many domains, establishing such appropriately documented design-time artifacts is mandatory due to legal requirements. For example, in the medical domain, for medical device software, the ISO/IEC 62304 standard requires various documentation artifacts based on the criticality of the medical device [7]. These artifacts range from the development planning documentation, the documentation of requirements through the planned software design to the concrete software implementation of the medical device. All these artifacts are created when following the model-driven development approach [8]. Unfortunately, the documentation artifacts created at model-driven development are often inconsistent with the software system's current state [9]. Such an inconsistency can lead to significant effort for harmonizing all artifacts before a certification.

One reason for this inconsistency lies in the way how software is developed. In the past, powerful IDEs, e.g., supporting near real-time syntax checks and fast compilation, were not available, requiring developers to think more about the source code upfront and write down large fragments in one go before executing and testing the new fragment. Although this allowed the implementation of amazing software systems, e.g., the Guidance Computer of the Apollo 11 mission [10], the manageable complexity was limited. In contrast to this, considering how software is developed nowadays, programming practices often incorporate consecutive steps of edits, updates, refinements, and other enhancements at the source code level to improve a program under development and meet ever-changing requirements incrementally [11]. In other words, programs consecutively evolve throughout their entire life-cycle due to the nature of modern software engineering [12, 13]. Moreover, continuous evolution also means that programs are prone to internal decay due to the often ad-hoc nature of program edits which may cause software systems to arrive at incomprehensible or even inconsistent states eventually. Such a decrease in design quality is called software aging [13] and often leads to an increase in the effort required for extending and maintaining a software system. Simultaneously, these low-level implementation changes are often not reflected in the software system's design-time models. Such inconsistencies might result in certification issues as the delivered design-time artifacts are not compliant with the implementation.

Usually, a software system is specified at the implementation level using a high-level programming language. These languages provide an abstraction from low-level languages close to CPU instructions, such as Assembler [14]. High-level languages mainly differ in their syntax as well as the programming paradigms realized for abstraction. Currently, one of the most used paradigms is the object-oriented (OO) programming paradigm [15]. This programming paradigm is an essential milestone towards improved program modularity and maintainability. Object-oriented programming concepts allow for enforcing essential program and data structures, e.g., through applying design patterns [16].

In practice, due to the continuous evolution, software systems need frequent restructuring to stay within the desired patterns. To support the efficient restructuring of a software system, refactorings have been proposed and documented in a human-readable form [17, 18]. As a consequence, tool-support for conducting (semi-)automated program refactorings has become an integral part of modern Java IDEs such as IntelliJ IDEA[1] and Eclipse[2]. Despite intense studies and widespread application, a verifiable specification of refactoring operations and the execution of this specification is still an open problem. The same applies to the interaction of refactorings with non-functional properties of the software system, such as security.

Furthermore, when a company develops a new product, the software is nearly never written from scratch. Instead, there is a significant amount of reuse among the company's different products [19]. Often, a company's products are developed as variants of a variant-rich software system, which is also often referred to as a software product line. Thereby, the software product line contains a base part contained in every product and variable parts specific only for one or more products. However, for a product's certification, this specific product's software will be reviewed and certified. Usually, there is no reuse among single certifications [20]. The variability introduced by this extensive reuse among products leads to a second challenge. For

---

[1] https://www.jetbrains.com/idea

[2] https://www.eclipse.org

products with many variants and variations, it is infeasible to check every product within a reasonable time, e.g., regarding OO design quality or security. For example, considering OO design-quality checks, a single anti-pattern detection for a medium-sized program with around 50k lines of code already takes around 20 minutes for a single product [21]. If we want to check the entire product line product by product, the test takes over 100 years if the product line contains 22 independent features. Every feature can be selected or not selected, giving two possible states per feature resulting in $2^{22} = 4,194,304$ possible feature configurations. As every check takes 20 minutes, checking all configurations takes 8.3886×10^7 minutes or 159.6 years.

To summarize, the increasing amount of security-critical data and faster changing environments are a burden to develop secure software systems. Nevertheless, there are already some approaches to tackle the single sub-problems.

1.1   Problem Identification

Considering the outlined trends one can assume that these are tackled by existing solutions sufficiently. Unfortunately, in summary, these different improvements in technology for supporting software development processes are not enough to compensate for all of these trends complicating the development of secure and long-living software. Especially, the demand for security planning and compliance in combination with continuous change throughout the whole life cycle, eventually, in combination with variants of a software system, is challenging. Considering existing solutions, we identify open problems regarding the development and maintenance of secure software systems.

Non-integrated solutions: For supporting the successful development of secure software systems, various approaches have been developed. First, there are high-level programming languages that allow effective structuring and reuse within a software system, e.g., following the OO paradigm. Refactorings support the structuring of the software for constantly preserving a maintainable structure of the software system throughout development. Also, approaches like MDD allow the planning of the software system's structure. However, such solutions mostly neglect essential aspects like security, have not been evaluated on more practical subjects, or do not cover the whole development life cycle of a software system. Considering MDD, there are approaches that allow developers to include security considerations from the very beginning [6]. In the best case, these security considerations can be reused until certification of the final product. In practice, there are many non-integrated solutions that do not allow reuse or might be entirely incompatible.

Inconsistency and missing traceability: Often, a software system's initial security requirements specification and the created documentation are inconsistent with the implementation's later versions [22, 23]. The continuous changes in the security assumptions and the design of software systems, for instance, due to structural decay [13], have to be reflected in both the design-time models, e.g., UML models, and the software system's implementation. Furthermore, the implementation can include additional artifacts such as program models, e.g., used for static analysis or verification. Currently, the developers need to manually trace among the different available artifacts to identify and apply a necessary change at proper locations in the software system concerning the corresponding artifacts. The effort to create such correspondences after the fact is still high even if this process is guided by tool support, e.g., for creating a correspondence model between design-time models and source code [23]. Also, there is no approach providing an assisted development methodology covering multiple phases and supporting roundtrip engineering. Thus, we have to maintain correspondences between different artifacts used in the different development phases from the very beginning and automate the underlying mapping process as much as possible.

Security-aware restructuring: As software systems are continuously subject to changes, we also have to continuously check their security compliance, e.g., with design-time security requirements or obligatory standards. In the best case, we can evaluate the desired change before applying it to the software system. A problem often mentioned by practitioners is that they cannot apply simple refactorings to a software system without losing the certification of the system. Although there are catalogs of well-defined refactorings [18] and approaches to check their applicability [24], we still have to solve two problems. First, even when the applicability of a refactoring has been checked, these are often applied in an ad-hoc manner. Accordingly, there is no guarantee for the correctness of the refactoring operation that is needed for preserving a certification. Second, current refactoring approaches do not take non-functional properties, e.g., security, into account. In summary, security-preserving restructurings of the software system are required for supporting the restructuring of security-critical systems without losing a certification or requiring a complete re-certification.

Variant-rich software systems: Last but not least, all of these discussed measures must also be applied to variant-rich software systems. The application of every single existing solution to each product of a software product line is possible, but due to the vast amount of possible products, this is not feasible within a reasonable time. Accordingly, we need means for applying security compliance checks and security-preserving refactorings to software product lines.

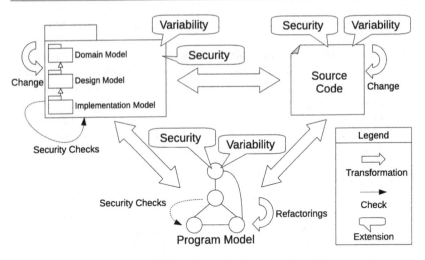

Figure 1.1 Concept of the GRaViTY software development and maintenance approach

1.2   Outline of the Approach

To overcome the discussed problems, we propose the GRaViTY approach to support developers in developing secure variant-rich software systems. The key idea is that developers should focus on their tasks while everything else is automatically handled in the background. In this thesis, we consider three kinds of tasks.

1. We consider the specification as well as the subsequent refinement of the software system's architecture,
2. the implementation of the software system following the specified architecture, and
3. the specification and enforcement of security throughout the whole development process.

Considering the discussed problems, multiple artifacts are involved in the development of a variant-rich software system. Figure 1.1 provides an overview of the artifacts considered in our approach, their relations, and activities executed on these. According to the figure, for performing the three outlined tasks, we consider three kinds of artifacts:

1. design-time models, e.g., specified in UML,
2. source code, e.g., written in Java, and
3. a program model (PM) of the source code for automatically performing analyses.

Changes on any of these artifacts are continuously synchronized for covering the different phases of software development, allowing developers to focus on their tasks. In the figure, this synchronization is indicated by bidirectional arrows connecting the artifacts.

For allowing our approach to consider security and variability, the different artifacts are extended with security as well as variability in terms of annotations. Here, we make use of existing approaches as far as possible. For example, considering design-time models, e.g., on UML models, we use the UMLsec profile proposed by Jürjens [6] for security annotations. For variability annotations, e.g., on Java source code, we benefit from preprocessor-like variability statements as defined in Antenna [25].

Using these extensions, we will present a synchronization between the different artifacts taking both security and variability into account. For this purpose, we utilize triple graph grammars (TGG), a model transformation language and tooling that allows incremental model synchronization, and the UML inheritance mechanism. Such transformation languages can also be used to specify and perform design analyses as already demonstrated for anti-pattern detection on a single product in [21]. Following this example, we specify security compliance checks and security-preserving refactorings for ensuring the software system's security throughout the whole development process.

For applying the developed checks and refactorings to SPLs, existing transformation technologies like Algebraic Graph Transformation (AGT) have to be extended to support variability. Here, we consider AGT as realized in the tool Henshin [26] or Triple Graph Grammars (TGG) of eMoflon [27]. Providing such an extension, we demonstrate how security compliance checks and security-aware refactorings can be executed on a software product line efficiently.

1.3   Research Questions

Based on the problems identified previously and the outlined approach, we formulate five research questions, that we will answer in this thesis. Figure 1.2 shows the location of the research questions in the proposed software development and maintenance approach. First, traces between security requirements on different system representations have to be established and maintained automatically. For this reason, RQ1 focuses on the tracing and synchronization of the different considered artifacts. In practice, many security-critical software systems have been developed in the past, are still in use, and under maintenance. Accordingly, the second research question (RQ2) aims to identify how we can support these legacy systems in the approach developed in this thesis. The goal of the desired synchronization is twofold. On the one side, we will use the generated trace links to propagate security requirements specified on the UML models into the implementation. These trace links allow us to check security requirements on the UML models and verify them on the implementation level using corresponding security checks considered in RQ3. On the other side, all artifacts have to be kept synchronized after changes. Thereby, following Figure 1.2, we consider manual changes on the UML models and implementation as well as refactorings performed on the program model. Utilizing the generated trace links, we can study the effects of changes on traced security requirements in RQ4. Finally, we study how we can apply the developed solutions to software product lines in RQ5.

RQ1:   How can security requirements be traced among different system representations throughout a software system's development process?

RQ2:   How can we apply model-based security engineering to legacy projects that have no or disconnected design-time models?

RQ3:   How can developers be supported in realizing, preserving, and enforcing design-time security requirements in software systems?

RQ4:   How do changes within a software system affect its security compliance, and how can these effects be handled?

RQ5:   How can we verify and preserve security compliance in variant-rich software systems?

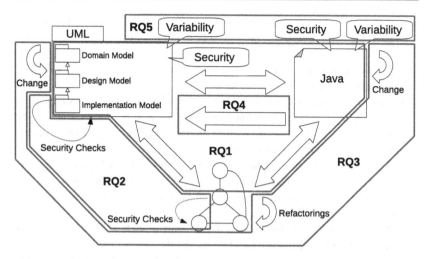

Figure 1.2 Location of the research questions in the GRaViTY approach

To be more precise, we introduce the research questions discussed in this thesis in detail in what follows.

RQ1: How can security requirements be traced among different system representations throughout a software system's development process?
Various artifacts, such as models or source code, are created during the development of a software system. Following approaches like security by design [28], already on the initial design artifacts, security requirements are planned and validated. These security requirements specified on model elements have to be fulfilled on later models giving more details on the elements or their concrete realization in the implementation. To ensure a software system's security, we have to trace the specified security requirements throughout all created artifacts. Thereby, we have to consider continuous changes on the software system, e.g., due to ongoing development activities or maintenance. Also, in the context of such changes, we have to preserve the validity of the created trace links. In principle, entirely reverse engineered UML models can be easily synchronized when changes in one of the tracked elements occur as one-to-one correspondences are possible. However, this is more challenging for elements not present in all system representations. Early design-time models are on a different level of abstraction than the software system's final implementation,

hindering the direct propagation of security requirements into the implementation. For answering this research question, we split it into three sub-research questions:

RQ1.1: How can we continuously create and maintain traces between design-time models and the implementation?
Security requirements specified in the design-time models of a software system must be fulfilled in the software system's implementation. Thus, we have to be able to retrieve all relevant parts of the implementation for a security requirement in the design models and all related model elements for an implementation artifact. As all artifacts are subject to continuous changes, we have to update the created trace links continuously. In the best case, we even can include a synchronization of the involved artifacts as part of the updates to avoid inconsistencies. (Section 6.2)

RQ1.2: How can trace links between design-time models with different levels of abstraction be represented and maintained?
Usually, during the development of an extensive software system, multiple design-time models with different abstractions are defined. Designers start with very abstract models and go into more detail afterward. Thus, the models that developers model in early phases have a different abstraction than later models or even models reversed engineered automatically. Nevertheless, not only the models that are close to implementation, but the models that are created early during design time have to be considered by our synchronization approach. As we consider only models using the same language, we can also use the same security extension. However, we have to study the tracing between models with different abstraction levels. (Section 6.3)

RQ1.3: How can trace links be used to propagate design-time security requirements into the implementation?
After creating trace links between all kinds of design-time models and the implementation, we have to leverage these trace links for propagating the specified security requirements. Different approaches might be suitable for propagating security requirements, depending on where the security requirement is specified and to which destination we want to propagate the security requirement. For example, during a static security check of the software system's implementation, we have access to all trace links and the design-time models, while this might not be the case at run-time. For this reason, we have to investigate different ways of propagating security requirements among the different artifacts. (Section 6.4)

RQ2: How can we apply model-based security engineering to legacy projects that have no or disconnected design-time models?
Many software systems that were developed decades ago, are still in use and are actively maintained. For such legacy systems, often no models are available or the existing models have been created in the early phases of system development and are disconnected from the implementation. As most legacy software systems have not been developed using the approach presented in this thesis, the question is how these legacy systems can switch to using the introduced model-based security engineering approach for further development and maintenance. As tracing between the design-time models and the implementation is essential, we have to reverse-engineer these trace links for legacy projects. Thereby, we distinguish between two kinds of legacy projects. Projects that do not have design-time models and projects for which early models were initially created but no traces have been maintained.

RQ2.1: How can we support legacy projects for that no design-time models exist in model-based security engineering?
In the first case, design-time models and the trace links have to be entirely reverse-engineered for applying the proposed approach. As in practice, many modeling tools come with the support of, e.g., reverse-engineering UML class diagrams, this usually happens in an ad-hoc manner. The extracted class diagrams are an independent snapshot of the current state of a software system's implementation. However, the two essential requirements of tracing and synchronization for applying our approach are not fulfilled. For this reason, we have to investigate how we can reverse-engineer models including a correspondence model between the reverse-engineered models and the implementation that is compatible with our approach. (Section 7.1)

RQ2.2: How can we migrate legacy projects that have models but that are disconnected from the implementation to model-based security engineering?
In the second case, we have to restore trace links to the existing design-time models. Although we could just reverse-engineer new models, it might be beneficial to integrate existing models as these contain information about the intended design and even can contain detailed information about the planned security. When we restore trace links with these design-time models, we enable compliance checks concerning the initially expected state of the software system. Furthermore, by transferring information, e.g., security requirements, specified in such design-time models, we can save redundant effort for specifying these again, e.g., on reverse-engineered models. Accordingly, we have to reconstruct trace links between early design-time models and the implementation in a format usable for our model-based security engineering approach. (Section 7.2)

RQ3: How can developers be supported in realizing, preserving, and enforcing design-time security requirements in software systems?
Various approaches have been developed to plan and verify required security mechanisms from the early stages of software design. However, when it comes to verifying the implementation of the security requirements in a software system, most checks have to be performed in manual code reviews. One reason is the local scope of the single security analyses and the lack of automated reuse. To effectively support developers in the implementation and verification of design-time security, automated reuse of the security specifications and suitable checks for checking the security properties on other system representations are required. Depending on where we want to apply such security checks and how we will specify these, we can divide this research question into three sub-research questions.

RQ3.1: How can we automatically verify a software system's compliance concerning design-time security requirements?
First, we have to find automated means to show the compliance between a software system's security design and its implementation. Here, the most relevant question is what do we have to check on the implementation to show that the specified security requirements are fulfilled. Also, we will study which other benefits we can gain from propagating design-time security requirements besides an immediate verification. (Sections 8.3, 8.4, and 8.5)

RQ3.2: How can formal approaches be used for the specification of security violation patterns?
One of the most significant issues with the current design- and security-analysis approaches is their informal specification. For example, in the OO design domain, anti-patterns or design flaws have mainly been specified in a textual manner [29] and later been captured using more formal approaches to overcome the incomprehensibility of the textual specifications [21]. The same applies to the domain of security. Security standards such as Common Criteria are a vague and hardly checkable automatically on a software system. As in the OO design domain, there are automatically checkable security rules, e.g., accompanying the SEI CERT security standard. However, currently, these are very fine-grained and locally checkable rules and still far away from common security standards. Moreover, existing security checks are often only available as ad-hoc implementations [29–33]. These complicate the study of the side effects and make it even harder to apply identical changes to all system representations. A promising approach to overcome these issues is graph transformations that have successfully been applied to specify design flaws on a formal basis [21, 34]. (Section 8.6)

RQ3.3:   How can design-time security requirements be enforced at run-time?
Until now, we have been focusing on the static verification of security requirements on the implementation level. However, when it comes to the security of
a software system, there are additional factors that interfere with the software
system's security. Specifically, we have to ensure security compliance regarding
design-time and development-time security requirements at run-time. For example, due to statically not checkable circumstances such as a change in a library
or a newly discovered attack type, security violations can occur in a software
system that passed all static security checks. (Chapter 9)

**RQ4: How do changes within a software system affect its security compliance,
and how can these effects be handled?**
The development of a software system consists not only of adding new elements, but
also of modifying existing elements. Both changes require the continuous update
of the traces studied in RQ1. However, as part of RQ1, we do not look at how such
changes might affect security requirements. Suppose we want to guide developers.
In that case, we have to inform them if some changes, which have automatically been
performed by our tool support or manually by them, affect security requirements.
For example, this is of particular interest in the certified software scenario [35, 36]
where it has to be ensured that a change violates no security requirement.

**RQ4.1:   How can behavior-preserving refactorings be specified on a formal
basis and this specification be used for executing the refactorings?**
Restructuring a software system to keep the system maintainable and extensible
is a common practice in developing a software system [18]. Such restructuring
operations are often performed in an ad-hoc manner and are likely to alter the
software system's behavior. Refactorings describe theoretically a systematic way
to perform restructurings without altering the behavior of the software system.
However, despite the existence of graph-based formal approaches to verify the
correctness of a refactoring operation [24, 37], refactorings are usually still implemented in an ad-hoc manner. The open question is how to apply a refactoring
operation that has formally been proven to be correct to a software system.
**RQ4.2:   How do refactorings interact with security requirements, and how can
malicious interactions be prevented?**
Furthermore, while correctly implemented OO-refactorings preserve behavior
by definition, they might affect security requirements, e.g., due to a necessary
increase in an attribute's visibility. This way, incorrect refactorings might not only
change a software system's behavior but could create vulnerabilities in a software
system. As refactorings will appear in this thesis only in the context of automated

tool support, e.g., to eliminate detected anti-patterns as described above, we have
to guarantee that the suggested refactorings will always be compliant with the
specified security requirements on all system representations. For this reason,
we have to study how graph-based refactorings can be specified in a security-
preserving way. (Chapter 10)

**RQ4.3: How can security requirements affected by arbitrary system changes
be identified end efficiently be rechecked for security compliance?**

For ensuring a software system's security, whenever a change is applied to a
software system, we have to check if this change violates any security requirements. The efficient verification of security requirements after arbitrary changes
is even more challenging than verifying refactorings. Since we cannot check
them in advance, we have to check every security requirement on every system
representation again. Especially for large software systems with many security
requirements, this can take much time. Using the trace links established before,
we can calculate which security requirements we have to check again and which
security requirements we do not have to check. Also, it regularly turns out that
previous security assumptions no longer apply. This leads to a situation in which
every published version has to be rechecked for security issues. If new security
requirements are specified on one system representation, trace links must be created to all relevant elements in every system representation. For this reason, we
have to study how we can efficiently identify and recheck elements affected by
changes for security compliance. (Section 8.6)

**RQ5: How can we verify and preserve security compliance in variantrich soft-
ware systems?**

Often software systems come in many variants that share huge parts in common.
Thereby, the number of possible variants can quickly reach an astronomical scale
making the security analysis of every single product infeasible [38]. Nevertheless,
for every single variant or product, we have to ensure that it does not contain any
security violation. Furthermore, we have to preserve security compliance also in
case of changes, e.g, in case of applied restructuring operations. Here, the goal is
to apply the developed security engineering approach also to variant-rich software
systems.

**RQ5.1: How can we specify variability throughout a software system, includ-
ing design-time models and security requirements?**

To verify security compliance of variant-rich software systems, first, we need to
specify variability on all considered artifacts consistently. Many approaches only
consider a single kind of artifact, when considering variability within variant-

rich software systems, e.g., source code. However, during the development of a software system various artifacts are created, e.g., design-time models or source code. To allow security compliance checks, we have to consider all of these artifacts in combination with the software system's security requirements. For this, it is necessary to express variability consistently across these artifacts but also concerning security requirements. Furthermore, we have to integrate these variability specifications into our approach for continuous tracing among all artifacts. (Chapter 11)

RQ5.2: How can security violations be detected on SPLs?
After the consistent specification of variability across all artifacts, we have to investigate approaches to check the product line for security violations. For scalability reasons, this check must be performed without iterating over every product. Thereby, we have to support design-level and implementation-level security checks to consider model-based security engineering to its full extend. (Chapters 12 and 13)

RQ5.3: How can we apply security-aware refactorings to SPLs?
Like single-product software systems, also variant-rich software systems require frequent restructuring to keep them maintainable. Considering their security, also in variant-rich software systems we have to ensure that the refactorings do not lead to violations of security requirements. For this reason, we have to investigate applying security-preserving refactorings to software product lines. Given a concrete refactoring operation, not only a single variant should be refactored but all variants in which the refactoring is applicable in terms of behavior preservation and security compliance. (Chapter 13)

1.4   Research Methodology

To answer the presented research questions and provide a solution to the outlined problems, we followed the design science research methodology [39–41]. The goal of this research approach is to develop artifacts that overcome current boundaries. Thereby, new knowledge is achieved by building and investigating the application of the developed artifact. Accordingly, this approach requires that, initially, a general solution concept is developed, which is afterward implemented and evaluated. If necessary, the developed solution concept is adapted based on the observations during application and evaluation until the desired goals are met.

We divided the topics of this thesis into small sub-problems with individual research questions that can be investigated separately for solving the identified problems. Therefore, we are going to solve them separately and incorporate them into one approach afterward. For every single sub-problem, we followed the design science research approach.

Henver et al. defined seven guidelines for applying the design science research methodology [39]. We followed these guidelines for performing the research presented in this thesis. In what follows, we shortly introduce these guidelines and discuss how we addressed these.

Design as an artifact: When following the design science research approach, the primary goal is to develop an artifact. The purpose of this artifact is to address and solve a relevant problem. By developing this artifact, new knowledge on how to solve the problem is gained. It should also be described effectively for allowing others to implement the artifact independently, follow the knowledge gained, and transfer it to other domains.

In our case, the developed artifact is a tool prototype. As we divided our overall problem into single sub-problems, we also developed artifacts for every single sub-problem. In chapters 5 to 11, for each chapter, we introduce the developed artifacts in *Tool Support* sections of the single chapters. Thereby, we present our artifact's conceptual design and its concrete realization for solving the sub-problems discussed in the single chapters. Among the thesis, we frequently reuse artifacts introduced in previous chapters for developing the next artifact. Finally, in Chapter 14, we show integrating all the single artifacts into one coherent artifact.

Problem relevance: For acquiring new knowledge, a relevant and yet unsolved problem must be addressed. Research following the design science research approach has to clearly outline the relevance of the addressed problem, what in state of the art solves already, and which open problems have to be overcome.

Following this methodology, we motivated the identified problem's general relevance at the beginning of this chapter and showed open problems when deriving research questions in Section 1.3. Chapter 3 discusses the state of the art in detail and explicitly showcases missing contributions for the identified open problems that have to be overcome. Also, at the beginning of every chapter, we summarize the relevance of the single sub-problems as well as missing contributions in detail.

Design evaluation: The feasibility of the developed artifact has to be demonstrated in a structured evaluation. For this purpose, among others, the evaluation's objectives can be functionality, completeness, consistency, accuracy, performance, reliability, or usability. The evaluation itself should be performed using standard design evaluation methods, such as case studies, controlled experiments, testing, or informed argumentations.

In this thesis, for every problem we solve, we present in detail how our solution works and solves the identified problem providing an informed argumentation on the feasibility of the developed artifact. In addition, we evaluate every artifact regarding quantifiable objectives in the *Evaluation* sections of every chapter. In total, we evaluate our artifacts regarding 18 evaluation objectives. These objectives comprise the scalability, efficiency, effectiveness, applicability, usability, usefulness, and correctness of the developed artifacts. Finally, we showcase the overall approach's feasibility using the combined artifacts on two subject software systems in Chapter 15.

One common problem in this thesis regarding the evaluation of the developed artifacts is the need for a suitable subject to perform an evaluation. We can easily get evaluation subjects for all sub-problems dealing with source code using the available source code from open source projects. For this purpose, first, we established an evaluation database containing more than 30 well-known open-source projects. However, open-source projects usually do not come with design-time models that play a central role in this thesis. To overcome this problem, we reverse-engineered the needed models. The models created from those open source projects are afterward used to study the graph transformation-related sub-problems from RQ1. The biggest issue to deal with if we want to apply the constructive design approach with a strong focus on evaluation is the lack of good sources for real-world security properties as needed in RQ2 and RQ3. Existing approaches for detecting critical sources and sinks in a program are promising solutions to this issue [42, 43]. We successfully applied those approaches for partly extracting security specifications. In addition, we manually extracted additional required information for the two case studies presented in this thesis.

Research contributions: Research following the design science research approach has to provide its contributions clearly. For contributions achieved using the design science research approach, possible categories are an artifact providing knew knowledge or applying existing knowledge innovatively, an extension of foundational knowledge, and the development of new methodologies for solving or evaluating a problem.

We mainly improve existing technologies to allow an application that was not possible before or overcomes the current state of the art. For this purpose, we usually innovatively apply existing technologies. Where necessary, we developed entirely new concepts. This development of new concepts mainly applies to applying transformation rules that contain variability themselves to product lines in Chapter 13. Finally, in the *Conclusion* sections of the single chapters and the overall conclusion in Chapter 17, we discuss and summarize the new knowledge gained at developing and evaluating the artifacts.

Research rigor: The design science research approach requires developing the artifacts and their evaluation to be performed with rigor to ensure the obtained results' validity. An essential key part is the effective use of theoretical foundations and research methodologies. Also, implications on the domain or a concrete application of the artifacts are essential.

When developing the artifacts presented in this thesis, we strictly followed the design science research approach. Where ever possible, we built upon existing foundational works. We only came up with new foundational extensions if the existing foundations were not sufficient for solving the problem in terms of innovative reuse of foundational works. We critically discuss our solution, its evaluation, and our implications in every chapter's *Threats to Validity* sections. We oriented all implications on our application scenario and tailored these to be as realistic as possible.

Design as a search process: In design science, problems are usually solved in an iterative process of developing a solution, evaluating it, and optimizing the solution based on the evaluation. Often, a problem is studied first in a simplified version that iteratively gets more realistic.

Throughout the whole research process, we followed this iterative approach. However, in this thesis, we only show the final results of the process. However, this thesis is still structured along with our division of the overall problem into sub-problems, their independent solution, and finally, the integration to an overall solution. This solution is a satisfactory solution for the identified problem. However, in additional iterations, the generalization, performance, or covered scope could be extended. We explicitly discuss possible future iterations in Chapter 17.

Communication of research: The presentation of the performed research plays the final essential role in the design science research approach. Based on the presentation of the research technology-oriented audiences should be able to reproduce the results obtained and management-oriented audiences should be able to apply the developed solutions to an organizational context.

This thesis builds the main presentation of the conducted research. However, most parts of the research have already been communicated to mainly the scientific but also business community in peer-reviewed conferences and journal publications. [207] lists the preliminary publications supporting this thesis. Also, all developed artifacts and evaluation data are publicly accessible on GitHub[3] to replicate the research.

---

[3] gravity-tool.org

1.5 Outline

This thesis is structured into parts that contain coherent topics of this thesis. In what follows, we outline the structure of the thesis and the contributions presented in the single chapters.

Prologue: This introduction is part of the prologue of this thesis. In the prologue we introduce the relevant background for reading this thesis and outline the presented approach.

- In Chapter 2, we introduce the iTrust electronics health care system used as a running example throughout this thesis.
- In Chapter 3, we discuss the state-of-the-art for the development and maintenance of secure software systems. Thereby, we also introduce the background common to all other chapters of this thesis.
- In Chapter 4, we demonstrate how the GRaViTY approach proposed in this thesis works from a developer's perspective. Thereby, we also show how it is supposed to integrate with common development practices introduced in Chapter 3.

Tracing: For the development of secure software systems, tracing is an important concept. In this part of the thesis, focuses on continuous tracing among a software system's artifacts.

- In Chapter 5, we introduce our program model for representing the implementation of a software system. This program model will be used by us to specify and apply implementation-level security checks and refactorings.
- In Chapter 6, we discuss the automated synchronization of design-time models, the implementation, and our program model. By applying the introduced synchronization, a correspondence model is built. Combined with the UML inheritance mechanism, we show how this can be used for tracing security throughout the whole development process of a software system.
- In Chapter 7, we discuss how our approach can be applied to legacy projects. First, by reverse-engineering design-time models from the implementation, and second, by restoring trace links between existing models and the implementation.

Security: In this part, we focus on security checks and security compliance throughout the software life cycle.

- In Chapter 8, we discuss how to statically verify a implementation's compliance with design-time security requirements. Moreover, we outline how we can generate additional benefits from tracing design-time security requirements into the implementation. Finally, we discuss in this chapter how we can specify security checks using formal mechanisms and how to incrementally check for security compliance after changes.
- In Chapter 9, we investigate how design-time security requirements can be enforced at run-time and how the design-time models can be adapted based on observations at run-time for investigating security violations.

Maintenance: For successful development of a software system on the long term, maintenance is an essential part of the development. In this part of the thesis, we focus on a software system's maintenance.

- In Chapter 10, we discuss how object-oriented refactorings can be specified on a formal basis and how our synchronization approach can be leveraged for actually executing the refactorings specified in the aforementioned way. In addition, we investigate the interaction of refactorings with security requirements and how we can specify security-preserving conditions for refactorings.

Variants: In this part, we focus on model-based security engineering and maintenance on variant-rich software systems.

- In Chapter 11, we introduce how variability can be specified throughout variant-rich software systems, including variability on design-time UML models, the implementation, and the program model.
- In Chapter 12 we discuss how we can efficiently verify the security of such UML model product lines.
- In Chapter 13 we introduce an approach for applying the security checks introduced in Chapter 8 and the refactorings from Chapter 10 to software product lines.

Tool Support and Application: In this part, we introduce integrated tool support for the model-based development and maintenance of secure software systems.

- In Chapter 14, we demonstrate how the single parts of our tool prototype, introduced throughout this thesis, integrate with each other.
- In Chapter 15, we discuss the application of GRaViTY to the iTrust running example as well as the Eclipse Secure Storage as a second subject system.

Epilogue: In this thesis' epilogue, we discuss related works and conclude on model-based security engineering covering a software system's life cycle.

- In Chapter 16, we discuss works related to the contributions of this thesis.
- In Chapter 17, we conclude and discuss the limitations and assumptions of our approach. Furthermore, we discuss future research directions.

Running Example: iTrust

2

In many software systems, security issues can have dramatic consequences. For example, in December 2019 a bug in a router led to 20,000 patient records being publicly available from the Internet [44, 45]. One of the main security issues was insufficient access control for the patient data in a management system for medical images. There was no internal access control implemented, and everyone who was in the network of the doctor's office had access to all patient data. Besides, due to a bug in the router, there were open ports in the firewall which allowed everyone on the Internet to get into the doctor's office network. As a consequence, everyone had unrestricted access to all the patient data.

During the treatment of patients, lots of data is generated that has to be stored and made available to various experts. This ranges from the notes of a doctor at an office visit to large images, e.g., created by imaging devices such as ultrasonic sensors or computer tomography scanners. For the management of such data, *Health Care System*s (HCS) are developed by various companies and are used everywhere from small doctor's offices to large hospitals. Besides the commercial systems, Aminpour et al. reviewed the utilization of open-source implementations for the management of *Electronic Health Records* (EHR) and identified 13 open-source Health Care Systems [46], e.g., the iTrust system [47]. Throughout this thesis, we use the iTrust system as the running example.

In what follows, we generally discuss the development process of such a Health Care System and possible pitfalls. Afterward, we introduce the iTrust open-source implementation of a management system for hospitals as a concrete running example. Throughout this thesis, we use iTrust for motivating and demonstrating the approaches we developed for answering this thesis' research questions. For this reason, in what follows, we not only introduce the development of software systems in the medical domain and particularly the iTrust system but also discuss the relation to the research questions.

© The Author(s), under exclusive license to Springer Fachmedien Wiesbaden GmbH, part of Springer Nature 2022
S. M. Peldszus, *Security Compliance in Model-driven Development of Software Systems in Presence of Long-Term Evolution and Variants*,
https://doi.org/10.1007/978-3-658-37665-9_2

2.1   Development of a Medical Management System

In this section, we look at the development process of a medical management system. For discussion purposes, we assume a fictive software company that is going to implement a new management system for patient data. Thereby, we focus on security-related decisions during the development process.

At first, the requirement engineers of the company collect requirements that the software system has to meet. Besides considering classical functional and non-functional requirements, domain-specific requirements from relevant standards must be observed, such as IEC 62304 [7] and IEC 62366 [48] for medical device software. Furthermore, all requirements on the software system must be checked for additional security implications, e.g., by automatically recommending and including relevant standards or measures. As the project is dealing with personal data, implementing appropriate access control is an example of such a security-implied requirement.

Afterward, in system design, software architects design the software system. The software architecture created in this step has to address all captured requirements. As a consequence, the required access control has to be reflected in the software system's architecture. In the above-mentioned vulnerable real-world system, access control for preventing outsider attackers had been considered (including a router with a firewall), but no access control for insider attackers had been planned. The fictive company lost track of this security requirement at working with architectural models having different abstractions. Such missing or neglected security mechanisms, as well as flawed and insecure security mechanisms, should be automatically detected at design time. This is a case of heuristic identification of conceptual or design problems during development. It requires a representation that is formal enough for automated analysis and allows software architects to connect different levels of abstraction to allow tracing.

The next pitfall for the fictive company occurs during implementation. The company skips the implementation of a (previously required) security mechanism to save time and effort. In addition, an inexperienced developer selects an inappropriate mechanism, e.g., a cryptographic hash function that is generally considered secure but not strong enough for the hashing of medical information according to a domain-specific standard. Automated tool support for developers, such as monitoring of source code for security issues and compliance violations with security requirements, could warn and help to prevent such security violations. If a security-related design concept like access control has no trace to an adequate part of the implementation, a warning can be provided to the developers. However, as such tool support was not available in the fictive company, the two security violations stayed undetected and remained in the developed health care system.

Configuration of the software system is yet another important part. In addition to internal access control, the company also implemented a limitation of accesses per hour to harden the software system against brute force attacks. However, the preconfigured number of accesses per hour might lead to a denial of service if the software is used without adaption to the context, e.g., a big hospital instead of a small doctor's office. At run-time, it has to be ensured that the security requirements are still fulfilled, in this case concerning availability.

Also, changes in the security assumptions will occur. For example, it has been recently shown that SHA1 has become an insecure hash algorithm due to new attack knowledge. New requirements may also be stimulated by unexpected observations at run-time, like several hundred access attempts from a single IP address which leads to all accesses being blocked by the above-mentioned access limit. Requiring dynamic IP address filters could be a decision by human experts. This representation of technical problems and solution attempts should be retrieved in a future case with a similar profile for informing problem analysis. While this example could be easy to inspect using traditional log files, other security violations, e.g, due to an attack might be harder to inspect.

Last but not least, the company started to develop custom-tailored variants for their customers. After starting a new variant by cloning another variant a few times. For avoiding duplicated effort, the company merged all variants into a single software product line from which the variants are generated. However, this exacerbated the security problems of the company as they had to generate all variants for inspecting them regarding security violations.

In summary, there are many pitfalls in developing a security-critical software system, and in the scenario, we demonstrated some of them. Suitable development approaches and tool support can help in preventing or mitigating the discussed security issues. However, as discussed in Chapter 3, the current state-of-the-art comes with significant limitations. In the next section, we introduce the iTrust system as a real-world example for a medical management system in detail.

2.2   The iTrust Electronics Health Records System

In this thesis, we present an approach for supporting developers in the model-driven software development (MDD) of secure software systems. A suitable running example has to provide a concrete implementation to which the approach can be applied but also suitable documentation to create the models required by the approach. For

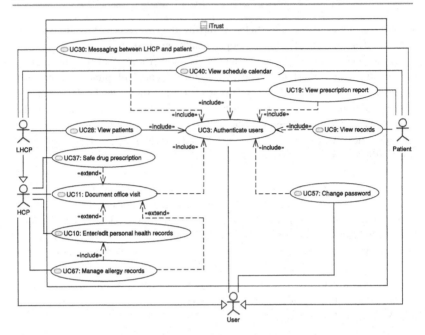

Figure 2.1 Excerpt from the use cases of iTrust

explaining our approach, we introduce the iTrust case study, realizing a software system comparable to the one described above. The iTrust electronics health records system is a web application for managing health data in hospitals. In the introduction of iTrust, we only focus on artifacts that have been created by its original developers. As the iTrust system has been used as a case study in various scientific publications [23, 49–51], additional artifacts, e.g., design-time models, are available.

The iTrust case study has been developed as a teaching project at the North Carolina State University, has been continuously extended by students over 25 semesters, and is publicly available [47, 50]. The first version of iTrust has been developed in the winter term 2004/05 and the last version in the winter term 2016/17. Due to structural decay and outdated technologies, starting with the summer term of 2017 iTrust has been superseded by iTrust2. Besides the source code of the implementation, documentation of the software system's design and requirements are available. At the writing of this thesis, only the requirements of iTrust2 have been publicly accessible [52]. The requirements of the original iTrust system have been provided to the author of this thesis by the responsible persons of iTrust[1].

The requirements of the iTrust system have been specified as use case descriptions. In the last version of iTrust (version 23) these requirements comprise 79 use cases of which 36 have been implemented in iTrust version 23. Figure 2.1 shows an excerpt from a use case diagram of the iTrust requirements. The shown use cases are selected to give an overview of the iTrust system and focus on the parts of the iTrust system used for explanations in this thesis.

The iTrust system comprises eleven roles of actors. In the shown use case diagram, we focus on the two most important users of the system, patients and doctors. While there is an actor role for patients in the system, doctors are represented with different roles based on their expertise and association with patients. In the diagram, we can see an actor representing arbitrary *Health Care Personnel (HCP)* such as doctors and the role of a *Licensed Health Care Professional (LHCP)* that is an HCP that has been allowed by a patient to access all of her health records. Other roles comprise additional medical staff, administrative staff but also representatives of official authorities.

Patients and doctors can exchange messages with each other (UC30) and can arrange appointments (UC40) using the iTrust electronics health care system. Furthermore, doctors but also patients can access the records created during the treatment of a patient (UC9 and UC28). Here, the patient can only access her records and an LHCP can access the records of the patients she has been licensed by. Regular HCPs cannot access any sensitive patient records. Any HCP can document the examination of a patient in the system (UC11). Besides basic information, such as the date and duration of the office visit, this can include the prescription of drugs (UC37), the record of health records like the blood pressure (UC10), or the management of allergies (UC67). All of these actions can also be performed by an HCP outside an office visit, e.g., during an emergency procedure. For managing allergies, the functionality of editing health records is used.

To execute all use cases it is required that the user authenticates herself in the system first (UC3). For the authentication, every user has a unique identifier, a medical identification (MID) name, and a password. In the implementation of the system, the authentication is realized as an initial login by the user. Also after authentication, the user can change her password (UC57).

As an example for a requirement from the iTrust specification, Figure 2.2 shows the requirement UC57 of a user changing her password. In iTrust, requirements

[1] Thanks to Sarah S. Heckman from NCSU for her quick response and for sharing iTrust's requirements with me.

57.1 Preconditions:

    A User is a registered user of the iTrust Medical Records system (UC2). The User
    has authenticated himself or herself in the iTrust Medical Records system (UC3).

57.2 Main Flow:

    The User selects the option to change his or her password [S1]. The User fills out
    required information to change the password [S2].

57.3 Sub-flows:

[S1] The user clicks link to change password.

[S2] The user enters the current password and the new password [E1].

57.4 Alternative Flows:

[E1] If the new password is less than 5 characters long and does not contain at least 1
letter and 1 number, the user is prompted to enter another appropriate password.

Figure 2.2 Use case description of the iTrust use case *UC57 Change password* taken from
the iTrust wiki

are defined as quadruples of preconditions, main-flows, sub-flows, and alternative
flows. The preconditions state what is necessary for the use case defined in the
requirement to be executable. In UC57, there has to be an account for the user and
the user authenticated herself at the system. Most times, these preconditions contain
references to other use cases that have to be successfully executed. The main-flow
summarizes the main objective of the requirement and thereby makes use of sub-
flows and alternative flows for detailing the overall objective. In the given example,
the main flow consists out of two sub-flows. An alternative flow is used as part of the
sub-flow S2 for specifying the behavior if the new password does not meet defined
security requirements. While main flows and sub-flows can be always executed
when the preconditions are met, alternative flows are only executed under defined
conditions.

The iTrust system has been implemented as a web application in Java using Java
server pages (JSP) for the front end. The application is executed on an Apache Tomcat HTTP web server. Data, such as medical records or authentication information,
is stored using a MySQL database.

Listings 2.1 and 2.2 show an excerpt from the Java implementation of the use
case UC57 of a user changing her password. The main functionality of this use case
is implemented in the class `ChangePasswordAction`. The most relevant part
is the method `changePassword`, shown in Listing 2.1. This method is called by
the server pages as soon as a user submits a change password form. Thereby, the
MID of the user, the user's old password, and twice the desired new password is
passed to the method. First, in line 13, the authentication service of iTrust is used
to authenticate the user using her MID and password. If the authentication was not

```
1  package edu.ncsu.csc.itrust.action;
2
3  public class ChangePasswordAction {
4
5      private AuthDAO authDAO;
6
7      public String changePassword(long mid, String oldPass, String newPass,
              String confirmPass) {
8          String containsLetter = "[a-zA-Z0-9]*[a-zA-Z]+[a-zA-Z0-9]*";
9          String containsNumber = "[a-zA-Z0-9]*[0-9]+[a-zA-Z0-9]*";
10         String fiveAlphanumeric = "[a-zA-Z0-9]{5,20}";
11
12         //Make sure old password is valid
13         if(!authDAO.authenticatePassword(mid, oldPass)) {
14             return "Invalid password change submission.";
15         }
16
17         //Make sure new passwords match
18         if (!newPass.equals(confirmPass)) {
19             return "Invalid password change submission.";
20         }
21
22         //Validate password. Must contain a letter, contain a number, and be
              a string of 5–20 alphanumeric characters
23         if(newPass.matches(containsLetter) && newPass.matches(containsNumber)
              && newPass.matches(fiveAlphanumeric)){
24             //Change the password
25             authDAO.resetPassword(mid, newPass);
26             return "Password Changed.";
27         } else {
28             return "Invalid password change submission.";
29         }
30     }
31 }
```

Listing 2.1 Excerpt from the Java class `ChangePasswordAction`, showing the method for changing a user's password

successful, an error message is returned. Otherwise, it is checked if the user entered two times the same password to prevent typing errors in the new password. Next, in line 23 the method checks if the new password meets all security requirements, e.g., has a suitable length. If this is the case the password is changed using the method `resetPassword` of the authentication service. The method `resetPassword` creates a connection to the iTrust SQL database and changes the password there.

```
 1   package edu.ncsu.csc.itrust.dao.mysql;
 2
 3   public class AuthDAO {
 4       public void resetPassword(long mid, String pass) throws DBException {
 5           Connection conn = null;
 6           PreparedStatement pstmt = null;
 7           try {
 8               conn = factory.getConnection();
 9               pstmt = conn.prepareStatement("UPDATE users SET password=?,
                     salt=? WHERE MID=?");
10               String salt = shakeSalt();
11               String newPassword = DigestUtils.sha256Hex(pass+salt);
12               pstmt.setString(1, newPassword);
13               pstmt.setString(2, salt);
14               pstmt.setLong(3, mid);
15               pstmt.executeUpdate();
16               pstmt.close();
17           } catch (SQLException e) {
18               throw new DBException(e);
19           } finally {
20               DBUtil.closeConnection(conn, pstmt);
21           }
22       }
23   }
```

Listing 2.2 Excerpt from the Java class `AuthDAO` showing the method for changing a password in iTrust's SQL database

The detailed implementation is shown in Listing 2.2. First, in line 8, a connection to the database is created. Next, in line 9, a statement for updating the user's password is prepared. The values of the SQL statement are set in lines 12 to 14. The password is not stored in clear text but hashed with a salt. This takes place in lines 10 and 11. In lines 15 and 16, the statement is executed and terminated and finally, in line 20, the whole connection to the database is closed.

Figure 2.3 shows a screenshot of the welcome screen of a doctor after the authentication of UC3. On the left-hand side, a navigation bar is shown, e.g., for accessing patient information as described in UC28 or managing office visits as described in UC11. On the right of the navigation bar, an overview of the upcoming tasks is shown for the doctor is given. For example, this contains messages exchanged with patients (UC30) or scheduled appointments (UC40). The top bar offers role-independent functionalities such as the change of the user's password (UC57).

Figure 2.4 shows a screenshot of a patient's view on her diagnoses following the use case UC9. For this patient, two diagnoses have been recorded. While the top bar

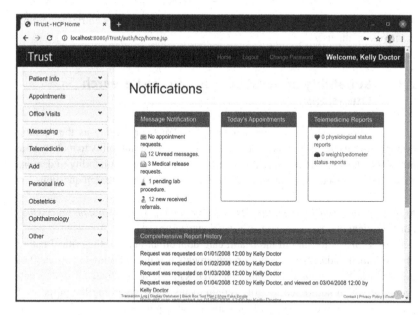

Figure 2.3 Welcome view for doctors in the iTrust system

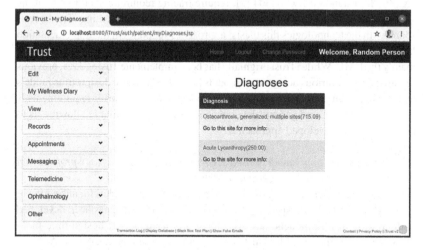

Figure 2.4 Patient view on her diagnoses in the iTrust system

is the same for every user of the system, the navigation bar offers entries according
to the role of the user.

2.3   Suitability of iTrust Concerning the Research
Questions

In what follows, we discuss the suitability of iTrust for serving as the running
example for this thesis. In this discussion, we focus on the suitability to motivate the
problems addressed by the thesis' research questions and the suitability to demonstrate the developed approaches on iTrust for answering the research questions.

*RQ1: How can security requirements be traced among different system representa-
tions throughout a software system's development process?*
Because iTrust is located in the health care domain and due to the critical nature
of this domain, addressing security requirements is crucial. Following article 9 of
the *General Data Protection Regulation* (GDPR) [53], medical data falls into a category for which additional security requirements apply regarding the purpose of
processing but also the secrecy of the data. These requirements make iTrust a typical software system in a security-sensitive domain. Furthermore, relevant standards,
e.g., the ISO standard IEC 62304 [7], require tracing requirements throughout the
software development. Also, the technologies used for implementing iTrust correspond with the technologies this thesis' approaches support. On the implementation
level, this technology is the Java programming language and for design-time models,
mainly the UML. While iTrust originally has been implemented using Java, previous
research created various design-time models [23, 49–51]. These design-time models
also include security requirements. Altogether, tracing of security requirements is
essential for iTrust, and various development artifacts are available allowing us to
demonstrate the developed approaches.

*RQ2: How can we apply model-based security engineering to legacy projects that
have no or disconnected design-time models?*
For motivating the research question and demonstrating approaches for answering it,
a legacy system with two specific characteristics is required: It has been developed
without design time models, however, there are disconnected design-time models available. In this regard, iTrust fulfills both of these characteristics. As there
are no design-time models available from iTrust's developers, we can investigate
their reverse-engineering as considered in RQ2.1 of this thesis. Furthermore, as
part of the case studies, various design-time models have been reverse-engineered

manually, allowing us to effectively study RQ2.2 regarding recreating correspondences between these models and the implementation.

RQ3: How can developers be supported in realizing, preserving, and enforcing design-time security requirements in software systems?
As iTrust is located in an inherent security-critical domain, security engineering is essential for developing software systems such as iTrust. In this regard, multiple previous works have investigated security engineering on single design-time models of iTrust [49, 51, 54, 55]. However, these works were restricted to single artifacts and mainly focus on the design-time planning of security requirements or the adjustment of planned security requirements and measures to changes in the security context knowledge. The enforcement of these planned or adapted security requirements throughout the whole is currently not considered. Nevertheless, the availability of design-time artifacts containing security requirements and changes within these requirements allow us to effectively study and demonstrate the developed approaches for supporting developers in realizing, preserving, and enforcing design-time security requirements in the iTrust system.

RQ4: How do changes within a software system affect its security compliance, and how can these effects be handled?
The iTrust system has been developed over a long time and shows significant structural decay that has lead to discontinuing its development. The fact that iTrust has been superseded by iTrust2 due to structural decay, makes it a perfect candidate to study the maintenance and security compliance of a security-critical long-living system as considered in this thesis. Particularly, this allows us to study the security-preserving refactoring of iTrust, as considered in RQ4, effectively. Also, the history of the iTrust implementation and changes in the health care domain, e.g., the release of the GDPR, can serve as sources for security-relevant changes.

RQ5: How can we verify and preserve security compliance in variant-rich software systems?
Considering iTrust's deployment in multiple hospitals, it seems reasonable that these are likely to have different requirements on the features supported by iTrust. For example, not every hospital is likely to provide patients with access to the iTrust system. For this reason, it could be that the iTrust system has to be deployed with this feature disabled. From a security perspective, it would be desirable that the deployed system does not even contain this feature avoiding exploits utilizing parts of the feature. Accordingly, there would be the need to create a version of iTrust that does not contain the implementation of the use cases UC9 and UC19 and contains

the use cases UC30 and UC40 only for doctors. Also, customers will likely request additional features tailored to their needs [56].

Altogether, if iTrust was developed in a commercial context, e.g., by the fictive company used for motivation at the beginning of this chapter, it would be likely that it evolves into a variant-rich software system. Considering iTrust as a variant-rich software system, it has the potential to contain variants in two dimensions:

time: As iTrust has been developed over 25 semesters, multiple versions of iTrust have been released. Each of these versions can be seen as a variant of iTrust. Except for the first version of iTrust, none has been developed from scratch but always based on the previous version. Accordingly, there is significant reuse among the different versions.

space: By making specific features optional, e.g., because a feature has been tailored for a specific customer, the possibility for multiple variants of iTrust emerges. While these variants differ in detail, there is significant reuse among them, e.g., all variants will likely contain the authentication of users as specified in UC3 of Figure 2.1.

While variants in time are present in the iTrust system, variants in space have not been realized. Nonetheless, as outlined there is a significant potential for variants in space. We investigate the introduction of iTrust variants in detail when answering RQ5 concerning model-based security engineering of variant-rich systems.

In this chapter, we outlined possible security issues in the development of security-critical software systems such as medical management systems. As a concrete example for such a medical management system, we introduced the iTrust electronics health records system. Throughout this thesis, we use iTrust to demonstrate the presented approaches that help the fictive company to avoid stepping into the outlined pitfalls.

State of the Art in Secure Software Systems Development

3

In the last decades, various concepts have been developed to support the development and maintenance of secure software systems. On the level of programming languages, concepts like *Object-Orientation* (OO) [57] have been introduced to improve the structuring and reuse in programs. Those concepts have also been reflected in modeling languages like the Unified Modeling Language (UML) [5]. On both, various kinds of security and design checks have been introduced to support developers in developing secure software systems. Also, different development processes have been proposed to structure the development and make it projectable. Besides, additional concepts for giving early and constant feedback to developers have been developed to follow these processes successfully. At this point, the most prominent one being continuous integration. While there is an overlap between all of these concepts, these are only partly integrated. In what follows, we give a short introduction to the enumerated concepts. Thereby, we focus on how the concepts contribute to the development of a secure software system and what are yet unsolved problems.

3.1 Object-Oriented Programming

Various programming paradigms have been developed to ease the implementation of a software system and allow more complicated software systems. Currently, one of the most widely used paradigms is Object-Oriented Programming (OOP). In the monthly TIOBE index of the most popular programming languages, in January 2021, 8 of the top 10 languages are object-oriented programming languages [15]. Among the considered languages, Java is the most popular object-oriented programming language.

© The Author(s), under exclusive license to Springer Fachmedien Wiesbaden GmbH, part of Springer Nature 2022
S. M. Peldszus, *Security Compliance in Model-driven Development of Software Systems in Presence of Long-Term Evolution and Variants*,
https://doi.org/10.1007/978-3-658-37665-9_3

The key idea of OO is the encapsulation of data and functionality [58]. Objects internally store data and communicate with each other through messages. Usually, fields of objects represent data and methods the functionality realized by the object. The invocations of methods realize the messaging between objects.

The object-oriented programming paradigm is an essential milestone towards improved program modularity and maintainability. Object-oriented programming concepts allow enforcing essential program/data structures, e.g., through design patterns [16]. Objects should comprise coherent functionality and can therefore be maintained independently and be reused in different contexts. However, in practice, especially when no detailed architecture has been defined upfront, design patterns are likely to be overused. Still aiming at designing a perfectly structured software system, developers can tend to compensate by locally over-engineering the software system leading to architectures hard to maintain. In contrast to this, OO-designs can also quickly get inextensible if patterns are underused. Object orientation often leads to complicated structures that might affect maintainability and security enforcement due to the manifold structuring possibilities that come with object-orientation. In general, it is likely to get more security issues the more complex a software system gets [59].

While the encapsulation of data and functionality was initially not thought of as a security concept [58], one could think about using an object's methods to add a security layer around the state or data of the object [60]. However, as in many programming languages encapsulation is not meant as a security feature, such mechanisms can be easily bypassed at run-time. For example, in the Java programming language one can use Java reflection to dynamically change the accessibility of members [61].

In general, object-orientation added language constructs to many languages that are not statically analyzable. One example is the polymorphism of objects, which is the possibility to use a child type in its parents' context. Together with constructs like dynamic class loading, we cannot foresee all possible objects implementing an invoked method [61]. If we have security assumptions on this invoked method, we cannot guarantee them statically. Such constructs give rise to new kinds of attacks such as object-hijacks where attackers generate new instances of objects, avoiding their proper initialization [59].

To summarize, in principle, object orientation allows the efficient creation and maintenance of large software systems. However, abuse or misuse of the object-oriented paradigm quickly leads to even more complicated and vulnerable software systems.

3.2   Restructuring and Adaption

Nowadays, practices in object-oriented programming incorporate consecutive steps of edits, updates, refinements, and other enhancements at the source code level for incrementally improving a program under development and to meet ever-changing requirements. In other words, programs consecutively evolve throughout their entire life-cycle. This evolution lies at the very core of modern software engineering [12, 13].

However, continuous evolution also means that programs are prone to internal decay due to the often ad-hoc nature of program edits which may cause software systems to arrive at incomprehensible or even inconsistent states eventually. To describe this effect, Parnas coined the term *Software Aging* [13]. In this regard, refactoring has been proposed as a countermeasure for the negative consequences of software evolution [17, 18]. Refactorings are behavior-preserving restructurings, usually, specified in a human-readable form.

Program refactoring aims at high-level restructurings of OO programs at the class–field–method level to fit previously defined structural patterns without altering the observable behavior. Most recent implementations usually rely on precondition-based program transformation rules directly applied to the program's abstract syntax tree (AST) [62]. Nevertheless, the complex nature of those rules, including an interplay between syntactic pattern matching at AST level and semantic constraint checking of properties that crosscut the AST, still makes refactorings prone to produce erroneous results potentially [63]. Although the problem of correctly specifying and executing refactorings for OO languages like Java has been extensively studied [62–71], a comprehensive and generally accepted OO refactoring theory is still an open issue.

Also, the effect of refactorings on non-functional aspects such as security is often neglected. While there are approaches for checking if a specific refactoring would change the observable behavior [69], such guarantees are often not given for security.

3.3   Model-driven Software Development

As OO programs require easy to extend and maintain structures, software architecture got an even more essential role than ever before. A common approach for structured development and documentation of software systems is *Model-driven Software Development* (MDD) [72], in which models are used in each development step. Models specified using the Unified Modeling Language (UML), are common

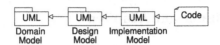

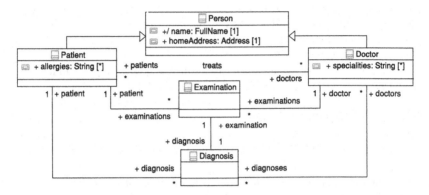

Figure 3.1 Artifacts used in model-driven software development

Figure 3.2 Excerpt of a domain model for hospitals based on the model presented in [78]

for the specification of software systems and can also be used in security analyses. For instance, the UMLsec approach, introduced in detail later in this section, defines a UML profile allowing developers to annotate UML models with security requirements and check their conciseness statically [73, 74].

A paradigm in which the role of models is even more emphasized is *Model-based Software Development* (MBSD). In MBSD, all details of the software system are expressed in models. The final running software system is generated from the models, or the models are executed at run-time [75].

In this work, we build upon the concept of model-driven software development [76]. Usually, models are iteratively refined until these reach an abstraction that allows an implementation of the architecture expressed by the models. In what follows, to give an overview of MDD, we will present different views on the iTrust case study following the classical MDD process. MDD allows developers to specify the software system and its properties on a higher level of abstraction than the source code level [8]. While MDD can cover many kinds of models, we focus on UML models [5]. Often, UML models with three different levels of abstraction [77] are used, as explained in what follows. Figure 3.1 shows the refinement hierarchy of the model kinds currently considered by us from the most abstract model at the left to the final implementation at the right.

3.3.1 Domain Model

The most abstract model is a domain model, specifying general properties of the domain in that the software system to develop is located [77]. Domain models are used in the earliest phases of software development to capture the general properties of a software system's domain. Often, domain models are specified using UML class diagrams to show common relations for all kinds of software systems placed in the domain.

Figure 3.2 shows an excerpt of a domain model for hospitals. In hospitals, two kinds of people play a central role, patients, and doctors who treat the patients. Both have a `name` and `homeAddress`. Usually, a list of `allergies` is stored for patients and a list of the doctor's `specialties`. A doctor can examine a patient in an `Examination` and create a `Diagnose` as part of such examinations.

When developers implement a software system for a hospital, e.g., like iTrust [47] for online management of patient data, they have to support the concepts captured in the domain model.

3.3.2 Design Model

After the specification of the domain model, the domain elements realized in the software are concretized in design models. Design models specify the design of the software system and how the functionality is distributed among the software system, e.g., by structuring the software system into components. Thereby, the foundation of an easily maintainable software system is set by the appropriate use of well-known design patterns [16]. The design model's definition is the first point where we have to start to continuously use design and security analyses to ensure the software system's maintainability and security as early as possible.

Figure 3.3 shows an excerpt of a design model for iTrust, based on a UML model reverse-engineered by Bürger et al. [51]. In this model, different controls are specified for using the iTrust platform, e.g., a login control, a control for documenting an office visit or for entering a diagnosis, as well as a more detailed data structure than in the domain model.

The different controls specify essential actions that can be performed, e.g., the option to reset the password in the login window. For a login of a user, the system needs the user information to identify and legitimate the user. For this purpose, the `LogInControl` accesses the data available in the `User`-object given to it.

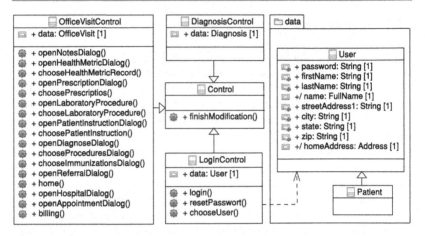

Figure 3.3 Excerpt of a design model for iTrust based on [51]

This model details the data used by the system. For example, the classes User and Patient can be seen as more concrete instances of the classes Person and Patient from the domain model in Figure 3.2. For example, on the Person class, it is explicitly specified that the homeAddress attribute, already known from the domain model, is derived from other attributes.

However, models with different abstractions are often created separately, leading only to implicit inheritance relations. For example, assuming that we semantically have a generalization, there should be an explicit inheritance relationship between the User in the design model and the Person in the domain model. Without explicitly capturing such relations, these are likely to be overseen and might result in errors.

3.3.3 Implementation Model

The precise functionalities of the planned software system are specified in an implementation model. The implementation model is usually the first platform-dependent model and contains information about the deployment or languages used to implement the software system. The implementation model can directly be executed, used for code generation, implemented manually, or a combination of all.

Figure 3.4 shows an excerpt of an implementation model showing how the iTrust platform could be developed in a hospital. The shown model is based on an implementation model created by the administrators of two hospitals as part of the VisiOn EU project [79]. We adapted the original model to support the iTrust system. The VisiOn EU project's goal was to create a platform for visual privacy management [80]. For the evaluation of the developed platform, the project included public administrations and private companies.

Inside the hospital, two servers are operated, one running the iTrust application and one running a database as well as an authentication service. Doctors access the iTrust system from the hospital's local network. Patients can get access to their data from the outside but have to authenticate themselves at the hospital's authentication service.

In our approach, we assume the single models shown in Figure 3.1 to be iteratively refined by developers until they reach a concrete implementation of the system. While it is a common approach to create UML models with different abstractions iteratively, these are often not connected explicitly, hindering the reuse of security-related information. The missing connection is likely to give rise to divergences between the models but also their implementation. These divergences can occur due to two reasons. First, they might already be introduced when a new model is created. Second, divergences manifest due to missing or wrong co-evolution after changes on one of the models.

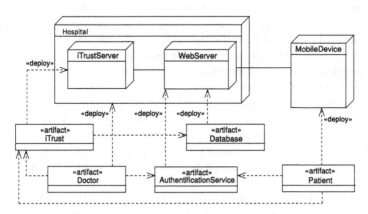

Figure 3.4 Excerpt of an implementation Model for iTrust based on the pilots of the VisiOn EU Project [79]

3.4   Development Processes

For the successful development of larger software systems, different development processes have been introduced. Currently, these development processes are mainly discussed regarding the structure of the flow through the development. On the one side, there are the classic sequential development processes with a strict order of development tasks. On the other side, the newer agile development processes focus on many fast iterations.

3.4.1   Sequential Software Development

Sequential development models comprise many well-known development processes. Among the most prominent processes are the waterfall model [81, 82] and the V-model [83]. The German government requires their version of the V-model for all of their software projects [84]. Furthermore, this development process is widely used to develop medical software [85]. Concerning these facts, the V-model is currently one of the most used development models. For this reason, in this section, we focus on the V-model.

Common to all sequential development processes is that the single development activities are performed in a sequential order defined by the process. For an enhanced version of the V-model that contains error handling, we show this order in Figure 3.5. Solid arrows depict the sequence of development steps considered in the process and dotted arrows to which step one has to return if an error is spotted. In general, the V-model is separated into two parts. First, on the left side of the V-model, the development of the software system. Second, on the right side, testing steps corresponding with the development steps from the left.

The execution of the development process starts on the top left of the V-model with requirements engineering, goes over the system-architecture specification, the system design, the software architecture, down to the concrete implementation of the software system at software design. If any error is spotted during the execution of a lower part of the development process, one has to go sequentially upwards to the step in which the error was made, fix it there, and then propagate the fix sequentially downward.

After the software system has been implemented, the software system's realization is sequentially tested by going upward on the right side of the V-model. Thereby, we first have very fine-grained unit tests at the beginning and coarse-grained acceptance tests at the end. If the acceptance tests are passed, the software system is deployed and goes into maintenance. If any test resolves an error, this error has to

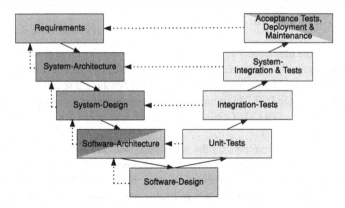

Figure 3.5 Concept of the V-model development process

be fixed in the development step corresponding to the test step in which the error was observed. For example, if we detect an error in an integration test, we have to start from the system-design step for fixing this error and start the development process from there again.

The design-time models considered at MDD perfectly fit the V-model steps and are classically developed following this process. First, the domain model is usually created in the requirements engineering step. Different versions of the system model are usually specified in the system architecture and system design steps. However, partly developers also tend to create a very detailed system model in the software-architecture step. The detailed implementation model is usually specified in the software-architecture step and software-design step.

One fundamental assumption of sequential development processes is that going to the next steps is only allowed after the current step has been completed. In the original V-model, even the error handling contained in our version is not included. Nevertheless, in practice, it is often infeasible to strictly follow this process. Among others, reasons for this are changing requirements, e.g., new functions wished by customers or changes in the security context knowledge that have to be addressed. It is often very challenging to predict the requirements on the models to be created in the current steps later steps might have. This challenging prediction tends to lead to complex architectures to avoid getting stuck in later steps. Also, it is essential to detect problems, e.g., possible security issues, early for the success of software systems developed using sequential software development processes.

3.4.2   Agile Software Development

To overcome the inflexibility of traditional sequential development processes, agile development processes have been proposed. The key idea of such development processes includes many and fast iterations instead of finishing a specific step before going to the next step [86]. This iterative way allows reacting to changes at the beginning of each iteration quickly. One of the most prominent agile software development processes is Scrum [87].

In Scrum, all requirements on the software system are collected in a *Product Backlog*. Based on the product backlog, a development goal is defined that can be reached with 2 to 4 weeks. The phase of reaching this goal is called a *Sprint*. During a Sprint, developers synchronize daily following strict communication rules. At the end of a Sprint, the developers assess together with the customers whether a Sprint's goal has been reached or not. Also, they assess what can be improved for future Sprints. After a Sprint, the subsequent development goal is defined based on the Product Backlog. Thereby, it is explicitly intended that the Product Backlog can change, e.g., due to the customer's new needs. Work continues this way until all requirements in the Product Backlog are fulfilled.

For working with Scrum, specific roles are defined for developers, customers, and management participating in the development of a software system [88]:

Product-Owner: A person only dedicated to communicating with the customers and collecting their requirements in the Product Backlog.
Team: A group of not more than 10 developers with different expertise required for successfully implementing a Sprint goal.
Scrum-Master: A person that organizes the developers and enforces the adoption of the Scrum rules within a team.

While, e.g., for many certifications, no specific development process is required, often artifacts that are usually created during MDD, are required for certification. Accordingly, the question is if it is possible to work with Scrum or other agile methods compliantly. Here, often the assumption is that Scrum only focuses on the Product Backlog and code. However, during a Sprint, any artifact required by a stakeholder can be created. These artifacts explicitly also include models, e.g., required for documentation or certification purposes. In contrast to sequential development approaches, all models will iteratively grow [89], and in this iterative process lies a considerable risk of inconsistency.

Scrum has been shown to be more efficient in adapting customer's needs than sequential development approaches due to the many fast iterations in rather small software systems [90]. Here, an often asked question is whether this also works for the development of large software systems. While a team of developers is small in Scrum to ensure efficient communication, it is explicitly considered that multiple teams can work in parallel. However, this even increases the challenge of integrating the work and keeping all artifacts consistent.

All in all, the main challenge for applying Scrum or other agile development approaches to software systems that require design-time models lies in the iterative way these will be developed.

Development processes aim at structuring the development of software systems for the successful development of software systems. Independent of the concrete used development process, keeping all artifacts consistent is an inherent challenge. However, this threat mainly impacts agile processes. While in sequential processes changes always occur on a specific artifact at a time and simple propagation rules can be used, in agile processes, all artifacts can be changed at any time. Also, detecting problems early is essential for the successful development of a software system. Here, agile processes can benefit from the many fast iterations but the detection of problems is still challenging.

3.5 (Security-)Compliance & Certifications

For showing that a software system is secure, compliance is an important term. In this thesis, we consider compliance in two different contexts. First, there is the implemented software system's compliance with its documentation and specification, e.g., the design-time models. This compliance is essential for successfully implementing, extending, and maintaining a software system. Usually, this compliance is a prerequisite for second context. This second context is compliance with legal obligations, e.g., security obligations derived from the GDPR. For this purpose, various standards and certifications have been developed. Such certification can show that a software system is compliant with a specific standard and be required for a software system to be released. For the development of secure software, various standards and certifications have been developed for verifying the security compliance of a software system.

3.5.1 Architecture Compliance Checking

Identifying the differences and equivalences between the planned and the implemented software architecture is the goal of architecture compliance checking. The compliance checks can be based on a static set of rules [91], dynamic monitoring of a running software system [92], or a hybrid of both [93]. Considering the model-based development of a software system, one can statically check the compliance of a software system's implementation with its design-level models. Generally, running compliance checks reveals the relations between a set of components from two models. In the end, such a compliance check is based on an analysis of observed correspondences between the design-time models and their implementation. In general, the outcome of an architectural compliance check includes three types of relations.

Convergence: A compliance check reveals an expected relationship among the implemented components. Convergence indicates that the implementation or a part of the implementation is compliant with the planned architecture.

Divergence: Divergence means that a compliance check reveals an unauthorized relation between the implemented components. In other words, the implementation diverges, and therefore, is not compliant with the planned architecture.

Absence: The compliance checks reveal a relation among design-level components that were not implemented. For this reason, a compliance violation is shown.

While it is easy to specify compliance in general, this gets more complicated when it comes to compliance among models with different abstractions. Concerning this, it is important to understand, what is the allowed degree of divergence due to the different abstraction and what is forbidden divergence. Furthermore, the next challenge is executing a compliance check and, in the best case, employing appropriate tool support for this compliance check.

3.5.2   Software Reviews and Audits

A common practice for the development of security- or safety-critical software system are reviews and audits. The IEEE Standard 1028-2008 for Software Reviews and Audits defines five types of software reviews and audits as well as how to perform these [94]. While a review usually targets the continuous internal evaluation of a software system, e.g., regarding security or quality criteria, and aims at improving the software system under development, an audit usually targets checking the compliance with some standard by a third party.

Software reviews and audits are usually performed in a systematic manual inspection of the implementation of the software system as well as its documentation. Accordingly, it involves a huge manual effort, making reviews and audits expensive. Furthermore, for effective reviews and audits specially trained experts are needed. Nevertheless, it has been shown that code reviews can lead to an improved quality of a software system and fewer errors [95].

While the considered review techniques are very formal, there are approaches to incorporate less formal reviews into every day's development activities for getting benefits of software reviews at a lower cost [96]. However, such reviews tend to focus on small defects that could also be detected automatically at a lower cost. Improved tool support could improve both traditional, structured software reviews as well as modern lightweight reviews.

3.5.3 Standards and Certifications

Usually, when we develop a software system for security- or safety-critical domains, we have to follow standards for being allowed to bring our product to market. These standards usually describe required development process steps, such as quality control, which we have to follow, and artifacts we have to deliver. By doing so, a standard should be achieved that prevents users of our software system from harm. Considering the iTrust example, in what follows, we will look into two relevant standards in detail. First, the ISO standard for developing medical device software, and second, the *Common Criteria for Information Technology Security Evaluation* (CC) as a widely used standard for security certifications.

ISO/IEC 62304: Medical Device Software – Software Life Cycle Processes

For medical device software, the ISO standard IEC 62304 specifies requirements for the development and maintenance of medical device software and which artifacts have to be delivered [7]. Thereby, a piece of software itself can also constitute a medical device. While the iTrust system itself does not consist out of hardware, its primary function is to plan and manage health data. The iTrust system has to be considered as a medical device since one of its purposes is to collect and analyze patient data collected from other medical devices and therefore has an immediate impact on the treatment of patients. What exactly has to be considered as a medical device and has to be developed following IEC 62304 is regulated in national laws [97].

Generally, the implementation of quality management, risk management, and a software safety classification is required by the standard when developing medical device software. Thereby, risk management explicitly includes software security. Furthermore, for the development of medical device software, the standard requires five different development activities:

Table 3.1 Required documentation artifacts for medical device software following IEC 62304 (×: Required Artifact)

Software Documentation Artifact	Medical Device Classification		
	Class A	Class B	Class C
Development Planning	×	×	×
Requirements Analysis	×	×	×
Architectural Design		×	×
Detailed Design			×
Unit Implementation	×	×	×
Unit Verification		×	×
Integration & Integration Testing		×	×
System Testing	×	×	×
Release	×	×	×

Software development: In the standard, the development is oriented on classical development processes. Activities like requirements engineering, software architecture, implementation, testing, and deployment are required but do not have to be executed following a specific development process.

Software maintenance: The maintenance of medical device software must be planned explicitly and not be performed in an ad-hoc manner. Before any changes, a problem and possible solutions have to be analyzed before realizing them.

Software risk management: The management of risks plays an essential role, as medical device software might cause serious harm to its users. Possible hazardous situations have to be explicitly analyzed, measures to be chosen and verified. In this thesis, we will only focus on security in this context. This analysis explicitly includes the risks caused by software changes. In principle, the security and reliability of medical device software should be achieved throughout software quality aspects, e.g., as defined in the ISO 25000 [98].

Software configuration management: Possible configurations of the medical device software have to be explicitly identified and controlled, e.g., different versions of the software system or possible configuration file values. While configuration might be considered partly in this thesis in terms of deployment in the implementation models, we will not focus on this.

Software problem resolution: At the development of any software system, usually, problems are faced that have to be documented, assigned to someone, solved, and their solution has to be verified and documented. For the development of medical device software, there is a specific process only focusing on this task. However, there are already reasonable solutions available for providing tool support in practice, e.g., various issue trackers [99, 100].

When developing medical device software, specific development artifacts have to be developed and delivered. Table 3.1 lists the development artifacts required by the IEC 62304. Thereby, the standard differentiates between medical devices with different classifications. In the medical domain, device software is classified into three categories based on the potential to harm people:

Class A: No injury or damage to health is possible.
Class B: Non-serious injury is possible.
Class C: Death or serious injury is possible.

Please note that there is also a classification of the medical devices themselves (Class I to III) that is independent of the software classification related to the medical device [97].

When looking at the required artifacts in Table 3.1, we notice these widely overlap with the artifacts considered at MDD. The same applies to the development processes that have to be performed for being compliant with IEC 62304 and the steps of the V-model. While the standard is clearly oriented on a development process similar to the V-model and using MDD, the standard does not require a specific development process. As long as quality management, risk management, and safety classification are performed, and the required artifacts are delivered, any development process can be used to develop medical device software. However, agile processes have a massive challenge in keeping all artifacts that have to be delivered consistent and compliant with each other. Also, risk management is a considerable challenge for the development of medical device software. For security risks, the *Common Criteria for Information Technology Security Evaluation* consider this challenge in more detail and are often applied to medical device software.

Common Criteria for Information Technology Security Evaluation
One of the most widely adopted security standards is the Common Criteria for Information Technology Security Evaluation, often referred to only as Common Criteria

(CC) [101]. The CC has been released as the ISO/IEC 15408 standard. The CC is meant to specify the *security functional requirements* (SFR) and *security assurance requirements* (SAR) on a software system and to verify if a software system complies with these requirements. For both, the CC provides recommendations that can be adapted to the specific software system.

Security Functional Requirements (SFR): SFRs specify concrete security functions the software system should implement. To guide the selection of necessary security functional requirements, the CC provides *Protection Profiles* that define security requirements for typical classes of devices. Thereby, a software system can be certified against one or more protection profiles. The specific security requirements that have to be implemented are captured as *Security Targets*.

Security Assurance Requirements (SAR): The CC provides a set of measures that should be considered to develop a secure software system to assure compliance with the security functional requirements. Thereby, SARs are assigned to protection profiles and security targets. Which amount of and to which depth the development has to be checked using SARs for showing the compliance with protection profiles is specified in *Evaluation Assurance Levels* of the CC.

In practice, the CC mainly specifies which processes, e.g., a security threat analysis, have to be performed and how these have to be documented. The CC does not specify specific security features that have to be implemented and verified for the software system to be secure [102]. However, this does not mean that security check results do not have to be delivered for certification but these are not inspected in detail as part of the certification. The CC focuses on whether such approaches are used during a software systems development and these reports indicate this. In conclusion, the CC is focused on security planning and documentation but not on verifying the implemented security mechanisms in a software system.

To generally summarize on state of the art for standards and certifications, many artifacts required in standards or certifications are tailored to these sequential development processes. However, none of these explicitly requires such a sequential development process. Nevertheless, there is a considerable challenge in preserving the consistency of the required artifacts during development. Here, vast parts of reviews or certifications are performed purely manually. One of the main challenges where tool support could help make these more efficient is the propagation of security knowledge between the different artifacts and automated verification by security checks.

3.6   Security Checks

Certifications, e.g., according to Common Criteria (CC) [101], play an essential role in ensuring the security of software systems. Usually, design specifications and test results have to be provided for the certification or a software audit. Which artifacts have to be provided depends on the assurance level of CC or other domain-specific standards, e.g., ISO/IEC 62304 for medical device software [7]. The certification is usually performed manually, and incremental re-certification or revocation is currently not supported in case of changed security context knowledge.

3.6.1   UMLsec Security Checks

Following the paradigm of security by design [28], security should be considered from the very beginning of the development of a software system as a first-class citizen. As a consequence, also, requirements engineering must address *security requirements*, which arise from three interacting dimensions: threats, security goals, and system design [103]. In this regard, UMLsec provides a UML profile for annotating UML models with security requirements and various checks for checking the consistency of those security requirements. In what follows, we introduce two of those checks that are particularly interesting for the design of a secure system, as they cover the security requirements of data on both the logical and physical levels of the software system: *Secure Dependency* and *Secure Links*.

Based on a variety of provided stereotypes, UMLsec supports various security checks, including the analysis of security policies, secure information flow, and secure communication in protocols. Stereotypes are one of the three extension mechanisms of UML and allow extension with domain-specific language elements. Such an extension can then be used to annotate UML model elements with those [5]. Similar to classifiers, stereotypes can have properties, which are called *tagged values*. UMLsec operates at the level of class diagrams, deployment diagrams, activity diagrams, sequence diagrams, and component diagrams. In the past, UMLsec has been practically applied for security analyses in diverse contexts such as protocol engineering [104], distributed information systems [105], and mobile communications [106].

Secure Dependency

UMLsec's *Secure Dependency* is a check concerning the static structure of the software system. It ensures that call- and send-dependencies between objects respect the security requirements on the data that may be communicated along with them. *Secure Dependency* can be thought of as a contract between calling and called objects. In the end, applying *Secure Dependency* results in structuring the software system into security levels, e.g., regarding *secrecy* or *integrity*.

The following definition adapted from [73] addresses *secrecy*; the *integrity* case is entirely analogous. We assume that objects have a set of members, that is, operations and properties, and a list of *secrecy*-stereotyped members, as can be specified using tagged values of the «critical» stereotype. To be more precise, every *Class* or *Component* in a UML diagram can be stereotyped with «critical» and the set of *secrecy*-stereotyped members is given as a list of signatures in the tagged value *secrecy*.

Definition 1 *(Secure Dependency) A subsystem fulfills* secrecy dependency *iff for all* «call» *or* «send» *dependencies d from an object C to an object S the following conditions hold:*

(i) for all s ∈ S.members: s ∈ C.secrecy ⇔ s ∈ S.secrecy,
(ii) for all s ∈ S.members: s ∈ C.secrecy ⇒ d is stereotyped «secrecy», *where s refers to the signature of a member.*

For instance, for the class diagram in Figure 3.6, showing an excerpt of Figure 3.3, secure dependency is not fulfilled: The class User specifies *secrecy* for the signature homeAddress:Address. However, since LoginControl does not specify *secrecy* for homeAddress:Address as well, and the «call»-dependency relating the two classes does not contain the «secrecy» stereotype, properties (i) and (ii) are violated.

Using CARiSMA[1], the tool support of UMLsec, security experts can find such violations against the application's structuring into security levels. The concrete violation of the example can be mitigated by removing the violating dependencies or by adding the LoginControl to the security level of secrecy for the violated security level of a member.

UMLsec secure dependency does not only allow us to detect such violations in the planned design but also to recognize bad design decisions. For example, for the class User considered above, we will likely get many dependencies like the one from LoginControl. For each of these dependencies, we have to consider starting from design-time until run-time the guaranties for classified properties and operations. This will not only dramatically increase the annotations needed by UMLsec but

---

[1] http://carisma.umlsec.de/

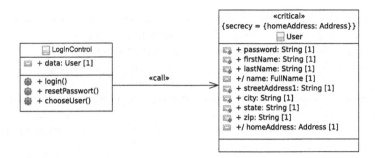

Figure 3.6 Application of the UMLsec *Secure Dependency* stereotypes to iTrust's design model

especially increase the effort needed for considering these in the upcoming phases and verifying compliance with them. Accordingly, the probability of not being compliant and creating a weakness will rise.

For this reason, requiring a tremendous amount of security annotations can also indicate problems. In the considered class diagram, it is unlikely that the Login-Control requires the property homeAddress:Address of the class Person for its functionality, but theoretically, has access to this property. Accordingly, we have to provide the security guarantees required to ensure the security of this potential access. If the same holds for other classes, it is a good idea to extract the security-critical properties in a separate class that provides high protection and is only accessed by entities that need access to the classified properties as part of their planned functionality. By doing so, we can reduce the amount of security-critical dependencies and already at design-time, start improving the software system's security.

Secure Links

Secure Links is a check concerning the physical deployment of a software system. It analyses whether the network of nodes with their communication paths respects the user-specified security requirements concerning a given attacker model.

The check is formulated relative to a given attacker type, such as *default* or *insider* attackers, with distinct capabilities of compromising the software system [6]. In Table 3.2, we show the attacker model considered in this thesis. For each pair of an attacker and a kind of communication path, a set of threats is specified. This section focuses on the threats posed by the default attacker, which represents an outsider adversary with modest capability. This kind of attacker can *read, modify*, and *delete* messages sent over a plain Internet connection, whereas in the case of an encrypted connection, this attacker can only *delete* messages, e.g., using a fake GSM base station to interrupt the connection between iTrust and the mobile device. However, a default attacker would not be able to read the plain text messages or insert messages encrypted with the correct key. Of course, this assumes that the encryption is set up in a way such that the adversary does not get hold of the secret key. The default attacker is assumed not to have direct access to the local area network (LAN) and, therefore, not to be able to eavesdrop on those connections nor on wires connecting security-critical devices, e.g. a smart-card reader allowing doctors to authenticate using their health professional card.

We recapitulate a definition of *Secure Links* for the security requirement «integrity» of UMLsec [73]. A corresponding definition for the security requirement «secrecy» is obtained by replacing the considered threat with *read*.

Definition 2 *(Secure Links) A subsystem fulfills* Secure Links *iff for all* «integrity» *dependencies d between objects on different nodes n, m, ∃ communication path p between n and m with a stereotype s s.t.* write ∉ Threats(s), *where Threats(s) is a set of threats posed by an outside attacker to s-stereotyped communication paths.*

Table 3.2 UMLsec *Secure Links* attacker model

	default attacker			insider attacker		
	read	write	delete	read	write	delete
«Internet»	×	×	×	×	×	×
«encrypted»			×			×
«LAN»				×	×	×
«wire»						

For example, in the deployment diagram in Figure 3.7, *Secure Links* holds under the condition that the communication path between Hospital and MobileDevice is annotated with «encrypted». Due to the «integrity»-stereotype dependency between Patient and AuthentificationService, *Secure Links* does not hold when only an «Internet» communication path is available because outsider attackers can perform a man-in-the-middle-attack to compromise integrity or threat secrecy by reading, e.g., the login data, on the unencrypted connection.

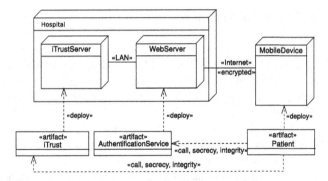

Figure 3.7 Excerpt of the iTrust implementation model showing the application of UMLsec *Secure Links*

UMLsec has been proven in various applications to be effective in detecting security violations in software systems. For example, among others, UMLsec has been successfully applied at the German telecommunications company O_2 [106] or the car manufacturer BMW [105]. However, these applications are limited to single independent models and do not consider the hierarchies created in model-driven development. For this reason, on every more detailed model, all security specifications made before have to be repeated. Using approaches like UMLsec, developers should specify all properties, like security assumptions, only once on the most suitable level of abstraction. This also includes other artifacts than the design-time models, such as the implementation of the software system. Also, the reuse between the different security checks can be improved. For example, *Secure Links* considers communications between different artifact and security requirements for these communications. In UML, internal details on artifacts can be described using a class diagram whose classes can be manifested in an artifact. For example, for a Java application, the artifact can be the executable jar-file of the application and other artifacts can be libraries or databases. The classes bundled into the jar file correspond to classes in UML class diagrams. The detailed class diagrams can contain dependencies between each other that are instances of the dependencies in the deployment diagram.

3.6.2   SecDFD Security Checks

At design time, the processing of system data can be specified with a variety of notations. Apart from UML activity diagrams [5], frequently used notations are and business process models (BPMN [107]) and data flow diagrams (DFD) [108]. Our rationale for focusing on DFDs and the SecDFD security extension is twofold: First, they are widely applied in practice, specifically in the automotive industry [109] and at Microsoft [110], as part of their STRIDE methodology. Second, they represent an essential set of concepts necessary for data flow analysis (processes and data flow between them), which can be mapped exhaustively to activity diagrams and business processes, rendering our mapping generation technique also applicable to these model kinds. We introduce our technique for DFDs, but it can be applied to a broad range of modeling languages supporting data flow modeling.

In what follows, we introduce DFDs and an extended notation that allows to include security-relevant information in DFD models, which is required for checking the consistency between planned security and implemented security requirements.

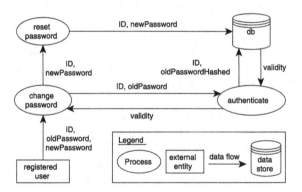

Figure 3.8 A DFD for changing a password in iTrust

Data Flow Diagrams

A Data Flow Diagram (DFD) is a graphical representation of the software architecture and the information it handles [110]. It represents how the information enters, leaves, and traverses the software system. The DFD consists of processes (active entities), external entities (e.g., third parties), data stores (where information rests), data flows (carrying the exchanged information), and trust boundaries (signaling trust levels). Figure 3.8 depicts a DFD for the iTrust electronics health records system. A registered user attempts to change her by sending a request including her identification number, the old, and the desired new password. The iTust system verifies the user by authenticating her ID and password against a database. Next, if the old password is valid, the password is reset to the new password and updated in the database.

Security Extension

To capture security requirements at the architectural level, we use the Security Data Flow Diagram (SecDFD [111, 112]). SecDFD is a notation that enriches DFD with security concepts to enable a formally grounded information flow analysis, focusing on the confidentiality and integrity of information assets. First, comparable to UMLsec, assets can be tagged with a *high* or *low* confidentiality label. Second, process nodes can be tagged with security contracts that define how the security requirements of assets change upon exiting the node.

The SecDFD notation defines four such contracts:

Encrypt or Hash contract: The contract for encrypting input asset(s) always results in propagating a low (public) label on the output flow(s).

Decrypt contract: If the input asset is labeled with low, decrypting it will result in propagating a low label. However, if the input asset is labeled with high, decrypting will propagate a high label on the output flow.

Join contract: The contract for joining two or more assets propagates the label equivalent to the most restrictive input asset. For example, if a confidential asset is joined with a non-confidential asset, the asset on the output will be confidential.

Forward or Copy contract: This contract will copy the labels of the input asset(s) to the output flow(s) carrying the corresponding forwarded asset(s).

Finally, the model elements can be grouped into attacker zones. An attacker zone specifies the groups of elements that an attacker of a specific profile can observe. The user of the SecDFD approach can define a hierarchy of attacker zones with different attacker profiles.

Figure 3.9 shows an excerpt (for clarity) of the SecDFD for the iTrust example. If a user resets her password, she enters secret information into the software system, for which its confidentiality has to be guaranteed. It has to be ensured that there is no unwanted data flow in the software system and the password is not stored in cleartext. Also, it has to be ensured that the new password not only stays secret but also cannot be maliciously modified. First, the designer must specify that the password is confidential. Second, the designer needs to specify the process contract, e.g., for the process authenticate. Since the password is confidential, it should

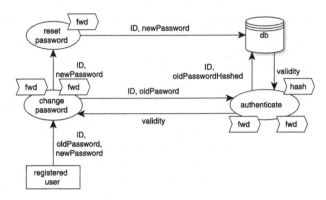

Figure 3.9 An excerpt of a SecDFD for iTrust

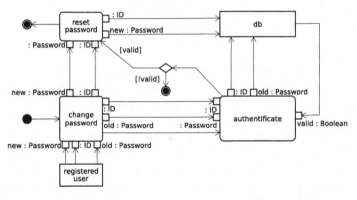

Figure 3.10 UML activity diagram corresponding to the DFD in Figure 3.8

not be leaked to other applications running in the environment or processes outside of the authentication service. These simple extensions allow us to identify such behavior in the model. The extended notation [111] is shipped with a simple label propagation (using a dept-first search) according to the specified process contracts. Once the labels have been propagated, a static check is executed to determine if any confidential information flows to an attacker zone. In Figure 3.9, the Plugin is not a malicious entity, i.e., it is not part of an attacker zone. The developer can manipulate the elements of attacker zones to change the design model and improve security. For the concrete syntax and semantics of SecDFD, we refer the reader to [111].

In contrast to UMLsec, SecDFD does not provide automated security checks but allows for propagating security labels through the diagram, which eases performing manual security analyses, such as STRIDE. While SecDFDs can support security analyses widely used in practice, the expressiveness of DFDs is very limited. For example, we know the sequence in which data flows are executed, but this information is not part of the DFD. Also, conditional flows are not supported. We do not know which data flows happen if the user's authentication fails in the DFD of Figure 3.9 and which flows in the case of success. To solve this issue, the generality of DFDs allows us to apply the SecDFD security contract also to UML activity diagrams. Figure 3.10 shows the same procedure as in the DFD of Figure 3.8 but contains additional control flow information. Every process is expressed by a corresponding activity and every data flow in the DFD by a data flow in the activity diagram. In addition, activity diagrams contain control flow, e.g., specifying what happens if the authentication fails.

An open issue for both approaches, UMLsec and SecDFD, is that a secure specification of a software system does not imply a secure software system implementation. All security requirements and measures have to be correctly implemented and verified in the implementation.

3.6.3 Implementation-Level Security Checks

Implementation-level security checks are realized often using static code analysis. Usually, such static security issues are used to detect actual security issues already during software implementation before executing the software system. Thereby, the analysis tools are often integrated within the development environments or build processes. Often IDEs already come with static code analysis or can be extended with such. One example of such a widely used static code-analysis that can be considered to contribute to the security requirement of availability is analyses for potential null-pointer exceptions. However, there are also implementation-level security checks that are only related to security. Besides such static security checks, three also exist security tests [113, 114] and dynamic security monitoring approaches [115, 116] that check a running software system in a test environment or the production environment. However, such security monitors got less attention in the security engineering community than static security checks that allow preventing security issues upfront. In practice, security tests are mainly executed as manual penetration tests and run-time security monitoring barely plays a role [117]. For this reason, we focus on static security checks. In what follows, we discuss three categories of static security checks.

Analysis of API Calls

Many approaches locally analyze calls to critical APIs and whether the chosen parameters have been selected securely. This covers, for example, calls to cryptographic APIs [118] or SQL queries [119]. While those approaches are essential for the development of secure systems, in this work, we are focusing more on whether, e.g., the use of a cryptographic API has been implemented at a specified location.

Secure Data-Flow Analysis

A common approach to detect leaks of secret data is a secure data flow analysis. The goal is to detect flows of sensitive information within the implementation into insecure sinks, e.g., a file in the file system or a socket [33, 120, 121]. While data-flow analysis tools have become very good at analyzing or approximating OO constructs such as dynamic class loading and Java reflection [122, 123], one of the main problems for a precise data flow analysis is the classification of critical sources and sinks. Many tools are based on shared libraries of well-known critical sources and sinks, created manually or by machine learning [42]. However, including project-specific information about sources of sensitive information and forbidden sinks is a substantial manual effort.

Dependency Analysis

In practice, many vulnerabilities of software systems arise from the use of deprecated dependencies containing the vulnerabilities. Due to the criticality of this issue, it was added to the OWASP Top 10 Security Issues in 2013. Several tools have been developed to mitigate this threat of deprecated dependencies for inspecting the dependencies of software systems for libraries with known vulnerabilities [124]. Among the most prominent tools are the OWASP Dependency-Check [125] and the GitHub Dependabot [126]. However, such tools cannot assist in detecting a malicious or accidental exchange of libraries at run-time.

While the single implementation-level security checks are very effective at their specific task, the scope of these is very narrow. All in all, the open question is if implementation-level security checks are suitable to check the high-level security requirements of the final software system. The idea is that security is planned already at design-time, using the introduced security checks and their tool support, and afterward are verified at the implementation level by suitable use of implementation-level security checks.

3.7 Conclusion on the State of the Art

The development of a secure software system involves multiple aspects of planning, realization, and verification. Considering all discussed aspects isolated, for every one of these different aspects, satisfactory solutions have been developed. However, there are many unconnected solutions for the individual local problems in total but no integration to apply these throughout the whole development and maintenance process. Currently, for most integration or transition steps, a massive manual effort is required. These manual tasks increase cost and the risk for errors. All together, keeping all artifacts consistent is an inherent problem for model-driven development, security certifications, and agile development processes. Another major challenge lies in the propagation of security properties between different development steps and artifacts.

A Walkthrough of the Proposed Development Approach

4

In the previous chapters, we discussed challenges in the development and maintenance of secure software systems and existing approaches for tackling the different challenges. The main issue lies in the tracing between different artifacts that are developed. Here, a huge manual effort is required for keeping the artifacts consistent. This distracts a developer's attention from her main task and, therefore, lowers the efficiency. Moreover, the requirement of considering too many things at the same time and the high effort required for preserving consistency might give rise to more errors in the long term.

To overcome these challenges, in Section 1.3, we identified five research questions, focusing on aspects required for improving the model-based development and maintenance of secure variant-rich software systems. To allow continuous model-based security engineering, we mainly focus on the automated tracing of security requirements throughout the whole development process and their continuous verification. Generally, the idea of the GRaViTY development approach is to create and maintain trace links between design and code artifacts automatically. The trace links are used to propagate security-related information between models and the software system's implementation. Also, the trace links allow to automatically reflect changes on any artifact to all other artifacts. Due to this continuous automated synchronization, that allows changing all artifacts of a software system at any time, the GRaViTY development approach supports both, sequential and agile development processes.

In this chapter, we discuss from a developer's perspective how a secure software system can be developed with GRaViTY to overcome the identified problems. As developers are a critical factor in the successful development of software systems, we consider our conclusion of this discussion when answering the research questions. For this purpose, first, we discuss our assumptions on how to allow developers to work efficiently at the development of secure software systems. By doing this, we derive key ideas on which we will build our solution. Afterward, we show

© The Author(s), under exclusive license to Springer Fachmedien Wiesbaden GmbH, part of Springer Nature 2022
S. M. Peldszus, *Security Compliance in Model-driven Development of Software Systems in Presence of Long-Term Evolution and Variants*,
https://doi.org/10.1007/978-3-658-37665-9_4

the development process for developing secure software systems using GRaViTY. Also, we show the provided tool support and how it is integrated into this process. Finally, we demonstrate the development using our approach from the perspective of a developer.

4.1   Key Ideas of the GRaViTY Approach

Developers play an essential role in the success of a software project. The more developers can focus on their tasks, the more efficient they can be in solving these tasks. The primary goal of GRaViTY is to enable the successful development and maintenance of secure software systems. Thereby, the key ideas for allowing developers to efficiently work on the development of a secure software system are:

Suitable Views: Developers should work on the most suitable view for their task. For every task, there is a view in which this task can be carried out most effectively. For example, when a security expert is planning or updating general security requirements of a software system, an abstract view of the software system is more likely to be suitable than the source code containing all details. However, due to circumstances from the used development process or tooling, all the required information might not be available in this view or the view cannot easily be created. For example, while a software system has initially been designed using UMLsec on abstract design-time models, due to missing trace links, changes in the security requirements have to be specified on the implementation level. Such situations should be avoided by the design of our approach and proper tool support. Software developers and experts, e.g., security experts or software architects, should always have to possibility to work on the most suitable view for their task.

Side effects: Developers should only focus on their tasks and should not have to care about potential side effects.
Nearly every task a developer performs comes with side effects she has to think about. In this thesis, we explicitly consider two kinds of side effects.

Local side effects: First, side effects within the artifact a developer is changing. These are essential for preserving the correct behavior of a software system. Automated tool support as part of a development approach can help in identifying such side effects. For example, UMLsec checks allow detecting side effects of model-level changes impacting design-time security requirements.

Global side effects: Second, in addition to local side effects, there might be side effects on other artifacts. If these artifacts do not immediately relate to the correct function of the software system, developers should not have to care about side effects on these. For example, consider a developer optimizing a software system's implementation-level design quality. Most changes might not affect the architecture of the software system, since they are too fine-grained and do not affect the borders of components. In this case, the developer should not have to care about the effects on the architecture during her task.

However, coming back to the suitability of views, an architect should also not have to review the local restructurings at the implementation level of the software system. Side effects that occurred and changed the architectural level should be propagated to the architectural level.

Furthermore, refactorings might have side effects regarding a software system's security requirements, e.g., by making sensitive information accessible. Here, the developer should still be able to focus on the code quality and tool support should take care of preventing changes with such side effects.

To this end, following the GRaViTY approach, a developer should not have to think about such side effects. The changes of the developer should be automatically propagated to all other artifacts and then be presented to the corresponding expert for review. Also, tool support should lower the risk of changes that lead to violations within other artifacts.

Synchronization: Developers can change artifacts in arbitrary order and their changes are automatically propagated for keeping all artifacts synchronized. Keeping all artifacts synchronized in case of changes usually requires a significant manual effort and is likely to give rise to inconsistencies. Also, this step is a prerequisite for allowing developers, architects, and security experts to work on the most suitable view of the software system as depicted in the previous two ideas. Accordingly, the synchronization of the artifacts should happen as far as possible in the background with as few user interactions as possible.

Continuous Security: Developers are consciously assisted by automated security compliance checks helping to preserve the software system's security. Continuous automated security checks are also an essential concept in other approaches, e.g., SecDevOps [127]. We consider these in our approach but our goal is to go even one step further.

Usually, when talking about continuous automated security checks, low-level security checks with a limited scopes are meant. In our approach, we target the security compliance of the implementation with the specification in design-time models. Nevertheless, security checks with limited scopes, such as UMLsec that only targets the model-level, are essential to ensure the consistency of the security specifications with which we check the compliance. However, these automated security checks should not replace manual reviews but support these. Also, continuous automated security checks allow to review changes quicker and studying their effects. This eases incremental reviews.

To summarize, we need a development process that allows developers to focus on their tasks and allows them to perform the tasks on the most suitable view on the software system. In addition, such an approach might also assist in performing the tasks themselves. The consideration of tool support can be a fundamental part of such an approach. However, in the intended GRaViTY approach, tool support is not meant to replace developers, security experts, or software architects but to assist them. While the desired tool support might not be easy to implement from a technical perspective, the main challenges lie in the design of a development approach supporting the outlined key ideas and in the underlying challenges that have to be solved for realizing the approach.

4.2   The GRaViTY Development Approach

Next, we show the general development process using the GRaViTY approach and the automatically executed tasks within this sequence. Figure 4.1 shows a concep-

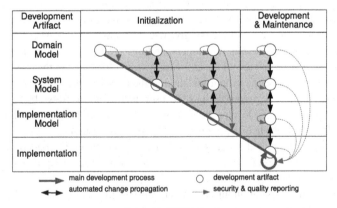

Figure 4.1 Development process of the GRaViTY development approach

tual overview of the development using the GRaViTY development approach. We assume that three levels of design models are used in addition to the concrete implementation of the software system. The artifacts that will be created are shown on the left side of Figure 4.1. As soon as a model is created, it is denoted by a circle representing an instance of the model or the software system's source code.

Following the figure, we assume, that all models are created in the order of their abstraction level and none is temporarily skipped. However, we do not assume that any of these models is completed before the next one is created. Incrementally, developing the models in iterations is explicitly possible and allows the usage of GRaViTY in agile development processes.

In agile development, the main development process has three initialization steps in which initial versions of all models are created. In the fourth step, the development and maintenance phase is reached, in which we iterate until the software system has been developed. If we want to consider the maintenance of the software system, we stay in this step and iterate until the software system's end of life.

The blue area above the main development process arrow contains all artifacts available in the current step of the main development process. Whenever a change is applied to any of the artifacts, this change is propagated to all other artifacts that have been developed automatically. The corresponding development activities are denoted in the figure by blue arrows.

A software system's development is supported by security and quality reports covering all artifacts that have been developed. Security and quality aspects are centrally reported into the main development process, which is denoted by red, dotted arrows.

Sequential Process Models: When using GRaViTY for the development of software systems following traditional development processes such as the waterfall model or V-model, the main development process only goes one step forward, after the model to be developed has been finished. Also, the iterations in the *development & maintenance* step of GRaViTY only take place at maintenance, meaning that the first iteration takes place when the entire implementation is done.

Agile Software Development: When using agile methods for software development, nearly all time will be spent in the *development & maintenance* step of GRaViTY. The initialization will take place in only a few Sprints, creating the basic setup of the required models. Afterward, these are iteratively refined in the following Sprints. Thereby, intense usage of the synchronization provided by GRaViTY takes place.

4.3   Developer Perspective on Using GRaViTY

In Figure 4.2, we show the interaction of a developer with the software system
under development while using GRaViTY. The software system under development
is depicted in the center of the figure. Thereby, the software system consists out of
the discussed development artifacts, namely different design models and the source
code of the software system. These artifacts as well as their relations are shown in
the center of the figure.

The GRaViTY framework is indicated by a cylindrical shape on the figure's
right side. This shape connects all development artifacts and operates invisibly for
a developer in the background. It takes care of synchronizing all artifacts in case of
changes, the propagation of security requirements, and security checks.

On the left of the figure, a developer is shown that can directly interact with the
development artifacts of the software system. In our case, interaction means that
the single artifacts of the software system can directly be edited by the developer,
using an IDE into which GRaViTY is integrated. This integration comprises user
interfaces allowing developers to make use of the GRaViTY tool support, e.g., by
using refactorings for restructuring the implementation. Currently, only the Eclipse
IDE in combination with the Papyrus model editor [128, 129] is supported. Within
this IDE, GRaViTY continuously provides reports to developers, e.g., on security violations currently present in the software system or details on the effects of
planned refactoring operations. Based on the reports, developers and experts can

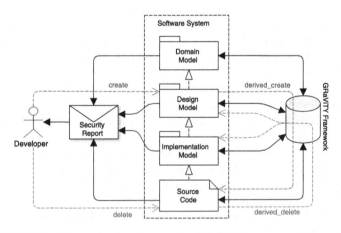

Figure 4.2 A developer performing changes using GRaViTY

plan improvements to the software system. For the generation of reports, GRaViTY considers all artifacts present in the software system.

Whenever a developer edits a development artifact, e.g., by deleting and adding elements in models or source code. These changes are propagated to all other artifacts by GRaViTY. For example, the developer's addition to the design model leads to a derived addition in the source code and a deletion of elements in the source code leads to deletions in the implementation model and design model. After every change, an updated report is created and presented to the developer. This report can then be used for estimating the impact of the change but also be shared with experts, e.g., software architects or security experts.

While working with GRaViTY, there should be no difference between working on a single product or a variant-rich software system. A developer can still change the software product line in her preferred way. Also, security and quality reports are continuously provided but now consider the whole software product line.

Part II
Tracing

Program Model for Object-oriented Languages

5

This chapter shares material with the PPPJ'2015 publication "Incremental Co-Evolution of Java Programs based on Bidirectional Graph Transformation" [130] and the TTC'2015 publications "Object-oriented Refactoring of Java Programs using Graph Transformation" [131] and "A Solution to the Java Refactoring Case Study using eMoflon" [130].

In this thesis, we study how to verify security compliance in the context of model-driven development of software systems. To make the implementation of a software system analyzable, we have to extract a suitable program representation from the source code of the software system. Common representations, such as UML models [5] or abstract syntax trees (AST) [132], are either too abstract for meaningful design-level quality and security analyses of the implementation or are too detailed and not providing direct access to relevant information. For example, an AST does not contain resolved references, which hardens analyses of access dependencies.

In this chapter, we introduce our program model for object-oriented languages. This program model has a level of abstraction between design-time models, such as UML models, and models close to the implementation, like ASTs. In the upcoming sections, we use this program model for tracing security requirements between the architecture and the implementation, security checks, and the specification and execution of security-preserving refactorings. In addition, this program model has been used in additional research for design flaw detection [34, 21].

© The Author(s), under exclusive license to Springer Fachmedien Wiesbaden GmbH, part of Springer Nature 2022
S. M. Peldszus, *Security Compliance in Model-driven Development of Software Systems in Presence of Long-Term Evolution and Variants*,
https://doi.org/10.1007/978-3-658-37665-9_5

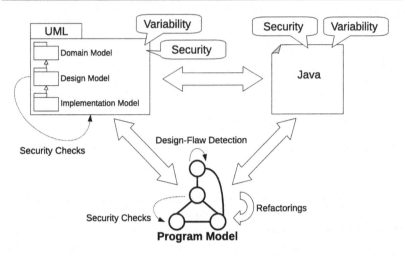

Figure 5.1 Location of the program model in the overall concept

One of the most significant issues when automatically checking and changing programs is defining and creating an appropriate program representation. According to Figure 5.1, the program representation has to be suitable for checking security and design-related problems and the effects of countermeasures to eliminate the identified problems. As a foundation to find answers for all five major research questions (RQ1–RQ5) of this thesis, we need a suitable representation of a software system's implementation on which we can work in the upcoming chapters. Also, in the best case, we can use this representation not only for a specific programming language but can achieve an abstraction allowing it to represent an object-oriented language. Altogether, such a representation must provide a suitable level of abstraction that allows easy structural queries without going to the statement level, and should be capable to represent arbitrary object-oriented programs by a single program model type?

In this chapter, we introduce a general notion for representing object-oriented programs and the dependencies within these programs on a method–field–class level. The notion is tailored to allow easy queries on a high-level abstraction of the statement-level details of a program. Although we orient on the Java programming language, we provide an abstraction to general OO concepts allow representing arbitrary OO programs and discuss this application.

5.1   Background on Program Representations

The creation of meaningful and easy to analyze program representations has been a subject in multiple different areas. First, the most native area comprises compilers that have to parse the source code to compile it. For this purpose, in the first step, a compiler creates an internal program representation of the source code, performs optimizations, and finally, transforms the (optimized) program representation into binary executable code [133]. In the first step, the compiler parses the source code and creates an *Abstract Syntax Tree* (AST) [132] from the source code. The AST is a tree representation of the source code's syntactic structure and is usually built per method. These trees represent the semantic relevant information and do not contain any interpretation of the information stored. For example, the execution sequence of the AST nodes and variable accesses are not resolved. Usually, the AST is used as an intermediate representation and is often converted into a *Control Flow Graph* (CFG) [134]. In a CFG, information such as local variable accesses have been resolved and is directly accessible. Still, information such as field accesses or calls of methods is not resolved. For these, the CFG only contains the information that a field or method with a given ID from a given namespace is accessed.

Next, program representations have been defined for special purposes, such as checking the validity of OO refactorings. To tackle the inherent problems of recent refactoring implementations operating at the AST level, graph-based program transformation has been proposed as a promising alternative for concisely and formally specifying and implementing OO refactoring rules comprehensively [24, 135, 136, 137, 24, 37, 138]. Here, the program under consideration is transformed into an abstract and custom-tailored program model representation that essentially (i) defines a restricted view on the AST containing only relevant high-level OO program entities, and (ii) adds additional cross-AST dependencies making explicit (static) semantic information being crucial to avoid behavior-scrambling refactorings [139, 137, 140, 141].

Furthermore, there are language-specific general-purpose program representations such as MoDisco [142] or JaMoPP [143] for Java. These representations are comparable to CFGs known from compilers. The significant difference lies in the scope of the model. While compilers focus on single methods, program models are on the scope of the whole program. For this reason, dependencies between methods and fields are resolved and explicitly represented by edges in the model. Also, models such as the MoDisco model usually contain syntactically irrelevant information such as comments. All in all, these models are specifically tailored to a version of a programming language and are likely to get very large.

To sum up, graph-based approaches to program transformation and analysis rely on a well-formed program representation through a program model that is suitable as an abstract view of programs. To this end, each possible program model instance has to conform to a predefined format, referred to as the *type graph*. The type graph can be seen as a metamodel of the corresponding programming language, where nodes represent first-class program entities and edges denote different kinds of relations between those entities. A concrete program model instance whose nodes and edge labels conform to the given type graph is said to be (well-)typed over the type graph. From a formal point of view, this requires a label-preserving graph morphism between the program model's nodes and edges onto the type graph, where graphs are labeled over sets of types [144]. From a practical point of view, the type graph serves as a template containing all node and edge types and their possible connections that can occur in program model instances. Edges may be further equipped with multiplicity constraints to restrict the number of edges of a given type. For instance, the multiplicity $0..1$ of a returnType edge, expressing an object of which type a method returns, denotes that each method definition has either exactly one or no (void) declared return type.

5.2   Program Model for Object-oriented Programs

Our program model provides a high-level abstraction from the pure Java source code [130]. This abstraction, in principle, also allows the application to other OO languages. First, details from the statement level are reduced to access edges between the single members. Second, easy to query structures are created, such as structuring methods and fields into a tree with names, signatures, and definitions.

Figure 5.2 shows our type graph for Java programs using a UML class diagram notation for convenience. The type graph represents a high-level abstraction for structural entities of object-oriented programs such as Java programs. The node TypeGraph serves as a common container for each program element, thus building the root of the containment hierarchy. The type graph contains an annotation mechanism that allows specifying annotations by extending the type TAnnotation. These annotations can be applied to all types with the attribute tAnnotation:TAnnotation for providing additional information. In the remainder of this section, we introduce the type graph elements in detail.

5.2.1 Namespaces

Object-oriented programs are usually structured into namespaces. Namespaces allow programmers to structure programs hierarchically, allowing them to group coherent functionality and reuse names in different contexts. Even on procedural languages that do not support namespaces, e.g., the C programming language, namespaces are often simulated using naming patterns. In many languages, such as Java or the UML, namespaces are realized using packages. Following these examples, we are also implementing namespaces using packages. The package structure is represented by the node `TPackage` and a corresponding self-edge for relating parent packages to their direct sub-packages. A package can contain an arbitrary number of types in terms of interfaces and classes. This containment means that the type is defined in the scope of the namespace represented by the package.

Listing 5.1 contains an excerpt from the Java class definition of the iTrust class `EditPatientAction` used for editing patient information such as the address of a patient. This class extends the class `PatientBaseAction` and uses the class `PatientBean` as a parameter in the `updateInformation` method. The method receives a `PatientBean` that contains the information entered in the UI of the iTrust system. For security reasons, the patient's medical identification number (MID) has to be set again to avoid the modification of the wrong patient in the database. Afterward, the data is validated, edited in the database and a notification e-mail sent.

```
 1  package edu.ncsu.csc.itrust.action;
 2
 3  public class EditPatientAction extends PatientBaseAction {
 4      public void updateInformation(PatientBean p) throws ITrustException,
            FormValidationException {
 5          p.setMID(pid); // for security reasons
 6          validator.validate(p);
 7          patientDAO.editPatient(p, loggedInMID);
 8          emailutil.sendEmail(makeEmail());
 9      }
10  }
```

Listing 5.1 Excerpt from the Java source code of the iTrust class `EditPatientAction` for updating the information about a patient

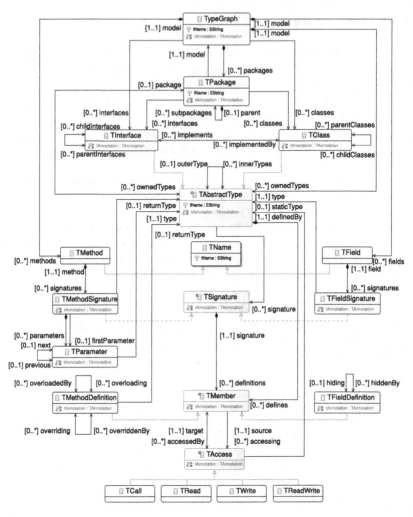

Figure 5.2 GRaViTY's metamodel for language independent object-oriented program models

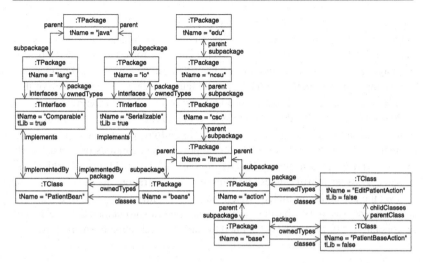

Figure 5.3 Excerpt from a program model of iTrust showing namespaces and the class hierarchy

For this class definition, Figure 5.3 shows the package hierarchy in the program model of these three classes and the interfaces `Serializable` and `Comparable` from the Java standard library. In the center of the figure, we can see the default namespace of the iTrust application: `edu.ncsu.csc.itrust`. The package `itrust` has two sub-packages, `action` and `beans`. The package `action` contains the class `EditPatientAction` from Listing 5.1 and has another sub-package `base`. We can see the packages representing the namespaces `java.lang` and `java.io` of the Java standard library on the figure's top left. As packages are only meant as representations of namespaces and could be used both in libraries and user code, the information where a package is defined is not encoded into the program model.

5.2.2   Types

As mentioned in the previous paragraphs, in our type graph, we define two kinds of types. The node `TAbstractType` represents arbitrary types that can be concrete classes represented by `TClass` or interfaces represented by instances of `TInterface`. It is a common practice to allow the separate specification of interfaces and concrete implementation of the interface. For example, in C-like languages, interfaces are specified in header files. The implementation of these interfaces is specified in *.c files for C or *.cpp files for C++. Also, Java-based languages allow the specification of interfaces that can be implemented by classes. For example, the program model excerpt in Figure 5.3 shows the realization of the interfaces Comparable and Serializable by the class PatientBean.

Many languages also describe some kind of enumeration for the definition of a finite amount of constants. As there is a vast difference in how exactly these enumerations are realized, we decided to represent enumerations by instances of TClass and to represent every enumeration constant with a field owned by this class instance. The selection of classes for representing enumerations instead of interfaces follows the possibility to include functionality in enumerations, e.g., as in current Java versions. To indicate that the specific class represents an enumeration, we define an annotation TEnumeration applied to classes representing enumerations.

5.2.3 Inheritance

As inheritance is one of the object-oriented paradigm's main features, this has to be captured in the type graph. Here, we consider two kinds of inheritance. First, inheritance between interfaces, and second, inheritance between classes. Both are expressed in the type graph by a parent-child relation (parentInterfaces/ childInerfaces and parentClasses/ childClasses). While multiple inheritance is only allowed for interfaces in many languages, we do not restrict the type graph to single inheritance for classes to be as general as possible.

A concrete example of inheritance between classes is shown in the program model excerpt of Figure 5.3. Following Listing 5.1, the class EditPatient Action extends the class PatientBaseAction. Accordingly, there is a parent-child reference between the corresponding two TClass nodes on the right of the program model excerpt.

5.2.4 Methods & Fields

In object-oriented languages, functionality is specified in methods, and data is stored in fields. The node TAbstractType contains an arbitrary number of members (abstract node TMember) in terms of method and field definitions (TMethodDefinition or *TFieldDefinition*, respectively). In addition, a *TAbstractType* refers to the abstract node TSignature, which is the common ancestor of method and field signatures. We split the name, the signature, and the definition of methods and fields into separate nodes within the program model. As object-oriented refactorings, for example, are mainly concerned with the high-level program structure, this separation facilitates reasoning about the feasibility of structural modifications of the program. Consequently, we support compact and modular definitions of refactoring rules concerning the class-method/field (de-)composition of Java programs concisely formulated over the corresponding program model. Methods and fields are represented by a graph structure consisting of three elements:

- The name of the method (field) is contained in the attribute tName of TMethod (TField), thus being globally visible in program model instances.
- The signatures of methods (fields) of a given name are represented by the type TMethodSignature (TFieldSignature). The signature of a method consists of its name and an ordered list of parameter types parameters, while the signature of a field consists of its name and its type. Different signatures with the same name, i.e., a common container TMethod or TField, facilitate overloading. Signatures play a central role in the OO language semantics as all method call dispatches and field accesses are resolved over signatures.
- TMethodDefinition (TFieldDefinition) is an abstraction encapsulating the entire method bodies occurring in the given program. The method body's implementation details are covered by a single definition node in the program model, while edges denote additional relevant (semantic) properties.

```
1  package edu.ncsu.csc.itrust.action;
2
3  public class EditOfficeVisitAction {
4      public String updateInformation(EditOfficeVisitForm form, boolean
           isERIncident) throws FormValidationException {
5          String confirm = "";
6          try {
7              updateOv(form, isERIncident);
8              confirm = "success";
9              return confirm;
10         } catch (ITrustException e) {
11             return e.getMessage();
12         }
13     }
14 }
```

Listing 5.2 Excerpt from the Java source code of iTrust class EditOfficeVisitAction

For example, Figure 5.4 shows a program model excerpt of the program model created from the iTrust implementation, focusing on the source code excerpts in Listings 5.2 and 5.1. The excerpt contains two different method signatures for the method name `updateInformation`. For the signature with the parameter types `EditOfficeVisitForm` and `Boolean`, a definition from the class `Edit-OfficeVisit` is shown, which calls another method definition. This allows the easy specification of, e.g., compliance checks with models [23] (Chapters 8 and 9), refactorings [145, 130] (Chapter 10), or design flaw detection [21] and elimination [146].

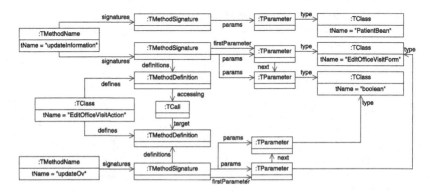

Figure 5.4 Excerpt from the iTrust program model

5.2.5 Member Access

One of the essential parts of every high-level programming language is access to data or calls of functions. These can be in sequential order as in Listing 5.1, but most times, such accesses are woven into a conditional control flow as in Listing 5.2. Generally, the control flow's precise structure is not important in many high-level applications, such as a vast selection of security checks, but it is sufficient to know which members are accessed. For this reason, in our type graph, access edges between member instances represent semantic dependencies between members. The node `TAccess` stands for all kinds of semantic dependencies among class members, i.e., essentially read, write accesses to fields, and call accesses to methods. For more sophisticated security analyses, it might be necessary to differentiate between different access kinds explicitly. Supporting such analyses, the type graph provides four specific kinds of accesses.

`TCall`: This access should be used for invocations of functionality such as method calls in Java.

`TRead`: Accesses, where a field's value is read but not modified, are represented by an instance of the `TRead` node.

`TWrite`: If there is an assignment to a field, then the `TWrite` node should be used.

`TReadWrite`: Often it is undecidable whether there is a read or write access to a field. For example, if a field is passed to the parameter of a method in a Java program, it is statically undecidable and depends on the method's concrete implementations. The `TreadWrite` node represents such cases.

For example, the `TCall` node in Figure 5.4 represents the method invocation of the method `updateOv` by the method `updateInformation` in line 7 of Listing 5.2.

5.2.6   Overloading, Overwriting and Hiding

To allow compact reasoning on a program model, e.g., as part of refactoring rule definitions, overloading, overriding, and hiding dependencies to other members are declared by corresponding edges between definition instances. However, the overloading/overriding/hiding structure is also derivable from the signatures, definitions, and inheritance relations.

In the context of overloading, we consider the definitions of methods with the same name but different parameters within the same type hierarchy. These definitions should reference each other using the `overriding` reference. Regarding the method overriding and field hiding, due to our focus on the Java programming language, we implement the specification of the Java programming language [61]. Methods have a hard override of methods with the same signature in parent classes, while fields are only hiding fields with the same name in parent classes.

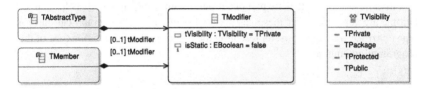

Figure 5.5 Modifiers and visibilities in the type graph

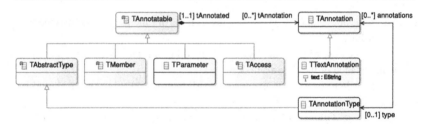

Figure 5.6 Annotation mechanism of GRaViTY's type graph

5.2.7   Modifiers & Visibilities

A low-level security concept in many programming languages is access restriction
to functionality or data realized in terms of visibilities. Methods, fields, or entire
types can be encapsulated from the outside. Access policies are specified using
the visibilities. Following Figure 5.5, in the type graph, we encode such visibilities
as modifiers on types and members. We orient the specification in the type graph
on the UML [5]. By default, the visibility is set to the lowest possible visibility
(TPrivate). Besides, we support the modifier static to indicate elements that can
be accessed outside of the context of an object.

5.2.8   Annotation Mechanism

As introduced at the beginning of this section, the type graph provides an annotation mechanism that supports defining custom extensions to the metamodel and
annotating elements in the program model. Figure 5.6 shows this annotation mechanism in more detail. Annotatable elements are the ones that extend an abstract
type TAnnotatable. Furthermore, this annotation mechanism is used to express
comments on the source code elements in terms of a TTextAnnotation on the
program model's corresponding elements.

Finally, annotations that are part of a programming language, such as Java annotations, are supported. For these cases, annotations in the type graph can have a
type (TAnnotationType) representing the corresponding annotation type of the
programming language.

5.3   Tool Support

We specified the program model's type graph as Ecore metamodel using the Eclipse
Modeling Framework (EMF) [147, 148]. The metamodel and generated Java classes
representing the type graph have been packaged to an Eclipse plugin. Besides the
default functionality of the generated type graph classes for accessing a program
model from Java applications, these have been extended with often used queries.
Among others, these queries comprise getting a TClass for a fully qualified name
such as edu.ncsu.csc.itrust.action.EditOfficeVisitAction, or
searching for methods signatures based on their String representations, like
updateInformation(EditOfficeVisitForm,boolean):String.

  While a direct interaction of developers with program models is not intended, it
can be useful to visualize excerpts of a program model, e.g., to visualize findings
of a security analysis or effects of a refactoring. Using the Sirius visualization
framework [149], we implemented a basic graphical editor for the program model.
Figure 5.7 shows a screenshot of this editor in the Eclipse IDE. In the center of the
figure, the model excerpt is visualized. In this case, the overriding hierarchy of the
method filter(List):List is shown. This method is invoked when doctors

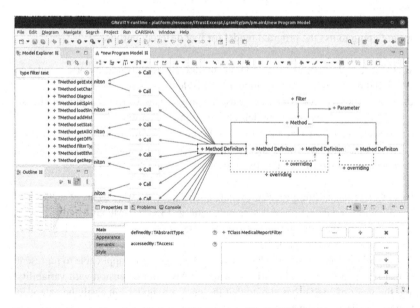

Figure 5.7 Screenshot of the Eclipse IDE showing GRaViTY's graphical program model
editor

want to filter medical reports or filter patients according to their demography. For the implementation of medical report filtering, the outgoing calls of the method definition are shown. At the bottom of the figure, in the properties view, details on the selected element are shown, e.g., the currently selected method definition is defined in the class `MedicalReportFilter`.

5.4   Evaluation of the Program Model

In this section, we evaluate the proposed program model and its type graph regarding two objectives. First, we evaluate whether the type graph is suitable to specify meaningful analyses. Second, we focus on the type graph's expressiveness and if it is applicable to represent real-world Java programs.

O1—Suitability of the Type Graph
The program model's idea is to provide a representation of object-oriented programs that allows the specification of analyses without going down to the level of statements. For this reason, the question is whether the specified program model is suitable for the application in the quality and security analysis of object-oriented programs.

Until now, the program model has been used for various purposes. In this thesis, we are going to use the program model for five different purposes.

1. In Section 7.2, we use the program model for establishing a correspondence model between design-time models and code.
2. In Section 8.4 and Section 8.6, we use the program models for compliance checks between the design-time models and the implementation.
3. In Section 10.2, we check the applicability of refactorings on the program model.
4. In Chapter 13, we extend the program model with variability annotations for checking refactorings on software product lines in Chapter 10.

Beyond this thesis, the program model has been used by Peldszus et al. for the specification and detection of design anti-patterns [34, 21] . Mebus extended in his master's thesis the program model with high-level data flows and used it to detect secure data flow violations [150].

Overall, the program model has proven to be flexible and applicable to represent object-oriented programs in various analyzes. Also, our extension with variability and the work of Mebus has shown that the program model can easily be extended to cover additional aspects.

O2—Applicability of the Type Graph to Real Java Programs

Besides being suitable to express meaningful analyses, it has to be possible to create program models for real-world object-oriented programs using the full range of OO features. As we focus on Java programs in this thesis, regarding this objective, we study whether real-world Java programs can be represented using the type graph.

As part of this thesis but also in other research, the proposed program model has been used to represent real-world Java programs. For this thesis, we created the program model for 22 Java programs from a broad selection of domains. In addition, in two related bachelor's theses, Wiebe and Ivanova studied the correlations between OO-design metrics and security aspects. For this reason, they created the program model for 50 Android applications [151] and 33 famous Java projects on GitHub [152].

In summary, the proposed type graph has been successfully used to create program models for 105 different Java programs and Android applications. This finding indicates good applicability to real-world Java programs. This assumption is backed by the fact, that we have corresponding program model elements to represent all constructs of the Java language in version 1.7.

5.5   Threats to Validity

The type graph has been designed to support arbitrary object-oriented languages but has not been applied to any other programming language than Java. Nevertheless, the generality of the program model and the extensibility, e.g., as demonstrated in the work of Mebus, are promising indicators for the applicability to other object-oriented languages. While the type graph itself should be expressive enough to represent, e.g., programs written in C++, problems can occur at the creation of program models at the resolution of constructs like pointers.

The reduction of the details from the statement level limits the applicability for analyses that require details from the statement level. However, first, the type graph has not been defined for such analyses and, second, there are plenty of alternatives. For example, MoDisco [142] or the Java model of the Eclipse Java Development Tools (JDT) [153] for Java programs provide program models containing resolved inter-method dependencies and all details from the statement-level of the methods. Second, if required, the type graph can be extended with additional information.

The type graph has been designed to represent the semantic structure of object-oriented programs in the presented version, but there are no trace links to source code files. For languages like Java, the location of a type usually can be calculated from the fully qualified name, e.g., multiple source folders can require an expensive search. Even more problematic is this issue if multiple Java classes are defined in the same compilation unit. However, without modification, the information about the location of a type on the file system can be encoded using the type graph's annotation mechanism. Alternatively, the type graph can be extended by additional elements for representing the desired information.

5.6   Conclusion on the proposed Program Representation

To conclude, the program model representation described in this section provides a reasonable trade-off between an appropriate level of abstraction on the one hand and the inclusion of further, initially implicit yet relevant, semantic program properties on the other hand.

This kind of representation coincides with an abstraction level, specifically tailored to reason about object-oriented refactorings and to perform high-level security analyses. This abstraction level has three significant advantages compared to conventional AST representations:

- It is restricted to those program entities being relevant for defining high-level program transformation rules and reasoning about their application to program graph instances.
- It is enriched with static semantic information between arbitrary program entities, being crucial for reasoning about behavior preservation as part of preconditions of graph-based program refactoring rules.
- The method signature is separated from the method definition to allow for a compact formalization of core concepts of object-oriented programs (especially those written in Java), namely inheritance, overloading, and overriding/hiding, within refactoring rules or security patterns.

In addition, the general and generic nature of graph-based representations allow for arbitrary application-specific adoptions and enhancements to be added to the type graph. For instance, if the program model has to incorporate complex inheritance structures or problematic visibility rules for class members [69], the type graph definition can be easily extended, e.g., by introducing a further directed accessibility edge between class members. For instance, additional information about semantic dependencies among class members is useful to check if a program transformation may obstruct non-obvious and even transitive access dependencies. This information can also be used for static security analyses when security requirements are given.

Model-Synchronization and Tracing

6

This chapter shares material with the PPPJ'2015 publication "Incremental Co-Evolution of Java Programs based on Bidirectional Graph Transformation" [130], the TTC'2015 publication "A Solution to the Java Refactoring Case Study using eMoflon" [130], and the EMLS'2020 publication "Model-driven Development of Evolving Secure Software Systems" [154].

One of the main challenges in developing and maintaining a secure software system is to keep track of all artifacts created during the development and their relations with each other. For example, consider a security certification of the iTrust system. For this certification, on the one side, we need to know which model elements from the design phase correspond with which implementation artifacts, e.g., to verify that all planned functionalities have been implemented. On the other side, we have to ensure that all security assumptions from any development phase are fulfilled in all other phases. To perform this compliance check, we have to trace security requirements between the design-time models and the source code. Also, in case of changes on any artifacts, the corresponding other artifacts must be changed to preserve compliance. Otherwise, a divergence between the design-time models and source code or divergence among the design-time models would manifest themselves and could lead to missed security violations in analysis results. For example, UMLsec security checks do not show any violations, but there are undetected violations in the implementation due to the divergence. These challenges are the subject of RQ1 of this thesis and answered in this chapter:

RQ1: How can security requirements be traced among different system representations throughout a software system's development process?

In Figure 6.1, the relevant parts for answering the research question are highlighted. First, there is the synchronization between the UML models, source code, and

© The Author(s), under exclusive license to Springer Fachmedien Wiesbaden GmbH, part of Springer Nature 2022
S. M. Peldszus, *Security Compliance in Model-driven Development of Software Systems in Presence of Long-Term Evolution and Variants*,
https://doi.org/10.1007/978-3-658-37665-9_6

program model. For this synchronization, we need a mechanism that gives us guarantees on the correctness of performed synchronization operations. For this reason, we look at formal methods that can give us such guarantees within a given specification. Second, we have to look at tracing between the different UML models considered in GRaViTY. Here, we focus on UML models describing a software system at different levels of abstraction. Finally, we have to look at how we can continuously trace concrete security requirements. This is essential to enable security compliance checks between the design-time models and their implementation. Accordingly, we have to consider three different tracing kinds leading to three sub-research questions:

RQ1.1: How can we continuously create and maintain traces between design-time models and the implementation?

RQ1.2: How can trace links between design-time models with different levels of abstraction be represented and maintained?

RQ1.3: How can trace links be used to propagate design-time security requirements into the implementation?

We support developers in applying the model-driven development approach, as described in Section 3.3, to develop and maintain secure software systems. As shown

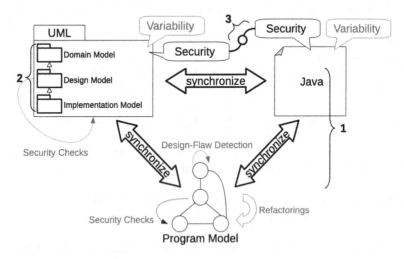

Figure 6.1 Location of the Tracing in the Overall Concept

in Figure 6.1, design models, source code, and a program model for performing sophisticated analyses, e.g., the security checks we will discuss in Chapter 8, are continuously synchronized to cover the different software development phases. As source code, we consider in this thesis Java source code and UML for specifying design-time models.

As introduced in Chapter 5, the program model provides a high-level abstraction from the pure Java source code [130], e.g., reducing details from the statement level to access edges between the single members. In addition, easy to query structures are created, such as structuring methods and fields into a tree with names, signatures, and definitions. Section 6.2 shows on this program model and UML class diagrams the realization of required synchronization.

While the synchronization introduced in Section 6.2 will allow us to trace between detailed UML class diagrams and their implementation, tracing within UML models of different abstraction is missing. Section 6.3 discusses the UML inheritance mechanisms regarding their suitability for tracing within GRaViTY and shows how to trace UMLsec security requirements.

In GRaViTY, security-related specifications are introduced into the different artifacts as annotations. On UML models, we use the UMLsec profile for security annotations proposed by Jürjens [6]. For making this information available at runtime, in Section 6.4, we introduce equivalent Java annotations. Also, we discuss dynamic tracing without enriching the source code with additional information, e.g., UMLsec security requirements.

However, providing a specification for the required models and the checks is only one challenge. The second challenge is to create the required models initially and to keep them up to date. In this chapter, we address this second challenge. First, we introduce our approach to create a program model or UML models from source code and keep the models and the code synchronized. Thereby, we generate the required traces for propagating security information. Afterward, we look at traces between UML models with different levels of abstraction. Last but not least, we discuss traces between security requirements on different artifacts.

6.1 Background on Tracing

This chapter mainly deals with tracing among different artifacts of a software system. For realizing the proposed GRaViTY approach, we have to come up with a suitable tracing approach that also allows synchronization in case of changes. For this reason, this section discusses the background on traceability, the general aim of traceability, and how to realize traceability. There are several definitions for tracing and traceability.

The ISO/IEC/IEEE standard 24765 [155], giving a vocabulary for systems and software engineering, contains three traceability definitions. The one that fits our needs best defines tracing as tracking relationships between multiple products of the development process [155]. For example, in the domain model of the iTrust system, we defined that there are patients in this domain. Tracing means here to find all elements related to this element, e.g., locations in the source code representing a patient and making these relations explicit.

Similarly, Spanoudakis and Zisman define software traceability as the ability to relate artifacts created during developing a software system with each other [156]. Thereby, the artifacts describe a software system from different perspectives and levels of abstraction. However, following their definition of software traceability, not only relating the different software artifacts is considered but also the stakeholders that have contributed to the creation of the artifacts and the rationale that explains the form of the artifacts.

In summary, possibilities to establish trace links range from simple references of complete documents to individual, identifiable, typed, and possibly attributed connections between particular elements within individual development artifacts [157, 158]. We aim at explicitly specified and typed trace links conforming to a traceability model defining the possible traces and traceable objects. When looking at how artifacts can be related among each other, five general types of traces can be identified [156, 159]:

Dependency: This trace kind comprises arbitrary relations between entities required for solving a problem. As all of such relations considered by us are explicitly contained within the artifacts, we do not have to trace these explicitly. However, our approach has to keep these relations consistent across all development artifacts.

Satisfaction: This comprises elements that satisfy other elements, e.g., the elements that satisfy a requirement. As there are usually multiple elements across all development artifacts that satisfy a requirement together, this trace type also includes the realization of an abstract element by a more detailed element. Going back to our motivation, this kind of trace is the most relevant for our approach.

Rationalization: As already motivated by Spanoudakis and Zisman [156], traceability also comprises the rationale for an artifact's existence. However, this kind of tracing is out of scope for this thesis.

Verification & Validation: This category comprises relations between parts of the software system, properties, and their verification, e.g., as part of test cases. In our case, these would be security checks used for the verification of security requirements.

Evolution: In this category, evolution steps are recorded for later inspection. In this thesis, we do not consider this type of trace link. However, we could record the changes propagated by the synchronization introduced in this chapter or applied refactoring operations.

To conclude, for our purpose, we have to develop an approach that can make satisfaction trace links explicit and maintain these in case of changes.

6.2   Inter-Artifact Tracing and Model-Synchronization

The proposed GRaViTY approach requires a continuous synchronization between UML models, the source code of the implementation, and a program model for performing analyses. Model changes, e.g., caused by a single restructuring operation of the software system's architecture, may substantially be very complex, involving various, arbitrarily fine-grained source code changes and harden the study of effects, e.g., as for security properties in RQ4: *"How do changes within a software system affect its security compliance, and how can these effects be handled?"*. Besides, the opposite direction may also hold: a developer's edit on a source code file, although only affecting a small part of the source code, may in some cases yield arbitrary complex program model modifications, e.g., due to subtle semantic changes caused by the edit.

A comprehensive technique is required for the postprocessing of changes to handle both cases. This technique has to automatically restore the other side's consistency for any possible modification applied to either side, whereas unaffected parts remain unchanged. Such an incremental consistency-preserving mechanism, which operates on the modeling language's level instead of the models itself, defines an exogenous bidirectional transformation [37]. In this context, bidirectionality means that, given two metamodels or grammars (referred to as the source and target languages), the underlying mechanism automatically synchronizes instances of the source metamodel with instances of the target metamodel and vice versa. Thereby, each transformation on the one side having an inverse transformation on the other side.

For the tracing and synchronization between the source code and program model, indicated by the lower right synchronize arrow in Figure 6.2, these two grammars or modeling languages are

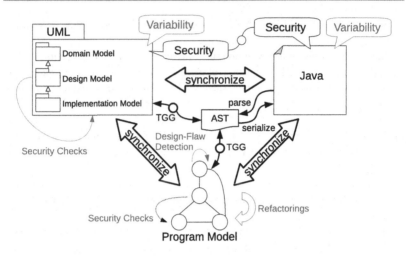

Figure 6.2 Concept for tracing using triple graph grammars

1. the Java grammar on the source code side, used to parse the source code and extract an AST from the parsed source code files, and
2. the graph language defined by our type graph on the program model side.

Altogether, in GRaViTY, we consider three kinds of artifacts, representing the software system under development or maintenance, that have different metamodels specifying the language's syntax. This metamodel is the UML Superstructure Specification released by the Object Management Group [5] for the UML models. For the program model, we use the type graph introduced in Chapter 5. As source code, we consider Java source code that complies with the Java language specification [61].

For the so-called forward and backward transformations of such a bidirectional transformation mechanism to be incremental, we require them to leave unmodified program parts unaffected by the transformation. This property of the bidirectional transformations ensures that, e.g., meta-information such as the formatting of source code is preserved. In addition, incremental approaches enable high performance of model synchronization even for larger software systems, as the execution time is proportional to the extent of the modification rather than the size of the software system's representations to be synchronized.

We employ *Triple Graph Grammars* (TGG) [160] for a bidirectional synchronization between the source code, the program model representation of Java programs, and UML models to keep the different artifacts consistent. In Figure 6.2, the

TGGs are denoted by bold circles that connect the artifacts translated by the TGG. In what follows, we first give a brief introduction to bidirectional graph transformations and introduce our approach for synchronization based on bidirectional graph transformation afterward.

6.2.1 Background on Bidirectional Graph Transformations

In a graph-based program transformation setting, the bidirectionality and incrementally properties required by us are guaranteed by a corresponding formalism for specifying bidirectional graph transformation rules. In particular, *Triple Graph Grammars* (TGG) [160] constitute an approach meeting those requirements. TGG constitutes a rule-based, declarative language for specifying bidirectional transformation rules. To this end, the TGG formalism provides a concise way to specify and maintain correspondences between instance elements of different metamodels. This is achieved by constructing a third graph (hence the name Triple Graph Grammars), a so-called correspondence graph, which establishes links between corresponding elements in the source and target models. Since these links express relations between corresponding elements from different artifacts, we can use the correspondence graph as a knowledge source containing all satisfaction trace links. Thereby, the transformation rules specify the satisfaction relations.

By convention, transformation rule-applications for synchronizing a target graph with a source graph are called forward transformations, whereas the rule-applications in the other direction are called backward transformations. Each pair of such complementing exogenous transformation rules are automatically derived from one declarative rule specification connecting both metamodels. TGG describes correspondences between source and target instances conforming to the given metamodels as usual.

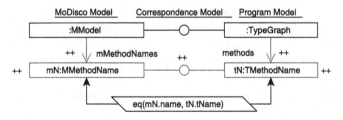

Figure 6.3 TGG transformation rule for method names from the MoDisco Java model ⇄ program model transformation

Thereupon, correspondences between elements from both metamodels are specified through the mediating correspondence graph.

Thus, a TGG specification consists of a set of declarative triple graph rules that simultaneously create the source, target, and correspondence graphs. These rules are operationalized each to a forward and a backward translation rule. In particular, a forward translation rule does not create the source graph but matches the elements of a given source graph and extends them to a triple by creating the correspondence and target element as specified in the rules.

6.2.2   Model-Synchronization with Triple Graph Grammars

In what follows, we introduce how we applied TGGs to synchronize the different software development artifacts considered in the GRaViTY approach. We specified TGG rules for two of the three synchronize arrows in Figure 6.2. We emulate the third synchronization by a subsequent execution of the other two. To be more precise, we defined TGG rules for translating between Java source code and UML models and between Java source code and the program model.

For instance, the TGG rules in Figure 6.3, 6.4, and 6.5a show an excerpt of the TGG rules of specifying the transformation between Java source code and the program model. These rules translate method name elements, method signatures, and method definitions, respectively, by creating the corresponding target elements and the correspondence graph elements to obtain a mapping between the source and the target model (a backward translation is executed analogously). In what follows, we describe the rules and their interaction in detail.

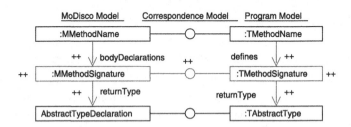

Figure 6.4 TGG transformation rule for method signatures from the MoDisco Java model ⇄ program model tramsformation

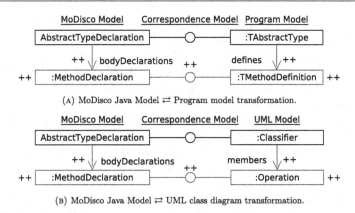

(A) MoDisco Java Model ⇄ Program model transformation.

(B) MoDisco Java Model ⇄ UML class diagram transformation.

Figure 6.5 Transformation rules for method definitions of the program model (A) and UML (B) TGGs

A TGG specification allows for propagating changes between source code and its program model representation or a UML model. In the following, we use the term synchronization for an automated mechanism for incrementally ensuring consistency between both views after arbitrary modifications on either side. As TGG rules are not directly applicable to textual inputs, to obtain an automated synchronization procedure, as well the Java source side has to be given in a graph-based format. For constructing a corresponding graph-based, yet much more AST-like intermediate representation of Java programs, several existing frameworks are available, cf., e.g., [141, 143]. Here, we consider the MoDisco metamodel and the corresponding transformation engine, for which parsing and serialization between Java source code and the graph-based MoDisco model have been already implemented [141, 161].

The transformation rules of the two TGGs implemented in GRaViTY use the same MoDisco metamodel for java source code and are structurally and syntactically very similar. Figure 6.5 shows two rules for translating Java methods. First, in Figure 6.5a, for translating methods into method definitions in the program model, and second, in Figure 6.5b, for translating these into operations in the UML models. While the source pattern matched in the MoDisco model is the same for the two rules, the target side pattern is very similar. This similarity also applies to most rules of these two TGGs. For this reason, in what follows, we only focus on the TGG rules of the Java source code to program model transformation. Thereby, we assume that our TGG rule's left-hand side refers to the MoDisco metamodel, and the right-hand side is defined by our type graph as described in Chapter 5.

Figure 6.3 shows a sample TGG rule consisting of a triple of graph rules. By convention, the source model part is depicted on the left, the target model part on the right, and the correspondence graph, with nodes being denoted by circles, in between. The circle-shaped correspondence graph reflects the mapping strategy between the two domains and is of high importance for translation purposes as it provides explicit traceability links between the models. The correspondences facilitate the iterative mapping of elements in two hierarchies, i.e., a correspondence created in a rule can be required as a context in another rule for further handling of child elements in the hierarchy. Black rectangles represent graph elements in the application context, i.e., elements that have to be present in the source graph to make the rule applicable, and green graph elements refer to those elements being created by the rule application. The parallelogram at the bottom of Figure 6.3 containing an expression represents a constraint. This constraint ensures that the name attributes of the referred elements on the left-hand side and the right-hand side have the same value. Intuitively, this rule's meaning is the following: for each yet unprocessed method name in the Java source code, a new method name node is created in the target program model.

Besides this basic rule in Figure 6.3, a complete TGG specification for synchronizing two graph-based model representations usually involves more complex triples to handle any possible case appropriately. For instance, as each element is translated only once during a TGG transformation, the given rule is not sufficient for synchronizing both sides as a single method instance in the program is represented by multiple elements in the program model (name, signature, definition). To illustrate that the expressive power of TGG specifications goes beyond simple one-to-one correspondences, we provide an example of two (interrelated) TGG rules for translating method definitions, shown in Figures 6.4 and 6.5a.

Rule MethodSignatureRule (Figure 6.4) defines the synchronization of method signatures. In a certain sense, this rule constitutes a successor rule of MethodNameRule (Figure 6.3) as it refers to elements created by MethodName-Rule as matching context. Please note that the translation of parameter lists from Java Source/MoDisco into a method signature and a corresponding parameter list representation in the program graph is specified in further rules. Nevertheless, this example shows a case where one element on the source side corresponds to multiple elements on the target side within a single TGG rule, thus ensuring correct correspondences while synchronizing both sides. This rule can be interpreted as: for each yet unprocessed method signature with an already processed name and type in the Java source code, an additional method name signature node is created in the target program model. This new element is connected with the respective signature node and type corresponding with the already processed ones from the source side of the rule.

The rule `MethodDefinitionRule` (Figure 6.5a) again constitutes a successor rule of `MethodSignatureRule` (Figure 6.4). Whenever `Method DefinitionRule` is applied, a new method definition is added to the program model for the corresponding method definition within the source, i.e., the respective MoDisco representation. This newly created method definition node is connected to the signature, previously created by `MethodSignatureRule` by inserting a new link within the correspondence graph. In additional rules, the relations to the classes defining the methods are created. All elements in the method definitions in the MoDisco model not translated by any TGG rule result in abstraction from the detailed model as there is no corresponding counterpart in the program model.

These three sample rules illustrate that in realistic application scenarios where both sides differ concerning the level of detail and/or the way information is represented, complete TGG specifications usually comprise more complex connections than just simple one-to-one correspondences. Consequently, on the one hand, it is challenging to develop TGG specifications that guarantee bidirectional model transformations, ensuring consistency preservation for any well-typed input models on both sides. On the other hand, once implemented, TGG rules are an expressive and powerful instrument for bidirectional model transformation scenarios, where incremental synchronization comes for free with the rules.

The (forward) transformation from Java program into the program model is applied if, for instance, a Java developer edits the source code, e.g., adding a new class. After such a source code modification is completed, the program model has to be updated, respectively, to incorporate a new node of type `TClass` representing the new class. This update is achieved by applying a corresponding TGG rule for translating class definitions (similar to the one shown for method definitions in Figure 6.5a) to insert a node for the new `TClass` into the program model. Additional rule applications might be necessary to capture all changes made by the developer.

In contrast, whenever the program model is modified, e.g., by applying a *Pull-Up Method* refactoring on the program model, the changes within the modified program model are incrementally propagated back into the Java source code. In a *Pull-Up Method* refactoring, semantically equivalent method definitions within child classes are pulled into their shared parent class, reducing duplicated code. Among others, this refactoring is discussed in detail in Chapter 10. For propagating the changes, the (backward) transformation, resulting from the same TGG specification, is applied. First, the differences between the original program model and the modified program model are calculated. For the *Pull-Up Method* refactoring, these differences comprise the deletion of all definitions realizing the method signature to be pulled up to the parent except one and redirect the remaining one's class edge. TGG synchronization is based on the previous execution of the forward transformation, and it consists of the following steps:

1. Withdrawing those rules that do not match anymore, i.e., rules that created elements that have been deleted through the modification. In our example, the *Pull-Up Method* refactoring results in one or more deleted method definitions, which have been created earlier by applying the `MethodDefinitionRule` in Figure 6.5a. Each additional element created by this rule application, i.e., the corresponding method on the MoDisco model side and the link to the method signature in the program model, has to be deleted while reverting this rule application. This procedure always yields a consistent state, as, after this synchronization step, no more necessary elements are removed, or unnecessary elements are preserved on either side.

2. Matching and translating those elements which have been added by the modification. In our example, another TGG rule (not depicted here) has to be defined to take care of the newly created membership edge between the method signature and its parent class by creating the corresponding membership edge on the MoDisco side. Thus, based on the intermediate MoDisco representation, we always arrive in a state of the source code that is the modified program model.

The shown TGG rules are appropriate in handling different granularity by not translating elements, e.g., all details from the method bodies available in the MoDisco model but not in the program model. Unfortunately, as illustrated in what follows, our experience at defining the TGG rules has shown that they cannot create structures that differ entirely on the two sides. Our solution for this issue comprises implementing multiple preprocessing steps extending the different models with such structural information.

One example of such an issue solved by preprocessing is the method representation as name, signature, and definition. Figure 6.6 illustrates this problem. In principle, it is possible to create this structure using TGG rules by creating the whole structure when a method name is translated the first time and inserting afterward. However, this way of creating this structure produces issues in synchronizing changes on the structure. Let us assume that the `TMethodName` node in Figure 6.6 has been created when the method defined by the class `EditOfficeVisitAction` has been translated using a TGG rule `TGG rule 1`. The other signature has been added afterward by `TGG rule 2`, reusing the `TMethodName` node created by the application of `TGG rule 1`. A refactoring, e.g., a *Pull-Up Method* refactoring [145], deletes the `TMethodDefinition` defined by `EditOfficeVisitAction`

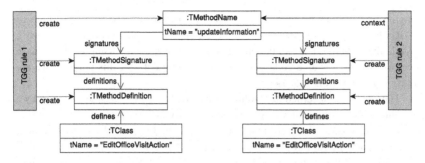

Figure 6.6 Illustration of the problem in creating method trees using TGGs

and synchronizes this change with the source code. For synchronizing this change, the TGG algorithm has to undo all rule-applications that initially lead to the creation of nodes or edges deleted by the refactoring. In this case, this is the application of the rule TGG rule 1. As the TMethodName node's creation took place in the same rule-application as the creation of the deleted TMethodDefintion node, after undoing the rule-application, it seems that the TMethodName node has never been created. Consequently, this undo also makes the creation of the other TMethodSignature node by TGG rule 2 invalid as its context does not exist anymore, leading to a situation in which no recovery without deleting and recreating the TMethodDefiniton node translated by the TGG rule 2 is possible. This pair of deletion and recreation is also reflected on the implementation side leading to a loss of all information from the statement level. To deal with this issue, we defined a preprocessing that already creates the required structure on the MoDisco model's side.

To conclude, TGGs provide an automated mechanism to preserve consistency between the two different program representations for managing co-evolving Java programs. As a result, we obtain a graph-based framework for arbitrarily interleaving program evolution and maintenance steps. We can also use this approach to translate and synchronize model elements' security requirements between different system representations, e.g., design-time models and source code.

6.2.3   Tool Support for the Model Synchronization

Our implementation of the synchronization between source code and the program model as well as UML models is based on the eMoflon graph transformation engine [162]. Among others, eMoflon allows the specification and execution of TGGs between models specified using the Eclipse Modeling Framework (EMF). While the UML models and the program model are specified using EMF, we have to parse the Java source code to create an EMF model. For this purpose, we are currently using MoDisco [141].

TGG rules are specified in eMoflon using a textual editor. Besides, support by a graphical visualization similar to the graphics of TGG rules is generated. Figure 6.7 shows a screenshot of the eMoflon rule editor in the Eclipse IDE. On the left, the classical package explorer is shown, giving an overview of the rule files. Right of the package explorer, the rule editor is shown. In the screenshot, an abstract parent of the rule from Figure 6.4 for the translation of method signatures is shown. The eMoflon tool supports inheritance between rules for minimizing the duplication of elements in rules. Comparable to abstract classes in Java, shared rule parts that are not executable on their own can be defined in abstract rules. In this case, signatures of methods and constructors are translating similar rules that only differ in the type of the node to create (`MMethodSignature` and `MConstructorSignature` in the MoDisco model). On the right of the figure, the visualization of the TGG rule is shown. Using this tooling, we developed the two TGGs discussed in this work. For synchronizing the program model with Java source code, we defined 109 TGG rules. Of these rules, 18 are abstract rules and 90 are concrete rules. The TGG for synchronizing Java source code with UML models is based on a TGG of Leblebici et al. [163] and has been extended with deployments of classes and various bug fixes. This UML TGG comprises 105 TGG rules, of which 88 are concrete rules and 17 are abstract rules.

The structure of the implementation is shown in the component diagram in Figure 6.8. Elements colored in white are elements that have been developed as part of this thesis, while gray elements are external dependencies. The two sets of TGG rules are located in the components `PM TGG` and `UML TGG`, respectively. The components `MoDisco`, `UML`, and `TypeGraph` contain the corresponding metamodels. These metamodels and related functionality, e.g., parsing and serializing of MoDisco, are exported through interfaces. For the MoDisco metamodel, we specified a wrapper that extends the MoDisco metamodel with additional elements such as the discussed nodes for method signatures and names and provides the extensions through an interface. The TGG components use the interfaces to export the extended MoDisco metamodel and the metamodel of their target language to realize the transformation. For the discussed preprocessing, six different interfaces are specified. We have two interfaces for every metamodel at which preprocessors that are executed before a transformation and postprocessors that are executed after a transformation can be registered. For example, the creation of the method-signature-

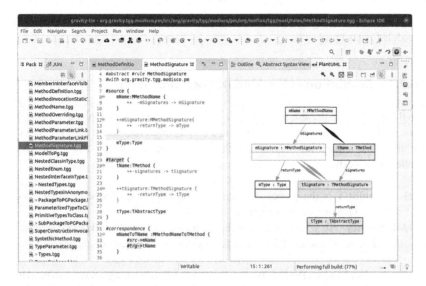

Figure 6.7 Screenshot of the eMoflon TGG editor in the Eclipse IDE showing the TGG rule for translating method signatures

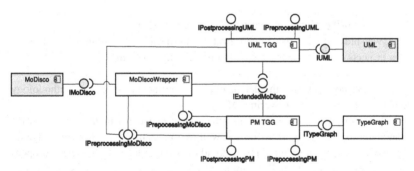

Figure 6.8 Component diagram of GRaViTY's artifact synchronization

name structure is registered at the interface `IPreprocessMoDisco`. Technically, these interfaces for preprocessors and postprocessors are realized as Eclipse extension points[1]. We provide a Java API for both transformations and implemented UI

---

[1] Eclipse FAQ: https://wiki.eclipse.org/FAQ_What_are_extensions_and_extension_points %3F

entries in the Eclipse IDE to create and synchronize UML models and program models for Java projects.

6.2.4 Evaluation of the Model Synchronization

In this section, we present the evaluation results of applying the implementation of our model-synchronization technique on a corpus of 20 real-world Java programs from various application domains (cf. the first column in Table 6.1) to consider the following objectives.

O1–Scalability: Is the proposed model-synchronization technique *applicable* to real-size Java programs in a reasonable amount of time?

O2–Efficiency: To what extent does incremental model-synchronization improve the *efficiency* of the model creation from source code in case of changes?

We present and discuss the results of our experiments concerning our objectives. All experiments have been performed on a Ubuntu 20.10 LTS mobile computer with an Intel i5-6200U dual-core processor, 8 GB DDR3 RAM and OpenJDK v1.14.0.

O1–Scalability of the Program Model Creation

First, we study whether the synchronization approach can be applied to real-world Java projects of different sizes in a reasonable amount of time.

Setup. We now describe the details on the experimental setup and methodology to obtain the results for answering **O1**.

Our selection of subject systems relies on former experiments performed for related approaches [164, 165, 166], as well as on a standard catalog for analyzing the evolution of Java systems [167], to address the objective. We selected open-source Java programs from different application domains, including software systems for software developers as well as for end-users. We also aimed at including a range of different program sizes. The particular program versions considered for the experiments, together with the URL for accessing source code, are included on our accompanying GitHub site[2]. We applied our proposed detection technique to all subject systems, monitoring the execution and measuring execution times.

---

[2] GRaViTY's GitHub site: https://github.com/GRaViTY-Tool

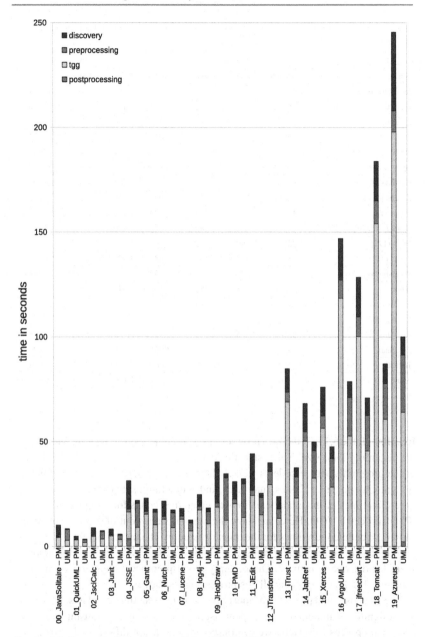

Figure 6.9 Runes for the program model and UML TGGs

Table 6.1 Program statistics and execution times of the program model and UML model creation

Project		Statistics				Duration in s	
Name	Version	LLOC	types	methods	fields	PM	UML
JavaSolitaire	1.3	1,197	27	115	109	12.88	11.17
QuickUML [168, 169]	2001	2,667	22	175	156	4.80	3.38
JSciCalc [170]	2.1.0	5,437	131	563	200	9.03	7.47
JUnit [171]	3.8.2	5,780	188	841	161	8.12	6.05
JSSE – OpenJDK	8	20,896	236	1,875	861	31.30	23.22
Gantt [172]	1.10.2	21,228	397	3,925	1,323	22.99	16.95
Nutch [173]	0.9	21,473	331	1,750	1,083	21.33	16.79
Lucene [174]	1.4.3	25,472	333	2,096	1,166	17.88	12.98
log4j [175]	1.2.17	30,662	459	3,190	1,226	24.73	18.83
JHotDraw [176]	7.6	32,434	480	3,781	900	40.16	34.47
PMD [177]	3.9	43,063	620	4,064	1,582	30.72	32.17
jEdit [178]	4.0	49,829	606	3,429	1,976	45.28	25.29
JTransforms [179]	3.1	71,348	610	1,509	396	39.99	23.65
iTrust	21	77,501	964	6,166	3,074	85.73	38.68
JabRef	2.7	77,813	1,371	5,702	3,669	68.33	49.96
Xerces [180]	2.7.0	102,279	865	8,267	4,676	76.75	47.76
ArgoUML	0.19.8	135,542	1,596	12,401	3,458	151.40	78.45
jfreechart	1.0.19	144,338	1,093	11,861	3,258	128.43	70.74
Tomcat	6.0.45	177,013	1,732	16,661	7,991	185.70	87.52
Azureus [181]	2.3.0.6	201,541	3,432	17,564	7,106	237.91	100.47

Results. Table 6.1 lists the Java programs used as subject systems along with statistics regarding their size. These statistics contain the logical lines of code (LLOC) of the program's source code as well as the number of types, methods, and fields. As types, we consider classes, interfaces, and enumerations. In the next column, the execution times of the model creation are given in seconds for the program model (PM) and UML TGG. Here, we show the median values out of 5 runs. Figure 6.9 shows the detailed run times for the transformations. The overall height of each bar is equal to the corresponding run time in Table 6.1. For every project, the amount spent for discovery using MoDisco, applying all preproccessings, transformation using the TGG, and applying all postprocessings is shown.

For all considered projects, the most time is spent executing the TGGs. However, also a significant amount of time is spent discovering the source code using MoDisco and for preprocessing. Here, we can observe a significant difference between the impact of the preprocessing required for the program model and the UML transformation. The postprocessing has only a minor influence on the recorded execution times. In summary, the TGG for UML models is faster than the program model TGG.

To study the effect of different properties of OO programs, we related the measured run time for creating a program model and extracting a UML class diagram to characteristics of the Java programs. Thereby, we considered the overall time as shown in Table 6.1. The first plot in Figure 6.10 depicts the relation between time for model creation and logical lines of code of the program, the second plot with the number of types in the program, and the third plot concerning the number of members as the sum of methods and fields from Table 6.1. It seems like the time needed for creating a program model correlates the strongest with the lines of code of the projects. While there is still a correlation with structural aspects of the projects, the data points in these diagrams are more varying. As this variation is more significant for the creation of the program model than for the UML models, this could be an indication of an impact of the details contained at the statement level of the programs. For the program model, we represent these details more fine-grained than in the UML class diagrams. Also, the higher slope for the program model is an indicator of this assumption.

To answer **O1**, the results show that the time required for initial model creation is reasonable also for larger-scale programs. As our implementation supports incremental model-synchronization, initialization costs might be omitted later on in the case of evolving programs. The run-time benefit of the incremental model-synchronization is the subject of objective **O2**, discussed in what follows.

O2–Efficiency of the Program Model Synchronization
In this part of the evaluation, we study if we can achieve a speedup by synchronizing changes instead of restoring the model from scratch.

Setup. To answer **O2**, we selected a set of fine-grained program edits which frequently occur during continuous software evolution. In this regard, evolution steps do not comprise complicated structural program changes in the large, but rather consist in introducing or deleting particular methods and/or fields, as well as renaming operations, as can be observed in the evolutionary history of the Qualitas Corpus, a standard catalog for analyzing object-oriented system evolution [167]. For our measurements, we initialize for every project a program model from an unchanged program state. Afterward, we perform a program edit and measure the duration of

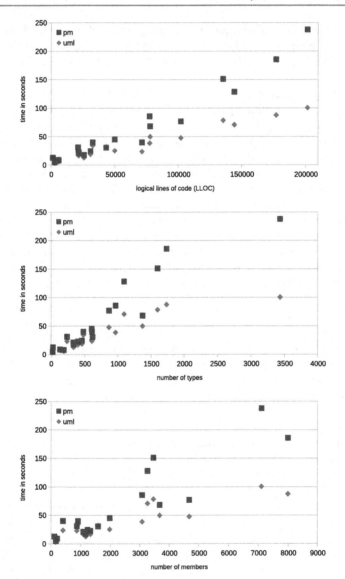

Figure 6.10 Relation between the time required for program model creation and different project metrics

the program model update as well as the time for the creation of a new program model.

The speedup $s_{evolution}$ is presumably obtained through *incremental model-synchronization* and is calculated according to the formula $s_{evolution} = 1 - (t_\Delta/t_0)$, where t_0 represents the complete initialization time of the unchanged program state and t_Δ denotes the time needed to update the program model after program edits. As edits are limited to very few program elements, we assume that re-creation without incremental model-synchronization requires the same time as for the unchanged program state, i.e., t_0.

For experimental purposes, we simulate the following implementation-level program edits:

- *Delete Method*: deletion of a random method and all invocations of this method,

- *Create Class*: inserting a fresh class into a new subpackage of the existing package hierarchy,

- *Create Method*: inserting a fresh method into a random class, that returns the value obtained from a call of the `toString` method of this class,

- *Rename Class*: renaming a random class.

Regarding the propagation of the changes from the model level to the implementation, usually, manual effort is included for resolving conflicts. However, this manual effort can be reduced by using our approach for propagating changes. For this reason, we measured the time needed for an initial propagation of changes into the source code but not the time needed for manual changes afterward. On UML models, we specified small changes oriented on typical security maintenance tasks concerning the UMLsec *Secure Dependency* security requirements. In this experiment, we considered the following changes in the iTrust UML model:

- Deletion of a security-violating dependency.

- Adding a new property to a class for separating sensitive from public information.

- Extraction of security-critical operations into a new class.

- Moving an operation to a different class to group security-critical functionality.

Results. Concerning **O2**, Figure 6.11 shows the measured time for synchronization (t_Δ) as a bar-chart for the four basic program edits per project. In the figure, we show the median value out of five runs per change. In general, the time required for synchronization increases with the size of the project and is in all cases much lower than the time required for initial translation. As the deletion of a method impacts more elements than the other changes, we observed higher execution times for this change.

Furthermore, while the measured times for changes only adding elements or not changing the structure of the already translated elements were very similar within a project, we observed huge differences for the deletion of methods. Here, the required time does not only depend on the size of the project but also the coupling of the deleted method has a significant impact. This coupling cannot only change between different projects but also within a single project.

Of the considered changes, the deletion of methods leads to a lower, but still remarkable speedup, than we observe for the other three kinds of changes. This difference is because the ratio of the edited program part to the whole is higher in this case. The achieved median speedup $s_{evolution}$ for the considered changes is as follows.

- *Delete Method*: 88.28%,

- *Create Class*: 98.1%,

- *Create Method*: 98.19%,

- *Rename Class*: 97.98%.

When looking into the single applied changes within a project, we noticed, that there is only a relatively small difference between the times needed for synchronizing the changes except for the deletion of methods. This can be explained by the fact that the number of the affected elements can vary for this change. As the deleted methods can have different amounts of dependencies with other members the amount of affected elements varies. For the other changes, the number of affected elements is always the same.

Next, we look at the differences between different projects. As the coupling of methods is different from project to project, we observed the highest variance in speedup across the different projects for deleting methods (0.014). The variance of the speedup for all other changes has been between 5.15E-5 and 9.61E-5. Anyways, for all considered changes there is a low variance across the different projects.

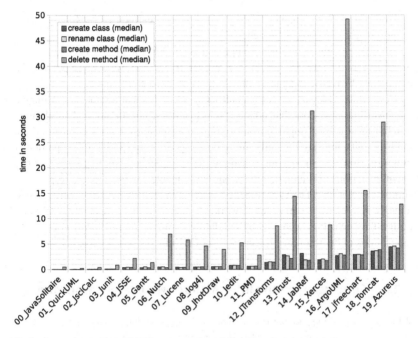

Figure 6.11 Time required for incremental model updates for program edits

In general, the achieved speedup factor for synchronizing source code changes into the program model is highly encouraging.

The propagation of a change from the UML models into the implementation took 50 seconds on average and 51.7 seconds in the worst case giving a speedup of 39.7% in the worst case. Currently, we use a non-incremental code-generator that takes most of the time (98.5%). For the pure propagation of the changes from the UML models into an implementation model, from which code is generated, only 0.75 seconds are needed. Thereby, we did not notice any significant difference between the changes applied to the UML models.

6.2.5   Threats to Validity

A general threat to internal validity may arise from the selection of subject systems not being representative; to address this issue, we thoroughly investigated related literature for our selection to cover a broad spectrum regarding both size and application domains. In addition, most of the programs have been considered for evaluation purposes by comparable approaches.

Another general issue for our approach is the NP-completeness of graph isomorphism used by pattern matching. However, in our case, we achieve polynomial complexity by restricting pattern matching using fixed entry points.

Concerning **O2**, we focus on a small set of self-defined program edits. Although our investigations show that typical evolution steps, not aiming at bug elimination but on structural improvement or program extensions, mainly comprise those kinds of edits, they are naturally limited in scope and are specific to the particular program. However, those edits constitute the most general building blocks of frequent evolution steps and, therefore, our experiments can be assumed to properly simulate evolution-related phenomena occurring in real-life evolving software systems. Nevertheless, as part of future work, we plan to further investigate continuous design-flaw detection scenarios by emulating entire version histories available in repositories of open source projects, e.g., at GitHub.

6.2.6   Conclusion on the Inter Artifact Model-Synchronization

While TGGs provide and mature mechanism for the translation between models and the synchronization of changes, they do not come without challenges. First, there is the discussed limitation regarding different granularity and structures between the source and target models. While this could be easily solved using preprocessings, it is desirable to enhance the TGG algorithm in a way we do not have to care about such issues. Nevertheless, we consider the proposed TGG approach as a powerful solution for the synchronization between the UML model, program model, and source code. Besides the pure synchronization of the different considered models, TGGs also allow generating source code structures from UML models and can be used for reverse-engineering UML models from legacy software systems. However, the supported UML class diagrams are on the same level of abstraction as the implementation and do not represent UML models as software architects would define. Nevertheless, when suitable views are created, these models allow to effectively use them, e.g., for annotating classes with UMLsec security requirements. Also, combined with tracing as introduced in the next section, these UML models allow propagating security requirements from more abstract UML models into the implementation and to detect inconsistencies after changes.

6.3   Tracing within UML Models of Different Abstraction

In model-driven development (MDD), as introduced in Section 3.3, a software system is developed by iteratively refining models until models close enough to contain all details necessary to implement the software system in executable source code are reached. In this thesis, we use UML models with the three different levels of abstraction that are common for software system development [77], as introduced in Section 3.3. To be more precise, we consider domain, system, and implementation models. Nevertheless, the user of our approach is not limited to use exactly this amount of levels but should have the freedom to choose to work with more or fewer levels. Also, we assume these models to be specified using the Unified Modeling Language (UML) [5].

These models are handed over to developers, that implement the concrete software system. To ease this task, from these models initial source code stubs might be generated that are manually extended with the specifications from the models that could not be generated automatically. Considering all models that have been created at MDD, there is a significant difference in detail between the very early UML models and those that are handed over to developers, are used for code generation, or are synchronized with the implementation using the mechanism presented in the previous section. While we presented a solution for tracing between the source code and fine-grained UML class diagrams, to allow the tracing among the different UML models, we need trace links comparable to the correspondence model of the TGGs for the inter-artifact tracing, introduced in Section 6.2. In what follows, we show how we can realize such traces by only making use of UML elements already specified in the UML Superstructure.

6.3.1   Background on Refinements in UML Models

The proposed workflow of iteratively refining models allows the systematic reuse of elements but also requires continuous tracing between the individual models. In this section, we first discuss the relationship types defined in the UML Superstructure [5] that could be used for defining the refinements considered by us. Afterward, as refinements can be used to establish some kind of inheritance hierarchy, we discuss polymorphism in the context of the UML as well as an implication for UMLsec.

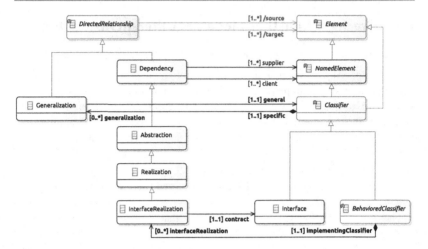

Figure 6.12 Excerpt from the UML Superstructure showing the specification of refinement relations

6.3.2   Refinement Relationship Types

The UML specifies various relationship types to define refinements [5]. Figure 6.12 shows an excerpt of the UML metamodel focusing on the refinement relations. On the left of the figure, the type hierarchy of the relationship types is shown and on the right the elements these can relate. In what follows, we discuss the semantic meaning of the non-abstract relationship types.

Dependency: This relationship kind represents one of the most abstract relations between elements. One or more elements require other elements for their realization. There are more specific instances of this relationship that concretize the kind of this requires relation.

Abstraction: Using this relationship, multiple elements that represent the same concept on different levels of abstraction or from different viewpoints can be connected.

Realization: This is a specific abstraction dependency that specified that concrete elements implement a more abstract element. Following the UML Superstructure, this relation should be used for the specification of refinement relations only considered for tracing.

InterfaceRealization: This is an even more specific kind of realization specifying that a classifier implements a concrete interface and offers its functionality over the contract specified by the interface.

Generalization: Using this relationship, we specify that one or more concrete classifiers are an instance of one or more general classifiers. This implies that the concrete classifiers can be used in the context of the generals. Also, the concrete classifiers inherit all features from the generals.

6.3.3   Polymorphism in UML

Comparable to object-oriented languages, inheritance within UML models leads to polymorphism. In UML, the inheritance between objects is expressed using generalizations as introduced in the previous section about refinement relations. While many programming languages, e.g., the Java programming language, allow multiple inheritance only for interfaces, the UML allows multiple inheritance in all cases.

Following OO languages, the UML specifies rules for overriding members between classes [5, 182]. In comparison to most OO-programming languages, there is a huge difference in the overriding mechanism. The UML specifies covariant overriding of features. This means, that a method or property can be overridden by a member with a narrower signature. In Java, for example, it is possible to specify a more concrete return type of a method in a subclass [61]. In the UML, this is not only possible for return parameters of operations but all parameters.

6.3.4   UMLsec Secure Dependency in the Context of Inheritance

The interface of a class considered in UMLsec comprises all features of the class itself as well as all features of generalized classes that have not been overridden. For example, the interface of the class `Patient` in the domain model of Figure 6.12 comprises the property `allergies` defined in this class as well as the two properties defined in its general `Person`, more precisely the properties `name` and `homeAddress`.

Following the UML Superstructure [5], stereotypes apply to a specific element and, therefore, clients do not inherit stereotypes from their generals. However, if we look at the domain model in Figure 6.13, from a security perspective, all security levels specified for features of `Person` should also apply to `Patient` as these features are accessible through the `Patient`'s interface. As the features are defined in the scope of the annotated class, assigning the security annotations to the features

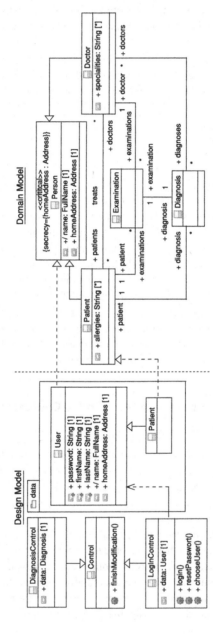

Figure 6.13 Model refinements between the UML domain model (Figure 3.2) and design model (Figure 3.3) of iTrust

is valid. Accordingly, even as inheritance is not explicitly considered in UMLsec and stereotype applications are not inherited, we assume UMLsec secure dependency to work as follows. The features are inherited together with their security level but security levels of features not defined within the class are not inherited.

Overriding is a second part in the area of inheritance not explicitly considered in UMLsec. A question to answer is whether it is allowed to override a classified feature, e.g., an operation or property, and if it is allowed which security level this overriding feature must be annotated. Also, it is unclear if we can override a non-classified feature with a classified feature. As the classified feature is usable in the context of the parent where no security information is available, this might rise issues. To avoid inconsistencies, we assume that UMLsec security requirements are consistent across inheritance hierarchies. Extending the definition of UMLsec secure dependency to consider such cases is out of scope in this thesis and could be done in future works.

Finally, considering the covariant overriding of UML, a challenge lies in relating signatures defined in a «critical» to the features contained in a class signature. While in this case the expected behavior is clearly given by the UML Superstructure, the technical realization is complicated and has not been realized in CARiSMA. For this reason, in this thesis, we do not make use of covariant overriding.

6.3.5   Refinements of UML Models

While we use TGGs to synchronize artifacts with different metamodels on a comparable level of abstraction, the single UML models created at MDD have the same metamodel but entirely different levels of abstraction. Accordingly, we need a different mechanism for realizing tracing. To keep things simple for developers, we do not want to introduce new language constructs or elements to the UML. For this reason, the single UML models are directly connected by explicit trace links based on standard UML language features. An example of these refinements is shown in Figure 6.13. On the left of the figure, the design model from Figure 3.3 is shown and on the right the domain model from Figure 3.2. The two models are visually separated by a dashed line. The User in the design model realizes the Person from the domain model. The described refinement relations are crossing the dashed line separating the two models.

In what follows we discuss the suitability of the different refinement relations for tracing between UML models with different abstraction. Thereby, we have to consider three constraints:

1. The usage of relations has to be within the semantic meaning of the relations as specified in the UML Superstructure [5].
2. There should be no conflicts with the synchronization between UML class diagrams and the implementation introduced in Section 6.2.
3. The tracing has to be integrated with UMLsec.

While the definition of *Dependency* in principle fits our needs, it is too abstract. Only based on this relationship type, we cannot easily distinguish between dependencies within a model and trace links across the different models. Here, the more specific versions of a dependency (*Abstraction* and *Realization*) fit our needs better. Considering models with different abstractions, the more concrete elements realize more abstract ones. For this reason, the more detailed *Realization* is even more suitable for our purpose of tracing than the more general *Abstraction*. The drawback of these two relationships is that none of the two has been integrated with UMLsec. Such an integration partly exists for the more classic inheritance relations *Generalization* and *InterfaceRealization*. However, as shown in Section 6.3.4 also this integration is not complete. In addition, there are two significant drawbacks of these two relationships. First, not every considered refinement relation is realized in the way that the more detailed element is an instance of the more abstract element. Considering the refinements between the domain model and design model in Figure 6.13, for the two classes Patient sub-typing might make sense, however, the User is not really an instance of a Person but only an element for representing Persons in the software system. Second, the two relationship types are part of UML class diagrams translated by the TGG presented in the previous section. If we use *Generalization* and *InterfaceRealization* for tracing, the challenge is to distinguish between uses of these relationships that should be translated by the TGG and those that are used for tracing.

In summary, there are cases in which the establishment of an inheritance relation makes sense and is beneficial but there are also cases in which this makes no sense. As inheritance is specified on a class level but overriding takes place on a feature-level, e.g., operations or properties, the security-related mapping between signatures gets complicated. In contrast to this, as visible in Figure 6.12, *Realizations* are specified between NamedElements its subtypes, including the types Operation and Property. For example, in Figure 6.13, the property name of the class Person is duplicated in the design model but also two more fine-grained properties firstName and lastName are specified for realizing the property from the domain model. Using Realization relationships, we can make this knowledge explicit. Afterward, these trace links can be used for propagating security information.

In what follows, we look at realizations in detail. Thereby, we consider realizations with a different level of detail, the interaction of realizations with inheritance, and security requirements specified using UMLsec. As an example, we use a realization of the design model by an implementation-level UML model that is synchronized with the source code using TGGs. Figure 6.14 shows the realization of a `Patient` in the implementation of the iTrust system.

As shown in Figure 6.14a, patients are represented in the implementation by beans that can be stored and loaded from a database. For this reason, the `Patient Bean` has to contain all data available in this database object. Among others, this includes the `homeAddress` of the patient, that `Patient` inherits from the class `User`. Please note that in UML an inherited feature is marked with a caret (^) when it is visualized. How exactly the `PatientBean` realizes the `Patient` is shown in Figure 6.14b. The property `homeAddress` of the class `User` is decomposed into more detailed properties in the implementation (`icAddress1` and `icCity`) for realizing this property. This realization is explicitly specified by two realization edges. Also, realizations can be used to show the internal structure of a class in more detail. For example in Figure 6.14b, it is explicitly shown that the getter and setter methods `getIcStreet1` and `setIcStreet1` realize the external interface for the property `icStreet1`. For ensuring architectural compliance, we can

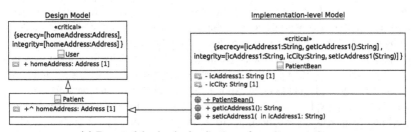

(A) Excerpt of the class-level realization and security annotations.

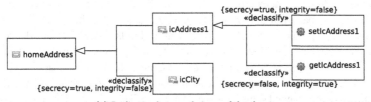

(B) Realization between features of the classes.

Figure 6.14 Realization of a class from the design model by an implementation-level class detailing features

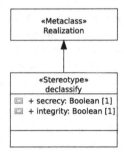

Figure 6.15 UML profile for security tracing

check whether the realized features are contained in the scope of the realized class. Furthermore, as shown in this example, we can use realizations to explicitly specify refinements also considering inheritance.

Next, we will look into the realization and impact of the security requirements specified on the class User using UMLsec. The specified security requirements have to be reflected on the realizing class. The most simple and naive solution is that every feature that realizes a classified feature has to be classified at the same security levels. However, in practice, this might not be suitable. For example, a decomposition into multiple features could separate sensitive information from non-sensitive information that was aggregated in a single property in the more abstract model. Considering the home address of a patient, it could be that the concrete address of the patient (icAddress1) is sensitive information but the city the patient lives in (icCity) not. As icCity is a more concrete refinement of icAddress, it inherits the security level and has to be explicitly specified as non-sensitive information. We call such an explicit specification of the non-criticality of a feature that refines a critical feature as declassification. To allow the specification of such a declassification, we introduce the stereotype «declassify». If a Realization is annotated with such a stereotype, this means that the realizing element only realizes a non-sensitive part of the realized element. Figure 6.15 shows the profile definition of this stereotype. For specifying which security levels of UMLsec are declassified, the stereotype contains a tagged value for every security level specified in UMLsec «critical». The figure shows the tagged values for secrecy and integrity. If there is a declassification regarding a security level, the value of the corresponding tagged value has to be set to true. The default value of the tagged values is false. In Figure 6.14b, we specified that there is no declassification for the property icAddress1 and the property icCity there is a declassification regarding *secrecy* but not *integrity*. Based on this information, we can derive the required security requirements for the refining class and can check their consistency with the security requirements of the refined class. For this purpose, we define the security requirement of *Secure Realization*.

Definition 3   *(Secure Realization) A system fulfills* Secure Realization *if for every feature f_a of a classifier A, that appears in the {secrecy} resp. {integrity} tagged value of a «critical» on A, the following conditions hold:*

(i)   *For each feature f_c of a classifier C that has a realization dependency to f_a which is not stereotyped «declassify» with the tagged value {secrecy} resp. {integrity} set to* true, *the feature f_c has to appear in the secrecy resp. integrity tagged value of a «critical» on C.*

(ii)   *There is either no feature f_c of a classifier C that has a realization dependency to f_a or at least one feature f_c of C that has a realization dependency to f_a that is not stereotyped «declassify» with the tagged value {secrecy} resp. {integrity} set to* true.

The first condition expresses that every feature that realizes a classified part has to be classified, too. The second condition expresses that a feature should either not be realized or there has to be at least one realizing feature that realizes the classified part of the realized feature.

Considering the example in Figure 6.14, *Secure Realization* is fulfilled for homeAddress. For the verification of the security requirement, we have to check the realization of the property homeAddress regarding the two security levels secrecy and integrity. First, we check the first condition of *Secure Realization* for every Realization dependency. We start with the realization by the property idAddress1. As this realization is not annotated with «declassify», the «critical» of PatientBean has to contain icAddress1 on both security levels (secrecy and integrity). These expected classifications are given in the example. The realization by the property icCity is stereotyped with «declassify» whereas secrecy is set to true. For this reason, icCity only has to appear on the security level integrity of the «critical» on PatientBean. As also this is given in the example, *Secure Realization*'s first condition is fulfilled. The second condition is also fulfilled as there are realizations of both security levels.

Please note, that the considered classifiers *A* and *C* are non-injective. Accordingly, we can use *Secure Realization* also for propagating security requirements within a class when the internal realization is specified as in the example in

Figure 6.14. In this example, the getter realizes the *secrecy* part of the property `icStreet1` and the setter the *integrity* part. Accordingly, the getter is added to the security-level *secrecy* and the setter to *integrity* of the «`critical`» stereotype on the class `PatientBean`.

In summary, the use of *Realization* relations for expressing refinements allows easy detection of changes that lead to inconsistencies, as the relations can be used as trace links. For tracing security requirements among UML models with different levels of abstraction, we introduced a new stereotype that allows the definition of detailed realization and decomposition rules and is supported by a security check that allows for checking the security compliance of the realizations. Unfortunately, unlike the correspondences using TGGs, we currently do not provide automation in updating the different UML models in case of changes.

6.3.6 Tool Support for Model Refinements

While for editing the UML models any UML modeling tool can be used, we are using Papyrus as it supports the CARiSMA plugin for checks of UMLsec. In addition, we provide support to the user in mapping elements between UML models and creating refinement relations. Our tool support is based on name mappings between Classes, Interfaces, Nodes, Actors, and Artifacts. This name mapping can be supported by providing a dictionary containing synonyms. Also, we discussed the tracing of UMLsec security requirements between UML models with different abstractions. For supporting the security tracing and realization, we specified a security realization profile that allows the detailed specification of security realization. This profile comes with a check that checks for the security compliance of the propagated security requirements at their realization.

We implemented a wizard that allows the selection of the models between which refinement relations should be established. Figure 6.16 shows two pages from this wizard. When the wizard is launched, it searches for all UML models within the current workspace selection. On the first page of the wizard, the developer has to select the model that should be refined, and on the second page the refining model. Figure 6.16a shows the page for selecting the abstract model that should be refined. The page for selecting the refining model looks the same but the already selected model is excluded from the list of models. On the third and last page of the wizard, developers can select a comma-separated file containing synonyms. Figure 6.16b shows the corresponding wizard page. When a file has been selected, a preview of the file is shown. In the example, `user` and `person` are defined as synonyms as well as `doctor` and `hcp`.

After all input data has been selected in the wizard, possible mappings are calculated based on the names of the model elements. Found mappings are presented to the developer in the view shown in Figure 6.17. For all elements, for those possible abstract elements they could refine have been found, an entry is shown. If this entry is opened, e.g., the class User in the second row of the view, possible refined elements are shown. For the class User, this is the class Person. Results that should be persisted in the models, can be selected with a tick. Afterward, realizations are created for the selected elements.

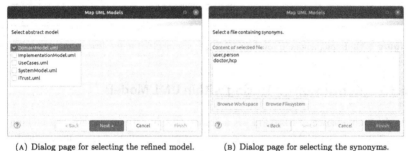

(A) Dialog page for selecting the refined model.   (B) Dialog page for selecting the synonyms.

Figure 6.16 Dialog pages of the UML model mapping wizard

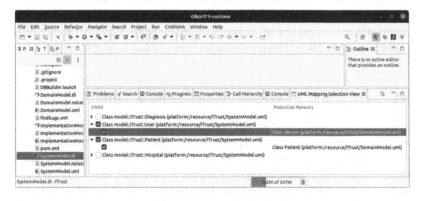

Figure 6.17 View for creating mappings between UML models

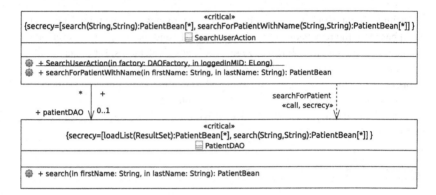

Figure 6.18 Implementation-level model of classes involved in the search for a patient as part of UC28

6.3.7   Conclusion on Tracing within UML Models

As the maintenance of trace links is a prerequisite in various domains, by making use of well-defined UML mechanisms we get tracing but also consistency checks between UML models with different abstraction in many projects for free. However, as we only provide a low level of automatization, a significant effort is required for maintaining trace links between the UML models. This effort might be infeasible for larger real-world software systems. Nevertheless, we demonstrated how tracing within UML models can be realized and exploited for propagating UMLsec security requirements. Also, there is the possibility for improved tool support in future works.

6.4   Tracing and Propagation of Security Requirements

In the previous two sections, we discussed how we can create and maintain trace links between the different UML models and the implementation. However, in the two sections, we mainly focused on the model-level or structural traces between the models and the implementation. Until now, we neglected the security tracing between models and the implementation. Here, practical observations show that tracing and maintaining security properties across system representations is manually laboriously and error-prone [183]. For this reason, using the GRaViTY development approach, security experts should specify security requirements only once on the most suitable system representation. Afterward, GRaViTY allows the reuse of security requirements across the different artifacts in the context of security analyses. For example, in Section 8.1, we will use the UMLsec security annotations to determine the sources and sinks of an implementation-level secure data flow analysis.

In this section, we utilize the introduced trace links for answering RQ1.3 of how to propagate design-time security requirements into the implementation. For this purpose, we show two possibilities of exploiting the generated trace links. First, we specify Java annotations equivalent to the UMLsec stereotypes on the source code level. Instances of these Java annotations are also available at run-time. In Chapter 9, we use these security annotations for a run-time security monitor. To create and maintain these security annotations, we show an extension of the TGG introduced in Section 6.2. Second, we show how the correspondence model can be used for dynamically propagating security requirements.

6.4.1   Persistence of Security Requirements in the Implementation

In GRaViTY, we mainly work on UML models and Java source code as well as its byte code and program model representation. In what follows, we introduce security annotations to support both kinds of artifacts.

To annotate UML models we make use of the existing UMLsec stereotypes [73], focusing on the *Secure Dependency* property, as exemplified in Section 3.6.1. More specifically, this contains the stereotypes «secure dependency», «critical», and «call». In Figure 6.18, we show the UMLsec security annotations on an implementation-level model used as an example for synchronization. UC28 of iTrust specifies that licensed health care professionals (LHCP) shall have the possibility to search for their patients in the iTrust system. This search is realized in the SearchUserAction class that utilizes a PatientDAO class for this purpose. Following Figure 6.14, some of the information about patients stored in

Table 6.2 Mapping between UMLsec and GRaViTY's Java annotations

UMLsec stereotypes		GRaViTY annotations		
stereotype	tagged values	annotated	annotation	parameters
«critical»	*secrecy, integrity*	Class	*@Critical*	*secrecy, integrity*
«critical»	*secrecy*	Member	*@Secrecy*	
«critical»	*integrity*	Member	*@Integrity*	

```
 1    @Critical(secrecy={"search(String,String):List"})
 2    public class SearchUsersAction {
 3
 4        private PatientDAO patientDAO;
 5
 6        @Secrecy
 7        public List<PatientBean> searchForPatientWithName(String firstName,
              String lastName) {
 8            try {
 9                if("".equals(firstName)) firstName = '%';
10                if("".equals(lastName)) lastName = '%';
11                return patientDAO.search(firstName, lastName);
12            }
13            catch (DBException e) {
14                return null;
15            }
16        }
17        ...
18    }
```

Listing 6.1 Source code with GRaViTY's security annotations of a class for accessing patients in iTrust

PatientBeans is classified. For this reason, the methods providing access to the patient beans are also classified regarding *secrecy*.

Mapping UMLsec Stereotypes to Code-Level Security Annotations

Java annotations provide a similar mechanism as UML profiles to annotate Java source code, that can be retained at run-time. We thus defined a set of Java annotations to support typical security requirements aligned with the set of annotations as introduced in UMLsec, so that source code (especially fields and methods) can be annotated.

Table 6.2 gives an overview of the Java annotations we define and their relation to respective UMLsec stereotypes. The Java annotations *@Critical*, *@Secrecy*, and *@Integrity* are used semantically identically to their UMLsec counterparts. UMLsec's «critical» provides all information regarding security levels within the tagged values *secrecy* and *integrity*. Similar to this we defined the parameters *secrecy* and *integrity* which provide, as well as «critical», arrays of member signatures. Usually, methods and fields are annotated by stating them as part of the respective values of «critical». To avoid errors by mistyping and keep clarity in larger classes, we also support that methods and fields can directly be annotated with @*Secrecy* and @*Integrity* respectively. As shown in Section 5.2.8, the program model used by us can also contain information about Java annotations, making these implementation-level security annotations also available in the program model.

In Listing 6.1, we applied the GRaViTY annotations to the Java source code of the class `SearchUsersAction` implementing the corresponding class from the UML model in Figure 6.18. This class allows legitimate users of iTrust to search for patients and access their data. The value `secrecy={searchForPatientWith Name(String, String):String}` of «critical» is represented by a `@Secrecy` annotation on the `searchForPatientWithName` method in line 6 of the example. Additionally, the security requirement *secrecy* is specified for a member with the signature *search(String, String):List* in the `@Critical` annotation in line 1 which is called in line 11, reflecting the corresponding entry in the tagged value `secrecy` of the «critical» in Figure 6.18.

Using the presented mechanisms, developers can specify the same security requirements on both UML models as well as Java source code. In the next section, we show how these two security specifications can be synchronized.

Propagation of Security Requirements

To synchronize the UMLsec annotations with GRaViTY security annotations in source code, besides the mapping between the different annotations from Table 6.2 a mapping between UML elements and Java source code is needed. Considering the problem of tracing UML elements to Java source code, mappings have already been defined in various reverse-engineering approaches [184, 163]. Unfortunately, existing mappings only consider a one-shot mapping. Thus, the challenge is to keep up with the continuous evolution of both, UML models and source code.

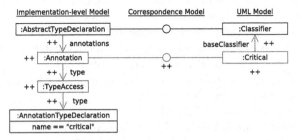

Figure 6.19 TGG Rule for translating @*Critical*-annotations in an implementation-level model to «critical»-stereotypes in a UML model

Furthermore, GRaViTY should not only be able to map ordinary UML elements and source code but should also cover UMLsec stereotypes and GRaViTY annotations.

Existing approaches use graph transformations providing model synchronization to deal with the issues arising from evolution [130, 163]. Similarly, we employ a *Triple Graph Grammar* (TGG) [160], a rule-based transformation supporting the synchronization of changes made on both the source and target model, as described before. When applying a TGG transformation between two models, a correspondence model is built between the two models, capturing which elements have been translated to each other. This correspondence model is used afterward to synchronize changes applied to any of the two models with the other model. We extended the TGG introduced in Section 6.2.2 to support security annotations and successfully applied this TGG to the example of the thesis generating the annotations shown in Listing 6.1. As an example of a TGG rule, we show in Figure 6.19 a rule from our extension and explain it in what follows. This rule is used to translate the @*Critical* annotation to a «critical» stereotype. The values of this annotation are translated using separate rules.

On the left side of Figure 6.19, are the elements from an implementation-level model shown, and on the right side the elements from the UML model. In between these two, the correspondence model is shown. Elements that will be newly translated by this rule are annotated with a ++ and are highlighted in green. In black and without annotations, we show the required context for the application of the rule. This context has to be translated using other TGG rules before this rule can be applied. In the shown rule, we assume as the context that an *AbstractTypeDeclaration* has been translated to *Classifier* and that an *AnnotationTypeDeclaration* with the name *Critical* has been translated. If we can find this context and there is an untranslated *Annotation* of the type *Critical* we translate it to a «critical» stereotype on the corresponding *Classifier*, meaning to add this stereotype to the model. The rule can also be applied in the opposite direction.

If after the initial transformation new elements are added, these can be translated as shown above. If elements are deleted, the rule applications for translating them are undone. This results in a deletion also on the other model.

Let us assume a change in the security knowledge and look at how the developed hospital system can be adapted to this change using the GRaViTY framework. Due to the introduction of the European General Data Protection Regulation (GDPR) [53], we got a stronger restriction in the ways how we have to deal with personal data. Before the GDPR became valid, it was legal to identify patients based on their names. This information has to be treated with more sensitivity now. This change in the security knowledge can, for example, be reflected in annotating the Patient in the domain model in Figure 6.13 with the UMLsec stereotype «critical» {secrecy={name:FullName}} expressing that the access to this information

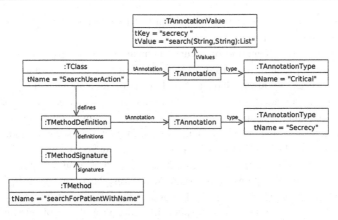

Figure 6.20 Program model excerpt with Java annotations

is only allowed for legitimate cases. As this security annotation is inherited by the more concrete subtypes, the secure dependency check will fail after this change, since there are no corresponding changes on the other elements. Accordingly, this gives a list of accesses to the developers, which have to be checked for this purpose. To do so, the developers have to look into the documentation and can follow the trace links generated by GRaViTY. Furthermore, they can use the TGGs to transfer the new security annotations into the code and re-execute the security analyses to get more detailed feedback about the compliance of the implementation.

Tool Support for Synchronizing Security Requirements

The presented TGG rules allow synchronizing security annotations between the UML models and the implementation. Propagation of the security annotations into the program model, e.g., for security checks, is already given by the TGG presented in Section 6.2. As the introduced security annotations on the implementation level are specified as Java annotations, these are handled by the transformation rules for Java annotations. Figure 6.20 shows an excerpt of the program model created from the example in Listing 6.1. The excerpt contains the class `SearchUsersAction`, the method `searchForPatientsWithName`, and the two security annotations (`@Critical` and `@Secrecy`). Both annotations are represented by instances of the type `TAnnotation` that have a reference to a `TAnnotationType` specifying the type of the annotation. The tagged values of «critical» respectively the parameters of `@Critical` are represented by instances of the node

`TAnnotationValue` where `tKey` identifies the parameter by its name and `tValue` holds the value.

This native representation of security annotations allows the propagation of these into the program model but is not easy to use. When we want to specify a security check, we always have to handle pairs of annotations and types. Also, the signatures contained in a «critical» are only present in textual form. To make the handling of security requirements on the program model level easier, we defined the security extension shown in Figure 6.21. For every security requirement contained in the Java annotations from Table 6.2, we define a corresponding subtype of the general `TAnnotation` in the type graph. This allows us to use the security-specific annotations as we would use arbitrary Java annotations but allows us to identify these by their type and to add additional explicit information. For the `TCritical` annotation, this explicit information is the resolved signatures (`TSignature`) put to a security level. Furthermore, to ease the usage in cases where it only has to be checked if an element is critical, we define a common parent type (`TAbstractCriticalElement`).

Figure 6.22 shows again a program model excerpt for the source code shown in Listing 6.1 but this time using the explicit security types. The `TAnnotation` nodes have been replaced by their typed equivalents and the *secrecy* classification

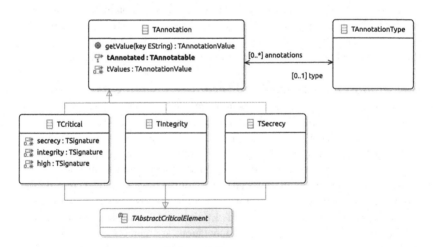

Figure 6.21 Extension of the type graph adding explicit types for UMLsec security requirements

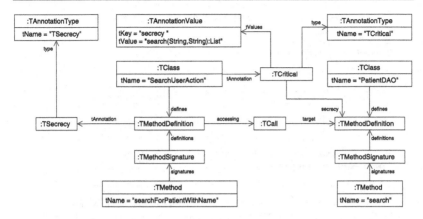

Figure 6.22 Program model excerpt with security annotations

of the method `search` has been made explicit by a `secrecy` reference from the `TCritical` node to the corresponding `TMethodDefinition` node.

Technically, we implemented the addition of these explicit types in terms of a postprocessor registered at the `IPostprocessingPM` extension point of the program model TGG. After the program model has been created, this postprocessor takes every `TAnnotationType` representing a security annotation and replaces all `TAnnotation` nodes instantiating this type with an instance of the corresponding type from the extension shown in Figure 6.21. While doing this, the preprocessor disables the change tracking of EMF to avoid triggering reactions, e.g., a change propagation by the TGGs. If a security annotation has been added to the program model, a preprocessor registered at the `IPreprocessingPM` extension point adds a reference to the corresponding `TAnnotationType` for allowing the propagation into the implementation.

Conclusion of the Security Persistence Mechanism

In conclusion, TGGs allow the propagation of security requirements between design-time models and the implementation. Using postprocessing, easily understandable security annotations can be propagated into the program model. Also, the security requirements are editable on any system representation and are available at run-time. As a drawback, the information contained in the single representations is significantly increased.

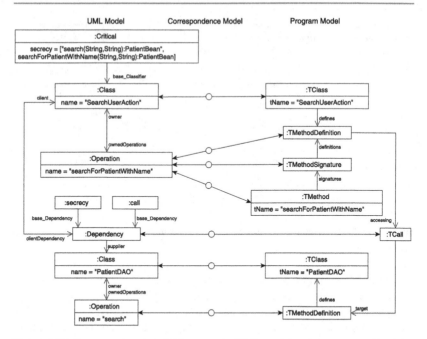

Figure 6.23 Correspondence model between the UML model and program model of the iTrust excerpt

6.4.2   Dynamic Tracing between UML Models and the Implementation

One drawback of persisting security requirements as Java annotations in the implementation is that it makes the source code more complicated and less readable. Often information about security requirements is not always needed but could be looked up dynamically when needed. Here, the correspondence model created between the implementation and the UML models by the TGGs cannot only be used for propagating changes between the artifacts but also for tracing security requirements.

Utilizing Correspondence Models for Dynamic Security Tracing

As the correspondence model holds the information about all structural correspondences, we can use this information to look up the corresponding implementation element for an element annotated with UMLsec security requirements. Accordingly, we can also look up the corresponding model element for given source code elements and if the corresponding model elements have UMLsec security requirements.

Figure 6.23 shows the correspondence model between the UML model excerpt shown in Figure 6.18 and the program model excerpt shown in Figure 6.22. The underlying graph structure of the UML model is shown on the left of the figure. The elements from the UML model are represented by typed nodes connected according to their relations in the visual UML model. On the right of the figure, the program model is shown. Correspondences are indicated by circles in the center of the figure that connect corresponding elements with arrows.

In the following, we assume that we develop the method `searchForPatient WithName` and want to know which security requirements apply for this method. In the program model, this method is represented by a triple of `TMethod`, `TMethodSignature`, and `TMethodDefinition` whereas the `TMethod` node contains the name of the method. The `TMethodDefinition` represents the implementation of the method and is the start point for tracing. Over the correspondence model, this operation is connected with the operation representing the method in the UML model. From this operation, we can navigate to the class defining the operation by following the `owner` reference. There we can check whether this class is annotated with security requirements. The class `SearchUserAction` defines the operation `searchForPatientWithName` and is annotated with a «`critical`» putting two signatures to a security level. Accordingly, the same security requirements have to apply to the implementation

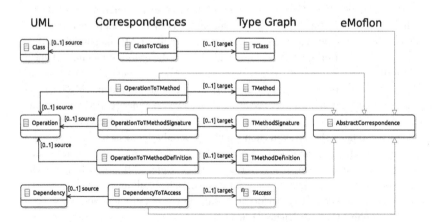

Figure 6.24 Excerpt from the metamodel for the correspondences between UML models and program models

represented by the program model. To check whether one of these applies to the method `searchForPatientWithName`, we have to calculate the signature of the operation we traced it to and have to check if this signature is contained in the list. For this operation, this is the case and we know that we develop a method that is on the security level of secrecy. In the same way, we have to check if any of the methods called by the `TMethodDefiniton` realizing `searchForPatientWithName` are put to a security level. Finally, we can trace every access relation in the program model to their corresponding dependencies in the UML model. In the figure, one `TCall` relation is shown that corresponds with a dependency in the UML model. For dependencies, we can immediately check whether these are annotated with UMLsec security requirements. In this case, the dependency is annotated with `secrecy`.

Tool Support for Dynamic Tracing
The implementation of the dynamic tracing is entirely based on the features of the eMoflon tool and the EMF implementation. When specifying a TGG, one step of the specification is specifying possible correspondences between the model elements. From this specification, an Ecore metamodel is generated by eMoflon.

One challenge at dynamic tracing using an eMoflon correspondence model is the reverse-navigation along the source and target edges of a correspondence. The correspondences, that are shown in Figure 6.23, build a separate model that connects elements from different models. Every circle indicates a correspondence node that has two outgoing references. Figure 6.24 shows the excerpt of the correspondence metamodel used in Figure 6.23. The correspondence metamodel itself only contains the types labeled with *Correspondences* all other types are referenced types from other metamodels. First, there are the metamodels of the models that should be related by correspondences. In the figure, these are the UML metamodel and the type graph of our program model. Second, there is the eMoflon metamodel specifying the type `AbstractCorrespondence`. All correspondences subtype this type to be usable in eMoflon. Also, an informal specification from the eMoflon metamodel is that every correspondence has to define two references called `source` and `target`. These two references indicate which element types the concrete correspondence relates. As eMoflon cannot add additional references to the metamodels between which a correspondence model is defined, the source and target references are only navigable starting from a correspondence. Here, EMF offers the possibility of reverse navigating edges which is based on a cache of all incoming references to an object. However, from a performance side, this is not efficient and might be an issue for applications of dynamic tracing.

One application in which we use a correspondence model for dynamic tracing is the creation of a correspondence model between the UML model and the program model. For synchronizing these two models we did not specify a TGG but emulate this synchronization by a subsequent execution of the other two TGGs. However, we also want to provide the possibility for direct dynamic tracing between these two models. For this purpose, we defined a correspondence model between UML models and the program model. An instance of this program model is created by dynamically tracing every MoDisco element to the corresponding elements from the UML model and the program model. For every pair, for that a correspondence type has been defined in the UML to PM correspondence model, we create the corresponding instances.

At creating the correspondence model between a UML model and program model we mitigated this risk of inefficiency due to reverse-navigation correspondence edges by adjusting the usage of dynamic tracing. First, we do not directly iterate over all MoDisco elements but overall correspondences of one of the two correspondence models. Starting from these correspondences, efficient navigation to two of the three models is possible. For the other correspondence model, we initially iterate over all correspondences and building our own cache structured according to our needs, namely a one-to-many map taking MoDisco elements as key.

Conclusion on the Dynamic Security Tracing

Dynamic tracing using the correspondence model created by eMoflon allows to trace between models and to propagate security requirements without enriching the source code with this information. However, there is the risk of inefficiency due to the need for reverse navigation along the edges of the correspondence model. This risk can be mitigated by constructing usages of dynamic tracing in a way that reduces reverse navigation to a minimum. Also, caching has been shown as an effective measure to deal with this issue.

6.4.3   Conclusion on the Propagation of Security Requirements

We have shown that we can propagate arbitrary security requirements within UML models of different abstraction but also between UML models and the implementation and program model. For this purpose, we investigated two different mechanisms for tracing security requirements. First, we extended the TGG transformation to create corresponding security requirements in the implementation as Java annotations. Second, we looked at how a dynamic tracing using the correspondence model works. Both mechanisms come with benefits and drawbacks and should be used complementary as discussed in what follows.

The dynamic tracing avoids enriching the implementation with additional annotations but it can have the disadvantage of being inefficient due to reverse navigation. If only a few traces are required across the correspondence model or an efficient cache has been created, dynamic tracing should be used to avoid distracting developers. This distraction by creating too many annotations in the implementation is the main disadvantage of propagating all security requirements into the implementation. However, if many annotations are required for analysis, the propagation is more likely to be efficient. Also, the created annotations are available at run-time. Altogether, small local look-ups should be realized using dynamic tracing, while for full compliance checks or at deployment the UMLsec security requirements should be propagated into the implementation using additional TGG rules. Unfortunately, current implementations of TGGs do not allow to dynamically enable and disable TGG rules but could be extended in this direction.

To conclude, our TGGs provide an automated mechanism to preserve consistency between the three different program representations for managing evolving Java programs. As a result, we obtain a model-based framework for arbitrarily interleaving program evolution and maintenance steps. Furthermore, we can use this approach to also translate and synchronize security requirements of model elements between different system representations to execute sophisticated security checks on them as discussed in Section 8.1.

Application to Legacy Projects using Reverse-Engineering

7

This chapter shares material with the MODELS'2019 publication "Secure Data-Flow Compliance Checks between Models and Code based on Automated Mappings" [23].

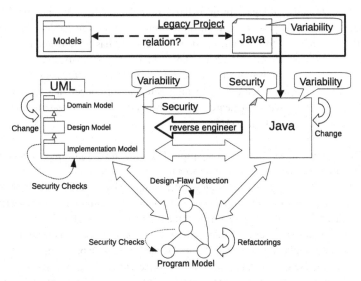

Figure 7.1 Concept for the application of GRaViTY to legacy projects

© The Author(s), under exclusive license to Springer Fachmedien Wiesbaden GmbH, part of Springer Nature 2022
S. M. Peldszus, *Security Compliance in Model-driven Development of Software Systems in Presence of Long-Term Evolution and Variants*,
https://doi.org/10.1007/978-3-658-37665-9_7

While the approach presented in this thesis allows developers to develop and maintain secure software product lines, it is limited to projects that have initially developed using GRaViTY. In practice, software systems are often developed not using models as essential development artifacts at all [9]. Nevertheless, informal modeling approaches are widely spread in the industry [185]. If models are created at design time, these are often not maintained in the implementation phase and do not reflect the current state of the software system. However, even in such software projects, migration to developing the software system using GRaViTY should be possible. For this reason, in this chapter, we investigate the reverse engineering of models and trace links required by GRaViTY. By doing this, we answer the second research question of this thesis:

RQ2:   How can we apply model-based security engineering to legacy projects that have no or disconnected design-time models?

As indicated and shown on top of Figure 7.1, legacy projects can be in various conditions. Usually, all legacy projects have source code, that can be used without changes. Some legacy projects might have some early design models. However, usually, their relation to the source code is unclear and has to be restored. If these early design models are too abstract or not present, it is necessary to reverse-engineer UML class diagrams with an abstraction suitable to GRaViTY's *Triple Graph Grammars* (TGG)s used for synchronization and tracing, as introduced in Section 6.2. In summary, there are two sub-research questions to consider if we want to cover the two described states of legacy projects:

RQ2.1:   How can we support legacy projects for that no design-time models exist in model-based security engineering?

RQ2.2:   How can we migrate legacy projects that have models but that are disconnected from the implementation to model-based security engineering?

In this chapter, we introduce reverse-engineering techniques allowing us to overcome this limitation for legacy projects. Following the sub-research questions, first, we discuss the application of the TGGs introduced in Section 6.2 to legacy projects for which no models exist and an entire reverse-engineering is necessary. Second, we consider projects for which models but no correspondence model with the implementation exists.

7.1   Reverse-Engineering UML Models Using TGGs

TGGs allow a bidirectional transformation between a source and a target model, meaning that TGGs can be executed in two directions. First, for propagating changes from the source model to the target model, and second, for propagating changes from the target model to the source model. If one of the two models does not exist, propagating the changes means the creation of the non-existent model as specified in the TGG rules. In Section 6.2, we introduced a TGG using the implementation-level MoDisco model representing Java source code as source model and a UML class diagram as target model. For reverse-engineering UML models from the implementation, we can execute the UML TGG in the Java to UML direction after parsing the Java source code. In Section 6.2.4, we successfully used the UML TGG to reverse-engineer UML class diagrams from 20 Java projects. This transformation not only extracts a UML class diagram but by nature also automatically creates the required correspondence model for the subsequent tracing of changes.

However, the created UML models are on the granularity of the implementation and additional more abstract models have to be extracted manually. The only abstraction from the implementation is the reduction of details from the statement level of methods and fields to dependencies between classes. Nevertheless, this abstraction provides a significant reduction in complexity in terms of used dependency types but also the number of considered dependencies. Size is one important aspect when it comes to the manual handling of models. For this reason, Figure 7.2 shows the size of the UML models created in Section 6.2.4 from software systems with different sizes. For relating these values to other models representing the same software systems, also the sizes of the corresponding MoDisco models and program models (pm) are shown. All models seem to grow more or less linearly with the number of code lines. But while the program model has on average 28 % of the number of nodes the MoDisco model has, this relation is only at 11 % for the extracted UML models.

Furthermore, using suitable views on the extracted models, these can effectively be annotated with UMLsec security requirements. The UML supports the concept of views that allow visualizing selected elements of a UML model [5]. A single UML element can be part of multiple views on the UML model. This allows developers to create views of a manually manageable size focusing on specific aspects of the software system, e.g., a security-critical dependency or classified class member.

Such views can be extracted automatically, e.g., using model slicing [186, 187] or clustering [188, 189]. At model slicing, starting from a given element all elements related to this element according to slicing rules are selected as part of this slice. At clustering, elements are grouped according to their coupling with each other. Given suitable slicing rules or coupling criteria, both approaches can be used to get all additional elements relevant to a developer when inspecting a specific UML model element. Based on these elements a suitable view can be created. However, there lies a significant challenge in defining suitable rules and criteria. Often, too many elements are selected. Here, the UMLsec stereotype can function as a source for additional coupling information improving the quality of the extracted views.

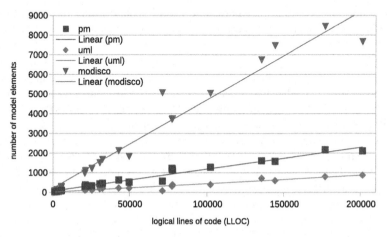

Figure 7.2 Model sizes in relation to the code lines of software systems

In summary, UML class diagrams that have been reverse engineered using our UML TGG are not as beneficial as manually created UML models but provide a foundation toward proper reverse-engineered models. Models with a higher degree of abstraction can be manually extracted from the reverse-engineered ones. Using the realization dependencies these extracted models can be connected to the reverse-engineered models as discussed in Section 6.3. However, often early design models exist but no trace links to the implementation exist and these might be deprecated. In the next section, we show how trace links between these early design models and the implementation can be restored in a semi-automated way. Of course, this approach could also be used to establish trace links between the reverse-engineered UML models and the early design models.

7.2   Mapping Early Design-Models to Code

In this section, we aim to support the reconstruction of a correspondence model between early design-time models and the implementation. We aim at the creation of a state allowing the application of GRaViTY. Furthermore, during the reconstruction, we can also discover secure data-flow compliance violations between the designed and the implemented security requirements in a software system. These violations can emerge if the models and code have not been kept synchronized using our approach introduced in Section 6.2.2 and divergences between the planned and implemented design manifested themselves. We present a technique that semi-automatically establishes a correspondence model between a *Security Data Flow Diagram* (SecDFD), a design-level model enriched with security-relevant information, and the implementation-level *Program Model* introduced in Chapter 5.

Our correspondence model and the proposed semi-automated reconstruction of the correspondence model support software architects in the early discovery of implementation absence, convergence, and divergence concerning the planned software design, including its security requirements. Furthermore, the correspondence model can be used to discover compliance violations of secure data-flow properties (typically, data confidentiality and data integrity properties) as follows: The designed data flow is captured in the SecDFD model. The actual data flow is obtained from implementation-level data-flow analysis tools. These tools typically require sophisticated meta-data, e.g., an explicit tagging of security-critical data and functions, as input, which can be obtained from our correspondence model. We discuss the leveraging of such correspondences in detail in Chapter 8. In this section, we focus on the creation of a correspondence model and make the following contributions:

1. We present an automated technique for establishing a correspondence model between design-time models in the SecDFD notation and program models. Thereby, we support the discovery of secure data-flow compliance violations as discussed in Section 8.2. The key idea of our technique is twofold. First, we define a mapping between SecDFD and program-model element types, constraining how elements of a concrete software system can be mapped to each other. Second, we combine similarity-based matching of element names with structural heuristics (based on data-flow properties) to automatically derive suggested correspondences between the SecDFD and the program model based on the previously defined mapping.
2. We present an incremental methodology, in which the user of the methodology, e.g., a developer that wants to reconstruct a correspondence model, is involved

to successively discover new correspondences and eventually derive an adequate correspondence model.

3. We present our implementation of the approach as a publicly available Eclipse plugin and the evaluation of its accuracy on five open-source Java projects (including the running example iTrust).

7.2.1 Background on Early Design Models

We aim at developing a semi-automated approach for reconstructing correspondence models between early design models and the implementation. For developing this approach, we have to select which design models we want to support. Here, we consider two criteria. First, we aim at models that are used in practice, and second, at keeping the approach as transferable as possible. For this reason, in this section, we discuss the background of early design models.

Security threats to software systems are a growing concern in many organizations, particularly due to the recent changes in legislation (GDPR) and upcoming security standards (ISO 21434). Therefore, one needs to consider security early in the design phase, when little is known about the software system. At the start of the development process, requirements are collected and use cases are defined. According to the principle of *security by design* [6, 190], the software system's assets and threats already have to be defined in this phase. The system architecture is then iteratively refined and finally implemented. Before any new functionality is released, it must be checked that every security assumption made in any of the phases is met. The state-of-the-art for these checks in practice is manual code reviews by security experts. Since such reviews are expensive and error-prone, they are only performed on selected code parts, leaving a large leeway for security threats [95, 96].

In the context of software architecture design, threat analysis techniques, like Microsoft's STRIDE [110], attack trees [191], CORAS [192], and threat patterns [193] aim to identify security threats to software systems. Threat analysis is very helpful to detect security threats early and plan countermeasures to mitigate them. Yet, empirical evidence shows that existing threat analysis techniques can be manually labor-intensive [194] and lack automation [195]. Furthermore, design-level models are seldom kept in sync with the implementation, potentially resulting in architectural erosion and technical debt [93].

Threat analysis is often performed on a graphical representation of the software architecture called *Data Flow Diagram* (DFD) [196, 197]). DFD-like models are extensively used in practice, e.g., in the automotive industry [109] and at Microsoft [110] as part of their STRIDE methodology. UML activity diagrams can be used for the same purpose. Still, the DFD notation is informal and lacks the ability to specify security requirements, which is needed to reason about security threats at the design level. To support the detection of problematic information flows at the design level, previous work extends the DFD notation with security-relevant information [198] and security semantics [111]. However, the outcomes of such detection are of limited value if the implementation does not comply with the security requirements described in the DFD. In contrast to DFDs, UML activity diagrams provide clearly defined semantics. However, if we only consider the activities and the data flow between them, they can be seen as a DFD.

7.2.2 Semi-Automated Mapping Approach

Assuming a correct DFD, the way it is implemented can vary depending on concrete design, e.g., depending on the selected architectural patterns, and implementation-specific decisions, e.g., the chosen programming language. Therefore, a full automatic generation of a correct and complete correspondence model between DFDs and code is not feasible. Yet, a manual specification of the same correspondence model is inefficient and error-prone. To this end, we propose an iterative methodology for interactively guiding the user in finding an adequate correspondence model by combining automated mappings with user decisions as shown in Figure 7.3.

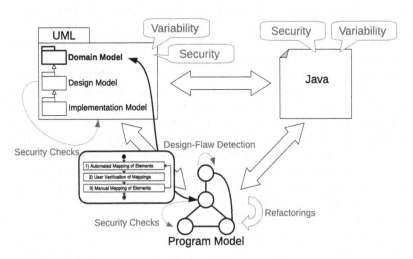

Figure 7.3 Semi-automated mapping of implementations to DFDs

Thereby, we assume that the domain model is specified using data flow diagrams or activity diagrams describing high-level processes in the domain as introduced in Section 3.6.2. As discussed in the background section, activity diagrams can be seen as DFDs with additional control flow and all approaches applicable to DFDs can be applied to activity diagrams. For this reason, in what follows, we only focus on DFDs. In step 1, correspondences between DFD elements and implementation elements are calculated using a heuristic technique. In step 2, these correspondences are presented to the user and manually checked by her. In step 3, the user can manually map additional elements. Afterward, the automated mapping is executed again, benefiting from the user input. The process terminates when the user cannot find any additional correspondence or finds a violation.

In this section, first, we define a mapping of DFD to element types that may correspond to each other as a basis for a correspondence model in concrete software systems. Second, we describe the steps of our methodology, including the automated technique, in detail. We show how our automated technique in step 1 establishes a concrete correspondence model between DFDs and their implementations by using naming- and structure-based heuristics and explain the interactive steps 2 and 3 of our techniques. As an example, we use the DFD showing the reset of a user's password in the iTrust system by the user. This DFD has been introduced in detail in Section 3.6.2. Figure 7.4 shows the same DFD as the one in Figure 3.8 used for the introduction of DFDs.

The implementation of this DFD has been shown in Listing 2.1 as part of the running example chapter of this thesis (Chapter 2). The most relevant excerpt from the method calls involved in the implementation of this DFD is shown in Figure 7.5. The update of a password starts with the call of the method `changePassword(long, String, String, String)`. As shown in the DFD, the implementation of this method has the user's MID, the new password, and the old password as parameters. In the implementation, the new password has to be entered two times to avoid typos, adding a fourth parameter. When this method is called, first the password of the user is checked using the `authentificatePassword(long, String):boolean` method. Next, it is checked if the new passwords are equal using the `equals` method. Afterward, the `resetPassword(long:String)` method is called. This method prepares an SQL statement and executes it to update the password in the database of the iTrust system. Among others, this is mainly realized by calling the methods `prepareStatement` and `executeUpdate`.

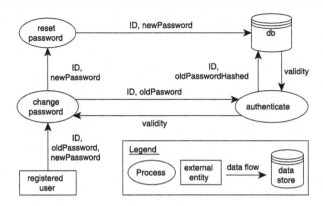

Figure 7.4 DFD for resetting a password in the iTrust system

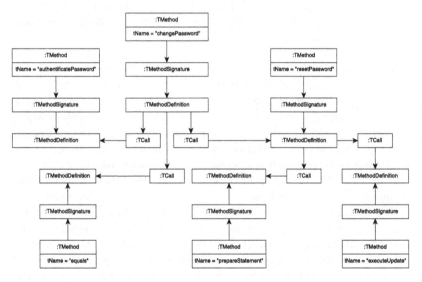

Figure 7.5 Program model excerpt of the implementation for resetting a password in the iTrust system

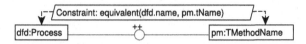

Figure 7.6 Rule describing the name matching for methods

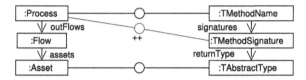

Figure 7.7 Rule for extending name matches based on return types

Identification of Corresponding Meta-Model Elements

As a prerequisite for mapping DFD elements to source code elements to find correspondences, first we have to define which DFD element can correspond with which source code elements. Here, the source code is represented by the program model introduced in Chapter 5.

Assets → types: The assets in a DFD are the elements holding critical data. On the level of implementation, data is usually stored in fields, processed using variables, and transmitted using parameters and return values. A single asset can be stored in many locations at the same time which makes it infeasible to map an asset to every single location. The only property of an asset which only changes rarely in programs, written in an object-oriented language, is the type of the asset.

Data stores → types & methods: Considering data stores like iTrust's database in the example DFD, it is quite obvious that this data store is reflected in the implementation by operations realizing queries. Also, the data store could be a field in a class, e.g., a map used as a cache. But it could also be implemented by an operation that, e.g., requests the cached values from an external server by creating HTTP requests. The common thing between these variants is the type used to represent the data at storing. The field has a type that provides getters and setters for using the data store, and the method used to get data from a remote server is implemented in a type. Therefore, we map data stores to types as well as to the methods used for accessing the stored data.

Processes → method(-names): Processes in DFDs describe functionalities that process data, like methods in implementations do. These two elements correspond with each other. While a concrete method definition in an implementation contains all details describing the functionality of this method, the processes only have a name describing the functionality. We assume that a developer implementing a process will choose a similar name for the methods implementing this process. This leads us to a correspondence between the names of processes and the names of methods.

Processes + Assets → method parameters: Between processes in a DFD, data can be exchanged using flows, where the exchanged data are represented by assets on the flows. In the methods implementing these processes, the same data have to be exchanged. Data between methods in implementations are usually exchanged using parameters and return values. Therefore, we can combine the name mappings between processes and methods with the assets flowing into and out of a process to method parameters giving us the corresponding method signatures.

Steps of the Semi-Automated Mapping Approach

Our semi-automated mapping approach is based on an iteration of three subsequent steps. First, an automated step, followed by two manual steps. In the first step, possible correspondences between the models and code are automatically detected. These correspondences are reviewed by the user of the approach in the second step and are partly extended in the third step. Afterward, the first step is executed again until the user has nothing to add in the third step. In what follows we discuss the three steps of our semi-automatic generation of correspondences in detail.

Step 1: Automated Mapping of Elements. The automated generation of correspondences is based on name matchings and structural heuristics, which are sequentially executed and complement each other in building mappings from which correspondences are derived. For illustration, we formalize two of our mappings using graph rules. For the specification of these graph rules, we use a notation inspired by algebraic graph transformation [199]. The other mappings can be formalized analogous.

Name matching: First, the names of elements from a DFD are mapped to the corresponding names in the implementation. Asset and data store names are mapped to the names of types and process names are mapped to the names of methods. Figure 7.6 shows a rule for mapping processes from a DFD to method names from a program model. A correspondence (visualized as a circle connecting the corresponding elements) between a process and a method name is created (denoted by ++) if the constraint at the top of the rule holds. In this case, the names of the two elements on the left and right of the rule have to be equivalent. The precise definition of this equivalence is described in what follows.

Names, both in a DFD and in a Java implementation, are usually built by concatenating multiple words. For example, a Java method name resetPassword consists of the word *reset* and *password*. These words can vary slightly in the names of the corresponding DFD processes, e.g., in plural form, *passwords* instead of *password*. In addition, the style of word concatenation can differ. In Java usually, the camel case (*resetPassword*) is used, whereas in DFDs this is not a prescribed style, so underscores may also be used (*Reset_Passwords*).

To deal with these issues, first, we split the strings at frequently used delimiters and upper-case characters. This gives us for our example the sets of words *[reset, Password]* and *[Reset, Passwords]*. Then we compare the lower-case versions of the words with each other using a fuzzy comparison based on the Levenshtein distance [200]. The Levenshtein distance is a measure of the minimal amount of characters which have to be removed, added, or flipped to change one word into the other one. For the given example this distance is zero and one as the first word is already identical and only the character *s* has to be added to change *password* into *passwords*. We accept different distances between words for considering them as identical according to the length of the words to be compared.

Finally, a DFD process is usually implemented in multiple methods, typically having slightly more concrete names. For example besides the method reset-Password, there might also be an additional method internalReset Passwod involved in the implementation of the process Reset_Passwords. But the name of a DFD process might also contain additional information, e.g., the process Reset_Password of the DFD in Figure 7.4 could be called Reset_Passwords_in_DB. To address this challenge, we compare all words from the two names with each other and count the similar words. If this number reaches a threshold of more than half the number of the average words of the compared names, we consider the names sufficiently equal.

For the example DFD in Figure 7.4 and the program model excerpt in Figure 7.5 we get a name match between the reset password process and the two method names authentificatePassword, changePassword, and *resetPassword* as well as a match between the process change password and the same three method names. While two of these matches are expected, the match between *rest password* and *changePassword* as well as authentificate Password are unexpected and should be dropped in the following steps.

Extending Name Matches to Method Signatures: For every method name, multiple signatures may exist. Even if our name matches were always perfectly correct, this would not imply that all signatures with this name are the ones corresponding to the matched process. For example, besides the relevant signature *resetPassword(long, String):void*, there is a second signature *reset-Password(long,String, String,String,String,String):String* defined in iTrust but belongs to the implementation of a different use case. Also, there could be additional signatures in libraries, e.g., the Java standard library, which might even are never used in the implementation of iTrust. To identify the actually relevant signatures, we use data-flow information about assets flowing into and out of a process. Information flowing into a process has to be passed to the implementation of the process, for example, as a parameter value. Likewise, information leaving a process can leave it over return values and parameters. Accordingly, we can use the mapped assets to identify relevant signatures. For every signature, we count how many mapped assets are compatible with the parameters and return types of the existing signatures. If we have at least one match we consider this signature for further mappings.

A rule for extending a process mapping based on an asset flowing out of a process is shown in Figure 7.7. On top of the rule, we can see an existing mapping between a process and a method name, e.g., created by the rule shown in Figure 7.6. A mapping to one of the signatures having this name is created if there is a mapping between an asset flowing out of the process and a type which is the return type of the signature.

If we look at the parameter types of the signature resetPassword(long, String) and assume that the newPassword asset from Figure 7.4 has been mapped to the implementation class java.lang.String and ID to long, we accept this signature as corresponding with the process reset password. The other method name mapped to this process was changePassword. While the parameter types match the expected assets, there are more parameters than data in the DFD. Also, the return type of this method signature is Status that has not been mapped to any asset. Accordingly, we do not create a mapping suggesting a correspondence between the two elements.

Finding Implementations of Signatures: The last step is to find concrete implementations of a signature corresponding with the process. For every signature, there might be several concrete implementations, all of which do not necessarily correspond to the process. We make use of the flows between different processes to find the concrete method definitions.

If there is a flow from one process to another, this does not only mean that there has to be a signature that has the capability to return or receive the corresponding asset. Also, there has to be a definition of this signature which is called from a definition mapped to the other process. Therefore, we search for two kinds of data flows between the concrete definitions of the signatures found before.

1. Parameters passed by a call from the source of a flow to the target of the flow.
2. Return values returned at a call from the target of a flow to the source of the flow.

The flow between two such definitions is not necessarily a single direct call between the two definitions. There can also be multiple definitions in between forwarding data. Matching such intermediate methods to one of the two involved processes is non-trivial. However, if we found such a flow, we can definitely assume that we found two definitions implementing at least parts of the two processes. The intermediate definitions can be partly mapped to one of the two processes by considering the internal coupling in a process. For every pair of signatures mapped to the same process, we look for pairs of definitions calling each other.

Cleanup: After mapping assets and processes, we have to decide which mappings are most likely to be correct and, therefore, should be presented to the user as proposed correspondences. For that reason, we introduce a certainty score for our mappings to be proposed as correspondences. This score is calculated concerning the quality of the underlying name matching as well as the coupling of mapped elements with other mapped elements. For every DFD element, we only present mappings whose score is higher or equal to the median score of all mappings for this element.

The mappings sorted out in this step are not presented to the user but may be discovered later again in the interactive process, based on future matches, which might have a coupling to the elements that are now discarded.

Step 2: User Verification of Mappings. The mappings created in the previous step are now presented as proposed correspondences to the user and verified by her. For every asset type, data store type, and process-definition mapping the user can perform three actions:

Accept: The user can accept the mapping as a correspondence. From then, the mapping cannot be discarded by the optimization step of the automated mapping approach anymore, and all mappings coupled to this mapping obtain a higher certainty score.

Reject: The user can reject the mapping. From then, this mapping is never presented to the user again and it is not considered anymore for extending it to other mappings. All other mappings to which the rejected mapping has been extended

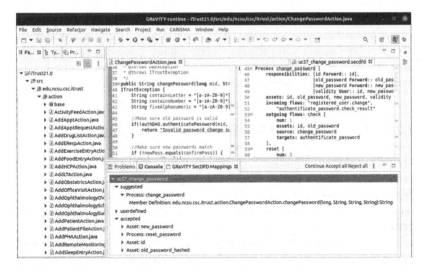

Figure 7.8 Screenshot of the semi-automated mapping UI in Eclipse

will be removed, too. However, these extended mappings might be presented to the user again.

Tolerate: The user can choose to ignore some suggested mappings. Mappings that are not explicitly accepted or rejected are suggested again and can be re-assessed in future iterations.

Mappings accepted or rejected by the user allow the heuristic to automatically discard related mappings that have only been found by following up the rejected mapping. This is how the search space is reduced in the next automated iteration. Conversely, manually accepting mappings can increase the score of related mappings and, for this reason, allows proposing new mappings which have not been considered as correct before. One limitation of our heuristic is that it cannot detect mappings that are outside the search space created by the initial name mappings. We overcome this limitation in our approach by including user feedback as described in what follows.

Step 3: Manual Mapping of Elements.   To increase the search space, an additional user step is conducted after the user manually verified the automatically created mappings that have been proposed as correspondences (or at least a part of them). In this step, the user has to add at least one new correspondence to give additional input to the automated mapping algorithm. The selection of this manually mapped element can have a large impact on the efficiency of the following automated mapping steps when starting over from step 1. Only, when all name matches are included in the search space, the automated mappings can detect all correspondences.

7.2.3   Tool Support for Semi-Automated Mappings

The presented semi-automated mapping approach is implemented and packaged as a publicly available Eclipse plugin[1]. The implementation leverages an existing implementation for modeling SecDFDs with an Xtext DSL with editor support [111]. We use the TGG presented in Chapter 6 for generating the program model from Java source code.

Figure 7.8 shows a screenshot of the user interface in Eclipse. On the left-hand side of the figure, users can see Eclipse's standard *Package Explorer*. The bottom windows are used for displaying and defining the mappings. The top two windows are used for displaying the source code (left) and the SecDFD (right). The target audience of the tool is software developers (or code reviewers) with training in the principles of software architecture. After the installation of the required packages, the program is started as a running Eclipse instance.

The developers first manually create one or several SecDFDs for representing the high-level architecture of a Java project, cf., top right window in Figure 7.8. Next, using context menu entries, the developers trigger the automated generation of a program model from the source code and start the first iteration of the semi-automated process for mapping the SecDFD elements to source code elements, see Section 7.2.2.

At the start of each iteration, the developers are shown a list of mappings suggested as correspondences, cf., bottom window in Figure 7.8. Since one SecDFD element is usually mapped to several program elements, the results are grouped by the SecDFD elements. For each SecDFD element, the list of mapped program model elements is shown, each with its path in the source code. The developers can interact with the tool by accepting, rejecting, and manually defining correspondences. All proposed correspondences that are not explicitly accepted or rejected are considered as tolerated. A mapping suggested as correspondence is accepted or rejected with a right-click on the entry and selecting *accept* or *reject*, respectively. Once

---

[1] Repository containing the implementation of the semi-automated mapping approach: https://github.com/SvenPeldszus/GRaViTY-SecDFD-Mapping/

Table 7.1 Projects considered in the evaluation of the semi-automated mapping approach

project	source code			DFD
	lloc	classes	methods	elements
jpetstore	1,221	17	277	47
ATM simulation	2,290	57	225	85
Eclipse Secure Storage	2,900	39	330	41
CoCoME	4,786	120	512	44
iTrust	28,133	423	3,691	31

a mapping is accepted, corresponding in-line markers are created on the SecDFD and in the source code. Double-clicking a mapping or correspondence will open the correct source file and navigate to the correct line in the file. Mappings accepted as correspondences can always be rejected. If all the suggested mappings are correct, the developers can select *accept all*. Rejected mappings will never be suggested again. The manual definition works by right-clicking and selecting *Map Selection to SecDFD* on source code elements. At the end of the iteration, developers can either stop or select *continue* to trigger a new search refining the present mapping.

7.2.4 Evaluation

In an experiment, we applied our approach to five open-source projects to evaluate the performance of our implementation. In what follows, we briefly describe the design of the experiment, the projects, and the results.

In our evaluation, we investigated the correctness of the automatically generated mappings proposed as correspondences. To this end, we set up an experiment to compare a ground truth of manually created correspondences with the generated mappings for each of the five considered projects. The iterative approach involves the user guiding the generation of mappings in the desired direction. As per this design choice, we intentionally investigate the correctness of the automated mappings and the impact of the user separately. Consequently, the evaluation aims to answer the following objectives.

O1–Correctness: What is the correctness of the automated mappings generated by the plugin?

O2–User Impact: What is the impact of the user on the correctness of mappings?

Table 7.1 depicts the characteristics of five open-source Java projects used in the evaluation. In what follows, we briefly introduce the considered software projects.

Jpetstore [201]: This is a web application built on top of MyBatis 3, Spring, and the Stripes framework. This is an example with very few classes, implementing the basic functionalities of a web store. In principle, the users can create their accounts, browse, and order goods online. Jpetstore has been designed as a minimal demonstration application for MyBatis, which should have a good design and documentation. The developers tried to strictly follow the MVC pattern.

ATM simulation [202]: This is an implementation of a simulation for an automated teller machine (ATM) developed for academic purposes. The ATM simulation implements the main procedure of a control system. Upon start-up, a new session is initiated, and the users can insert their bank card and PIN. The session continues upon a correct PIN entry and provides the users with the option of a withdrawal, deposit, balance inquiry, and money transfer. After the completion of desired transactions, the ATM returns the bank card and optionally prints the receipt.

Eclipse Secure Storage [203]: Eclipse Secure Storage is used for ensuring secure storage and management of sensitive data within a developer's Eclipse workspace. The secure storage allows for plugins to authenticate and have controlled access to workspace resources.

CoCoME [204]: CoCoMe is a platform for collaborative empirical research on information system evolution [205]. This platform helps engineers manage different aspects of software evolution, such as the software system life-cycle, versioning artifacts, and comprehensive evolution scenarios. The implemented software system is a cash register.

iTrust [47]: As described in Section 2, the iTrust example is a web application for a hospital that allows the hospital's staff to manage medical records of patients, based on 55 use cases. The example originally stems from a course project, has been maintained by a research group at North Carolina State University, and was used as an evaluation example in research papers before [51]. Detailed requirements describing different activities are available online [47]. However, the available requirements and use cases mostly describe very simple tasks and only a few of them are realized in the implementation.

The experiment was executed by the author of this thesis and the second author of [23]. The authors worked on the projects individually and compared their results at each step. First, the authors modeled the SecDFDs for all five projects manually. To this aim, the authors inspected all available documentation (including the source code) and reverse-engineered a high-level architecture. Second, the ground truth was created for each SecDFD by following the execution of the modeled scenarios, and manually mapping the executed methods and transferred data to the processes and assets of the according step. The ground truth is a JSON file with a list of expected correspondences the elements of the SecDFD and a uniquely identifiable location of the source code element. Third, the implemented plugin was used to find the automated mappings in several iterations. Each iteration included accepting, rejecting the automated mappings, and defining correspondences manually by highlighting elements in the source code and specifying the corresponding SecDFD elements. After each iteration, the precision and recall of the automated mappings were logged.

This study shows promising results for guiding the user in the discovery of compliance violations. In particular, Table 7.2 shows measurements of high precision and recall only after a few iterations for realistic Java projects. Each iteration consists of an automated, and a manual (user input) phase. We present the precision and recall for the automatically suggested correspondences in each iteration. We also depict the amount of manually accepted, user-defined, the sum of all accepted and user-defined, rejected correspondences, and the impact of the user-defined correspondences on recall (in that order). The later iterations make use of the manually defined correspondences for finding additional mappings that can be proposed as correspondences.

O1–Correctness

In what follows, we discuss the recorded data of our experiment regarding the first objective. First, we introduce our methodology for measuring the correctness of the mappings proposed as correspondences, and afterward, we discuss the results.

Setup. We measured correctness in terms of *precision* and *recall* (dependent variables). Conventionally, precision ($TP/(TP + FP)$) is measured as a ratio between the true positives (i.e., mappings correctly proposed as correspondences) and all generated mappings proposed as correspondences (including the false mappings). A true positive TP is a correct correspondence between the source code and the SecDFD element which is listed in the ground truth. A false positive FP is a mapping between the source code and SecDFD element that is not listed in the ground truth. Recall ($TP/(TP + FN)$) is measured as a ratio between the true positives and all correct correspondences, including the overlooked correspondences. A false negative FN is a mapping between the source code and the SecDFD element which is present in the ground truth but has not been identified.

Table 7.2 Results of the mapping after each iteration

project	it.	automated		manual			
		precision[%]	recall[%]	accept+u	($\sum$)	reject	recall[%](Δ)
jpetstore	1	56.1	51.1	23 + 3	(26)	18	57.8 (+6.7)
	2	96.4	60.0	1 + 3	(30)	1	66.7 (+6.7)
	3	96.8	66.7	0 + 5	(35)	1	77.8 (+11.1)
	4	97.4	82.2	2 + 3	(40)	1	88.9 (+6.7)
	5	100	93.3	2 + 3	(**45**)	0	**100** (+6.7)
ATM simulation	1	72.0	40.0	18 + 3	(21)	7	46.7 (+6.7)
	2	67.6	51.1	2 + 5	(28)	11	62.2 (+11.1)
	3	70.5	68.9	3 + 5	(36)	11	80.0 (+11.1)
	4	76.6	80	0 + 4	(40)	13	88.9 (+8.9)
	5	95.5	93.3	2 + 3	(**45**)	2	**100** (+6.7)
Eclipse sec. storage	1	73.0	90.5	40 + 1	(41)	14	92.9 (+2.4)
	2	67.7	**100**	1 + 0	(**42**)	12	—
CoCoME	1	27.9	77.3	17 + 1	(18)	44	81.8 (+4.5)
	2	86.4	90.5	1 + 1	(20)	2	90.9 (+0.4)
	3	90.9	83.3	0 + 2	(**22**)	4	**100** (+16.7)
iTrust	1	23.5	80.0	8 + 1	(9)	26	90.0 (+10.0)
	2	81.8	90.0	0 + 1	(**10**)	2	**100** (+10.0)

Results. We start by reporting the correctness of the automated mappings in the first iteration. The average precision of the first iteration is 50.5%. On average, the recall of the first iteration is 69.8%. Yet, both the precision and the recall increase after the first iteration. On average, the final precision and recall of the automated phase are very good (87.2% and 92%, respectively).

The average difference between the recall of the second iteration and the user-impacted recall of the first iteration (last column in Table 7.2) is 4.5%. This means that on average, the automated search was able to increase the recall between the first and second iteration by 4.5%. On the other hand, the average difference between the user-impacted recall of the second iteration and the recall of the third iteration is minimal. This means that the automated search was not able to increase the recall significantly between the second and third iteration.

O2–User Impact
For evaluating the user impact on the created mappings, we discuss the recorded data as described in what follows. First, we introduce how we calculated the user impact based on the recorded data and discuss the results afterward.

Setup. Our approach's implementation automatically derives trivial mappings from the user-defined correspondences, raising the recall before a new iteration starts. Therefore, the impact of the user-defined correspondences is measured as the difference in recall before, and after the added correspondences.

Results. On average, the user accepted less (7) mappings as correspondences than they rejected (9.6) and defined only 2.6 correspondences manually. However, in three cases (jpetstore, ATM simulation, Eclipse Secure Storage) the user accepted more mappings than rejected. This means that the user could quickly scan the suggested mappings and eliminate the ones that are obviously wrong. Overall, adding a few correspondences manually resulted in a more fruitful next iteration. For instance, adding three correspondences manually in the first iteration of evaluating the ATM simulation resulted in two new correct mappings proposed as correspondences (see accepted mappings of the second iteration).

On average, the user impact on the recall was an increase of the recall by 7.9%. This means that the users were indeed able to guide the discovery of compliance violations. Further, the users had a larger impact on increasing the recall in later iterations compared to the automated search (7.9% vs 4.5%). Notice, that on average 75% of all correct correspondences (TP) are suggested to the user and do not have to be manually defined.

Additional Observations
While we were executing the evaluation we made different observations that are not directly covered by our research questions but give further proof for the effectiveness of our approach.

1. All DFDs were created based on the available documentation. At executing the evaluation on the ATM simulation we recognized an absence between the

created DFD and the implementation. Further investigations revealed that there is really an absence between the documentation of the ATM simulation and its implementation.

2. At studying the different examples from our evaluation we noticed big differences between the different implementations. The more realistic or real examples (Eclipse Secure Storage, CoCoME, and iTrust) have a source code structured much better than the other two more artificial examples. While in the realistic examples functionalities are implemented in multiple methods, in the artificial examples single methods realize multiple functionalities. These differences are one of the reasons why our technique performed better on the realistic, larger examples. A hypothesis to be studied in the future is that writing the code with the DFD in mind can help structure it better and get better mappings.

3. In the experiments, we had to manually accept and reject mappings proposed as correspondences repeatedly. Thereby we learned that users can reduce the number of necessary clicks by first rejecting asset mappings, then accepting process mappings, and in the end accepting asset mappings and rejecting process mappings. This order ensures that a maximal amount of rejects and accepts is performed automatically.

7.2.5   Threats to Validity

We identified threats to the validity of our experiments regarding three categories. In this section, we discuss these threats.

External Validity

The main threat to *external validity* is our selection of samples, based on a limited number of open source projects, partially originating from a teaching context. The rationale for our selection was the manual effort for creating the ground truth of our technique, a full correspondence model between high-level DFD elements and low-level program elements. However, as a result, the generalizability of the results to larger projects in other domains is limited. To mitigate this threat, the considered projects were chosen to be representative of realistic projects by providing good documentation, including architectural information, such as wikis, use cases, scenarios, requirements, state charts, and the like. The available documentation enabled building good design models, close to the intended architecture. We plan to extend the evaluation in the future to include a more comprehensive set of projects.

Internal Validity

Regarding *internal validity*, the main threat of our evaluation is researcher bias. In absence of pre-existing ground truths and design models, the ground truth and design models for our evaluation were created manually by the authors, possibly introducing a risk of creating a biased result. To mitigate this threat, the ground truths and the design-level models were carefully discussed between all authors. The created models and ground truths are of similar size and complexity and are available online[2].

Construct Validity

Concerning *construct validity*, we consider the threat of misinterpreting divergence, absence, and convergence compliance violations in the context of design-level models and implementation-level models. However, to the best of our knowledge, our interpretations are in line with the existing literature [93]. As such, the implementation of the approach does not perform low-level static or dynamic checks to verify the intended security requirements of SecDFD assets. This threatens the intention of the approach to holistically analyze security requirements. We discuss the possibilities to extend the plugin to include static and dynamic checks as future work. The implemented plugin only notifies the user about the accepted, defined, and missing correspondences with in-line information markers. Thus, the user decides what compliance issues the correspondences identify. Yet, the implementation can be easily extended to support active proposals of compliance violation types.

7.2.6 Conclusion on the Semi-Automated Mappings

We presented an interactive, semi-automated approach for mapping concrete implementations to SecDFDs with the aim to reconstruct a correspondence model and to perform conformance checks of the implementations with the SecDFDs as well as security checks on the implementations. In the proposed approach mappings are iteratively calculated by heuristics and are presented as proposed correspondences to a user for verification. Furthermore, the user guides the automated mapping by actively adding additional correspondences.

The approach has been evaluated on five open-source projects (including Eclipse Secure Storage [203]) and shows good precision and recall for the initial, automatically created mapping. Our evaluation shows that new mappings can be found by

---

[2] Semi-automated mappings implementation and evaluation data: https://github.com/SvenPeldszus/GRaViTY-SecDFD-Mapping/

considering the user input in later iterations. Consequently, both the user and the proposed heuristics contribute to the discovery of new mappings. All in all, the user is not only guided through the implementation by our tool, but also assisted in creating the correspondence model between SecDFDs and their implementations.

Using this semi-automated approach, users can interactively discover convergence, absence and divergences between the SecDFDs and their implementations. Also, the security information available in the SecDFDs can be used for executing security analyses on the source code level. We discuss these applications in detail in Chapter 8.

7.3   Conclusion on the Application to Legacy Projects

In this chapter, we discussed the application of GRaViTY to legacy projects considering two different scenarios. First, we considered software projects in which no design-time models describing the software system exist. Here, we discussed how the required models and correspondence models between the design-time models and the implementation can be reverse engineered using GRaViTY's synchronization mechanism introduced in Section 6.2. Second, we considered legacy projects in which early design models are available but are disconnected from the implementation. To restore this connection in terms of a correspondence model, we introduced a semi-automated mapping approach.

The two approaches can be used complementary with each other in projects containing early design models. First, developers can reverse engineer UML class diagrams using the TGGs, and afterward, reconstruct the correspondence model between the DFDs and the implementation. These correspondence models can then be used to create trace links between the DFDs and reverse engineered UML class diagrams. This allows to transfer security requirements from SecDFDs into the class diagrams and avoids specifying these again. However, currently, this is not included in the presented reverse engineering approach.

To conclude on the application of GRaViTY on legacy projects, the proposed reverse engineering approaches allow reconstructing models and correspondence models that allow the application of GRaViTY. The reverse-engineered UML class diagrams can continuously be synchronized with the implementation using GRaViTY's synchronization mechanism without any adaptions. The correspondence model created between early design models and the implementation is a snapshot of the current state and cannot be automatically synchronized. However, as outlined, they build a basis for propagating security requirements and reconstructing the model hierarchy used by GRaViTY.

Part III
Security

Static Security Compliance Checks

8

This chapter shares material with the FSE'2017 publication "Model-based Privacy and Security Analysis with CARiSMA" [74], the' MODELS'2019 publications "Secure Data-Flow Compliance Checks between Models and Code based on Automated Mappings" [23], the DKE'2021 publication "Ontology-Driven Evolution of Software Security" [206], the EMLS'2020 publication "Model-driven Development of Evolving Secure Software Systems" [154], and the SoSyM'2022 publication "Checking Security Compliance between Models and Code" [207].

The continuous checking of a software system for security violations is one important task for ensuring the security compliance of a software system under development. Traditionally, security compliance is checked in manual security audits, e.g., as specified in the IEEE 1028-2009 standard for software reviews and audits [94]. As the effort for such audits is very high, audits are only performed from time to time. For this reason, approaches like SecDevOps encourage system developers to make use of frequent and automated security checks [127]. In the GRaViTY approach of this thesis, we follow the same principle of frequent automated security checks but in combination with automated reuse of security specifications among these security checks. Furthermore, while approaches like SecDevOps mainly focus on local fine-grained security checks as discussed in the state of the art (Section 3.6), GRaViTY aims at security checks covering the design-time models and implementation.

S. M. Peldszus, *Security Compliance in Model-driven Development of Software Systems in Presence of Long-Term Evolution and Variants*,
https://doi.org/10.1007/978-3-658-37665-9_8

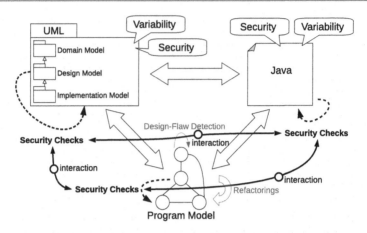

Figure 8.1 Interaction of security checks in the overall concept

To enforce the appropriate implementation of security requirements, there are various kinds of security checks available in existing works that can be integrated into GRaViTY. According to Figure 8.1, in GRaViTY, we perform security checks on all three artifacts considered in the overall concept. The key idea is to follow the principle of security by design and to specify and verify security requirements from the very beginning [28]. In GRaViTY, we not only support the verification of security requirements within an artifact but also continuously check security compliance within all specified security requirements in later software design phases. Thereby, no security check stands on its own, but they interact with each other and should be used complementary. Currently, the process of transferring security requirements among different phases of system development is being performed manually. To reduce the required effort and the probability of mistakes but also to allow further reuse of security requirements, developers should be assisted by automated tool support. In this chapter, we focus on how such automated assistance be realized for static security analysis. As most established security checks have been implemented using high-level programming languages, the verification of their correctness is challenging. While this verification can be suitable for standard checks that are widely used, this can limit the application of project-specific security checks. For this reason, we aim at putting specifications of security checks on a formal basis and investigate the suitability of algebraic graph transformations for specifying security checks. In this section, we address the third and fourth research questions of this thesis:

RQ3:   How can developers be supported in realizing, preserving, and enforcing design-time security requirements in software systems?

RQ4:   How do changes within a software system affect its security compliance, and how can these effects be handled?

In this thesis, we consider the third research question from two perspectives. First, in this chapter, from the perspective of static security analysis, and second, in the next chapter from the perspective of dynamic security analysis at run-time. For answering this research question for static security analysis, we address the following two subquestions:

RQ3.1:   How can we automatically verify a software system's compliance concerning design-time security requirements?

RQ3.2:   How can formal approaches be used for the specification of security violation patterns?

Considering the development of a software system, it is continuously subject to change. For all changes applied to a software system, it is essential to check the security compliance after the application of changes to ensure the software system's security. As complete security compliance checks tend to be expensive, we have to find means for effectively only rechecking the changed parts of a software system after changes. As developers are capable of arbitrary changes, besides the two subquestions of RQ3, we consider the third sub-question of RQ4 in this chapter as well:

RQ4.3:   How can security requirements affected by arbitrary system changes be identified end efficiently be rechecked for security compliance?

In what follows, we recapitulate different kinds of security checks introduced in Section 3.6 and in which stages of model-driven software development they can be applied. Afterward, we discuss our understanding of security compliance within the GRaViTY approach and discuss the supported security compliance checks in detail. In Sections 8.2 to 8.5, we focus on different compliance checks for answering RQ3.1. Afterward, we answer RQ3.2 and RQ4.3 in Section 8.6 by applying the formal approach of graph transformations to specify security checks and execute these incrementally.

8.1   Background on Static Security Analysis

To verify a software system's security and enforce the appropriate implementation of security mechanisms, we can use various security checks. This section gives an overview of the existing security checks reused in GRaViTY, structured by the artifacts on which these are used.

8.1.1   Design Model-based Security Checks

To address security effectively, the paradigm of *security by design* emphasizes that security cannot be addressed merely retroactively, by identifying and fixing security loopholes [28]. Accordingly, developers should address a software system's security already from the earliest phases of software design. Design-time models are one of the earliest artifacts created during the development of a software system. In the following, we review approaches that aim at checking security requirements in the targeted software system early during its development.

UMLsec
The UMLsec [6] approach, integrated into GRaViTY, allows the specification and verification of essential security requirements already at design time. In UMLsec, UML models are annotated with security requirements like security levels of class members (attributes and operations). These security annotations are then checked for compliance with different security policies provided by UMLsec. For example, UMLsec allows, as part of the *Secure Dependency* security policy, to check if a UML model contains insecure uses of attributes or operations, that are annotated with security requirements. In the implementation model, we also annotated the calls and communication paths with UMLsec stereotypes. For example, in the iTrust electronics health records system, all data transferred from and to doctors is sent over an internal LAN connection and all data sent from and to patients is sent over an encrypted Internet connection.

On the design-models level, we can utilize refinement relations between the different model kinds for detecting security violations at no additional cost for considering multiple models as discussed in Section 6.3. Also, if a security requirement is changed in one representation we can immediately see the impact on the other UML representations. However, automated verification of the security requirements at the implementation level is an open issue.

Detailed information about the UMLsec is provided in Section 3.6.1. Besides UMLsec, there are approaches like Security Data Flow Diagrams (SecDFD), making use of similar concepts for the early verification of data flows in a data flow diagrams [111].

Security Data Flow Diagrams

Comparable to UMLsec, Security Data Flow Diagrams (SecDFD) allow the specification of security requirements at design time. In contrast to UMLsec, in the SecDFD approach, data flow diagrams are annotated with security requirements instead of UML models. Thereby, SecDFD is based on security labels for data and processing contracts specifying the intended data processing. As discussed in Section 3.6.2, UMLsec and SecDFD can be used complementary or the SecDFD annotations could be applied to UML activity diagrams.

In this chapter, we use the security labels of SecDFD and the data processing contracts for compliance checks of the implementation. The specified security requirements can also be propagated from the SecDFD to the implementation using the correspondence model created by GRaViTY as introduced in Chapter 6. Furthermore, we use the contracts as an input to a code-level analysis tool. Thus, we enable compliance checks between planned and implemented security requirements, see Section 8.4.1.

8.1.2 Static Code Analysis

While design-time security can make security planning controllable, they do not allow security violations to be actively detected and prevented. In contrast to this, static code analysis is usually used to detect actual security issues during software implementation. Thereby, the analysis tools are often integrated within the development environments or build processes.

Analysis of API Calls

Many approaches locally analyze calls to critical APIs and whether the chosen parameters have been selected securely. This covers, for example, calls to crypto APIs [118] or SQL queries [119]. While those approaches are important for the development of secure software systems, in this work we focus on whether, e.g., the use of a crypto API, has been implemented in a specific location specified as in the design-time models.

Secure Data Flow Analysis

A common approach to detect leaks of secret data is a secure data flow analysis. One of the main problems for a precise data flow analysis is the classification of critical sources and sinks. Many tools are based on shared libraries of well-known critical sources and sinks, created manually or by machine learning [42]. However, more precise information, especially about critical sources, is available in design-time models, e.g., annotated with UMLsec. For example, in Figure 3.6 we declared the property `homeAddress` to contain secret values, which has to be considered during a secure data flow analysis.

To conclude, multiple suitable approaches for the specification and verification of security requirements have been developed. On the architectural level, we can use UMLsec and SecDFDs to design a secure architecture. These approaches allow specifying, propagate, and verify security requirements. After a software system's architecture has been implemented, it can be checked in detail on the source code level. Among others, in GRaViTY, we can analyze the correct usage of cryptographic methods and analyze data flows within the implementation using existing security tooling. However, what exactly is analyzed is up to the developers. The successful verification of the implementation's compliance with the security requirements specified at design time depends on the experience of the developers executing such an analysis.

8.2   Structural Compliance between Models and Code

After a secure design of a software system has been created using approaches like UMLsec or SecDFD, the software system has to be implemented. Thereby, a correspondence model between the implementation and the design-time models should be created and maintained. For this purpose, the tool support introduced in Chapter 6 can be used. For successfully certifying a software system, the implementation must be compliant with the architecture specified in design-time models. Usually, this compliance is reviewed manually during the certification process. Since this is tedious and time-consuming, such reviews are expensive and are only performed if necessary [96]. GRaViTY's correspondence model between the design-time models and source code can be used to perform structural compliance checks automatically. At first, it can be checked if the implementation corresponds with the specification in a DFD or UML activity diagram. Afterward, the correspondence model can be used to perform more sophisticated security analyses on the code using security requirements from design-time models.

Identifying the differences and equivalences between the planned and the implemented software architecture is the goal of software architecture compliance checking. The compliance checks can be based on a static set of rules [91], dynamic monitoring of a running software system [92], or a hybrid of both [93]. In our work, we statically check the compliance of design-level models with their corresponding implementation. Running compliance checks reveals the relations between a set of components of the design-level model and a set of components of a program model extracted from the software system's implementation.

In what follows, we describe the check we developed to determine if the implementation corresponds with the specification in the models.

8.2.1   Automation of Structural Compliance Checks

For performing structural compliance checks, we use the trace links contained in the correspondence model between the design-time models and the program model representing the implementation. These trace links allow us to get the corresponding implementation elements for every model element and to check if they are as expected. Using the structural compliance checks, we check for the presence of the three relation types introduced in Section 3.5 (convergence, absence, and divergence). Furthermore, in combination with the semi-automated reverse engineering technique introduced in Section 7.2, developers can interactively check the compliance of the implementation with design-time models.

Convergence

The easiest case are convergences between the models and implementation. In the context of a correspondence model between design-time model elements and implementation elements, convergence means that the user has accepted a suggested correspondence or has manually defined a correspondence. In the context of security requirements, convergence means that a planned security contract is implemented at the correct location and no leaks have been detected, e.g., by a data flow analyzer. All model elements which have been mapped to implementation elements in the correspondence model and have not been rejected by a user are allowed correspondences. Following the definition of convergence, the convergences between the design-time models and the implementation are described by the set of all allowed correspondences. More precisely, we consider all correspondences in the correspondence model and refinement relations between the UML models as convergence.

Absence

If our approach is neither able to map a model element to the code automatically and the user is not able to map the same element manually when asked to do so, we discover an absence of specified functionality in the code. Assuming the correctness of models, we only have to consider the model to code direction of absence (concerning the opposite direction, see *divergence*). However, there can be cases of absence that do not result in a violation but are intended abstractions. For example, the domain models created before developing the software system might capture concepts that are common for the domain but are not realized in the software system.

Divergence

Absence indicates that the source code is not compliant with the planned architecture due to a missing implementation. In the context of the security requirements, absence means that security mechanisms specified on the model level have not been implemented or security requirements are not fulfilled. Elements present in the source code of the implementation, but not specified in the design model represent a divergence between the model and code. Here, one can look for model elements that relate to existing correspondences to find the relative parts of the implementation. In the context of security requirements, we identify divergence when

(i) there exists an implemented data flow that does not comply with the specified security contracts at a process node in a DFD or an activity in a UML activity diagram, or

(ii) the analysis with a state-of-the-art data flow analyzer reports a leak of potentially confidential information.

To help the user in discovering divergences between design models and the implementation, it is possible to show all data flows from members mapped to a design-time element to other members not mapped to this element. If the target of such a flow has not been mapped to any process, there seems to be a divergence. But, a divergence also arises if there is a flow between two processes or activities in the code that has not been specified in the design-time model. If a critical asset is communicated along with such a flow, this is not only divergent from the intended design but a security violation.

Using these checks, a developer or code reviewer can detect a compliance issue between models and the implementation at hand. However, regarding security, these checks are not precise enough: They might not reveal flows of confidential assets that are not supposed to take place. For example, if a developer uses a full representation of an object, instead of a stripped one, all information stored in this object flows into the location of the usage regardless of if this information is needed there. If this unused information is sensitive it might not be allowed to flow to this specific location. To this end, we can perform more sophisticated security checks, as described in the next sections.

8.2.2   Tool Support for Structural Compliance Checks

We implemented a structured view of recorded correspondences for data flow diagrams allowing developers to inspect the correspondences for divergences. Thereby, the developer is supported in automatically navigating to the source code locations of selected correspondence. Also, in the data flow diagrams correspondences are shown in information markers and elements for that no correspondence exist are highlighted with a warning marker for this absence.

A component diagram of our implementation and its integration with the other components of GRaViTY as well as external components is shown in Figure 8.2. The structural compliance checks are implemented in the Structural Compliance component. This component analyzes the correspondence model created by the Semi-Automated Mappings component, discussed in detail in Section 7.2.3, regarding, convergence, divergence, and absence.

Figure 8.3 shows a screenshot of the tool support for structural compliance checks. Whenever a correspondence model between a SecDFD and the implementation is loaded, this correspondence model is automatically checked for convergence and absence. Convergences and absences are shown in terms of information and warning markers in the DFD. In the example shown in Figure 8.3, our tooling identified an absence for the change password process.

8.2.3   Conclusion on the Structural Compliance Checks

In this section, we discussed how the correspondence model maintained by the GRaViTY approach can be leveraged for verifying the structural compliance of the implementation with the architecture specified in design-time DFDs. This verification is the most effective when it is executed dynamically using the semi-automated mapping approach presented in Section 7.2. Developers are assisted with structured

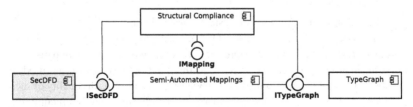

Figure 8.2 Component diagram of the structural compliance checks

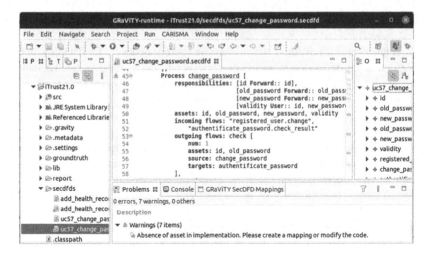

Figure 8.3 Screenshot of the tool support for structural compliance checks

views on the existing correspondences and can dynamically navigate between the models and source code. Currently, only the combination with the reverse engineering of a correspondence model provides an automatization in the verification of structural compliance. However, as long as developers continuously apply the GRaViTY approach, structural inconsistencies should not be possible, as all changes are automatically propagated. Nevertheless, a frequent analysis for structural compliance is beneficial. In future works, one can provide an extended automatization of this task.

8.3   Leveraging Correspondence Models for the Calculation of Security Metrics

The planned structure of a software system's design has a significant impact on the software system's security [28, 208]. One approach to achieve a secure software system is to structure it into different security levels where only some parts have to be maintained by security experts, e.g., this kind of structure can be used to isolate subjects for manual security code reviews. Unfortunately, the quality of such a security design is hard to judge. Furthermore, a software system's structure into security level also might erode and increase the effort required for maintaining security [13]. To deal with such challenges in general software design, OO design-quality metrics have been developed [209], e.g., the well-known metrics *Coupling Between Objects* (CBO) or *Lack of Cohesion in Methods* (LCOM). Comparably, to continuously measure and quantify security aspects for detection of such erosion, security metrics have been defined [210–212].

In what follows, first, we introduce security metrics that have been proposed in the literature and discuss their limitations in Section 8.3.1. In Section 8.3.2, we discuss how the correspondence model created by the GRaViTY approach can be leveraged for calculating the discussed security metrics. Afterward, in Section 8.3.3, we introduce a prototypical implementation of the security metrics as part of GRaViTY. Finally, we conclude in Section 8.3.4.

8.3.1 Background on Security Metrics

When talking about security metrics, we often think about security metrics such as the ones from the *Common Vulnerability Scoring System* (CVSS) [213], measuring the potential impact of a reported vulnerability (CVE) on the security of a software system using the software. Such metrics can be useful to decide whether a specific version of a library should be used or comes with a security risk too high for using the library. However, these metrics do not directly consider the security of the software system under development.

In this section, we introduce two categories of security metrics that allow us to estimate specific security properties of a software system itself. First, we introduce metrics that consider the attack surface of a software system. Second, we introduce a metric that quantifies the distribution of security-critical implementation parts among a software system.

Attack Surface of Object-Oriented Programs
The first category of security metrics considered by us is related to a software systems exposure to the outside. Thereby, the key assumption is that the greater this exposure is, the higher is the risk for security issues. In this context, the *attack surface* of a program comprises all conventional ways of entering a software system from the outside [214]. A larger attack surface increases the danger of exploiting vulnerabilities, either unintentionally by some user or intentionally by an attacker. Concerning Java-like programs, in particular, explicit restrictions of accessibility of class members provide an essential mechanism to control the attack surface. However, the attack surface covers many other aspects such as used sockets, libraries, or files [214]. In these cases, the attack surface is significantly impacted by a software

system's deployment, e.g., how a firewall is configured and where other systems the software system communicates with are located. Based on the assumption that visibilities can indicate a software system's attack surface, metrics have been developed to quantify the attack surface in terms of visibilities.

Total visibility: One idea is to assign numerical values to the visibilities and to sum them up or average them before and after a change [146]. If the value increases, the visible Java API increased, too. Accordingly, the total visibility of the Java API can function as a proxy for the attack surface.

Inappropiate generosity: More sophisticated metrics compare the assigned visibilities of types and methods with the theoretically possible values [215]. In this approach, the metrics *Inappropriate Generosity with Accessibility of Types* (IGAT) and *Inappropriate Generosity with Accessibility of Methods* (IGAM) quantify the degree of divergence per type or method. On the scope of a package or project, the average values can be used. However, there are two reasons for visibilities higher than possible:

1. The visibility is too wide by mistake, e.g., due to developers not paying attention to the visibility of the element.
2. The element belongs to the software's intended API and has to be wider than on the scope of only the software.

While the first case is clearly an issue, it cannot be solved easily due to the second reason. By calculating these metrics, one cannot distinguish between the two kinds of reasons when only relying on the source code. Another limitation of the two metrics is that these do not reveal unnecessarily high visibilities due to a bad structuring of the implementation. A high coupling within the implementation technically requires higher visibilities which makes these valid for the two *Inappropriate Generosity with Accessibility* metrics.

Considering this discussion, visibilities can provide indicate the attack surface of a software system but might only have a minor influence on initially entering the software system. Nevertheless, strict visibilities might play an essential role in preventing harm after malicious code has been injected into the software system. Their application can help developers in reducing the API that can immediately be invoked from this injected code. However, these metrics do not consider the security design of a software system.

Distribution of Classified Properties

Metrics explicitly considering the security design of a software system usually quantify the distribution of security-related elements among the software system or entities belonging to the software system. Depending on the degree of distribution, the security design of a software system can be rated.

As an example for this category of security metrics, we consider the *Critical Design Proportion* (CDP) metric. This metric measures the ratio between security-critical and not-security-critical classes [212, 216]. Here, the idea is that this metric is an indicator of the security of the software system. One can assume that a software system that concentrates security-related data and functionality in a few security-critical classes is easier to implement and maintain. It is less likely that changes in a non-security-critical part of the software system have side effects in security-critical parts of the software system. However, classes that have a higher ratio between security-critical elements and non-critical elements should be tested more intensively [217]

The *Critical Design Proportion* (CDP) metric is defined at the scope of a software system's class-level design D as follows [216]:

$$CDP(D) = \frac{SC}{C} \tag{8.1}$$

Whereas C is the number of classes in the software system and SC is the number of security-critical classes within all classes such that SC $\in$ C. Accordingly, the metric can be applied to both, the high-level class design such as specified in UML models but also to the detailed low-level class design of an OO program.

All discussed security metrics are beneficial from an administrative perspective, as these allow to utilize security experts more efficiently as they can focus on small security-critical parts of the software system. However, measuring such metrics is usually not easily possible as it is not known which classes are security-critical and which not. This kind of information is required for all presented security metrics.

8.3.2   Leveraging Traces for Security Metric Calculation

The introduced security metrics (as many other security checks) need information about what are security-critical parts of the software system, therefore, their application is often not possible. Most projects do not explicitly provide a detailed security classification on the level of single classes within the application. Usually, this classification is part of a software system's documentation and rather high-level.

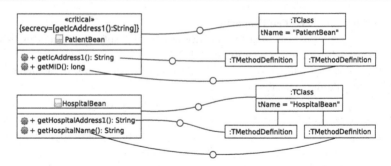

Figure 8.4 Correspondences between a UML class diagram containing security requirements and the program model

When approaches like UMLsec or SecDFD are used, detailed security requirements are available in design-time models. In what follows, we demonstrate how we can transfer security-related information from the design-time security models to the implementation. For this purpose, we use the correspondence model between design-time models and the implementation created by our approach. Chapters 6 and 7 discuss these correspondence models and their creation in detail.

As an example for leveraging security-related information, we use the *Critical Design Proportion* metric, specifying the ratio between security-critical and non-security-critical classes [212]. To calculate this metric on the low-level class design, we have to classify all classes within the implementation as security-critical or not security-critical. For this purpose, we leverage the correspondence model between the implementation of the software system and design-time models containing the software system's security requirements.

In this thesis, we consider two model-level security specifications that can be used to obtain the information required for calculation the CDP metric at the implementation level. First, UML models annotated with UMLsec stereotypes, and second, the SecDFD security specifications, introduced in Sections 3.6.1 and 3.6.2.

UMLsec: As the UMLsec secure dependency stereotypes are applied at the class diagram level, these are of special interest for propagation security requirements suitable for calculating the intended security metric. Considering UMLsec's «critical» stereotype, this procedure is straightforward. In Section 6.4.1, we discussed this propagation of security requirements in detail. Figure 8.4, shows correspondences between a UML class diagram and a program model for a security-critical class (PatientBean) at the top of the figure and a non-security-critical class (`HospitalBean`) at the bottom of the figure. The class `PatientBean` is considered as security-critical as it is stereotyped with «`critical`», putting the operation `getIcAddress1` on the security level of secrecy. This class and the operations specified within the class correspond with the upper instances of `TClass` and `TMethodDefinition` on the upper right of the figure. In the same way, the `HospitalBean` corresponds with a `TClass` at the implementation level. Accordingly, we consider every `TClass` that corresponds with a `Class` stereotyped with a «`critical`» that contains a signature of a feature (`Operation` or `Property`) of this class as security-critical class.

```
1  class PatientBean {
2    @Secrecy
3    String getIcAddress1(){
4      ...
5    }
6
7    long getMID(){
8      ...
9    }
10  }
```
(a) Security-critical class.

```
1  class HospitalBean {
2    String getHospitalName(){
3      ...
4    }
5
6    String getHospitalAddress(){
7      ...
8    }
9  }
```
(b) Non security-critical class.

Listing 8.1 Security annotation propagated into classes with and without security-critical members.

Although the security metrics' calculation is possible using this dynamic tracing, for simplicity, we assume that the security requirements have been propagated to the implementation using the Java security annotations introduced in Section 6.4.1. This allows to immediately calculate the security metric on the program model without explicitly considering the UML models. An example for a security-critical and non-security-critical class is shown in Listing 8.1. In both classes, the security requirements from the design-time models, such as shown in Figure 8.4, have been propagated into the implementation as Java annotations. While Listing 8.1a shows with `PatientBean` a critical class, as it contains the method `getIcAddress1` on the security level of secrecy, Listing 8.1b shows the non-critical class `HospitalBean` that does not contain classified members. Considering the explicit propagation of the security

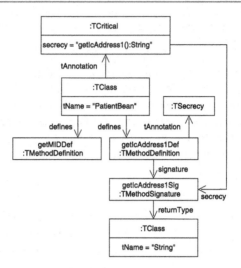

Figure 8.5 Program model extended with security annotations

requirements, the program model shown in Figure 8.4 is extended as shown in Figure 8.5 for the security-critical class `PatientBean`. The «critical» stereotype is represented by an `TCritical` node. In addition, the specified signature is resolved and this information is explicitly added. First, by adding an explicit reference from the `TCritical` to the resolved signatures (`TMethodSignature`). Accordingly, In the example, a secrecy reference is added from the `TCritical` note to the `TMethodSignature` node. Second, by annotating `TMethodDefinitions`, whose signature is put to the security level of secrecy by the class that defines these method definitions, with `TSecrecy`.

SecDFD: While the correspondence model between class diagrams and source code and the secure dependency security requirements are between comparable entities, there are significant differences for SecDFDs. Even though the SecDFD assets are mapped to types, they do not necessarily represent security-critical classes. For example, the class `String` is used in the implementation of iTrust to represent both secret assets, e.g, the address of a patient as shown in Listing 8.1a, but also other public data, e.g., the name of the hospital in Listing 8.1b.

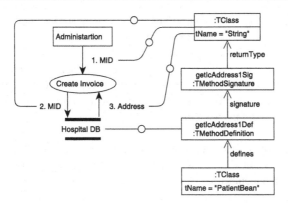

Figure 8.6 Correspondences between a SecDFD and the program model

Figure 8.6 shows the correspondence model between a SecDFD excerpt describing the creation of an invoice and a corresponding excerpt of the program model representing the implementation. For example, this figure contains the correspondence between the asset `Address` and the type `String`. As part of creating an invoice, the address of the patient has to be retrieved from the hospital's database. Here, the method `getIcAddress1` of the class `PatientBean` provides access to this information in the database. Accordingly, there is a correspondence between this method and the data store in Figure 8.6.

We can automatically derive the security-critical classes from the correspondence model by first identifying the security-critical methods and afterward the classes defining these methods. If we are going to consider the assets as specified in a SecDFD, the critical methods are exactly all methods mapped to a process, data store, or external entity in the SecDFD that is processing an asset tagged as confidential. In the example, the method `getIcAddress1` has the return type `String` that is mapped to the secret asses `Address`. Also, the method is mapped to the database that is the source of a data flow propagating the asset `Address`. As a consequence, this indicates that the returned `String` really represents this asset. Accordingly, we identified a security-critical method in the implementation. Consequently, we can annotate this method with `@Secrecy` and the classes with `@Critical` as we do for the UMLsec secure dependency stereotypes. Finally, for the considered example, this results in the same annotations on the program model as the ones derived from the UMLsec stereotypes.

Figure 8.5 also shows the security annotations derived by leveraging the SecDFD to program model correspondences shown in Figure 8.6.

Regardless of using a SecDFD or UMLsec, in the program model, the security requirements are represented in the same way, using both the @Critical and @Secrecy annotations. Accordingly, for counting the number of security-critical classes, we can count two patterns:

1. the number of classes that define a member annotated with @Secrecy
2. or the number of classes annotated with @Critical that has a secrecy reference to a member defined in the class.

As both patterns represent the same information, we can use any of these two patterns for calculating the desired metric. After counting the number of security-critical classes, the *Critical Design Proportion* metric for a program can simply be calculated by dividing this number by the number of classes.

8.3.3   Tool Support for the Calculation of Security Metrics

We implemented the discussed metrics as an extension to the design-flaw detection tool *Hulk* [21, 34]. Hulk is an incremental rule-based design-flaw detection tool based on the type graph presented in Chapter 5 of this thesis. The annotation mechanism of the type graph is used to define annotations representing metrics, code-smells, and anti-patterns. Thereby, more detailed design flaws are calculated based on locally restricted flaws, e.g, anti-patterns are derived from the presence of multiple code-smells, and code-smells are usually derived from metrics.

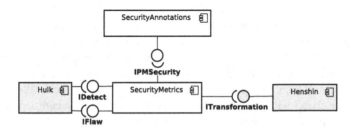

Figure 8.7 Component diagram of the security metrics implementation

Figure 8.7 shows a component diagram of our implementation of the security metrics. Our implementation resides in the `SecurityMetrics` component. This component implements two interfaces defined by `Hulk`. First, the `IDetect` interface specifies the methods that have to be implemented by our extension to allow Hulk to execute a design-flaw detection or metric calculation. Second, the `IFlaw` interface is implemented to provide information about the annotations defined by us for representing instances of the calculated metrics, e.g., the *Critical Design Proportion* metric. While the calculation of the total visibility, IGAM, and IGAT has been implemented by us in handwritten Java source code, for calculating the metric, we defined the metric in a Henshin rule. For executing this rule, the `SecurityMetrics` component uses the `Henshin` component.

Figure 8.8 shows the rule for calculating the *Critical Design Proportion* metric. The program model, represented by a node of the type `TypeGraph`, is annotated with a new instance of this metric (`CriticalDesignProportion`) whose value is calculated by a constraint.

For the calculation of the metric's value, we make use of the concept of amalgamation offered by Henshin [218]. Amalgamation allows matching a graph pattern as often as possible within a rule. Such a pattern is denoted by a * in a rule element's action type, e.g., «`preserve*`». In the rule shown in Figure 8.8, we use amalgamation two times. First, to match all types defined in a program model, and second, to match all elements denoting security-critical types.

In the variable `all`, we match every `TAbstractType` in the program model (`TypeGraph`) that is not from a library. In the constraint for calculating the metric value, we count all instances of `TAbstractType` matched this way giving us the total number of types in the program. For this purpose, we use the function `COUNT` provided by Henshin. This function counts the number of instances assigned to a variable.

For counting the number of security-critical types, we make use of an amalgamation nested into the almagation already described. This nesting is denoted by giving a path after the specification of the amalgamation action. The previously described level of amalgamation is on the first level (`/types`). On the second level (`/types/security`), we count the number of security-critical types. If a type is security-critical, it is annotated with an instance of `TCritical`, that has a `secrecy` reference to a signature implemented by the type. Also, every type can only be annotated with one instance of `TCritical`. However, this `TCritical` can point to multiple signatures. Accordingly, for counting the number of critical types, we can count the number of `TCritical` instances matching the described pattern. Using second-level amalgamation leads to the following semantics: For each `TAbstractType` matched to `all`, every `TCritical` with a reference

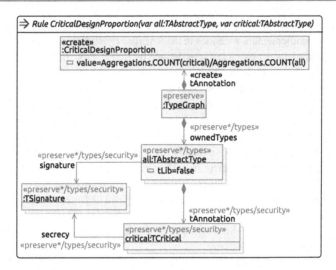

Figure 8.8 Henshin rule for calculating the critical design proportion metric

to a TSignature that is implemented by the type are matched to the variable critical. When we count the number of different TCritical assigned to critical, again using the function COUNT, we get the number of critical types in the program model.

Finally, to get the proportion of security-critical types we can divide the number of security-critical types (COUNT(critical)) by the number of types (COUNT(types)). The outcome of this calculation is assigned to the value property of the CriticalDesignProportion node created by the rule in Figure 8.8.

8.3.4 Conclusion on Security Metrics

In this section, we have shown how to leverage the traces created and maintained by GRaViTY to calculate security metrics on the implementation level. While these security metrics can be of practical importance, due to the lack of explicit security knowledge they have been challenging to calculate before. Also, this might be the reason for only a few implementation-level security metrics being specified in the literature that considers the security design. In contrast to this, OO design properties have been intensively studied regarding maintainability and extensibility resulting in widely accepted catalogs for OO design metrics [209]. Furthermore, the security metrics we found, are practically important but still limited.

The *Critical Design Proportion* metric discussed by us in detail allows us to quantify a structural security property. Until now, its application was mainly limited to UML class diagrams explicitly containing security requirements. Using our approach, we can also calculate it at the implementation level. However, this also reveals some of its limitations. Following the metric's specification, a software system's design is better the smaller the portion of classes is that hold security-critical elements. While this might hold at the design level, at more detailed levels, we should avoid combining unrelated security elements, e.g., secret information. Whenever a part of the implementations accesses a piece of secret information, it also gets access to the other unrelated information although this access is not required. As a consequence, this could cause serious security issues. For example, consider the administration of a hospital implicitly getting access to detailed medical records at the creation of invoices.

However, considering the detailed information about accesses available at the implementation level, we could detect such unrelated secrets to which implicit access is given. To allow the continuous improvement of a software system's security design, in future works, it would be beneficial to study approaches to leverage structural implementation-level information for calculating security metrics on the design-model level. For example, a useful metric would be the average amount of classified assets communicated along with a dependency in a UML class diagram. If there is a significant difference between the communicated classified assets and the

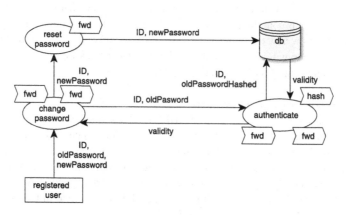

Figure 8.9 SecDFD for updating a user's password

number of classified assets specified in the accessed class, this might be an indicator
of a security issue in the security design.

8.4 Security Compliance Checks between Models & Code

Using approaches like UMLsec or SecDFD, security experts specify security
requirements such as data processing contracts on the design-time models of the
software system. These contracts are then checked for consistency using the tool
support of the approaches. If these checks reveal inconsistencies or vulnerabilities,
the design-time models have to be adapted until a secure state is reached. However,
for the final software system to be secure, it has to be compliant regarding the structure as discussed before but also with these contracts specified on the design-time
models. To be more precise, the contracts have to be implemented as planned. Usually, such compliance checks are performed manually. In this section, we show how
the SecDFD contracts can be verified in the implementation showing compliance.

8.4.1 Verification of SecDFD Contracts

In the used model-based security approaches, security contracts are specified on
the design-time models and are verified at design time. This procedure allows software architects and security experts to build a secure design of the software system.
However, for the final software system, it is not enough to consider design-time
security requirements at design-time but it has to be verified that the implemented
software system is compliant with these design-time security requirements. In what
follows, we show how the security compliance of the software system's implementation can be automatically checked regarding the data processing contracts and the
cryptographic contracts of the SecDFD approach.

SecDFD Data Processing Contracts
The forward and join contracts at the SecDFD level describe local data flows within
a process that have to be present in the implementation. To check if the specified
contracts have been implemented, we propose a two-step procedure. First, we extract
the relevant asset-communicating flows from the process's implementation. In what
follows, we refer to the flows in the implementation as *i-flows*. Second, we compare
the implemented flows (i-flow) with the expected flows specified in the SecDFD.
To flows in the DFDs, we refer to as *d-flows*.

Algorithm 1: Algorithm for extracting i-flows *i* for a given process *p*.

Input : Process *p*, Correspondence Model *m*
Output: i-Flows *i*

1 *methods* ← *m*.methods(*p*)
2 *in* ← inFlows(*methods*)
3 **foreach** flow ∈ in **do**
4 | *type* ← communicatedType(*flow*)
5 | **if** m.*correspondence*(type) = ∅ **then**
6 | | **remove** *flow* **from** *in*
7 | **end**
8 **end**
9 *out* ← outFlows(*methods*)
10 **foreach** flow ∈ out **do**
11 | *type* ← communicatedType(*flow*)
12 | **if** m.*correspondence*(type) = ∅ **then**
13 | | **remove** *flow* **from** *out*
14 | **end**
15 **end**
16 *i* ← { }
17 **foreach** target ∈ out **do**
18 | *sources* ← reachableBwd(*target*, *in*)
19 | **if** sources ≠ ∅ **then**
20 | | **add** (*sources*, *target*) **to** *i*
21 | **end**
22 **end**
23 **return** *i*

The main challenge in checking forward and join contracts is that one process can be realized by multiple methods but also many methods do not belong to any process but interact with multiple processes. Furthermore, an asset in the SecDFD can be realized by different types in the implementation. For example, the hashed old password (`oldPasswordHashed`) in Figure 8.9 is realized by instances of the Java classes `String` and `byte[]`. In addition, a single type in the implementation can be used to create instances of different assets. This is especially a problem for frequently used types like strings that can be used to represent nearly every asset as shown in the previous chapters of this thesis.

In Algorithm 1, we show the pseudo-code for extracting implemented flows (i-flows) for a given DFD process. We define an i-flow as a pair of the flow's target and a set of the sources of a flow in the implementation. The inputs to this algorithm are the DFD process for which we want to extract the implemented flows and a correspondence model between the design-time model and the source code. Following Chapter 6, such a correspondence model is automatically created if the software system is developed using the GRaViTY approach. However, it is also possible to work on a manually created correspondence model between the design-time model and source code as introduced in Chapter 7.

First, in line 1, we retrieve the methods implementing the DFD process *p* from the correspondence model *m*. For each method, we search in line 2 for the relevant incoming and outgoing data flows in the implementation. To this aim, we implement operations *inFlows* and *outFlows* which collect all flows into the parameters of the methods and all incoming or outgoing return flows. Next, we filter the collected flows in lines 3–8 and 10–14. For the forward and join check only the flows that can be used to communicate assets from the SecDFD are relevant. This means that the type communicated along a data flow has to be mapped to an asset in the correspondence model. Accordingly, we filter out the flows which communicate unmapped types. At this point, it is not important which assets can be communicated along with the single data flow.

After filtering, in line 18, for every outgoing flow (*traget*), we perform a backward search and check if we found reachable incoming flows (*sources*) in line 19. The pair of the found sources and the target represents one i-flow that is added to the result set *i*. If exactly one incoming data flow is propagated to the outgoing data flow, we found an *implemented forward* contract, and if multiple incoming data flows are propagated to an outgoing data flow, we found an *implemented join* contract. We only consider patterns with one outgoing flow. If there are SecDFD contracts with multiple outgoing flows, these have to be split into multiple contracts. Finally, in line 23, we return all found i-flows.

After we extracted the i-flows, we compare them to the expectations from the SecDFD using Algorithm 2. The input to this algorithm is the process, the correspondence model, and the extracted i-flows. The output is a set of identified violations (absence and divergence).

Algorithm 2 is again based on two steps. First, we collect all possible matches between the i-flows and the expected flows from the SecDFD contracts (d-flows). We consider the implementation of a contract to be *convergent* with the SecDFD if and only if there exists a bidirectional one-to-one mapping between the d-flow of the contract and an i-flow. We call this property a biunique mapping. But, the matches are usually not biunique because of the overlapping asset type mappings, therefore we have to reduce the initial set of matches to a set of biunique mappings in a second step.

Algorithm 2: Algorithm for checking the implemented flows *i* for a given process *p* against the specified contracts.

Input : i-Flows *i*, Process *p*, Correspondence Model *m*
Output: Violations *v*

1 $v \leftarrow \{\}$
2 *matches* $\leftarrow \{\}$
3 **foreach** contract $\in$ *fwdJoinContracts(p)* **do**
4 | *inAssets* $\leftarrow$ *contract*.inAssets()
5 | **foreach** outAsset $\in$ contract.*outAssets()* **do**
6 | | *flows* $\leftarrow \{\}$
7 | | **foreach** iflow $\in$ i **do**
8 | | | *type* $\leftarrow$ communicatedType(*iflow*.trg())
9 | | | **if** outAsset $\in$ m.*correspondence(type)* **and** $\forall$ s $\in$ iflow.*src()* : (m.*correspondence(communicatedType*(s)) $\cap$ inAssets) $\neq \emptyset$ **then**
10 | | | | **add** *iflow* **to** *flows*
11 | | | **end**
12 | | **end**
13 | | **if** flows $= \emptyset$ **then**
14 | | | **add** "Absence: Not implemented" **to** *v*
15 | | **end**
16 | | **add** (*contract, outAsset*)$\rightarrow$*flows* **to** *matches*
17 | **end**
18 **end**
19 *solution* $\leftarrow$ findSolution(*matches*)
20 **if** solution $= \emptyset$ **then**
21 | **add** "Divergence: No biuniqe assignment" **to** *v*
22 **else**
23 | **foreach** flow $\in$ (matches $\setminus$ solution.*flows())* **do**
24 | | **add** "Divergence: Not in DFD" **to** *v*
25 | **end**
26 **end**
27 **return** *v*

To collect the matches we iterate over every SecDFD contract and every outgoing asset of the contract in lines 2 and 5. For each of these pairs we select i-flows if their possible outgoing assets contain the expected asset and if for every incoming flow at least one possible asset is contained in the set of expected incoming assets, see line 9 in Algorithm 2. If such an i-flow does not exist, the contract is not implemented for this outgoing asset, and we detect a *divergence* (lines 13 and 14 in Algorithm 2).

After collecting all possible matches, we have to find a biunique solution within the created mappings between the d-flows and the i-flows. This is implemented in the function *findSolution*. The easiest implementation is to iteratively assign i-flows to d-flows and to check if a solution is still possible. If so, we can assign the next i-flow to a d-flow, else, we have to backtrack. If we cannot find such a solution, we report a violation as there is at least one unimplemented contract and we detected an *absence* (lines 20 and 21). If we found a solution, all specified contracts have been implemented and we found a *convergence*. However, all i-flows that are not part of the solution are still reported as violations, as they are unspecified forwards or joins of assets and represent a *divergence*.

Cryptographic Contracts

The cryptographic contracts in the SecDFD describe at which location in the implementation the use of encryption, decryption, or hash-function is expected. In what follows, we introduce how we can check if the implementation meets this expectation defined at design time. When our proposed check is executed, all encrypt and decrypt process contracts will be checked against the implementation.

For each process with such a cryptographic contract, we collect all the mapped method implementations that call at least one method signature performing an encrypt or decrypt operation. If at least one such method implementation exists, we consider that the process contract has been implemented, and mark it as *convergence*. If no such method implementation has been mapped to this process, we consider that the process's SecDFD contract has not been implemented, and mark this occurrence as an *absence*.

We provide a list of common methods that are called during cryptographic operations. Table 8.1 aggregates an excerpt of these lists relevant to the iTrust example. We compiled this list by inspecting the Java standard security library and packaged it together with the plugin. In addition, the user can add project-specific methods to this list (at run-time) via the user interface. We remark that state-of-the-art static analysis tools, e.g., SonarQube[1], maintain similar rules for checking implemented encryption logic. However, these tools are restricted to locally accessible information in their analysis. In contrast to this, using our approach users can automatically verify their expectations regarding the planned security by leveraging the correspondence model for transferring expectations into an analysis on the implementation level.

---

[1] https://www.sonarqube.org

Table 8.1 Excerpt of well-known cryptographic signatures

Library	Signature	Kind
OpenJDK – JSSE	javax.crypto.Cipher.doFinal(byte[]):byte[]	Encrypt, Decrypt
	javax.crypto.Cipher.init(int, Key, AlgorithmParameterSpec):Object	Encrypt, Decrypt
	javax.crypto.SealedObject.SealedObject (Serializable, Cipher)	Encrypt
	javax.crypto.SealedObject.getObject(Cipher)	Decrypt
Apache Commons[2]	org.apache.commons.codec.digest.DigestUtils .sha256Hex(String):String	Hash

8.4.2 Tool Support for the Verification of Contract Implementations

The tool support for the verification of implemented SecDFD contracts is implemented as an Eclipse plugin. Figure 8.10 shows the architecture of the SecDFD contract check implementation.

The general management and execution of checks are implemented in a `ContractVerification` component. The component specifies an interface `ICheck` at which SecDFD compliance checks can be registered. This interface allows the integration of additional SecDFD compliance checks. For executing compliance checks, this component accesses the SecDFD and the Program Model and provides access to these for all registered checks.

This main component (`ContractVerification`) providing the compliance checks is separated into two sub-components. One for the verification of the forward and join contracts (`ProcessingContracts`) and one for the verification of the encrypt and decrypt contracts (`CryptoContracts`). In both sub-components, we implemented the checks as introduced in Section 8.4. For this purpose, both check components implement the external `ICheck` interface of the `Contract-Verification` component.

Figure 8.11 shows the integration of the contract verification in the Eclipse IDE as an extension of the semi-automated mapping implementation presented in Section 7.2.3. The contract verification can be executed by clicking the `Check process contracts` after creating a correspondence model between a SecDFD

---

[2] https://commons.apache.org/

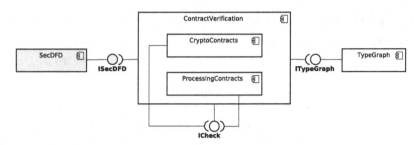

Figure 8.10 Component diagram showing the implementation of the SecDFD contract verification

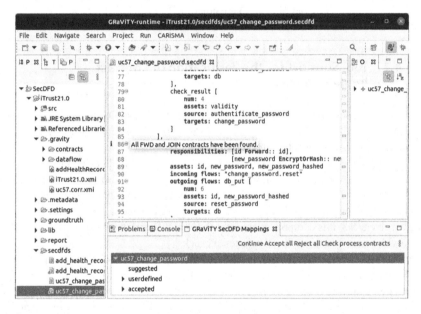

Figure 8.11 Screenshot of the static security compliance checks

and its implementation. The information marker on the SecDFD in the center of the figure shows that the `Forward` contract in line 87 has been found in the implementation and is implemented as expected accordingly. When no violations are shown, the implementation can be considered compliant with the specified contracts.

8.4.3 Evaluation of the Contract Verification

In this section, we evaluate if the proposed contract checks (Section 8.4) can effectively detect convergence, absence, and divergence between the planned security requirements and the implemented security mechanisms. We focus on the effectiveness of the SecDFD contract verification to answer the following objective.

O-Effectiveness: How effective is the proposed approach in the verification of SecDFD contracts specified on data flow diagrams?

Setup. It is important to evaluate if the proposed checks can effectively be used in the context of realistic projects. To this aim, we have used open source Java projects, as opposed to illustrative projects. Further, as we are interested in the effectiveness of the proposed compliance checks, we execute the evaluation for all process contracts, encrypt, decrypt, forward, and join. We evaluate the approach with perfectly compliant SecDFDs (i.e., verification results only include convergences, and there are no absence or divergence violations) and with SecDFDs with injected process contracts. In case of the fully compliant SecDFDs, all the detected compliance violations are false positives (FPs). Injecting the process contracts allows us to measure expected compliance violations (e.g., an absence of a join contract), which we mark as true positives (TPs). If the expected compliance violation is not found (according to the injected contract), we mark it as a false negative (FN). Finally, if we find unexpected compliance violations we mark them as false positives (FPs). As a term of measure, we adopt the well-understood precision ($TP/(TP + FP)$) and recall ($TP/(TP + FN)$) of detected compliance violations.

Execution. Two projects are used as subjects for this evaluation. The first subject is the *iTrust* project, which is used as the running example in this thesis and introduced in detail in Chapter 2. The second subject is *Eclipse Secure Storage* that provides the capability to store and read sensitive data to other Eclipse plugins. Eclipse Secure Storage is introduced in detail as a second case study for the GRaViTY approach in Section 15.2. For both projects, we created based on the documentation and implementation of the projects two SecDFDs each, a total of four SecDFDs. As the created SecDFDs (all four) have been reverse-engineered from the implementations, these are perfectly compliant and are contained in the repository associated with this thesis. An example of such a SecDFD for iTrust is shown in Figure 8.9. An example of a SecDFD for Eclipse Secure Storage is provided as part of a second case study in Chapter 15.

First, to verify the initially security-compliant state, we applied the contract verification to the two projects. We expected to detect no divergences or absences between the SecDFD and the implementation.

Afterward, we injected violations into the software systems and checked if these are detected. The violations are injected by adding random contracts to the SecDFDs that are not implemented. After every injection, we executed the contract verification and checked if the expected violation has been detected, if additional false alarms have been raised, or if expected convergences are not detected any longer. We generated injections of all contract types (encrypt, decrypt, forward, and join). Regardless of the contract type, we injected all possible contracts that have not been specified on the initial SecDFD.

New encrypt and decrypt contracts can be injected independently of each other. An encrypt contract can be injected to every process that has no encrypt contract in the initial SecDFD and a decrypt contract to every process that has no decrypt contract. Accordingly, it can happen that we injected a decrypt contract to a process that has already an encrypt contract and the other way around.

For the injection of forward and join contracts, we injected for every process of a SecDFD all possible contracts that have not been already specified. To do so, we calculated all possible combinations with one outgoing flow. To calculate the combinations we considered all incoming and outgoing assets. For instance, for a process with two incoming and two outgoing assets (and no specified forward, or join contract), we injected 6 possible contracts. Every incoming asset can be forwarded to every outgoing asset (4 forward contracts) and the pair of incoming assets can be joined with both outgoing assets as target (2 join contracts). If a combination is equivalent to an existing contract, it is omitted.

Table 8.2 Results of evaluating the cryptographic contracts verification

	Eclipse		iTrust		
	1	2	1	2	Overall
TPs	12	48	59	70	189
FPs	0	0	0	0	0
FNs	0	0	11	0	11
precision	100%	100%	100%	100%	**100%**
recall	100%	100%	84.28%	100%	**94.5%**

Table 8.3 Results of evaluating the processing contracts verification

	Eclipse		iTrust		
	1	2	1	2	Overall
TPs	1	29	55	67	152
FPs	0	28	1	10	39
FNs	14	29	23	14	80
precision	100%	50.88%	98.21%	87.01%	**79.58%**
recall	6.67%	50%	70.51%	82.71%	**65.52%**

Results. Tables 8.2 and 8.3 depict the results of the contract verification based on the injected contracts. We show the results per SecDFD and overall. The results of the evaluation are in favor of using our approach to execute security compliance checks between the design and implementation of a software system. For the execution of the verification on the fully compliant SecDFDs, we achieved 100% precision and recall. Since the effectiveness of the proposed contracts must also be studied in the context of imperfectly mapped SecDFDs. In what follows, we discuss the effectiveness of the approach in detecting absences of specified contracts.

For evaluating the verification of *encrypt* and *decrypt* contracts, we injected 200 additional encrypt and decrypt contracts into the SecDFDs. Most injected contracts (except 11) were correctly detected as absent. The 11 undetected absent contracts belong to the same SecDFD of the iTrust project. After investigating them, we noticed that all of them have been injected into processes that already have a encrypt or decrypt contract. The reason for this defect is that in the list of well-known cryptographic operations the project-specific specified signature for encryption is also specified for decryption. As iTrust uses a crypto-function that can be used for encryption and decryption, this is a correct classification. In this function, a parameter specifies whether encryption or decryption should be performed. Since we only check for at least one method call for encrypt/decrypt, we can not detect an absence in this particular case.

To evaluate the forward and join checks we injected 232 contracts into the SecDFDs. In contrast to the verification of cryptographic contracts, the results presented in Table 8.3 paint a more diverse picture. On the one hand, the processing contracts verification reaches a very good precision (98.21% and 87.01%) and recall (70.51% and 82.71%) on the iTrust project. On the other, the verification performs below par on the Eclipse Secure Storage project. In addition, there is a huge difference between the two SecDFDs on the Eclipse Secure Storage.

In particular, the verification showed a poor performance for the SecDFD called `Eclipse 1`. Two reasons handicap the verification:

First, external entities are not part of the software system and can not be mapped to elements from the software system. For example, the external entity `registered user` in Figure 8.9 represents an arbitrary iTrust user that is accessing the software system from her internet browser that is not part of the software deployed on the iTrust server. Similarly, the data can be accessed over a local Java API that allows plugins to access data. In such cases we attempt at guessing possible incoming flows by considering, e.g., every parameter of the methods mapped to a process as a possible source but also all returns of called methods that have not been mapped to any process. For instance, the `change password` process (iTrust 1) is heavily interacting with an external entity and the processes `reset password` and `authenticate` interact with a data store which results in very many guesses weakening the results.

Second, despite the reduction when extracting flows, described in Section 8.4, the overlapping asset types caused both FPs and FNs. In the example, this communication of `change password` is implemented by mainly using assets whose correspondences are overlapping (mainly strings). In general, representing sensitive objects with string values is prevalent in Eclipse Secure Storage. This also affected the performance of the processing contracts verification on the second SecDFD (Eclipse 2). Yet, the verification still achieves a recall and precision of 50%. This happened because the asset types of injected contracts overlapped with the asset types of the implemented contracts. For instance, consider two existing and fulfilled forwards of assets that are both mapped to the type `String`. In Figure 8.9 for instance, these are the forward of `ID` on the `change password` process and the forward of the `newPassword` and `oldPassword`. In addition to these expected forwards, there are some additional uses of strings that are not representing assets, e.g., a parameter representing a second submission of the new password *change password* process. As discussed in Chapter 2, this second submission of the new password is used to avoid typing errors by comparing the two versions of the new password. Now we inject a join of `ID` and `newPassword` to `newPassword`. As the default value is a guessed flow, we could easily ignore it before this injection but now it exactly contributes to the injected join contract and we have to report this contact as convergence. However, we cannot any longer report the forward of `data` as convergence as the flow pattern is now mapped to the injected join contract. Accordingly, we now report a false divergence. In this case, at least the user would have been warned about a violation but the information about the assets was not entirely correct.

As the iTrust project does not have as many overlapping asset-type correspondences and the SecDFDs have fewer external entities, the results are much better for this subject than for the Eclipse Secure Storage. Again, the missed violations are mainly due to overlapping asset correspondences as shown in the previous explanation.

Overall, the contract verification is fairly precise (80%) and reaches a recall of more than 65%. Generally, the presented contract verification works and can bridge the huge gap between early design models and concrete implementations. Though, it suffers from overlapping correspondences. Also, missing API specifications of the software system, i.e., the issue of mapping external entities, harms the performance of the contract verification.

8.4.4   Threats to Validity

In this section, we discuss internal and external threats to the execution of our experiments as well as threats to their construction that might threaten the validity of our evaluation.

External Validity

The main threat to *external validity* is our selection of samples, based on a limited number of open-source projects, partially originating from a teaching context. Regarding the validity of the studies conducted to evaluate the security compliance checks, the open source projects do not contain well-known security violations, thus we consider them secure in this respect. The rationale for our selection was the manual effort that was required for creating the ground truth of our technique, a full correspondence model between high-level DFD elements and low-level implementation elements. However, as a result, the generalization of the results to larger projects in other domains is limited. To mitigate this threat, the considered projects were chosen to be representative of realistic projects by providing good documentation, including architectural information, such as, wikis, use cases, scenarios, requirements, state charts, and the like. The available documentation enabled building good design models, close to the intended architecture. Further, we partly mitigate this threat by experimenting with contract injections in evaluation.

Internal Validity

Regarding *internal validity*, the main threat of our evaluation is researcher bias. In absence of pre-existing ground truths and design models, the ground truth and design models for our evaluation were created manually by the authors, possibly introducing a risk of creating a biased result. To mitigate this threat, the ground truths and the design-level models were carefully discussed between all authors involved in the publication [207]. The created models and ground truths are of similar size and complexity and are available online[3].

Construct Validity

Concerning *construct validity*, we consider the threat of misinterpreting compliance violations in the context of design-level models, implementation-level models, and violations detected by static code analysis. However, to the best of our knowledge, our interpretations are in line with the existing literature [93].

8.4.5   Conclusion on the SecDFD Contract Verification

We introduced a novel approach for tackling the problem of automating the code-level verification of planned security mechanisms. In particular, we have developed a solution with tool support for executing security compliance checks between an abstract design model and its implementation (in Java). Once defined, the correspondence model is leveraged for an automated security analysis of the implementation against the design. Two types of security compliance checks are executed: a rule-based check for a set of cryptographic operations, and a local data flow check for data processing contracts specified in the model. The results of the compliance checks (convergence, absence, and divergence) are lifted to the attention of the user via the user interface of our tool.

Our approach was evaluated with two studies on open source Java projects, focused on assessing the performance from different angles. The rule-based security compliance checks are very precise (100%) and rarely overlook implemented cryptographic operations (recall is 94.5%). In addition, the local data flow checks are fairly precise (79.6%) but may overlook some implemented flows (recall is 65.6%), due to the large gap between the design-time SecDFD models and the implementation.

Regarding future improvements, we note that extending the SecDFD with strongly typed assets could improve the performance of the security compliance checks. The introduction of strongly typed SecDFD assets could allow a more precise correspondence model to the implementation, which would make the local data flow checks cleaner. Such strongly typed assets are, e.g., given in detailed UML

---

[3] Contract verification implementation and evaluation data: https://github.com/SvenPeldszus/GRaViTY-SecDFD-Mapping/

activity diagrams that support the typing of dataflows with types defined in class diagrams. In addition, the missing correspondences to the external entities could be better approximated by relying on parsed API specifications (e.g, JavaDoc). Finally, the evaluation of the security checks could be improved by including more open source projects, especially projects with known security violations.

8.5 Optimized Data Flow Analysis

Secure information flow analysis dates back to the 70s and has been heavily studied ever since [219–221]. In principle, the idea is to perform a static analysis of the program to show that if executed, a program does not leak confidential information. Data flow analysis computes the data dependencies, i.e., which variables are dependent, to determine how data propagates in a program. Data flow analyzers take as input an abstracted representation of the code, e.g., an abstract syntax tree or a control flow graph, to perform the analysis. *Taint analysis* is a kind of information flow analysis where data objects are tainted at the source and tracked to the sink using data flow analysis [221]. It is one of the most used data flow analyses and has even been integrated into some programming languages, e.g., perlsec [222] in Perl. *Source methods* are characterized by reading data from a system resource, e.g., a remote database or user input, and returning them to the caller. Contrarily, *sink methods* write to system resources. An alarm is raised if a tainted object (i.e., source) flows into a forbidden location (i.e., sink) in the program.

8.5.1 Optimizing Data Flow Analysis based on Security Requirements

To perform a data flow analysis, a developer needs to identify the sources and sinks of secret data in the implementation. More importantly, to perform a meaningful and precise data flow analysis, the sources and sinks must be *identified correctly*. For instance, we have found the standard substring method in Java (`java.lang.String.substring(int, int):String`) as one of the sink method signatures in an existing list of identified sinks[4]. This will result in many false alarms raised by the analyzer since it seems unlikely that data can leave the software system through this method and it is a very common operation over strings in Java. Dually, overlooking an important source may result in overlooking true leaks. Though some

---

[4] SuSi repository: https://github.com/secure-software-engineering/SuSi

sources and sinks can be extracted from library APIs [223], finding project-specific sources still remains a challenge. In addition, many data flow analyzers work with a flat security policy. Specifically, they raise an alarm if there is an access path between *any* of the source methods and *any* of the sink methods. But, certain tainted data might be expected to flow to some sinks, e.g., writing a hashed password to iTrust's database, but not others. If all the tainted objects are treated equally, the analyzer raises false alarms. In response to this challenge, we aim to automatically extract project-specific sources and sinks *for each SecDFD asset*.

Project-specific sources
The SecDFD modeling approach requires the user to specify confidential assets, thus their source element (in the model) can easily be determined. There are three possible types of source elements: an external entity, a data store, or a process. If the asset source is an *external entity* and it is mapped to method definitions, their signatures are collected as sources. But, if no correspondence with the external entity exists, e.g., for the entity `registered user` from Figure 8.9, the signatures of the mapped method definitions of the processes reading from that entity are collected instead. If the asset source is a *data store*, it can be mapped to methods or types. First, the signatures of method definitions mapped to the data store (if any) are collected. Second, if the data store is mapped to a type, e.g., a class, the signatures of method definitions defined by this class are also collected, but only if the return type matches the asset type. Finally, an asset source can be a *process* element, e.g., a random number generator. If there is no process contract with this particular asset on the output, then the signatures of the method definitions mapped to the process are collected. But, the asset may originate in the process as a result of a transformation, e.g., a join of two assets. In this case, the assets on the contract inputs are *traced backward* reaching either an external entity, a data store, or a process with no contracts impacting the traced asset. The signatures of the method definitions mapped to the traced element are collected as sources.

Allowed sinks
We collect the sink method signatures from [223] (excluding methods of Android-specific packages) and exclude the allowed sinks. The allowed sinks are maintained *for each* confidential asset. These are method implementations mapped to SecDFD elements where the confidential asset exits the software system, i.e., external entities and data stores. For example, the secret flowing into the data store `db` in Figure 8.9 is expected to flow there. Therefore, we consider the data store `db` as an allowed sink for this specific asset.

8.5.2   Tool Support for Optimized Data Flow Analysis

Figure 8.12 shows a component diagram of the implementation of the optimized data flow analysis. We implemented the optimized data flow analysis in a component DataFlowAnalysis as an extension to the SecDFD contract checks presented in Section 8.4. For this reason, the new DataFlowAnalysis component is registered at the ICheck interface of the ContractVerification component. This allows an execution of an optimized data flow analysis when the implementation is checked for compliance with a SecDFD. In this work, we perform the data flow analysis using FlowDroid [33], a state-of-the-art taint analyzer for Android applications, but also applicable to Java programs. The 2.7.1 release of FlowDroid was obtained from its release site[5] and is imported as a library in our plugin.

FlowDroid raises an alarm if and only if an object flows from a predefined list of *source* methods, i.e., these objects are tainted, into *sink* methods, i.e., they violate the security policy. The sources and sinks must be identified and are passed as parameters to the analyzer. To simplify the analysis, FlowDroid relies on the capabilities of the Soot compiler framework [224] which converts Java bytecode into the Jimple [225] intermediate code representation. This makes FlowDroid's analysis precise as it is flow-sensitive, i.e., the call graph is aware of the order of statements, and context-sensitive, i.e., the call graph is enriched with the context of the callees. In addition, the Jimple representation can handle Java reflection, but only for reflective calls where the types of all referenced classes are known. The analysis in FlowDroid is also object-sensitive, meaning that the call graph distinguishes method invocations on different object instances since it uses access paths as taint abstractions. In general, taint analyzers consider only explicit flows for performance

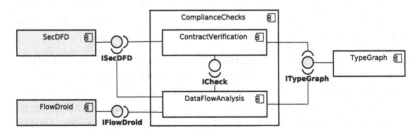

Figure 8.12 Component diagram for the optimized data flow analysis

---

[5] FlowDroid   release   site: https://github.com/secure-software-engineering/FlowDroid/releases

reasons [226], but FlowDroid also supports tracking implicit flows and shows good results on benchmarks (86% precision and 93% recall on DroidBench [33]). We refer the interested reader to [227] for more details.

The `DataFlowAnalysis` component of our implementation executes Flow-Droid over its Java API. Following Section 8.5.1, we execute FlowDroid for every asset in the SecDFD taking its set of allowed sinks and possible sources into account.

8.5.3 Evaluation of the Optimized Data Flow Analysis

The purpose of this study is to evaluate whether using our approach helps to reduce the number of false alarms raised by an existing data flow analyzer. In this section, we present the design, execution, and results of this study for answering the following objective.

O-Effectiveness: To what extent can the mapped design model (with our approach) be used to reduce the number of false alarms raised by a data flow analyzer?

Setup.
We investigate the performance of analysis with FlowDroid [33] initialized with project-specific sources and sinks. To this aim, we built three configurations of sources and sinks. Apart from the first configuration (PLAIN), we execute the analyzer *for each SecDFD asset* separately. This experiment was conducted with the same two projects as the evaluation of the contract checks in Section 8.4.3, namely, Eclipse Secure Storage [203] and iTrust [47]. To the best of our knowledge, both projects are free of data flow leaks. Therefore, all the reported leaks by the analyzer are by default labeled as false alarms (FPs). In what follows, we introduce the three configurations of sources and sinks handed to FlowDroid in detail.

PLAIN. We execute the analyzer with the list of source signatures shipped with Flow-Droid [223] (herein *Default sources*) and sink signatures extracted from [223] as described in Section 8.5.1 (herein *Default sinks*). Apart from Java method signatures, this list contains signatures of methods specific to Android source packages. We removed such signatures to avoid unnecessarily searching for them with FlowDroid. Note, that this reduced the list of source signatures from 18,077 to 1,229 and sink signatures from 8,315 to 1,310. As a result of this filtering, the Android SQL database API (SQLite) was also removed. To analyze Java projects, we manually added signatures from the Java SQL API to the above list of sources and sinks.

PARTLY OPT. We execute the analyzer (for each confidential asset) with project-specific source signatures (herein *SecDFD sources*) and *Default sinks*. The *SecDFD sources* are extracted per SecDFD asset, as described in Section 8.5.1. Note that the *SecDFD sources* are extracted independently, and therefore may not include any of the *Default sources*.

FULLY OPT. We execute the analyzer (for each confidential asset) with *SecDFD sources* and without allowed sink signatures (herein *SecDFD sinks*). The list of allowed sink signatures is extracted per SecDFD asset, as described in Section 8.5.1. The *SecDFD sinks* are obtained by *removing* the allowed sink signatures from the *Default sinks*.

The results are compared concerning the number of FPs, as no actual leaks (TPs) exist in the analyzed projects. In addition, we measure the number of extracted project-specific source signatures and the number of removed sink signatures. A false alarm (FP) is a detected leak with a *unique pair of source and sink method signatures*, regardless of the access path where the leak is detected. The rationale for counting unique signature pairs is that comparing access paths would be computationally expensive and not useful for this study. For instance, consider an implementation of a function where the number of recursive calls depends on a conditional. In this case, at least two access paths (when the conditional evaluates to `true` and `false`) are detected. But the DFD does not specify such a level of detail, thus we can not distinguish between the access paths of the detected data leaks. The false alarms are aggregated per SecDFD, to enable comparison with the PLAIN configuration.

As we execute the analysis for each SecDFD asset, we measure the project-specific sources and sinks in the same manner. Specifically, to measure the number of project-specific sources we count each discovered source signature per SecDFD asset. Similarly, to observe the number of times we can remove an allowed sink, we count each signature that has been removed for a unique asset.

```
1   Infoflow result = new Infoflow("", false, null);
2   result.setSootConfig((options, conf) -> {
3       conf.setCallgraphAlgorithm(CallgraphAlgorithm.AutomaticSelection);
4       conf.setImplicitFlowMode(ImplicitFlowMode.AllImplicitFlows);
5       conf.setAliasingAlgorithm(AliasingAlgorithm.FlowSensitive);
6       conf.setStopAfterFirstKFlows(100);
7   });
8   result.setTaintWrapper(new EasyTaintWrapper(Collections.emptyMap()));
9   return result;
```

Listing 8.2 Configuration of FlowDroid used in this study

Execution. Both projects used in this study include two SecDFDs, representing two different scenarios. Listing 8.2 shows how we configured FlowDroid for all our executions. This configuration was set up to achieve the best performance and most conservative analysis, following the literature [227]. We configure FlowDroid to use the default call-graph construction algorithm (SPARK). In addition, we have

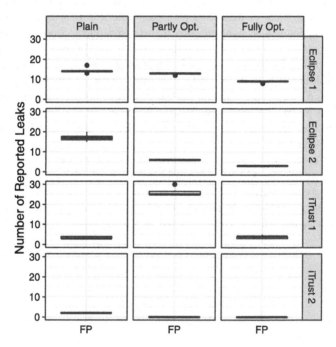

Figure 8.13 False alarms (FPs) raised by the analyzer after three configurations of sources and sinks per SecDFD (Eclipse Secure Storage on Top, iTrust on Bottom)

Table 8.4 Average false alarm reduction for the different configurations (aggregated per project)

Configuration	FPs on Eclipse		FPs on iTrust		Overall
Plain	15.65		2.7		9.18
Partly Opt.	9.45	(↓ 60%)	13.1	(↑ 485%)	11.28
Fully Opt.	5.95	(↓ 37%)	1.9	(↓ 85%)	3.93
Total		(↓ **62%**)		(↓ 30%)	(↓ **57%**)

enabled implicit flow tracking and flow-sensitive aliasing. Note that, without tracking implicit flows, FULLY OPT. produces no false alarms, while PLAIN still reports many. Finally, we limit the static analysis to the projects, excluding third-party libraries (cf. line 8 in Listing 8.2), and stop the analyzer after identifying 100 leaks per run. We have implemented and executed the experiments using the JUnit Plugin Test framework with a limit of 6 GB of memory consumption (for each execution of the analyzer). The amount of allowed memory and the maximum number of identified leaks were determined empirically. We have executed random parts of the experiment with different configurations repeatedly and didn't get different results.

Results.
Figure 8.13 shows the false alarms raised by the analyzer after three configurations per SecDFD model as box plots. The average number of false alarms is aggregated per project in Table 8.4 and the change in the number of false alarms is presented. The main takeaway of the evaluation is that using our approach we were able to

a) extract project-specific sources of secret data and
b) reduce the number of false alarms (up to 62%) raised by the data flow analyzer.

In what follows, first, we discuss the reduction with only project-specific sources. Second, we discuss the reduction with removing allowed sinks.

Our measurements from the PARTLY OPT. configuration show that deriving project-specific sources from the SecDFD is possible and can reduce the number of FPs. For instance, in the case of Eclipse Secure Storage, we achieved an average 60% reduction of false alarms (Table 8.4). However, adding project-specific sources can also lead to a rise in false alarms (as observed on iTrust). The number of project-specific sources is realistic considering the project size (11 for Secure Storage and 10 for iTrust). In addition, the project-specific source methods are in fact accessing

sensitive resources, e.g., the `java.sql.PreparedStatement.execute`
`Query()` is called when iTrust authenticates the confidential credentials entered
by a user. But, the derived sources depend heavily on the correspondences. Since
iTrust is implemented with the dynamic Java Server Pages, FlowDroid can not
analyze the entire behavior of the program. Therefore, we are only able to reduce
the number of FPs after removing the allowed sinks.

We found that the number of FPs can be further reduced by removing allowed
sinks from the list of sinks passed to the analyzer (FULLY OPT. configuration).
We have been able to remove 3 sinks (all from `java.lang` package) for Eclipse
Secure Storage and 36 sinks (all from `java.sql` package) for the iTrust project.
These sinks were included in the previous configurations but were derived in this
configuration as allowed for certain SecDFD assets. In particular, we observed a
further 37% average reduction of FPs for the Eclipse Secure Storage project, when
comparing the analysis results to the previous configuration (PARTLY OPT.). Compared to the first configuration (PLAIN), considering only project-specific sources
and removing allowed sinks reduced the number of false alarms on average by 62%.
As project-specific sources were hard to find for the iTrust project, we compare the
analysis results to the initial configuration (PLAIN). Removing the allowed sinks in
iTrust reduced the number of FPs on average by 30%.

8.5.4   Threats to Validity

In this section, we discuss threats to the validity of our experiments. We identified
threats regarding three different categories.

External Validity

The main threat to *external validity* is our selection of samples, based on a limited number of open-source projects, partially originating from a teaching context.
Regarding the validity of the studies conducted to evaluate the security compliance
checks, the open source projects do not contain well-known data flow leaks, thus
we consider them secure in this respect. The rationale for our selection was the
manual effort that was required for creating the ground truth of our technique, a full
correspondence model between high-level DFD elements and low-level program
elements. However, as a result, the generalizability of the results to larger projects
in other domains is limited. To mitigate this threat, the considered projects were
chosen to be representative of realistic projects by providing good documentation.
The available documentation enabled building good design models, close to the
intended architecture.

Internal Validity

Regarding *internal validity*, the main threat of our evaluation is researcher bias. In absence of pre-existing design models, the design models for our evaluation were created manually by the authors, possibly introducing a risk of creating a biased result. To mitigate this threat, the design-level models were carefully discussed between all authors involved in the publication [207]. The created models are of similar size and complexity and are available online[6].

Construct Validity

With respect to *construct validity*, we consider the threat of misinterpreting compliance violations in the context of design-level models, implementation-level models, and violations detected by static data-flow analysis. Also, there could be issues with the selected initial source and sink sets for the taint analysis. However, to the best of our knowledge, our interpretations are in line with the existing literature [93].

8.5.5   Conclusion on the Optimized Data Flow Analysis

Once defined, the correspondence model is leveraged for an automated secure data-flow analysis of the implementation against the design-time data-flow specifications. The mapped design is leveraged to initialize and execute a state-of-the-art data flow analyzer over the entire Java project. The results of the data-flow compliance checks are lifted to the attention of the user via the user interface of our tool.

Our approach was evaluated on two open-source Java projects, focused on assessing the performance from different angles. Our approach enables a project-specific data flow analysis with up to 62% fewer false alarms.

Regarding future improvements, we note that as for local data-flow analysis strongly typed SecDFD assets could be mapped to the implementation more precisely, which would make the initialization of the data-flow checks cleaner and more precise. In addition, the missing correspondences to the external entities could be better approximated by relying on parsed API specifications (e.g, JavaDoc) for improved identification of sources and sinks. Finally, the evaluation of the optimized data-flow analysis could be improved by including more open source projects, especially projects with well-known data leaks.

---

[6] Optimized data flow analysis implementation and evaluation data: https://github.com/SvenPeldszus/GRaViTY-SecDFD-Mapping/

8.6   Specification of Incremental Security Checks

The presented solutions allow to effectively check for the security compliance
between security requirements specified in design-time models and their implementation by leveraging the correspondence model between the design-time models and
the implementation. However, these checks are hard-coded, lack a formal foundation, and are not trivial to understand. In this section, we introduce security violation
patterns that allow the specification of security violations using the notation of graph
transformation and their detection (RQ3.2). Also, the security violation patterns are
designed to allow an incremental application to the changed parts of a software
system (RQ4.3). This allows efficient security compliance checks after changes, as
it allows us to only check the changed parts.

8.6.1   Background on Henshin Model Transformations

Using a graph-based representation of the program model, correspondence model,
and UML model, we consider the detection of security violations as in-place graph
transformation. We use the transformation language Henshin [228] to specify security violation patterns of interest. Henshin is based on graph transformation concepts,
which enables us to specify security violation patterns as declarative graph transformation rules. A Henshin rule $r : L \rightarrow R, NAC$ consists of two graphs L and R
referred to as left-hand side and right-hand side, respectively, and a set of negative
application conditions on L. The notation $L \rightarrow R$ symbolizes a partial mapping
which, by adopting notations from set theory loosely, induces the graph patterns to
be found and preserved ($L \cap R$), to be deleted ($L \setminus R$), to be created ($R \setminus L$) by a rule,
and those that are forbidden (NAC). In the visual Henshin transformation language,
the left- and right-hand side of a rule are integrated into a "unified graph", the graph
patterns $L \cap R, L \setminus R, R \setminus L$, and NAC are marked by stereotypes «preserve»,
«delete», «create», and «forbid», respectively.

8.6.2   Incremental Security Violation Patterns

During development but also maintenance, software systems are continuously subject to changes. While GRaViTY allows the propagation of structural changes
into the implementation [130, 154], we need a verification of the adapted design-
time security requirements on the implementation level. As a first idea, we could
re-execute all implementation-level security checks. However, this comes with

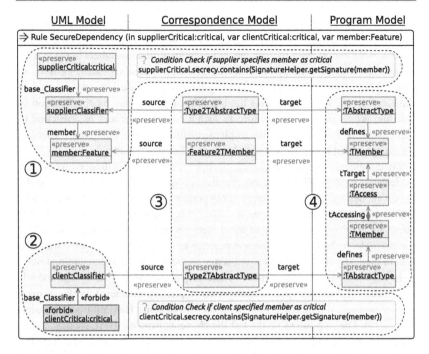

Figure 8.14 Rule-based specification of a security violation pattern for detecting violated design-time security requirements in the implementation

two drawbacks. First, even when these have been adapted to reflect the current security context knowledge, e.g., using security maintenance rules [206], these implementation-level security checks are usually disconnected from the security requirements specified on architectural models of the software system. Second, a full compliance check is usually very time-consuming. For this reason, following RQ4.3, we need an efficient verification of the compliance of the software system's implementation with the architecture in case of changes.

One example of such a UMLsec security specification is the *Secure Dependency* check [6]. As introduced in Section 3.6.1, secure dependency aims to structure the application into different security levels for critical class features. Access to features on such a security level is only allowed by entities that obey these security levels according to their security specifications.

To show the compliance of a software system's implementation with the security levels specified at design time, we have to prove that the implementation does not contain violating accesses to elements representing critical members in the system model. This can be done by either a blacklist or whitelist approach, meaning to specify all violating access patterns or all allowed access patterns. As we want to show violations, we are going for the blacklist approach and the specification of violating access patterns. If we execute such a compliance check as a reaction to changes on the model level or the implementation, an entire compliance check is not necessary but it is sufficient to only check all changed parts.

For compliance checks, we leverage the information stored in the correspondence model between the UML system model and the program model. For every class in the system model, we have one or more corresponding classes in the implementation. The same holds for the operations and attributes of classes in the system model. These are corresponding to one or more methods or fields in the implementation. For example, in Java, it is a common practice to encapsulate a property from the system model by the use of getter and setter methods at the implementation level.

In Figure 8.14, we show a rule for detecting a violation of the system model-level secure dependency specification on the implementation level for the security level of secrecy. We specified this violation pattern using Henshin transformation rules [228]. The rule shows on the left the elements from the UML models, in the center the correspondences from the correspondence model, and on the right the elements from the program model.

On the UML model, the rule matches in part ① of the rule every feature (operations or properties) contained in a class `supplier` with the stereotype critical, that contains the signature of the feature in the list of signatures on the level of secrecy. Thereby, the containment is expressed in the condition on top of the rule. Also on the UML model, in part ②, the rule matches a `client` class that does not specify the feature's signature in a critical stereotype and which is connected with the other class over the implementation. This connection to the implementation is expressed in part ③ showing the correspondences between the matches in the UML model and the match in the program model that have to be present. In part ④ of the rule, the access from a member of a type in the implementation corresponding with the class `client` to a member corresponding with the feature of the class `supplier` is matched. If this rule matches, we found a security violation in the implementation regarding the model-level security specification.

If we have a closer look at the name of the rule, we can see that this is followed by parameters of the format `kind name:type`. These parameters make the rule elements with the same name accessible to the conditions of the rule and the caller of the rule. The parameter kinds in the rule are `var` and `in`. While `var` parameters only serve as internal variables, parameters of kind `in` can be bound to an element when calling the rule. For the shown rule, the parameter `supplierCritical` may be bound by the rule's caller. This allows us to bind this parameter to the «`critical`» stereotypes that have been modified as part of a security maintenance step and to restrict the compliance check only to the changed security requirements. Similarly, we can bind other nodes for incremental security verification, e.g., to a changed class in the implementation or UML model.

To answer RQ3 of how to support developers in preserving a software systems security regarding an efficient verification of a software system's implementation compliance with the design-time security requirements after changes, we introduced security violation patterns. Following RQ3.2, the security violation patterns use algebraic graph transformation rules as a formal basis. As shown in this section, using security violation patterns, we can specify security violations on the implementation level concerning to security properties specified in design-time models. In case of changes, a matching of these patterns can be initialized with the changed parts to restrict the search space and only execute compliance checks on the changed parts.

8.6.3   Tool Support for Security Violation Patterns

As we specified security violation patterns using the Henhsin transformation language, these can manually be executed using Henshin. Henshin provides a wizard, that provides a graphical interface for executing Henshin rules on selected models. However, in our case the manual execution of the security violation patterns is infeasible. For this reason, we make use of the Java API of Henshin. Whenever any tracked artifact is changed, and a changed elements type is compatible with one of the parameters of a security violation pattern, this element can be assigned to the parameter and the security violation pattern be executed.

Figure 8.15 shows a component diagram of the implementation of security violation patterns in GRaViTY. The security violation patterns are implemented in the component `Security Violation Patterns`. The use of the Henshin API for matching the security violation patterns is represented by the use of the `ITransformation` interface of the `Henshin` component. For matching the security violation patterns, a program model (`TypeGraph`), UML model (`UML` component), and the correspondence model between them (`PM-UML` `Correspondence`) are used. To allow the manual execution of the security violation patterns, we integrated these into the CARiSMA tool [229] and the Hulk design-flaw detection tool [21, 34].

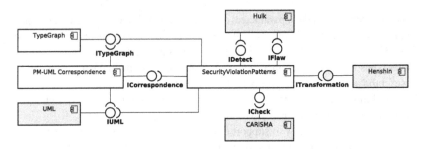

Figure 8.15 Component diagram of the security violation pattern implementation

CARiSMA provides check implementations for UMLsec, among others, for secure dependency. All checks implement an `ICheck` interface and are centrally managed and executed through this interface. To allow the extension of CARiSMA this interface is exported to the outside. As security violation patterns aim at checking the compliance between UMLsec security requirements and the implementation, we implemented this interface to allow the execution of the security compliance patterns from CARiSMA.

Hulk provides design-flaw detection on program models using the `TypeGraph` also used by the security violation pattern implementation. For this reason, we also integrated the detection of the security violation patterns into `Hulk`. For this purpose, `Hulk` specifies two interfaces. First, the `IFlaw` interface allows specifying program model annotations that will be added to the program model as part of a registered detection to specify the findings. Second, the `IDetect` interface specifies the operations that have to be implemented to execute the security violation pattern detection by Hulk.

8.6.4   Evaluation of Incremental Security Violation Patterns

In this section, we study if our solution as implemented in our prototype is feasible to solve the identified problems on a real-world software system. We want to show that security violations due to real-world security knowledge changes can be detected using our approach. Furthermore, it has to be possible to execute the detection with a reasonable time after a change has occurred. In summary, we consider feasibility regarding the following two objectives:

O1–Feasibility: The evaluation should show that the approach can be applied to an evolution scenario on a real-world software system.

O2–Performance: Our evaluation should show the benefit of incremental security violation patterns in the verification of changes.

We evaluated security violation patterns regarding two objectives. First, we studied whether security violation patterns are feasible for detection security violations on the implementation level regarding security requirements specified in design-time models. Second, we studied the run-time benefit of the incremental security compliance checks using security violation patterns.

O1–Feasibility

As an example to demonstrate the feasibility of our approach, we use a legal change, namely the release of the EU General Data Protection Regulation (GDPR) in which the European Parliament has adopted stricter regulations for the use of personal data [53]. For simplicity, in the considered scenario, we assume that the protection of personal data has not strictly been regulated by now and it is only regulated that medical records have to be treated as sensitive information and require explicit protection against their disclosure. This protection should be realized by assigning a security level to sensitive information and restricting access to this security level. Technically, this can be done by applying UMLsec secure dependency.

Figure 8.16 shows an excerpt from the system model of the iTrust medical application [47] with applied UMLsec secure dependency stereotypes. On the right, the users of the software system are shown. These can be doctors or patients. For both, a hashed version of the password and personal information like their home address is stored. On the left, we see different actions that can be performed in the software system. These actions are realized as controls. One of these controls is the `DiagnosisControl` that allows users, depending on their rights, to read or edit medical diagnoses. To access this control, a user has to log in using the `LoginControl`. To check if a user can log in and determine her rights, the `LoginControl` accesses the `User` object captured as «call» dependency (shown on the bottom of the diagram). Thereby, the `LoginControl` potentially has access to all information captured by the `User` class.

From a security perspective before the change of the regulation, only the password stored in the `User` class is sensitive and access has to be limited, e.g., by restricting access to this information to entities that are on a required security level. Accordingly, in Figure 8.16, we put the information stored in the property `password` on the level of secrecy by adding the signature of this property to the `secrecy` tag of the «critical» stereotype on the class.

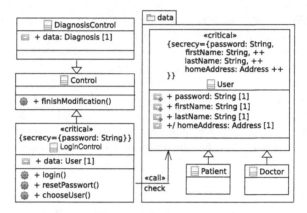

Figure 8.16 Excerpt from the design model of iTrust after adaptation to new regulations by adding new security requirements

After a release of the GDPR adopting stricter regulations for the use of personal data, sensitive information also comprises every kind of personal data. This security context knowledge change is reflected by the execution of security maintenance. In this maintenance the following actions are performed, taking the new kind of sensitive information as input:

1. Detection of every instance of the new kind of sensitive information in the software system's design-time models. In the example shown in Figure 8.16, these are the properties `firstName`, `lastName`, and `homeAddress`.
2. Adding the detected instances to the security level of secrecy, as shown in Figure 8.16. The changes are highlighted in green and indicated by a ++.
3. Inspecting all incoming dependencies of the changed classes for the mitigation of the introduced violation of *Secure Dependency*. Here, the CARiSMA can be used to detect violating dependencies. For the shown example the considered mitigations comprise:

   a. Deletion of the dependency called `check`.
   b. Extending the security level to `LoginControl`, the source of the violating dependency.
   c. Extraction of sensitive information into a new class.

As the class `LoginControl` has to access the class `User` to verify the password of the user, the deletion of the dependency in step 3 (a) is not possible. Also, for the implementation of this class, the developers have already to consider the security level of the class `User`. For this reason, a security expert decides to extend the security level as proposed in option (b). For all other dependencies, she decides similarly.

4. After mitigation has been performed by a developer, the security violation pattern shown in Figure 8.14 is executed to detect violations of the new security level on the implementation.

Afterward, matching the security violation pattern against the program model of the iTrust implementation detects the occurrence illustrated in Figure 8.17, meaning that a concrete security violation has been detected on the implementation. The elements in Figure 8.17 are arranged as in the security violation pattern shown in Figure 8.14: On the left, we see the elements from the design-time UML model, the center shows the elements from the correspondence model, and the right-hand part comprises the elements from the program model. The concrete violation is the access to a getter method of the property `lastName` by the method `updateAllergies` of the class `OfficeVisitControl`.

The corresponding source fragment of the violating access is shown in Listing 8.3. The detected security violation takes place in the implementation that allows doctors to edit health records as part of an office visit. To be more precise, in a method implementing the update of a patient's allergies. The concrete violation is the call to the method `getName` (line 6). This method is part of a `PatientDAO` that is a data access object for patient data. As no access to personal information has been planned in the system model, the whole editing of health records should be done over a patient ID which is resolved at line 6 and violating the defined security level. Even more dangerous is that the only use of the personal information is as part of a status message (line 10) if an allergy has already been recorded which might even be written to log files. As mitigation of the security violation, personal information has to be removed from this status message which makes access to personal information obsolete.

O2–Performance

For applying continuous security checks in practice, the execution times of the security checks are essential. As part of this objective, we study whether the execution times of the security violation patterns are feasible and what is the benefit of incremental execution of the security violation patterns.

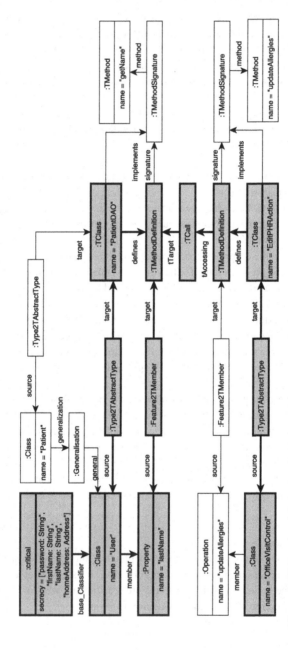

Figure 8.17 Security violating match of a security violation pattern

```
 1 public class EditPHRAction extends PatientBaseAction {
 2     private PatientDAO patientDAO;
 3     ...
 4     public String updateAllergies(long pid, String description){
 5         ...
 6         String patientName = patientDAO.getName(pid);
 7         List<AllergyBean> allergies = allergyDAO.getAllergies(pid);
 8         for (AllergyBean current : allergies){
 9             if (current.getDescription().equals(bean.getDescription())) {
10                 return "Allergy " + bean.getNDCode() + " - " + bean.
                     getDescription() + " has already been added for " +
                     patientName + ".";
11             }
12         }
13         ...
14     }
15 ...
16 }
```

Listing 8.3 Security violating source code fragment from iTrust.

Setup. Regarding the application of security violation patterns, for the verification of UMLsec secure dependency on the implementation level, two violation patterns are required for each security level. First, for the client not being annotated with the required security requirement, as shown in Figure 8.14. Second, for the opposite direction, the supplier not being annotated with the required security level. We applied these two patterns after two kinds of changes. First, changes that resulted in a security violation and, second, changes that did not affect the security compliance. Here, we did not change the structure of the implementation but edited the security annotations to introduce a security violation. To quantify the benefit of incremental security violation patterns, we executed the security violation patterns incrementally and in terms of a complete security compliance check.

We measured the execution of the security violation patterns on an Intel Core i5-6200U mobile CPU running at 2.30GHz with 8GB of memory. As the execution environment, we used Ubuntu 20.04LTS and OpenJDK 14.

Results. For a security-compliant implementation, the incremental security violation patterns' execution took on average 235 seconds, while the complete security compliance check did not terminate within 60 minutes. When investigating a change that led to a security violation, the execution time of the incremental security violation patterns increased to 440 seconds on average. The full security compliance check did not terminate within a reasonable time.

When discussing dynamic tracing in Section 6.4.2, we identified the potential for inefficiency due to reverse navigation along the correspondence edges. In this experiment, we faced this issue. For the considered security violation pattern a reverse-navigation is necessary. In the incremental case, the amount of required reverse-navigations is one time from the changed UML model element to a method in the program model and then for each other method involved in an access relation into the program model. In contrast to this, in the full application, the amount of required reverse-navigations is in the worst case the cross product of all methods.

All in all, reconsidering objective **O2**, our tool prototype shows a run-time sufficient for automatic execution, e.g., as part of a continuous integration pipeline. While there is still potential for optimizing the prototype's implementation, e.g., an incremental code-generation, we already achieved feasible execution times on a consumer computer. Furthermore, we assume a continuous integration pipeline to be executed on a server with relatively high computing power.

8.6.5 Threats to Validity

The validity of our demonstration of feasibility might be subject to some threats discussed in what follows. Thereby, we differentiate between internal and external threats.

Internal Validity

An internal threat to validity is that all experiments have been performed by ourselves, precisely knowing how our tool prototype works. Nevertheless, this still shows that our prototypical tool is suitable to solve the problem. However, this might not be the way external users want to use the proposed approach.

Also, the run-time measurements are subject to an internal threat to validity. The run-time performance of the automated tasks supported by our tooling and carried out in terms of our feasibility study has been evaluated in a non-closed system. Thus, we cannot rule out other computational tasks or processes we were unaware of to impact our measurements negatively. Moreover, performance measurements could be biased by just-in-time compilation overheads of the Java run time. However, we did not aim for high-precision micro benchmarking in terms of our feasibility study but to report about the maximal run times that we could observe in terms of our study to showcase the applicability of our tooling in a real-world setting.

External Validity

The selection of iTrust as a subject system to demonstrate our approach's feasibility gives rise to an external threat. We cannot guarantee that iTrust is representative of all other software systems our approach could be applied to.

With UMLsec *Secure Dependency*, we selected only one security check for demonstrating the feasibility of graph transformation rules for security compliance checks. This limitation gives rise to another threat. Again, we cannot guarantee the generalizability of our results, this time to other security checks.

Finally, there is a threat that the considered changes in our feasibility study do not represent all possible kinds of real-world changes. However, we cover notable changes with different feasibility study effects, still showing our approach's practical applicability.

8.6.6 Conclusion on Security Violation Patterns

We demonstrated the applicability and usefulness of the developed techniques in a feasibility study on a medical information system. Thereby, we focused on two aspects of feasibility. First, we considered the application to real-world problems and, second, whether execution times are acceptable. Also, we studied the benefit of the incremental execution of security violation patterns. We introduced how security compliance checks leveraging security specifications on the system model can be specified using security violation patterns. For these security violation patterns, we demonstrated how to apply these incrementally to detect security violations on the implementation level in case of changes in the system model.

Verification and Enforcement of Security at Run-time

9

In today's software, security is one of the most important quality aspects [51, 54]. Several approaches exist to support security at design-time [73, 230, 231], e.g., using design-time models, but also statically during implementation [232, 233] and at run-time [234–236]. Unfortunately, few approaches cover coupling these phases so far [123, 237]. Here, we have shown in the previous chapters how to couple the design time with the implementation time but did not look at the run-time, yet.

Following our approach, during software development, different representations of a software system are created, e.g., to plan the security of a software system before implementing it. All of these single representations have to be kept in synchronization in the case of changes and compliance with all security requirements has to be re-verified. As discussed in Chapters 6 and 8, we provide tool support for this step. An automatization of this process is usually called round-trip engineering [238]. Relevant changes can occur as part of the normal development process but also due to unexpected changes like the deployment of the software system with an unexpected version of a library or due to an attack. To the best of our knowledge, no existing approach for secure software engineering supports round-trip engineering considering run-time information, albeit this is important for several security-related reasons.

First, it is desirable to find vulnerabilities as early as possible [239]. For this reason, support to automatize detection of and reaction to breaches should be provided starting from the design time. Unfortunately, many security violations are hard to detect in the system design or source code [240–242]. This especially applies to vulnerabilities based on concepts as Java reflection, which are statically not analyzable to their full extent. Here, we need the possibility to enforce design-time security decisions at run-time.

Second, as the source code is usually not generated from the design-time models, divergences between the design-time security assumptions and the implementation

S. M. Peldszus, *Security Compliance in Model-driven Development of Software Systems in Presence of Long-Term Evolution and Variants*, https://doi.org/10.1007/978-3-658-37665-9_9

likely appear [23]. To ease the investigation of the violations, the design-time models should be automatically adapted to also contain the observations made at run-time.

All in all, this breaks down to our third research question of how to support developers in the development of a secure software system.

RQ3: How can developers be supported in realizing, preserving, and enforcing design-time security requirements in software systems?

To be more precise, in this chapter we are going to answer the third sub-question of RQ3:

RQ3.3: How can design-time security requirements be enforced at run-time?

In what follows, we introduce the run-time security enforcement of GRaViTY, called UMLsecRT. As shown in the previous chapters, the GRaViTY approach enables developers to specify security requirements in design-time models or source code. UMLsecRT takes these security requirements and monitors compliance with them at run-time. Violations and findings at runtime, like possible attack sequences and monitored calls, not covered by the design-time model, can be synced back to the model by adapting it. If a security property is violated, e.g. by a vulnerability introduced during an update or an attack, the system operator is notified and the software system is brought into a safe state. What is considered a *safe state* in which situation, is also handled within the security requirements.

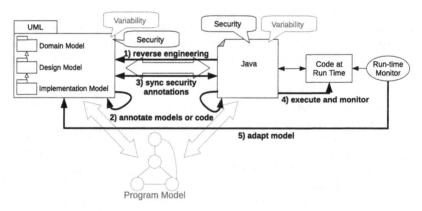

Figure 9.1 Concept of the run-time monitoring in the overall approach

Figure 9.1 visualizes our approach for enforcing security at run-time and adapting system models based on run-time information. We explain the usage of the approach step by step:

1. For round-trip engineering, a UML model consistent with the source code is required, e.g., a class diagram for the UMLsec security requirements considered in this thesis. If such a model is not available, our approach supports reverse engineering it from Java source code as discussed in Chapter 7. If only security monitoring is required (not the possibility for round-trip engineering), working only on the source code is also possible. In this case, the security annotations can be applied directly and only to the source code.
2. A developer annotates, assisted by tool support [74], the UML model, the source code, or both with security requirements derived from the project's requirements. Thereby, the UMLsec annotations can be directly used for static security checks using the tooling of UMLsec and the static security compliance checks introduced in Chapter 8.
3. Annotations added to the model are automatically synchronized with the source code and vice versa. If only the UML model has been annotated, source code annotations can be generated automatically from the model.
4. The annotated Java source code is executed and the execution is monitored for security violations concerning the security annotations added in the earlier steps.
5. The design-time models are adapted based on the security-relevant data gathered at runtime. For example, by adding sequence diagrams describing detected violations.

Using the proposed approach, developers cannot only enforce compliance with the security requirements specified during the development of a software system but also adapt the design-time models to inspect and react to security violations observed at run-time. Including UMLsecRT, the GRaViTY approach proposed in this thesis contains integrated tool support covering all phases from early software design over the implementation of a software system to its execution.

The remainder of this chapter is organized as follows: Section 9.1 discusses background on security compliance at run-time. Afterward, we introduce an explanatory security violation in the iTrust system in Section 9.2. We will use this security violation to demonstrate our run-time monitoring approach. Section 9.3 introduces this run-time monitoring approach and covers how to monitor for violations at run-time, and how to perform countermeasures if security violations occur. Section 9.4 presents a prototypical implementation of UMLsecRT. In Section 9.5 we evaluate the run-time monitoring approach. We elaborate on threats to validity in Section 9.6. In Section 9.7, we conclude and give an outlook on future work.

9.1   Background on Security Compliance at Run-time

Many security-related issues are related to concepts like Java reflection or dynamic class loading. As such concepts are statically not analyzable, these have to be checked at run-time.

```
1   public static Object reflectiveCall(Object instance, String name,
        Object[] params) {
2       Class<?>[] types = new Class<?>[params.length];
3       for(int i = 0; i < params.lengt; i++) {
4           types[i] = params[i].getClass();
5       }
6       Method method = instance.getClass().getMethod(name, types);
7       method.setAccessible(true);
8       return instance.getClass().invoke(instance, method, params);
9   }
```

Listing 9.1 Example for Java reflection

Listing 9.1 demonstrates the infeasibility of static analysis for Java reflection. The method `reflectiveCall` allows invoking an arbitrary method of any class. For this purpose, the object instance on which the method should be invoked, the name of the method, and values for the parameters are required. First, in lines 2–5, the type of the method's parameters are calculated. Afterward, in line 6, the method retrieves an object representing the method to invoke and sets it to accessible in line 7. This allows to not only invoke public but also private methods. Finally, in line 8, the method is invoked and the return-value forwarded. In this implementation, no specific value is given, that can be used to calculate the method to be invoked. Possible values, e.g., for the method name, have to be traced across all call locations of the method `reflectiveCall`. Thereby, the construction of the method name can be arbitrarily complex and in the worst-case depend on external data, e.g., user input.

Accordingly, many run-time checks have been developed. All of these checks come with a high overhead making them infeasible to monitor the whole software system. For example, the JBlare monitor has an overhead of a factor of 12 for class loading and 4 for execution [243]. Again, the information about the most sensitive parts of the software system, that should be monitored under any circumstances, and parts not relevant for the software systems security is available in the design-time models.

While all these different security checks on the different artifacts can help in the development of a secure software system, they are often limited to their area of focus. However, such security checks are more powerful when they are combined. For example, often information required by a security check on a lower level has already been defined at design time. This information should be reused to avoid misunderstandings and divergence in the security assumptions but also to improve the effectiveness of the checks. Unfortunately, doing so is challenging and should be assisted by tool support.

9.2   Example Security Violation

As part of the UC28, iTrust allows doctors to search for their patients. This search has been implemented in the `SearchUsersAction` shown in Listing 9.2. A search can be performed by calling the `searchForPatientsWithName` method. While it has been planned that the functionality of this class is only available for legitimate users, e.g., licensed health care professionals (LHCP), a check should be performed when an instance of the class is created (line 7), this check of the MID has not been implemented.

For the hashing of passwords, e.g., at the creation of new users in an iTrust installation or changing a password as described in UC57, the external library Apache Commons[1] is used in iTrust. Line 10 of Listing 9.3 shows one usage of this library. The `sha256Hex` method of the library is used to hash a salted password at resetting a user's password in the database of the iTrust system. In the rest of the method, an SQL statement for updating the hashed password and salt for a MID is created and executed.

In Listing 9.4, we show how a malicious library can exploit the iTrust system every time a new password is created, e.g., by executing a search for user information and sending it to the outside. We assume that the Apache Commons library has been replaced by a malicious version at deployment time. Whenever the `sha256Hex` method of the malicious library is called, the malicious implementation tries to query the data about patients in the iTrust system. For example, we use the home address of a patient, that has been classified at the security level of secrecy. To access this critical information, the malware makes use of the circumstance that it

---

[1] Apache Commons: commons.apache.org

```
1    @Critical(secrecy={"search(String,String):List"})
2    public class SearchUsersAction {
3
4        private PatientDAO patientDAO;
5        private PatientDAO personnel;
6
7        public SearchUsersAction(DAOFactory factory, long loggedInMID) {
8            this.patientDAO = factory.getPatientDAO();
9            this.personnelDAO = factory.getPersonnelDAO();
10       }
11
12       @Secrecy
13       public List<PatientBean> searchForPatientsWithName(String firstName,
                String lastName) {
14           try {
15               if("".equals(firstName)) firstName = "%";
16               if("".equals(lastName)) lastName = "%";
17               return patientDAO.search(firstName, lastName);
18           }
19           catch (DBException e) {
20               return null;
21           }
22       }
23
24       ...
25   }
```

Listing 9.2 Source code of a class for accessing patients with security annotations

has been called from a sensitive method deeply in the iTrust system and the missing authentication in the constructor of the `SearchUserAction` class.

The malware is implemented as follows. In line 6 of Listing 9.4, the malware makes use of the missing authentication in the constructor of the class `SearchUserAction` and creates an instance. This instance is then used to search for arbitrary patients in the iTrust system. To avoid detection by static analyses, it now uses the `reflectiveCall` of Listing 9.1. This method uses the Java-Reflection API for invoking arbitrary methods. In line 9, the `getIcAddress1` method of the class `PatientBean` is invoked in this way to access the critical data. Afterward, the retrieved data is passed to a `send` method that sends the information to the outside. Finally, in line 13, the original implementation of the library method is executed and its return value forwarded.

```
1    public class AuthDAO {
2
3        public void resetPassword(long mid, String password) {
4            Connection conn = null;
5            PreparedStatement pstmt = null;
6            try {
7                conn = factory.getConnection();
8                pstmt = conn.prepareStatement("UPDATE users SET password=?,
                     salt=? WHERE MID=?");
9                String salt = shakeSalt();
10               String newPassword = DigestUtils.sha256Hex(password+salt);
11               pstmt.setString(1, newPassword);
12               pstmt.setString(2, salt);
13               pstmt.setLong(3, mid);
14               pstmt.executeUpdate();
15               pstmt.close();
16           } catch (SQLException e) {
17               throw new DBException(e);
18           } finally {
19               DBUtil.closeConnection(conn, pstmt);
20           }
21       }
22
23       ...
24   }
```

Listing 9.3 Source code of the method for resetting a user's password in iTrust's database

```
1    package org.apache.commons.codec.digest;
2
3    public class DigestUtils {
4
5        public static String sha256Hex(final String string) {
6            final List<PatientBean> patients = new SearchUsersAction action =
                 new SearchUsersAction(DAOFactory.getProductionInstance(), −1);
7            action.searchForPatientsWithName("%", "%");
8            for(final PatientBean bean : patients) {
9                String address = (String) reflectiveCall(bean, "getIcAddress1",
                     new Object[0]);
10               // do something evil with the address
11               send(address);
12           }
13           return sha256Hex_original(string);
14       }
15
16   }
```

Listing 9.4 Sourcecode of a Malicious Implementation of a Library

In the succeeding section, we introduce a realization of secure dependency on code level which prepares run-time monitoring of this security requirement.

9.3   Verification at Run-time and Model Adoption

We propose to couple security at design-time with security at run-time by using the notation for specifying security requirements in Java source code introduced in Section 6.4.1. This notation maps the UMLsec secure dependency stereotypes to corresponding Java annotations with the same semantics. When the retention of these Java annotations is set to RUNTIME, these are contained in the Java bytecode and can be monitored at run-time. Additionally, we utilize the reverse engineering and synchronization of UML models annotated with UMLsec stereotypes and Java source code annotated with security annotations (Section 6.2 and Section 6.4.1). We further demonstrate how we realize countermeasures to mitigate security violations at run-time. At the end of this section, we discuss how we automatically evolve the software system's architecture based on the information about security violations collected at run-time.

9.3.1   Security Monitoring at Run-time

After the specification and static verification of security requirements, the next step is to execute the annotated source code and to monitor the execution for security violations (step 4 in Figure 9.1). To ensure that we detect every security violation wrt. secure dependency, we have to check all method calls and field accesses for their compliance with the specified security requirements. There are built-in security mechanisms in Java, such as the Security Manager, but these are insufficient for realizing UMLsecRT, because they cannot be configured fine-grained enough (only on jar-file or classpath-entry level) and are only executed when the method *check-Permissions* is explicitly called [61]. We need to take action as soon as any method is entered or exited or any field is accessed. According to *Secure Dependency*, we have to consider two cases that can appear at the same time:

1. the accessed member is missing an annotation, or
2. the accessing member is missing an annotation.

We reify monitoring by instrumenting the compiled code using Javassist, a framework for bytecode manipulation of Java programs [244, 245]. Instrumentation needs to take place at run-time because it is not foreseeable which classes will be loaded, e.g., due to dynamic class loading. We encapsulated the run-time part of UMLse-cRT into a Java agent which is called before the main method of a Java program is called. The byte code instrumentation provided by our agent is triggered every time a class is loaded and instruments appropriate code to conduct the secure dependency check at run-time. An excerpt from the code injected into methods is summarized in Listing 9.5 and explained in what follows.

   While the JVM maintains call stacks for all threads [246], required information as the annotated security requirements are not accessible from these stacks. For this reason, the UMLsecRT agent provides a global set of stacks for call traces, one stack per thread. The corresponding stack for a method is retrieved as soon as the method is entered (line 1 of Listing 9.5). Whenever a method is entered, the conditions of secure dependency are checked in line 5. To accomplish this, whenever such a relevant event occurs, we need to investigate the call trace backward and check both if the originating method is annotated as required and if the accessed member is annotated as requested by the originating method. In line 2, the security annotations of the originating member are read from the stack, and in lines 3–4, the annotations of the currently instrumented method are built by reading them from the bytecode and hard-coding them into the injected code. Additionally, the method is pushed to the stack (line 6). After all statements of the methods have been executed, but

before the return statement in line 8 is finally initiated, the method is removed from
the stack.

```
1    RTStack stack = RTStackManager.getStack(currentThread());
2    RTAnnotation originating = stack.peek();
3    String[] secrecy = ... // Signatures on the secrecy level
4    RTAnnotation accessed = new RTAnnotation("Signature of this method",
         secrecySet);
5    check(originating, accessed);
6    stack.push(accessed);
7    ... // Original method code
8    stack.pop();
```

Listing 9.5 Code for monitoring security, injected before and after methods

As field accesses are statically analyzable [61], we check them whenever a new
class is loaded. Depending on the developer's preferences, we can directly throw
security exceptions or instrument the field access in a way that a security exception is
thrown when the access is executed. An exception to this is reflective field accesses.
Here, we instrument the Java reflection library methods to execute the required
checks.

In Figure 9.2, we demonstrate the security monitoring for the execution of iTrust
use case UC57 of changing a user's password. The figure shows a control flow graph
excerpt on the left and the executed monitoring steps on the right. Due to numerous
involved methods and fields, we only look at the excerpt already considered in the
previous chapters. To be more precise, we use the methods discussed in the program model excerpt of Figure 7.5, which has been used in Chapter 7 to introduce
the correspondence model between the DFD describing UC57 and the implementation. Among others, the considered excerpt contains the usage of the method
resetPassword, which is shown in Listing 9.3 of this section, by the method
changePassword. The implementation of the changePassword method has
been shown in Listing 2.1 when introducing iTrust in Chapter 2. In addition to
these methods, we consider the usage of the sha256Hex method by the method
resetPassword.

First, we look at the execution sequence depicted in the control flow graph.
At the beginning of the execution, the method changePassword of the class
ChangePasswordAction is called by the user through the web UI to change her
password. The user's MID as well the data entered into the web-form (old password
and two times the new password) is passed to this method as parameter values. This
method accesses the field authDAO and calls the authenticatePassword
method on the field to check the correctness of the entered password to decide if a
change is permitted. The called method executes additional calls, we do not consider

now. Afterward, the `changePassword` method compares the two new passwords by calling the `equals` method on the first password. In the considered execution sequence, the passwords are equal and the reset of the password to the new password is triggered by a call of `resetPassword`. As shown in Listing 9.3, this method first calls a method for initializing an SQL statement and retrieving a salt, which we do not consider in detail in this example. After these calls, the method `sha256Hex` of the class `DigestUtil` is called. This method calls additional methods that are beyond the considered scope of the example and are not depicted in detail in Figure 9.2.

After, discussing the considered execution sequence, we now look at the executed agent calls. To the beginning of every method a `check` and `push` functionality has been written at instrumenting the classes. Accordingly, when entering the first method of the considered sequence (`changePassword`), in agent call 1), the security compliance of this method with the method on top of the stack is checked. Afterward, the method `changePassword` is pushed to the stack at the end of this agent call.

Next, the field `authDAO` is accessed. As all fields have been statically checked at class loading, in agent call 2), the results of this check are loaded for the accessing method `changePassword`.

For the call of the method `authenticatePassword`, agent call 3a) takes place as soon as the body of this method is entered. Again, the top of the stack is retrieved and the compliance between the current method and the top of the stack is checked. In this case, the top of the stack is `changePassword` that we pushed to the stack in agent call 1). After the compliance has been checked, `authenticatePassword` is pushed to the stack. The same behavior takes place for all methods invoked by `authenticatePassword`. When the execution of `authenticatePassword` ends, the top element is removed from the stack in agent call 3b). As this takes always place as soon as a method is left, this removed element is always the method whose execution ends, in this case, `authenticatePassword`.

Afterward, the execution goes back to `changePassword`, that calls the `equals` method. Again, the security compliance is checked in agent call 4a) and the method is pushed to the stack. This method does not call any other methods and is removed from the stack in agent call 4b).

Next, `changePassword` calls the method `resetPassword`, that is checked for security compliance and pushed to the stack in agent call 5). This method now calls some methods before calling `sha256Hex`. Here, we can see how the stack grows with the dept of calls. The `resetPassword` method has not been removed from the stack yet. In addition, when it comes to agent call 6), `sha256Hex` is also

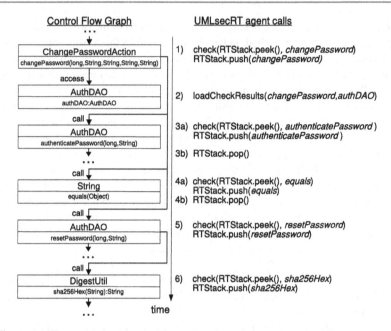

Figure 9.2 Events monitored at run-time and performed check steps

pushed onto the stack. Only considering the methods shown in Figure 9.2, after agent call 6) the methods `changePassword`, `resetPassword`, and `sha256Hex` are on the stack.

In case one of the validations on the right of the figure fails, we provide various reactions to mitigate the violation. We discuss these reactions in the next section.

9.3.2   Countermeasures

If a violation of secrecy or integrity is detected, we provide four different kinds of countermeasures to study the violation and to prevent harm:

1. Log actions of potential attacks for future evaluation
2. End the attack by shutting down the application
3. Provide a statically defined value instead of the real value
4. Call operations implementing countermeasures

The simplest reaction is to log the call or access leading to a violation and all calls and accesses which take place after the violation. This could be a classical textual log file or sequence diagrams as generated by our automated system evolution, described at the end of this section. Logging will not prevent damage caused by the occurred violation but enables system developers to study the violation and adapt the software system to prevent future damage. To actively encounter a violation, we provide several reactions to stop exploiting a software system and thus combine logging with additional countermeasures we discuss in the remainder of this section.

The first active reaction is to terminate the software system and notify the system operator. Surely, the termination of a whole software system is in many cases undesired. Considering software systems used in critical contexts, the damage caused by a not running software system can be quite high, and considering a risk assessment higher than a maybe limited data loss. For example, in September 2020, the EHR system and many other systems of a German hospital have not been available due to a ransomware attack. As a consequence, emergency patients were redirected to other hospitals that may have played a role in the death of one patient [247]. In this sense, an attacker could knowingly cause a security incident to ultimately provoke a shutdown as the actual goal. For this reason, shutting down the system is no option for iTrust. However, in software systems with low requirements regarding availability, in combination with logging, a controlled shutdown might be a valid option. As an alternative to keep the software system running and to actively prevent it from harm, we support changing return and field values in case of a violation. For instance, returning `null` is a well-known reaction in case of unforeseen or unusual situations. This prevents the software system from disclosing real data to an attacker. For this reason, our security annotations support having statically defined early return or field values.

In many cases, realistic data cannot be specified statically but has to be generated dynamically to pass simple plausibility checks and not cause exceptions to be thrown. For example, an array has to contain an expected amount of entries that can depend on run-time information. Furthermore, there can be a need for additional countermeasures to bring the software system into a fail-safe state and to protect other parts of the software system from an ongoing attack.

Early return values are defined in both cases by a parameter `earlyReturn` of `@Secrecy` and `@Integrity`. This parameter can be any primitive type, String, `null`, or the name of a parameterless method within the class, which should be called. This method can perform any operation accessible from the scope of the accessed member. To avoid accidental use of methods providing countermeasures at the regular program execution, we additionally provide `@CounterMeasure`: whenever a method annotated in such a way is entered, UMLsecRT prohibits this call by returning `null`.

```
 1      public class PatientBean {
 2
 3          @Secrecy(earlyReturn = "secure")
 4          private String icAddress1;
 5
 6          @Secrecy(earlyReturn = "secure")
 7          public String getIcAddress1() {
 8              return icAddress1;
 9          }
10
11          @CounterMeasure
12          public String secure() {
13              StringBuilder s = new StringBuilder();
14              Random random = new SecureRandom();
15              for(int i = 0; i < 10 + random.nextInt(10); i++) {
16                  s.append((char) random.nextInt('z' - 'a') + 'a');
17              }
18              SecurityManager.startSafeMode();
19              return s.toString();
20          }
21      }
```

Listing 9.6 Specification of a countermeasure

Listing 9.6 exemplifies the usage of calling an additional method to determine an early return value: `secure():String` will be called if a security violation of the secrecy property of the field `icAddress1` or the method `getIcAddress1` occurs at run-time. This method generates a random string that is returned instead of the real address of the patient. Also, the software system is set into safe mode at a central class `SecurityManager`. For example, this could mean that only a limited set of functionality is working in this mode and non-essential functionality that might have a critical impact if exploited, e.g., the changing of passwords is not permitted.

9.3.3 Automated Software System Evolution

After the detection of a security violation, even if it has been mitigated by UMLse-cRT, the software system has to be adapted to reduce the attack surface regarding this violation. Especially for software systems extensible with plugins or accessible over the Internet, system models might not cover all possible ways the software system can be extended or how it can be accessed, which makes adaptation difficult.

Here, the data logged by UMLsecRT can be helpful but a simple log file stating what happened can be hard to understand and mappable to the architecture. For the specification of call sequences, UML provides sequence diagrams [5]. Sequence diagrams allow developers easily to understand which parts of the software system are involved in a specific call sequence as the corresponding model elements are directly used in the diagram.

To cope with these issues we suggest as the fifth step in Figure 9.1 an automated evolution of the UML system models reverse-engineered in step 1. This automated evolution covers:

1. addition of missing UML elements to the design-time models,
2. and documentation of security violations as sequence diagrams with explicit references to involved UML elements.

As generating such diagrams might be time-consuming and requires the usage of additional libraries such as the UML library, at run-time, UMLsecRT stores data in a custom format that is used for model adaption afterward. Figure 9.3 shows the format of the information recorded at run-time, specified as a class diagram.

For every application that is monitored using UMLsecRT, as soon as a security violation is detected, a `Protocol` is created, containing information about the date and time at which the security violation occurred (`date`) and the monitored application (`application` and `path`). Also, the current call stack is stored in the `Protocol` and extended as long as the monitored application runs.

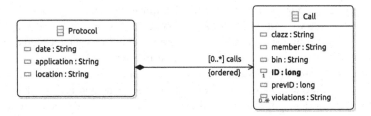

Figure 9.3 Format used by UMLsecRT for recording call-sequences

For every member on the stack or accessed later, a `Call` is recorded. These calls are stored in the order of their addition. For the identification of the member, this `Call` contains the signature of the member `member`, the fully-qualified name of the class defining the member (`clazz`), and the path from which the class has been loaded (`bin`). Also, each call has a unique `ID` and contains the `ID` of the last call to the member from which the current call originates (`prevID`). Finally, information about violations or countermeasures is stored (`violations`).

In the remainder of this section, we discuss how these evolution steps can be realized using the gathered data.

Addition of missing Elements

For the addition of missing elements, we consider two different UML diagrams available in system models. First, the UML class diagram on which the secure dependency property has been specified. On this diagram, we add the classes discovered at run-time as well as observed dependencies. While this immediately allows visualizing the violation of secure dependency, the concrete identification of the classes missing in the system model might not be possible if these are not contained in the known classpath but have been side-loaded maliciously. For this reason, we also generate a deployment diagram showing from which artifact, e.g, a class file or library, the class has been loaded. Furthermore, this allows distinguishing between classes that have accidentally or maliciously the same name and namespace. Also, we show from which device the missing classes have been loaded.

Figure 9.4 shows a deployment diagram of the running example combining the class diagram with the deployment relation. The shapes with white background resemble the elements coming from the (reverse-engineered) model. On top of the figure, the adapted class diagram is shown, and at the bottom of the figure, the adapted deployment is shown. Thereby, the deployment is a more detailed version of the general deployment architecture shown in Figure 15.3, focusing on the internal structure of the `iTrust` artifact. These two diagrams are connected by «`manifests`» relations, expressing which artifacts contain which classes.

For the known part of the software system, it shows the usage of the `PatientBean` by the class `SearchUsersAction`, for which a source code excerpt is shown in Listing 9.2. Below those two types, we can see on which artifacts those are deployed and on which execution environment they are manifested. Both are expected parts of the iTrust implementation and are deployed on the `iTrustServer`. Also, the class `DigestUtil`, which comes from the Apache Commons library (`commons-codec-1.9.jar`), is an expected part of the iTrust system. However, the call to the class `PatientBean`, that the maliciously exchanged version of the library from Listing 9.4 performs, is not defined in a design-time model. For this reason, UMLsecRT added a dependency expressing this call to the model and highlighted it with a comment.

The shapes with a gray background on the right side of the figure were also automatically added as evolution steps by a UMLsecRT guarded execution and represent entities not present in the design-time models. These show further actions of the malware introduced in Listing 9.4 that has not been considered by the system's developers. In this case, the `DigestUtil` calls an additional class `Send` that is not contained in the design-time models.

For the identification of unknown and known elements comparing their fully qualified names is not sufficient. A Java class that has the same fully qualified name as a UML Classifier might still be injected by an attacker using a weakness of the implementation. Also, there might be two Java classes with the same name and namespace at run-time. Here, we improve the identification of elements by considering their manifestation dependencies specified in deployment diagrams such as Figure 9.4. In addition to comparing the fully qualified names, we compare the manifestation of UML elements in artifacts with the protection domains of Java classes. A protection domain contains the information from where the classloader loaded the class and is represented by the manifestation in the UML model. Based

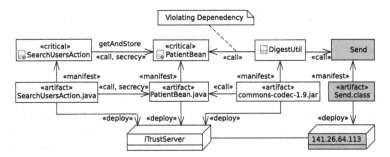

Figure 9.4 Deployment and manifestation of classes with evolution

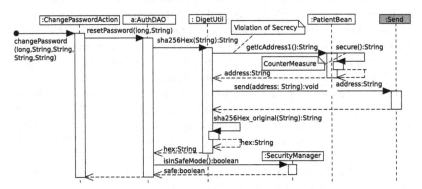

Figure 9.5 Sequence diagram automatically generated by UMLsecRT

on the protocol over which a class has been loaded, e.g. a file or socket, we can even check if the deployment of the artifact manifesting a Classifier is the expected one. In the deployment diagram shown in Figure 9.4, we can see that the class `Send` has been loaded from a class file that came from an external server. In such cases, the name of the node is set to the URL or IP address of the server it represents. In the recorded data, this information is stored in the property `bin`.

Documentation of Security Violations.
To understand an attack it is not only necessary to show which method call or field access leads to a security violation but it is of special interest which sequence of actions the attacker performed. In what follows, we first show a sequence diagram that has been generated for the example security violation. Afterward, we show how such sequence diagrams can be generated from the data UMLsecRT collects at run-time.

Example for a generated sequence diagram: Figure 9.5 is a sequence diagram generated by UMLsecRT during monitoring execution of the running example, cf. Listing 9.4. It outlines a call sequence leading to a security violation and the mitigation carried out against it. The call of the method `getIcAddress1():String` by the method `sha256Hex` is the source of the security violation. For highlighting this violation for developers, a *Violation of Secrecy* comment has been added to the message representing this call. While this call is obfuscated by the use of Java reflection in the implementation, we can show the effective calls in the generated sequence diagrams. Which countermeasure has been executed is also shown in a comment. In this case, the method `secure()` has been called as specified in Listing 9.6. After the violating call, the attacker called `send(String)` but due to the countermeasure not with the secret value. As the software system has been set into safe mode as part of the countermeasure, the user's password is not changed using the potentially malicious hash of the new password. Here, we assume that `resetPassword` asks the `SecurityManager` about the current safe mode state before changing passwords in the iTrust database.

Due to efficiency reasons, we do not keep track of all methods already being returned but beginning with the violation all future accesses are recorded and will be visualized. In this case, for the methods that have been called after the security violation, this is just one additional call of `send`. An example for a method that is not part of the generated sequence diagram but shown in the control flow graph of Figure 9.2 is the method `authentiatePassword`, that already terminated before `resetPassword` has been called.

Generating sequence diagrams: To generate sequence diagrams, we have to translate our internal stack structure as shown in Figure 9.2 and recorded in the format shown in Figure 9.3 into a sequence diagram. To do so, we translate every method call into a synchronous message in the sequence diagram. For every accessed field we generate a lifeline, e.g. the lifeline a of type AuthDAO in Figure 9.5. Also, we create lifelines for classes if static members of those are accessed or we cannot determine the variable the method is called on. For the first element on our stack, we create a message from a start node. All other elements on the stack have always exactly one predecessor from which the corresponding message originates and to which the return message goes. Before the return message is added to the diagram, first all successors are added to the diagram. As the list of predecessors is ordered, we automatically get the correct sequence of messages. Listing 3 shows this procedure in detail as pseudo-code.

As input for the generation of a sequence diagram, we take a Protocol compliant to the specification in Figure 9.3 and return a UML Interaction containing the sequence diagram. First, we initialize three maps in lines 1–3. The first map names2lifelines, maps pairs of protection domains and class names to lifelines. The second map allows immediate access to every processed Call using its ID, and the third map, provides access to the return message generated for a Call, using its ID. Afterward, we initialize a new Interaction in line 4.

Next, we iterate over all calls in the order of their addition, starting with the first added call. In each iteration, we first lookup in the map names2lifelines whether we already created a lifeline in the interaction I for the current Call or not. If there is already a lifeline, retrieve this lifeline or create a new one otherwise. Afterward, we lookup if we already translated the predecessor of the current Call of this iteration. This should always return a Call except for the first recorded call that has no predecessor.

In lines 8–17, we determine the kind of message suitable for representing the current Call, and if suitable, the lifeline from which the current call originates. If we process the call sequence's first call, prevCall is not defined, and we create an *asynchronous* message. Also, there is no lifeline from which this message will originate. Otherwise, in line 9, we retrieve the lifeline for the source of the call. Afterward, we distinguish between calls to constructors and methods or fields. Here, we assume, that a constructor has the same name as the class in which it is defined. For constructors, we create a *create* message and for all other members a *synchronous* message.

In line 18, the message representing the Call is created using the previously determined information. Please note that UML always handles a message, whose source is not set, as found message, and no special treatment for the initial call is required. Next, in lines 19–23, we create the reply messages for synchronous messages as well as the highlighting for active times of a lane. Also, we add the reply message to the map containing all replies.

Algorithm 3: Generation of a sequence diagram from UMLsecRT's protocol.

Input   : Protocol P
Output: Interaction I

1   *names2lifelines* := Map<(String,String),Lifeline>$\rightarrow$**new**;
2   *ids2calls* := Map<long,Call>$\rightarrow$**new**;
3   *ids2replies* := Map<long,Message>$\rightarrow$**new**;

4   I := Interaction$\rightarrow$**new**;

5   **foreach** call $\in$ P.calls **do**
6   *rhs* := *names2lifeline*$\rightarrow$getOrCreate(*call*.bin, *call*.clazz);
7   *prevCall* := *ids2calls*$\rightarrow$get(*call*.prevID);

8   **if** prevCall = *null* **then**
9   kind := ASYNCH_CALL_LITERAL;
10   **else**
11   *lhs* := *names2lifeline*$\rightarrow$get(*prevCall*.bin, *prevCall*.clazz);
12   **if** *getNamme(*call*.member)* = call.*clazz* **then**
13   kind := CREATE_MESSAGE_LITERAL;
14   **else**
15   kind := SYNCH_CALL_LITERAL;
16   **end**
17   **end**

18   *message* := createMessage(*lhs*,*rhs*,*call*.member,*call*.violations,*kind*);
19   **if** kind = *SYNCH_CALL_LITERAL* **then**
20   *reply* := createReply(*lhs*,*rhs*,*call*.member);
21   createBehaviorExecutionSpecification(*message*,*reply*);
22   *messages*$\rightarrow$put(*call*.ID,*reply*);
23   **end**

24   *successor* := *ids2replies*$\rightarrow$get(*call*.prevID);
25   **if** successor $\neq$ *null* **then**
26   *message*$\rightarrow$getOccurrenceSpecification()$\rightarrow$setToAfter(*successor*);
27   **end**

28   *ids2calls*$\rightarrow$put(*call*.ID, *call*);
29 **end**
30 **return** I;

As the last creation step, in lines 24 to 27, we arrange the ordering of the messages. If no explicit order is given, the messages are added to the end of the lifeline.

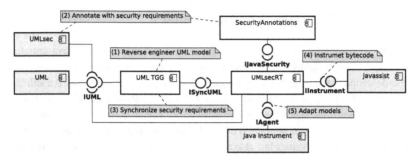

Figure 9.6 Structure of the UMLsecRT implementation

However, if a message has been called within the active time of another message, we have to adjust this order. For doing this, we retrieve the return message of the predecessor, in line 24, and move the message created in this iteration before the retrieved reply. If there was no reply message for the predecessor, no adjustment of the order is required.

Finally, at the end of each iteration, we put the `Call` to the map of already processed calls (`ids2calls`). After processing all calls in the protocol, we return the generated `Interaction`.

9.4   Tool Support for Monitoring and Adaption

To evaluate UMLsecRT, we implemented prototypical tool support for UMLsecRT. Generation of monitored call sequences as sequence diagrams and missing model elements that appear at run-time is supported, too. We present the prototype in detail in this section. In Section 9.5, we elaborate on the evaluation of UMLsecRT in detail, based on this prototype.

In Figure 9.6, we show the structure of our implementation, realizing UMLsecRT as introduced in Figure 9.1, in detail. In both Figures (Figure 9.1 and Figure 9.6) we use the same number labels for respective steps. In what follows, we elaborate on the implementation's key features in order of the number labels.

9.4.1   Java Annotations and IDE Support

For the security annotations on the source code level, we used the Java annotations specified in Section 6.4.1 and added the support for countermeasures. To ease development and further support the developer, we also implemented a validation plugin for the Eclipse IDE[2] to validate GRaViTY annotations. This validation mainly ensures if the types specified in early return values fit the types of annotated fields and return types of annotated methods. This check covers not only statically specified early return values but also return types of methods that are called in case of security violations.

9.4.2   Validation at Run-time and Countermeasures

As soon as a developer annotated the UML model and Java source code with the UMLsecRT annotations and synchronized the annotations as described before, he executes the program and monitors it using UMLsecRT, cf. step 4.

To realize monitoring, we make use of bytecode instrumentation as provided by the bytecode manipulation framework Javassist [244]. To access the running software system, we implemented a Java agent, which can be called, e.g., via the JVM's -javaagent command-line, and is documented in the package java.lang.instrument [248].

The JVM calls our agent whenever a class is loaded. Our agent then transforms the bytecode of the class by injecting the code to keep track of the call stack, issuing checking of the *Secure Dependency* conditions at appropriate times, as shown in Figure 9.2 and Listing 9.5, and also to produce report data to realize model adaption (step 5). Static checking of potential malicious field accesses is also executed when the class is loaded. As the agent is also called on dynamically loaded classes, the analysis we provide is a hybrid analysis not depending on the local availability of all classes. Which of the discussed countermeasures should be performed, when a security violation is detected, is specified as an argument when launching the application with the agent.

A threat regarding security is that attackers can inspect the software systems and add UMLsecRT annotations to their malicious code to avoid detection. This issue can be solved by the addition of cryptographic signatures to the annotations. If UMLsecRT annotations are only used as an internal security mechanism, commits containing changes to security annotations can be only accepted from developers

---

[2] Website of the Eclipse IDE: https://www.eclipse.org

with sufficient rights. As the signature check only has to take place at the loading of a class, this is a static overhead and has only a relatively low impact on long-running programs of a software system.

9.4.3   Automated Adaption of Design-Time Models

While we support synchronization of model and code, there may be associations between the model and code that still are not covered and cannot be detected statically. This especially applies to dynamic behavior introduced by libraries and reflective calls. While program execution is monitored, cf. step 4 in Figure 9.6, our implementation of UMLsecRT keeps track of every method which has been entered and not exited yet.

The prototype facilitates the graphical presentation of the observed call flows by creating sequence diagrams (cfer. step 5 of Figure 9.6). As our tool can keep track of every method and field that is accessed, we can check continuously if a call edge detected in the monitoring has respective elements in the model. If not, the tool can feed this information into the model by adding respective elements.

9.5   Evaluation of the Security Monitor

We evaluate the applicability of UMLsecRT and its tool support regarding three objectives:

O1–Effectiveness Can we detect real-world security violations using UMLsecRT?
O2–Applicability Can we monitor real-world Java programs with a reasonable run-time overhead using UMLsecRT?
O3–Usability How useful are the adapted UML models for investigating security violations observed at run-time?

In the following we introduce the evaluation objectives in detail, present the methodology and the evaluation's results. We performed the experiments on a system equipped with an Intel i5-6200U CPU, 8 GB RAM, and running Oracle JDK 8 on Ubuntu 20.04.

9.5.1   O1–Effectiveness of the Run-time Monitoring

At first, we study the effectiveness of UMLsecRT for the detection of realistic vulnerabilities and compare it to the Java security manager.

Setup. For this evaluation, we studied the causes of real-world security violations, reproduced them, and evaluated the detection and mitigation of them as performed by UMLsecRT and the Java security manager.

Common weaknesses of software are collected in the common weakness enumeration (CWE) using a unique ID for every entry [249]. However, the presence of weaknesses does not imply that the weakness can be actively used to perform malicious actions. Nevertheless, weaknesses in software should be detected and fixed. In Table 9.1, we briefly summarize the CWEs considered in our evaluation and how they are mitigated by UMLsecRT if they are exploited.

To study the effectiveness and precision of static weakness detection approaches the Juliet tests suite has been created. For many CWEs, the Juliet test suite provides a database of good and bad code examples [250, 251]. Unfortunately, it does not contain examples to exploit the weaknesses maliciously. Such an exploit is needed to violate *Secure Dependency*.

For example, the weakness *CWE470 – Unsafe Reflection* states that using the Java reflection API to load classes based on external data is dangerous. To detect this violation statically, it has to be determined if the values passed to the reflection API, e.g., the name of a class to be loaded, are created from external data. A small change in how the name of a class is passed to the API can have a huge impact on the detection and this is what the Juliet test suite is designed for. While the detection of all these different variations of a single weakness is challenging statically, the concrete values can be inspected at run-time. As the Juliet test suite is designed for static analysis tools, the examples for CWE470 end as soon as a class has been loaded based on external data. The same applies to the other CWEs considered in Juliet.

At run-time, we cannot change the underlying implementation of a software system to remove exploits of weaknesses but have to mitigate the exploits. As we can perform checks as soon as a class is loaded, we do not have to evaluate if we can detect the loading of a class based on external data but if we can detect malicious actions this class performs after it has been loaded. Here, we have three possibilities to consider malicious method calls as well as write and read accesses to fields. While for CWE470 all three are possible, for other CWEs this is not the case. For example, write accesses cannot be used to expose sensitive data as considered in CWE200.

Table 9.1 Considered CWEs and their mitigations by UMLsecRT

CWE	description & mitigation
200 – Exposure of Sensitive Information	UMLsecRT prevents the exposure information by checking every access to data declared as sensitive.
209 – Sensitive Information in Error Message	If @*Secrey* is required from *print* methods of exceptions, calls to those not compliant are prevented.
226 – Sensitive Information Uncleared in Resource	UMLsecRT prevents illegal access to fields declared as sensitive.
327 – Broken Cryptography	If required security guarantees of a hash or encryption/decryption function have been removed, e.g.,
328 – Reversible One-Way Hash	due to an update of a library, UMLsecRT prevents calls to those.
470 – Unsafe Reflection	UMLsec Checks Accesses at run-time and Prevents Forbidden Ones.
481 – Assigning instead of Comparing	All assignments from locations not having the required guarantees are prevented by UMLsecRT.
486 – Comparison of Classes by Name	As UMLsecRT does not rely on names, malicious classes loaded due to comparison by name cannot perform accesses they do not have the rights for.
491 – Object Hijack Using Cloneable	As UMLsecRT uses the security requirements on the level of members, classes injected using clonable cannot perform accesses they do not have the rights for.
498 – Clonable Class Containing Sensitive Data	While usually security checks are implemented in constructors, we check all accesses to sensitive data.
499 – Serializable Class Containing Sensitive Data	As every access is checked, no sensitive data can be accessed during a malicious serialization.
502 – Deserialization of Untrusted Data	Methods of injected malicious classes can only perform accesses they have the rights to.
586 – Explicit Call to Finalize	As explicit *finalize* calls threat integrity, only calls from methods guaranteeing @*Integrity* are enforced.
829 – Functionality from Untrusted Control Sphere	Also for external functionality, compliance with specified security requirements is enforced at runtime.

For this reason, based on the Juliet test suite and our research on CWEs, we created executable test cases to study the effectiveness of the run-time monitoring. Thereby, we consider two kinds of test cases, positive test cases and negative test cases. Every positive test case contains an exploit that has to be detected at run-time monitoring. In summary, we created test cases utilizing the 13 CWEs shown in Table 9.1. For example, the violation shown in Listing 9.4 of the running example is an instance of CWE829 utilizing CWE470 to perform an illegitimate method call that leads to disclosure of data (CWE200). According to Listing 9.6, it is mitigated by the call of a countermeasure. In this experiment, we always throw a *SecurityException* as soon as a violation of *Secure Dependency* has been detected by UMLsecRT. In Table 9.2, this case is used to test the secrecy case of a method call for the violation in the first row. Every negative test case corresponds with a positive test case by covering the same language construct but not containing a security violation, e.g., as the security annotations are consistent.

All test cases are around the size of this example and have been created wherever possible for secrecy and integrity cases of field accesses and method calls. Our examples cover calls from and to external libraries, reflective accesses to fields and methods, reflective instantiation of objects, code injections into a Javascript engine as well as a deserialization attack. All in all, we specified 13 different kinds of tests with 37 expected security violations. For every expected security violation, there is also an additional test case where the same action takes place but no security violation is expected, giving us 74 test cases in total. All tests are available in our replication package [252]. Table 9.2 gives an overview of the tests and which CWEs they address.

Results. While the specification of the test cases using UMLsecRT was straight-forward and UMLsecRT has been able to detect all expected security violations without getting a single false positive, this was more challenging using the Java security manager. The results of the experiment are shown in Table 9.2. A check-mark stands for successfully mitigated and a cross for not possible to mitigate. In some cases not all cases make sense, e.g., the test case for CWE209 – Sensitive Information in Error Message cannot lead to a violation of integrity.

While UMLsecRT supports different kinds of security requirements, the standard Java security manager does not support these. For this reason, we implemented the security checks using the Java security manager without differentiating between the different security requirements.

The second general limitation of the Java security manager we observed is that it is not possible to check field assesses. Accordingly, we consider all test cases with forbidden field accesses as failed. An exception to this is reflective field accesses.

Table 9.2 Effectiveness of UMLsecRT and the Java security manager: ✓ – mitigated, (✓) – partly mitigated, × – not mitigated, N/A – no test case

	Kind of Action Executed in the Test Cases	CWEs	UMLsecRT Field Read Secrecy	Field Write Integrity	Method Call Secrecy	Method Call Integrity	Security Manager Field Read	Field Write	Method Call
1	A plugin accesses critical members of the host	200, 226, 486, 807, 829	✓	✓	✓	✓	×	×	✓
2	Internal bug: Security properties of source violated	200, 807	✓	✓	✓	✓	×	×	×
3	Internal bug: Security properties of target violated	200, 807	✓	✓	✓	✓	×	×	×
4	Accidental assignment to field but only read rights	481, 807	N/A	✓	N/A	N/A	N/A	×	N/A
5	Dynamic loaded class accesses data	200, 226, 486, 807, 829	✓	✓	✓	✓	×	×	✓
6	Injected JavaScript code into the Rhino engine	200, 226, 807, 829	✓	✓	✓	✓	×	×	✓
7	Call *printstack trace* of sensitive exception	200, 209	N/A	N/A	✓	N/A	N/A	N/A	✓
8	Reflective access to critical members	200, 226, 470, 807	✓	✓	✓	✓	(✓)	(✓)	(✓)
9	Call to finalize with insufficient privileges	586	N/A	N/A	✓	✓	N/A	N/A	(✓)
10	Cloning of a class containing sensitive data	200, 498	✓	N/A	✓	N/A	×	N/A	N/A
11	Serialization of class containing sensitive data	200, 499	✓	N/A	✓	N/A	×	N/A	N/A
12	Replacing class at deserialization	200, 807, 829	✓	✓	✓	✓	×	×	✓
13	Unsecure method/field in new library version	200, 327, 328, 807	✓	✓	✓	✓	×	×	×

However, here the Java security manager only provides the possibility to check if the use of Java reflection is allowed for the location the class has been loaded from but not to check against the security requirement of the field. However, as some kind of security check can be expressed, we consider this as partly successful. The same applies to method calls executed via Java reflection.

One main goal of UMLsecRT is to not only protect from attacks but also to mitigate security violations caused by bugs within the implementation. Here, the granularity of the Java security manager does not allow us to specify security checks within a single classpath entry. Last but not least, the security manager only allows us to check invocations of methods that are under our control but not if an external method invoked by us provides the expected security requirements.

To sum up, while the Java security manager can be effectively used to check incoming method accesses originating from classes stored at a different classpath as the code we want to protect, it provides not a sufficient granularity and expressiveness to enforce UMLsec security policies at run-time. On the other hand, the proposed security policies can be effectively enforced at run-time using UMLsecRT. Also, if the software system has been developed using UMLsec, there is no additional effort included in enforcing the UMLsec security requirements.

9.5.2   O2–Applicability of the Run-time Monitoring

To use UMLsecRT in practice, it is vital to be able to monitor real-world programs with reasonable overhead and without facing issues, e.g., due to exceptions. Thus, the second evaluation objective targets to confront UMLsecRT with different real-world applications. More specifically, we aim at constituting which part of UMLsecRT is responsible for the overhead to what extend and which programming constructs are problematic to monitor.

Setup. To consider both real-world programs as well as realistic program executions, we applied the monitoring component of UMLsecRT to the DaCapo benchmark suite [253]. The DaCapo benchmark is a benchmark suite which is actively maintained since 2006 and supported by industry. In version 9.12 DaCapo consists of 14 real-world open source applications (the tomcat benchmark is currently broken and therefore excluded by us [254, 255]) on which typical tasks are executed. It, for instance, contains indexing of or search in large documents like the King James Bible using Apache Lucene (*luindex* and *lusearch*) and XML to HTML transformation (*xalan*). A list of the benchmarks is given in Table 9.3. As the majority of the monitoring code is executed regardless of UMLsecRT annotations being

Table 9.3 Benchmarks of the DaCapo benchmark used for the evaluation of the run-time monitoring

benchmark	project characteristics			execution time in ms		slowdown
	classes	methods	fields	plain Java	UMLsecRT	
avrora	1,741	19,575	27,789	4,576	12,213	2.7
batik	2,121	66,734	350,799	4,195	14,145	3.4
eclipse	407	5,357	3,359	47,625	399,534	8.4
fop	1,204	29,814	86,919	2,137	15,749	7.4
h2	441	13,745	6,884	7,906	17,699	2.2
luindex	491	6,313	2,869	1,994	6,472	3.2
lusearch	491	6,313	2,869	3,839	15,967	4.2
pmd	644	35,606	49,432	4,138	13,595	3.3
sunflow	220	1,653	990	7,154	19,251	2.7
xalan	1,419	52,200	72,989	4,879	19,046	3.9

present in the code or not, we do not need to annotate the applications of the DaCapo benchmark to evaluate the overhead of UMLsecRT.

As part of this objective, we conducted two experiments. At first, we measured for every DaCapo benchmark the time needed to finish execution both with and without monitoring. In the second experiment, we profiled, which percentage of the DaCapo benchmark's execution time has been spent on which tasks, to learn about reasons for the expected slowdown.

Results. We have been able to monitor 10 benchmarks successfully and had problems on 3 benchmarks using *jython* or *Geronimo*. In these, a *java.lang.VerifyError– Inconsistent stack height* exception is thrown when the programs themselves use byte code instrumentation after UMLsecRT performed changes. As this exception is also thrown if we insert only non-behavior-changing code, the cause seems not to be UMLsecRT. Despite these 2 programs, there seem to be no problems with monitoring real-world programs.

The execution times with and without security monitoring are denoted on the right of Table 9.3. On average the execution with security monitoring is 4.1 times slower than without security monitoring. If we look into the details of the different benchmarks we can see that there is a notable difference in the slowdown between the different benchmarks. With a factor of 2.2, *h2* has only a relatively small slowdown while the *Eclipse*-based benchmark has the biggest slowdown with a factor of 8.4.

Figure 9.7 shows the distribution of time needed for central parts of UMLsecRT among the benchmark executions. These are instrumenting the classes, checking security annotations, creating new annotation objects, representing members and their annotations, as well as the retrieval of the stack corresponding to the current member. The benchmarks in the figure are sorted by their slowdown with the benchmark with the highest slowdown on the top. We can see that the slowdown does not directly depend on a single activity. On average, 56% of the slowdown is due to the instrumentation of the loaded classes, 2.7% for checking the security annotations, 5.4% for creating new annotation objects, and 35.9% for stack retrieval. However, there are huge differences between the individual projects. Whilst analyzing the data, we can make out two groups, one mainly spending time for the retrieval of the stack and one where the instrumentation of the classes takes the most time.

At looking closer into the execution times, we notice that the projects with the lowest overhead are the ones running the longest already in the unmonitored execution. An exception to this is *Eclipse*, where the OSGi classloader and the structuring into plugins cause a high instrumentation overhead. A second exception to this is *fop*, here the high instrumentation overhead due to the many classes in combination with the short run-time of the benchmark leads to a high slowdown. The very high instrumentation overhead for *batik* can be explained by the excessive amount of fields that are all checked at classloading and many methods that have to be instrumented. The same applies to *fop*, *pmd*, and *xalan*. All in all, it seems like the slowdown is decreasing with the execution time. This and the average static instrumentation overhead of 56%, indicate that UMLsecRT has a lower slowdown for long-running applications than the measured average slowdown.

9.5.3   O3–Usability

The possibility to adapt the design-time models based on the observations at run-time allows developers to easily study violations that have been observed and mitigated. To study the usability of the adaption for the investigation of security violations, we performed a user study and asked the participants for their opinion.

Setup. In our user study, we introduced the Eclipse secure storage, explained in detail as the second case study in Chapter 15, to the participants. Afterward, we showed them three representations of a security violation caused by an Eclipse plugin executing an implementation, comparable to the one shown in Listing 9.4, in a start-up action. The first representation was the stack trace of a security exception that has been thrown at the beginning of the *get(String,String)* method of the Eclipse

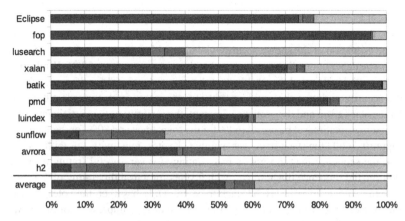

Figure 9.7 Distribution of execution time for run-time monitoring (sorted by slowdown)

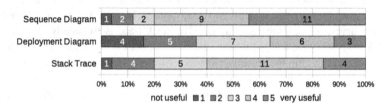

Figure 9.8 Usability of representations of a software system for the investigation of a security violation

secure storage. The second representation was the generated deployment diagram, comparable to Figure 9.4, and the third one the generated sequence diagram, comparable to Figure 9.5. For all three representations, we asked the participants to identify key aspects of the security violation. Next, we asked the participants to write down the benefits and disadvantages of all representations. Finally, the participants had to rate the usability of the different representations for the investigation of a security vulnerability on a scale from one for not useful to five for very useful.

In total, 25 experienced software developers participated in our user study. Of these developers, 56% had an experience of more than 10 years and another 28% had more than 5 years experience. Two participants had less than 3 years of experience.

Results. In Figure 9.8, we show the results of the usability rating of our user study. While the answers of the participants have low variance for the usability rating of the well-known stack trace, the answers are more diverse for the proposed models. Both, the stack trace and the sequence diagram, have been rated to be useful for the investigation of the shown security violation with an average value of 3.52 and 4.08. The deployment diagram was rated with an average rating of 2.96. While 36% of the participants rated the deployment diagram to be useful for the investigation of a security violation the same amount of participants tends towards not useful. For the stack trace and the sequence diagram, the majority of the participants rated these representations to be useful (60% for the stack trace and 80% for the sequence diagram). While the stack trace was mainly (11 votes) rated with a usability rating of 4, the sequence diagram got as many ratings for very useful (rating of 5). In addition, the sequence diagram got, with 9 votes for a usability rating of 4, nearly the same amount of votes as the stack trace got. Only based on the votes, we can conclude that the participants of our study have a diverse impression of the shown deployment diagram but still see some use in it. The well-known stack trace is seen as being useful, but the votes for the sequence diagram are even more positive.

When we look into the benefits and disadvantages identified by the participants of our survey, we can see some trends. The stack trace is frequently rated as a well-known structure that is linked to the code but does not provide very detailed information regarding the security violation. Also, the deployment diagram does not provide detailed information but is rated as a very simple entry point that is also suitable for non-technical stakeholders. Also, the sequence diagram might be suitable for non-technical stakeholders. Many participants agreed on the sequence diagram giving a very detailed description of the security violation but at the cost of readability for larger violations. Also, the models might require trained personal for productive use. In summary, many participants commented that for them the integration of all representations would be the best. While this was not explicitly given as an option to the participants, this reflects the practices at developing a software system using the proposed GRaViTY approach.

In summary, the participants of our case study rated the sequence diagram as the best representation for providing details about the detected security violation. However, for a practical application, the integration of all representation seems to be the favorite of the participants. Here, we have not shown to the participants that the deployment diagram and the sequence diagram are already integrated as they are adoptions of the same model reusing the same elements. As the sequence diagram uses methods as messages it provides the same integration with the code like the stack trace and integration with the stack trace is straightforward.

In this evaluation, we showed that UMLsecRT can be used for effectively monitoring Java applications for compliance to security requirements specified at design time. Furthermore, in our evaluation of the applicability we have shown that depending on the program size there is a huge initial overhead that relativizes with time. Accordingly, an efficient implementation of UMLsecRT seems feasible for long-running programs.

9.6 Threats to Validity

While evaluating UMLsecRT, we identified threats to validity that we discuss in this section. First, we discuss threats to the internal validity of our evaluation, and afterward, threats to the evaluation's external validity.

9.6.1 Internal Validity

For studying the effectiveness of our approach in detecting security violations (**O1**), we might have not covered all relevant cases. Here, we used the Juliet Testsuite as a guideline for selecting relevant security violations that can be detected using UMLsecRT. While there might be other relevant weaknesses that could be detected and mitigated using UMLsecRT, we currently only consider the selected ones as possible. If UMLsecRT is suitable to detect security violations due to other weaknesses, will be subject of future works.

Regarding **O2**–Applicability, we successfully showed that it is possible to monitor for vulnerabilities and breaches in real-world Java programs. However, we did not conduct the evaluation based on security breaches that have been documented to be seen in the wild on real applications. Nevertheless, as part of the first experiment regarding **O1**, we have shown that UMLsecRT is suitable to detect real-world security violations in minimal examples.

The design of our user study (**O3**) did not allow the participants to interactively apply our approach but was based on generated views on a security violation selected by us and presented in a survey. Also, we asked to consider all three presented representations exclusively. These design decisions for the user might affect the participants' answers regarding the usability for inspecting security violations.

9.6.2 External Validity

On the one hand, it might seem like annotating the whole code basis is a huge overhead and might threaten practical applicability. However, large amounts of annotations are heavily used in industry, e.g., in the context of the Spring framework [256] or Jackson [257]. On the other hand, most of the data needed by us has already been collected at thread modeling and can not only be reused at low cost but even improved by our approach. The suitability and usability of UMLsec to specify this information have been evaluated in different contexts. In a public report of the EU project VisiOn [80], the pilots write to feel able to analyze complex aspects of privacy and security [79]. In a comparison of models for data protection by Pierre Dewitte et al., the CARiSMA tool used by us ranked the highest for tool support, indicating good applicability [258].

Regarding the performance of our implementation, we measured an overhead for monitoring of 4.1x. While we have shown that the overhead for instrumenting the classes gets less relevant for long-running applications there is space for improvement in the performance of the checks, this threatens the applicability to real applications. This is mainly the retrieval of the UMLsecRT stack for the current thread. Currently, this happens twice for every method call, when a method is entered and when it is left. A possible solution could be to introduce a field to every class holding the stack. For single-threaded applications this is simple, but if objects are shared between multiple threads it gets more complicated.

The relevance of the slowdown could be reduced if, comparable to Bodden et al. [259], only the critical core parts of an application are monitored. Here, again the models used in UMLsecRT could be utilized to identify these parts.

Another possibility to implement UMLsecRT is to extend the existing Java annotations to be used with aspects [260]. A drawback of this approach is that the monitoring will be part of the target program. Also, the steering of a monitored application is might not possible in a sophisticated manner as the aspects always run on the application level. Apart from that, this has the immanent security risk that an attacker gets to know that UMLsecRT aspects are part of the program and uses reflection to deactivate or, even worse, taints them.

An external threat to the validity of our user study is the limited number of participants that might not result in generalizable results for other groups of participants. Nevertheless, the user study indicated good usability of the adapted system models for investigating security violations. The usability from the user perspective can be studied in detail in future works.

9.7   Conclusion on the Run-time Security Monitoring

In this chapter, we introduced an approach for coupling model-based security analyses with the code level, lowering the effort needed for annotating the code base and supporting round-trip engineering by providing feedback into the models.

The approach supports reverse engineering of models from code and synchronization of security annotations in model and code as well. Reaction to detected security issues is supported by passive reactions like call trace logging or actively by providing modified return values to protect real application data. Round-trip engineering is supported both by feeding additional associations monitored during execution back into the model as well as automatically generating sequence diagrams of attacks to support developers in investigating attacks with graphical support and related to the model. Thus, software system evolution detection is also tackled.

We introduced UMLsecRT by realizing support for checking secure call dependencies, by extending the realization *Secure Dependency* for the UMLsec extension which could only be checked statically (and thus partly) by now. Our approach is supported by a prototypical implementation. We realized support for the source code level by utilizing the Java security annotations introduced in Section 6.4. Run-time monitoring is provided by the UMLsecRT Java agent, while synchronization of model and code is realized using triple graph grammars.

We applied our approach successfully to the iTrust EHR system and the Eclipse Secure Storage. Details on the application to Eclipse Secure Storage are shown in Chapter 15, in which we discuss the application of the GRaViTY approach to two case studies. Also, we evaluated UMLsecRT in terms of effectiveness and applicability against real CWEs and DaCapo benchmark. Results show that UMLsecRT can be used in realistic application scenarios. However, during analyzing the evaluation results, we identified potential for additional research.

Future work can primarily target a more efficient implementation to reduce the current monitoring overhead and thus increase the applicability in real-world environments. Apart from that, the evaluation can be expanded by both supporting additional security requirements and evaluate off-the-shelf applications having actual security issues. Also, the applicability of UMLsecRT to other domains, like safety or real-time processing guarantees, can be investigated.

Part IV
Maintenance

Security-aware Refactoring of Software Systems

10

This chapter shares material with the FASE'2018 publication,,Controlling the Attack Surface of Object-Oriented Refactorings" [146] , the PPPJ'2015 publication „Incremental Co-Evolution of Java Programs based on Bidirectional Graph Transformation" [130] , and the TTC'2015 publications „Object-oriented Refactoring of Java Programs using Graph Transformation" [131] and „A Solution to the Java Refactoring Case Study using eMoflon" [130]

In the previous chapters, we discussed the development of software systems using a model-based security engineering approach. As part of this approach, we considered the synchronization of changes among all artifacts of the software system as part of incremental software development. Such changes do not only occur during development but also at the maintenance of the software system after initial development.

Maintaining software systems over a time is challenging. Due to continuous changes in the software system, it is prone to structural decay which might give rise to anti-patterns [21]. Anti-patterns qualify architectural decay in the large, involving several classes spread over the entire program and result in a higher effort for maintenance [13]. Also, there is the widespread assumption that software systems prone to many anti-patterns are more likely to contain vulnerabilities [261]. The reasoning behind this assumption is that such software systems are more challenging to understand and therefore to maintain. As a consequence, more errors are made, including errors that lead to vulnerabilities.

© The Author(s), under exclusive license to Springer Fachmedien Wiesbaden GmbH, part of Springer Nature 2022
S. M. Peldszus, *Security Compliance in Model-driven Development of Software Systems in Presence of Long-Term Evolution and Variants*, https://doi.org/10.1007/978-3-658-37665-9_10

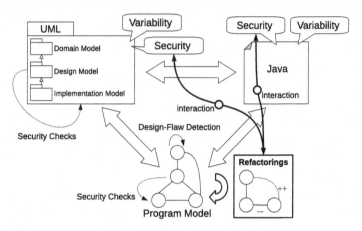

Figure 10.1 Location of refactorings in the overall concept

Refactorings are a common measure to mitigate the effects caused by anti-patterns and to improve the quality of the implementation [18]. However, as refactorings lead to changes in the software system, they might affect security requirements as studied in the previous chapters. As shown in Figure 10.1, refactorings interact with the security requirements specified on the design-time models and source code. For investigating the impact of arbitrary changes on a software system's security requirements, in Section 8.6, we introduced security violation patterns that can be executed to check changed parts of a security system for security violations. While this allows detecting security violating changes efficiently, their mitigation has to be performed manually or the change has to be undone which might not always be possible. In the best case, we can investigate changes before applying these to the software system. Accordingly, we have to study the interaction of refactorings with security requirements and have to find means to prevent refactorings from negatively impacting security. We answer our fourth research question in the context of object-oriented refactorings.

RQ4 How do changes within a software system affect its security compliance, and how can these effects be handled?

The key idea is that whenever a developer applies a refactoring using our approach, not only the behavior but also the software system's security is preserved. For this reason, we have to study the interaction between refactorings and security requirements. To study this interaction, we have to formalize refactorings first. This formalization builds the basis for studying the effects of refactoring systematically and incorporating security-preserving constraints. Accordingly, the research questions of this chapter are as follows.

RQ4.1: How can behavior-preserving refactorings be specified on a formal basis and this specification be used for executing the refactorings?

RQ4.2: How do refactorings interact with security requirements, and how can malicious interactions be prevented?

In what follows, we first give a brief introduction to object-oriented refactorings in Section 10.1. In Section 10.2, we introduce our formalization of behavior-preserving refactorings and how these can be applied to a software system. Finally, in Section 10.3, we study the interaction of refactorings with a software system's security requirements and show how security-preserving refactorings can be specified.

10.1 Background on Object-Oriented Refactorings

Opdyke was the first to propose refactoring as a countermeasure for the negative consequences of software evolution, by defining 23 program restructuring rules in a human-readable form [17]. Fowler expanded this catalog of refactorings (by retaining its informal nature) in his seminal work [18], which serves as the de-facto standard by now. Guided by such refactoring catalogs, software systems are restructured manually by applying the described refactorings.

For example, the iTrust system has been developed as a class project over 25 semesters. Between the semesters, among others, the teaching assistants refactored the iTrust implementation through manual restructurings for preparing a more easily extensible version for the next semester's class [50]. An example of a restructuring, performed after the summer term of 2009, is the relocation of test cases that do not access iTrust's database to their own classes. By doing this, the initialization of the database has been avoided for these test cases, and as a consequence, a significant speedup has been achieved. In this case, the benefit of the refactoring was twofold. First, an unnecessary initialization could be avoided by reducing the coupling. Second, if a developer works on the relocated test cases, she does not have to care about this initialization of the database and possible interactions, which eases the work.

While refactorings as described before are often performed manually, tool support has been developed to assist at refactoring. Most recent refactoring implementations usually rely on precondition-based program transformation rules directly applied to the abstract syntax tree (AST) [62]. Nevertheless, the complex nature of those rules, including an interplay between syntactic pattern matching at AST level and semantic constraint checking of properties that crosscut the AST, still makes refactorings prone to potentially produce erroneous results [63].

To tackle the inherent problems of recent refactoring implementations operating at the AST level, graph-based program transformation has been proposed as a promising alternative for concisely and formally specifying and implementing OO refactoring rules in a comprehensive way [24, 37, 135, 137, 138, 140, 144]. Here, the program under consideration is transformed into an abstract and custom-tailored program graph representation that essentially

(i) defines a restricted view on the AST containing only relevant high-level OO program entities
(ii) and adds additional cross-AST dependencies making explicit (static) semantic information being crucial to avoid behavior-scrambling refactorings [137, 139–141, 143].

On this basis, refactorings are formalized in terms of endogenous transformation rules at a program-graph level [37, 140]. However, for a graph-based program refactoring approach to finally become established in practical tools, seamless integration and co-evolution of program source code and the accompanying program graph representation are required.

10.2　Formalization of Object-Oriented Refactorings

Modern Java IDEs aim at assisting object-oriented software development workflows with continuously interleaved co-evolution steps of program editing and program refactoring. Program editing usually comprises manually performed program changes applied by a programmer at the source code level. In contrast, refactorings consist of behavior-preserving program restructuring rules with complex preconditions, usually formulated over an appropriate program abstraction. However, an example of behavior-preserving manual restructuring is the teaching assistant restructuring the iTrust system.

To integrate both steps into a comprehensive program evolution framework, we present a graph-based approach for incremental co-evolution of Java programs. Our approach is based on the concise graph-based representation of Java programs in terms of the program model introduced in Chapter 5. On this basis, a precise formal specification of object-oriented program refactorings can be defined in terms of endogenous graph-transformation rules. To propagate the changes performed by a refactoring on the program model into the software system's implementation, we use Triple Graph Grammars (TGG) for automated incremental synchronization between a program model and the corresponding source code, as discussed in Section 6.2.

Based on three refactoring operations, namely *Create Superclass*, *Pull-Up Method*, and *Move Method*, we illustrate the applicability of graph-based program refactoring and the incremental synchronization as a basis for a comprehensive co-evolution methodology for Java programs. In our experimental evaluation, we compare our approach with the refactoring implementation of the Eclipse IDE [1], uncovering a case that is handled incorrectly by Eclipse but handled correctly by our technique. The experiments show that our framework builds a promising basis for designing, formalizing, and implementing existing and novel OO refactorings for Java-like programming languages comprehensively.

In what follows, we first discuss in Section 10.2.1 the challenges in refactoring Java programs in general but also especially using formal approaches. Afterward, in Section 10.2.2, we introduce the specifications of three refactorings using the notation of graph transformations. In Section 10.2.3, we discuss the propagation of the changes made by refactoring application into a software system's implementation as part of the software system's co-evolution using the TGG transformation presented in Chapter 6. A prototypical implementation of the discussed refactorings is presented in Section 10.2.4. In Section 10.2.5, we evaluate the proposed refactoring approach. Finally, we discuss threats to validity in Section 10.2.6 and conclude on our formalization of OO refactorings in Section 10.2.7.

10.2.1 Refactoring of Java Programs

In this section, we illustrate challenges arising during the evolution and maintenance of Java programs, namely the erosion of a software system's implementation [13]. To overcome the negative effects of code erosion, object-oriented refactorings have been proposed. Refactorings comprise a methodology for incrementally maintaining and improving high-level structural properties of continuously evolving objected-oriented programs while preserving their observable behaviors.

As illustrated by the restructuring example on iTrust in Section 10.1, refactoring aims at restructuring a software system's behavior without changing its external behavior to improve the software system's structure or other non-functional aspects,

---

[1] Website of the IDE: https://www.eclipse.org

e.g., execution times as in the concrete example. At refactoring a software system in terms of manual restructuring operations, developers have to constantly deal with reasoning whether the desired change is possible without altering the behavior or even ending in a not compiling or not executable state. In the concrete case, for every method included in the test suite, it had to be judged whether the method can be executed without the database running. This reasoning about the applicability of planned restructuring can get arbitrary complex and challenging.

At the development of a software system, program evolution usually happens in an ad-hoc manner in terms of small and local edits on certain parts of the source code, whereas subsequent program maintenance steps consist of a predefined set of arbitrary complex precondition-based program transformation rules, specified on an appropriate abstraction of the concrete program such as an Abstract Syntax Tree (AST) [62]. However, using the AST representation as a basis for the design and application of program refactoring rules has two major drawbacks, namely:

1. Usually, object-oriented refactorings are applied to coarse-grained program entities, limited to the class-field-method level, whereas details of method implementations at the statement-expression level are out of scope. As a result, the information represented in the AST is usually far too fine-grained and contains many details being irrelevant for reasoning about refactorings.
2. To reason about behavior preservation of refactorings, additional (static) semantic information, e.g., call dependencies among methods, has to be taken into account. Those dependencies go beyond the pure syntactic structure of programs and, thus, massively crosscut the tree hierarchy of the AST.

In this regard, graph-based program transformation has been proposed as a promising alternative to AST-based refactoring rules [135, 136]. When using graph-based program transformation, the program is transformed into a restricted, more abstract, and thus custom-tailored program model representation that

(i) only contains those program elements being relevant for object-oriented refactorings and, thus, facilitates concise formalization of high-level program transformation operations, and
(ii) makes explicit additional semantic cross-AST (control and data) dependencies among methods and fields, being crucial to reason about behavior preservation of refactorings.

Based on this representation, program transformations are defined in terms of endogenous graph transformation rules [37].

The general applicability of such a graph-based representation for Java programs in combination with graph transformation rules to express program refactorings has already been shown, e.g., in [24, 138, 140]. However, those existing works leave open how to obtain a graph-based representation from the source code of a given Java program and, conversely, how to propagate changes applied to that graph presentation back into the source code.

As our running example illustrates, Java programs continuously undergo interleaved edit operations on the source code and consecutive maintenance steps in terms of refactoring rule applications. Hence, there is a strong necessity for a comprehensive graph-based program refactoring framework to include an automated mechanism for incrementally synchronizing changes both of the source code, as well as its respective program model representation to keep both views consistent. In particular, an appropriate synchronization mechanism must be bidirectional in the sense that arbitrarily interleaved changes in terms of source code edits, as well as in terms of program model transformations are continuously propagated between both representations in a consistency-preserving and automated manner.

Here, we employ *Triple Graph Grammars* (TGG) [160], a declarative way of expressing bidirectional graph transformation rules, to facilitate incremental synchronization between the AST and the program model representation of evolving Java programs. Our implementation is based on eMoflon, a graph-transformation engine incorporating support for TGG [162], and discussed in detail in Chapter 6.

In the next section, we show how to formalize refactorings using graph transformation rules. Afterward, we solve the open problem of propagating changes made by refactoring operations into the implementation through using the bidirectional exogenous graph transformation rules introduced in Chapter 6 to formalize the correspondences between Java source code and its graph-based abstraction concisely.

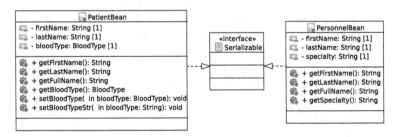

Figure 10.2 Class diagram showing an excerpt of the `PatientBean` and `PersonnelBean`

10.2.2 Program Refactoring based on Graph Transformation

Program models, such as our program model introduced in Chapter 5, are designed to contain sufficient information for reasoning about particular program transformation scenarios such as refactorings. To this end, program models provide an appropriate abstraction layer for an intuitive and precise specification of program modifications using declarative graph transformation rules. Here, the declarative nature of a rule means that it only describes preconditions (patterns) under which the transformation should be executed and how the expected result is supposed to look like but leaves open how to actually check and execute those rules on a given input program.

As already mentioned in Section 10.2.1, object-oriented refactorings are an ideal example for predefined program transformation operations which can be effectively specified by program model patterns on the type graph. Those graph patterns are supposed to identify all places in a program that may be refactored. Moreover, graph transformation rules further comprise specifications of the actual program modifications corresponding to refactoring operations. The theoretical framework of graph transformations provides a declarative, rule-based technique for modifying graph-based models such as program models [144]. In particular, a graph transformation rule consists of a left-hand side (LHS) and a right-hand side (RHS), both constituting typed graphs, i.e., program models in our case, conforming to a given type graph of the underlying modeling language. In this thesis, we use the type graph introduced in Chapter 5 to specify transformation rules that express refactorings. The application of a graph transformation rule on a given input program model consists of

1. finding a match of the LHS within the given input program model, i.e., an occurrence of the respective graph pattern specified by the LHS, and
2. transforming the input program model by replacing the match by an image of the RHS which essentially imposes the deletion and creation of particular nodes and edges, thus yielding the output program model.

In addition, the LHS and/or RHS part may contain negative application conditions (NAC), i.e., graph patterns which are not allowed in the input and/or output graph, respectively, for a successful transformation rule application. Intuitively, the LHS and RHS of a graph transformation rule can be conceived as preconditions and postconditions, limiting the applicability of the graph transformation operation specified by that rule. Generally, the precondition has to be fulfilled by a given input graph for the transformation to become applicable. Similarly, the postcondition has to be fulfilled by the transformation's resulting output

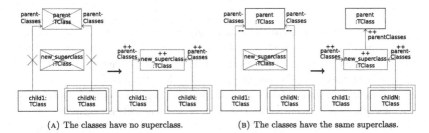

(A) The classes have no superclass. (B) The classes have the same superclass.

Figure 10.3 Schematic representation of a *Create Superclass* refactoring – Left-hand side and right-hand side

graph. In what follows, we show how this notation can be used to specify refactoring operations based on three examples.

Create Superclass Refactoring

The first refactoring considered by us is the *Create Superclass* refactoring [18]. For example, the iTrust system contains different kinds of users. Among others, these are patients and personnel such as doctors. In the implementation, data about patients is represented in terms of the class `PatientBean`, which we already investigated in more detail in Chapter 9. Similarly, as for patients, data about personnel is stored in a `PersonnelBean`. As shown in Figure 10.2, both beans implement the `Serializable` interface but do not have a common parent in which shared functionality could be implemented. The *Create Superclass* refactoring specifies the conditions under which such a common parent can be created.

In general, *Create Superclass* is used to create a common superclass for a set of classes that share a considerable amount of functionality [18]. This refactoring can be seen as the first step towards an improved program structure. A new common superclass of these classes sharing functionality is created, that can then be filled with shared data or functionality.

Figure 10.3 shows a schematic representation of how the *Create Superclass* refactoring is performed, considering two starting situations in the program model. The black elements (without additional annotations) appearing in both the LHS and the RHS, correspond to those entities within a given program model whose matches are part of the rule context but remain unaffected by the program model transformation. In contrast, red elements (annotated with – –) in the LHS (on the left in Figure 10.3 are deleted, while green elements (annotated with + +) in the RHS (on the right in Figure 10.3) are created during rule application. The crossed-out blue edge in the LHS represents a negative application condition. The patterns within cascaded boxes on both sides are recurring patterns, i.e., those patterns might occur zero or more times in a valid match (respectively output) of the rule. The nodes of the LHS and RHS graphs are identified using the notational style name:type, where name is a unique identifier of an object at the level of program instance entities and type is the node type in the type graph to which the object refers.

The semantic meaning of the two refactoring rules is as follows. The child classes either have to have the same superclass in the program model or none of them has a superclass. From a technical point of view, each Java class has a superclass except for java.lang.Object, which is the uppermost parent of all classes. However, an explicit generalization of the class Object is not necessary in Java programs.

In case the refactoring's preconditions and postconditions (see below) are fulfilled, a new class new_superclass will be created which becomes the superclass of the child classes in the set classes, containing child1 and all classes that have been matched to childN (classes := [child1] ∪ childN). Note that a *Create Superclass* refactoring does not necessarily represent a valid refactoring. It marks merely a part of the input program where it is looked for a possible refactoring operation.

In addition to the conditions shown in Figure 10.3, the following precondition has to be fulfilled for a *Create Superclass* instance:

– The classes contained in classes are implementing the same superclass. Note that classes with no explicit superclasses reference in Java are implementing java.lang.Object. However, specifying this superclass explicitly in the source code is a developer decision that does not influence the conditions for *Create Superclass*.

Additionally, the result of a *Create Superclass* has to fulfill the following postconditions:

1. Each class in [child1] ∪ childN has an inheritance reference (parent Classes) to the class new_superclass.
2. In case the classes in [child1] ∪ childN had an explicit inheritance reference to a superclass parent before the refactoring, their new superclass new_superclass has an inheritance reference to this parent.

Figure 10.4 shows a UML class diagram focusing on the classes PatientBean and PersonnelBean, that has been extracted from the iTrust implementation after the application of a *Create Superclass* refactoring. Their new superclass UserBean has

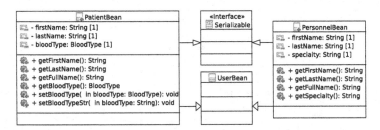

Figure 10.4 `PatientBean` and `PersonnelBean` after the application of a *Create Superclass* refactoring

been inserted by the refactoring but does not contain any features, yet. Also, the two generalizations of `UserBean` have been added by the refactoring. While the classes `PatientBean` and `PersonnelBean` have `public` visibility in the extracted UML model, the `UserBean` is shown with `default` visibility as currently no visibilities are considered in the specification of the refactoring. Also, the name of the created superclass has not been discussed yet as well as the package containing this new class. All three properties are not necessary for checking the applicability of the refactoring but are required when it comes to propagating the changes into the source code.

Figure 10.5 shows a concrete realization of the two refactoring rules using the Henshin notation. In this notation, the LHS and RHS of the rules are combined into one single representation, using a similar notation for create (labeled «`create`» instead of ++), delete (labeled «`delete`» instead of −−) and NACs (labeled «`forbid`»). For simplicity, only rules considering exactly two child classes are shown. In these two Henshin rules, we added conditions and patterns to handle the properties neglected until now, e.g., regarding the visibility of the created superclass.

libraries: We can only create a superclass for classes that we can modify but not for classes that are defined within a library. In the program model, the property `tLib` is set to `true` for types that are defined within a library. Accordingly, the Henshin rules contain conditions for assuring that `tLib` is set to `false` on all nodes representing types that will be changed by the refactoring.

packages: The new superclass should be added to a package. While this could be handled in the two rules identically, differentiating allows a more precise outcome regarding the aggregation of coherent functionality. As the child classes can be in different packages and the new class is common to all of them and not only to a single child class, in the case we already have a superclass, the package this

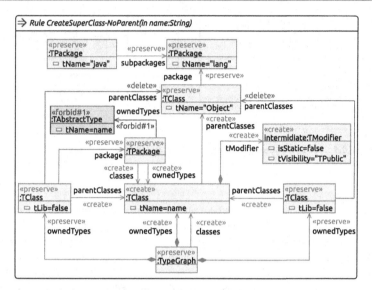

(A) For classes with no explicit parent.

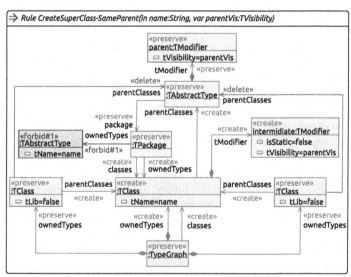

(B) For classes with the same parent.

Figure 10.5 Model-transformation rules for *Create Superclass* refactoring including preconditions

superclass resides in is selected. If we do not have a common parent, this is not possible. In this case, we select randomly the package of one of the child classes.

superclass name: In both rules, the desired name of the new superclass can be specified using a name parameter specified on the rules. The name of the created superclass will be set to this name specified before matching by the developer. Also, the NAC from Figure 10.3, ensuring that the class to be created does not already exist, is detailed using this name parameter. It is checked that no type with the name specified in the parameter (name) is defined in the package to which the new class will be added.

default parent: Figure 10.3a specifies a *Create Superclass* refactoring for classes that do not have an explicit superclass, meaning that these immediately extend java.lang.Object. As in Java this does not have to be specified but can be specified, in the program model this relation is made explicit in all cases. Accordingly, Figure 10.3a checks whether the child classes extend java.lang. Object instead of the NAC specified in Figure 10.3a. This is necessary as the next conditions require a differentiation between the two cases.

visibilities: At setting the visibility of the newly created class, we have to ensure that this class is accessible for all child classes. If the child classes have an

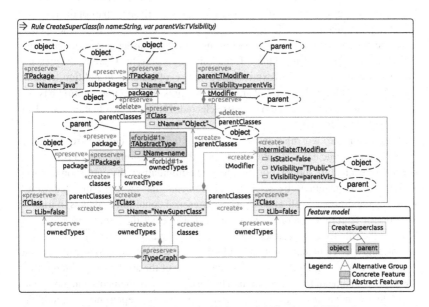

Figure 10.6 *Move Method* refactoring specified as variability-based (VB) rule

explicit parent, the new superclass will get the visibility that is set for this parent. As the new class resides in the same package as the old superclass, using this visibility, it is accessible for all child classes. In case the child classes have no explicit parent, the new superclass is located in the package of one of the child classes. In this case, we cannot easily give such a guarantee for accessibility. If one of the other child classes is in a different package, `public` is required while `protected` would be sufficient when all child classes are in the same package. For simplicity, when there is no explicit superclass, the visibility `public` will be used.

While the two discussed versions of the *Create Superclass* refactoring are very similar, it is still necessary to specify these in two different rules. Also, our discussion has shown that there is the possibility to specify additional more detailed versions of this refactoring. However, a user should not have to understand all of these different versions of the refactoring and select the correct one. Here, variability-based (VB) transformation rules allow specifying multiple transformation rules that share common parts but also have individual parts within one transformation rule, reusing the shared parts [262].

Figure 10.6 shows such a VB rule, that combines the two versions of the *Create Superclass* refactoring. This rule has a base part that is always a part of the rule, and variable parts that are specific to one of the two rules in Figure 10.5. The specific parts are annotated with presence conditions, shown as dashed circles in the figure, specifying in which variant of this VB rule this part is present. Thereby, the presence conditions can contain logical expressions over a set of features. In addition, a feature model gives additional constraints over the features. In our case, the rule has two features of which exactly one has to be selected. Here, the two features stand for the two rules we have.

In the end, the two rules shown in Figure 10.5 can be derived from this VB rule. Therefore, one has to iterate over all possible feature combinations concerning the VB rule's feature model. For each feature combination, the corresponding rule variant can be generated by selecting all elements that are not annotated with a presence condition as well as those whose presence condition evaluates to true for the current feature selection. For example, if we select the feature `object`, we will get the rule for child classes having no explicit parent, shown in Figure 10.3a. Accordingly, all elements annotated with `object` will be added to the rule variant, e.g., the packages with the names `java` and `lang` or the attribute condition setting the expected name of the old superclass to „`Object`". All elements annotated with `parent` will not be added to the rule variant, e.g., the node representing the modifier of the old superclass.

When such a VB rule is applied to the program model, first, the base part of the rule is matched. If there are matches for the base part, these matches are extended to all possible variants of the rule. Accordingly, we get the same matches as we would match the two rules shown in Figure 10.5. For each of the matches, the deletions and additions specified in the rule variant can be performed. Accordingly, VB rules can be used to check the refactoring for all possible variations of the rule and to execute one of the possible outcomes.

Although *Create Superclass* is a refactoring that only requires a few preconditions, we include this operation to demonstrate that our synchronization mechanism can cope with newly created class nodes in the program model during backward transformation. Since those endogenous refactoring transformation rules only modify the program model (in the first place), we do not (yet) require bidirectional synchronization for this step.

Pull-Up Method Refactoring

In this section, we discuss the *Pull-Up Method* refactoring [18] as the second refactoring considered by us. When looking at the iTrust system after applying the *Create Superclass* refactoring, shown in Figure 10.4, we notice that the `PatientBean` and `PersonnelBean` contain similar functionality. For example, both contain a method (`getFullName`) to calculate the full name from the first and last name of a patient or personnel. As the idea of creating a shared superclass for these two classes was to implement shared functionality there, it is a good idea to implement the currently duplicated functionality in this new superclass. By performing such a restructuring, the amount of duplicated code can be reduced and the risk for independent evolution of code duplicated can be lowered. The *Pull-Up Method* refactoring specifies how such a restructuring can be performed systematically and which conditions for applicability have to be considered. For example, the proposed pull-up of `getFullName` is not immediately possible, as this method has to access the getters `getFirstName` and `getLastName` that are defined on the child classes.

As motivation for the challenges that come with this refactoring, consider the synthetic Java program in Listing 10.1. The Java program initially consists of four classes: A, B, C and E, assuming that all classes reside in the same package. The classes A, B and C are in the following inheritance relation:

- Class B extends class A.
- Class C extends class B.

In this inheritance hierarchy, methods m and member variables `mult` are defined as follows:

```java
public class A {
    int mult = 3 ;

    public int m(int a) {
        return mult * a;
    }
}

public class B extends A {
    int mult = 2;
}

public class C extends B {
    public int m(int a){
        return mult * a;
    }
}

public class E {
    public void main (String[] args) {
        A a = new A();
        System.out.println(a.m(2)); // output: 6

        C c = new C( );
        System.out.println(c.m(2)); // output: 4
    }
}
```

Listing 10.1 Example Java program containing the possibility for a *Pull-Up Method* refactoring

- Class A implements a method m which receives as argument an integer value a and returns the value resulting from multiplying this value with the value 3 of the member variable mult.
- Class B inherits the implementation of method m from class A, but redefines the value of mult to 2.
- In contrast, class C overrides the implementation of method m, but (accidentally) uses the same method body as the one in class A.

While the two implementations of m are clones, both implementations of method m return different values as C.m accesses the redefined value of the member variable mult in class B. These differing behaviors are demonstrated by the main method in

```
1    . . .
2    // class D has been added
3    public class D extends B {
4        public int m(int a){
5            int tmp = 0;
6            for (int i = 0; i < mult ; i ++){
7                tmp += a ;
8            }
9            return tmp ;
10       }
11   }
12
13   public class E {
14       public void main (String[] args) {
15           A a = new A();
16           System.out.println(a.m(2)); // output: 6
17
18           C c = new C();
19           System.out.println(c.m(2)); // output: 4
20
21           D d = new D();
22           System.out.println(d.m(2)); // output: 4
23       }
24   }
```

Listing 10.2 Example Java program after evolution

class E, calling both A.m and C.m with the same parameter value 2 which produces different results.

As an evolution step, assume a developer to insert a further class D, shown in Listing 10.2, which also extends class B and overrides the implementation of method m, similarly to class C. To demonstrate the execution of the newly inserted method implementation, a corresponding call of D.m has been added to E.main. While D.m uses an alternative way of computing the multiplication, the method body of D.m implements the same functionality as C.m. As a result, we have two sibling classes implementing the same methods with equivalent behaviors. Hence, as a consequence of program evolution, the source code may exhibit undesirable decay, e.g., duplicated/redundant code in this example, which potentially obstructs maintenance and comprehensibility throughout subsequent development steps.

For instance, as motivated before, the *Pull-Up Method* refactoring proposed by Fowler in [18] is concerned with situations such as observed for the example in

```
1    . . .
2    public class B extends A {
3        int mult = 2;
4
5        public int m(int a){
6            int tmp = 0;
7            for (int i = 0; i < mult ; i ++){
8                tmp += a ;
9            }
10           return tmp ;
11       }
12   }
13
14   public class C extends B {
15   }
16
17   public class D extends B {
18   }
19
20   public class E {
21       public void main (String[] args) {
22           A a = new A();
23           System.out.println(a.m(2)); // output: 6
24
25           C c = new C();
26           System.out.println(c.m(2)); // output: 4
27
28           D d = new D();
29           System.out.println(d.m(2)); // output: 4
30       }
31   }
```

Listing 10.3 Example Java program after the application of a *Pull-Up Method* refactoring for method m

Listing 10.2 after inserting class D. In particular, developers may execute a *Pull-Up Method* refactoring in a consecutive maintenance step to eliminate code duplication. As the concurrent implementations of method m in the classes C and D are semantically equivalent, it is possible to move one of their implementations into superclass B and to erase the redundant code from C and D. The result of this refactoring operation is shown in Listing 10.3.

For such program transformations to constitute correct refactorings, several preconditions must be met to ensure behavior preservation. For instance, before applying *Pull-Up Method*, it has to be ensured that any call to the affected method is resolved in exactly the same way before and after the refactoring. In our example, the results of all three calls to the refactored method m in E.main yield the same results as before the refactoring. In contrast, consider the slightly adapted implementation of E.main in Listing 10.4, where the *Pull-Up Method* refactoring is not executed yet. Here, method m is called on object b of type B instead of D. In this case, a pull-up of method m from C to B must be neglected as it would alter the result of calling m on b as m would access a different field after the refactoring.

An example of a graph transformation rule for the *Pull-Up Method* refactoring is shown in Figure 10.7 using the same notation as for the *Create Superclass* refactoring. This rule is a simplified version of the *Pull-Up Method* refactoring rule specified on our type graph.

```
1  public class E {
2      public void main (String[] args) {
3          A a = new A ();
4          System.out.println(a.m(2)); // output: 6
5
6          B b = new B();
7          System.out.println(b.m(2)); // output: 6
8
9          C c = new C();
10         System.out.println(c.m(2)); // output: 4
11     }
12  }
```

Listing 10.4 Example Java Class Containing an Access Prohibiting a *Pull-Up Method* (PUM) Refactoring

To summarize, the rule in Figure 10.7 is interpreted as follows: For a *Pull-Up Method* refactoring to be applicable on a given input program model, there must exist a superclass with at least one (but possibly more) subclass(es) child1...N, each having a method represented by the corresponding method definition(s) definition1...N. Those definitions are supposed to refer to method implementations in sibling sub-classes, but having equivalent functionality.

In general, checking whether a given set of methods implement equivalent functionality, is undecidable and, consequently, out of scope of preconditions for object-oriented refactoring rules. In contrast, declaring a given set of sibling methods as equivalent is usually obliged to the developer before invoking the refactoring operation. Hence, we require those methods matched by definition1...N to share the same signature signature. The NAC edge between parent and signature in the LHS further ensures that no method with the same signature already exists in the parent which would, otherwise, obstruct the pull-up operation.

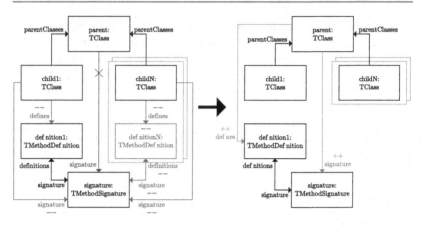

Figure 10.7 Transformation rule of a *Pull-Up Method* refactoring

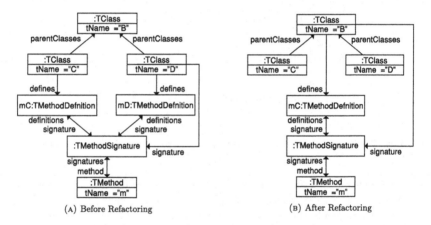

Figure 10.8 Program model before and after a *Pull-Up Method* refactoring

When executing this transformation rule, all method definitions (including all their connections) except for one are deleted from the sibling sub-classes, and the preserved method definition1 (together with its `signature`) is moved (pulled up) into the class `parent`.

Figure 10.8 shows a concrete example for an application of the *Pull-Up Method* rule to the input program model corresponding to the source code in Listing 10.2. For convenience, Figure 10.8 only contains a relevant excerpt of both program models.

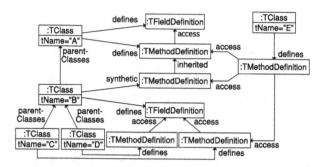

Figure 10.9 Excerpt of the program model of the program in Listing 10.4

As the LHS of the refactoring rule in Figure 10.7 matches the input program model in Figure 10.8a, the *Pull-Up Method* rule is applicable to this program. As a result, one of the method definitions is deleted and the definition and signature of the common method m are attached to the common superclass B. The resulting output program model shown in Figure 10.8b corresponds to the source code in Listing 10.3.

When considering the modifications shown in Listing 10.4, cf. the corresponding program model excerpt in Figure 10.9, the refactoring rule is not applicable anymore on this program model. To simplify the shown program model excerpt, instances of TAccess are visualized as an edge labeled access from the source to the target of

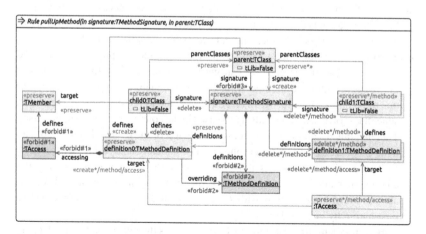

Figure 10.10 Model-transformation rule for *Pull-Up Method* refactoring including preconditions

the access. This inapplicability is because that method B.m is accessed now, which is inherited from the class A. A pull up of m from class C and D to class B, therefore, changes the program behavior as m accesses different instances (and thus values) of field mult before and after the pull-up operation. Such a potential violation of behavior preservation is not directly detectable on a plain AST, whereas it is explicitly recognizable by investigating the additional access edges in the program model.

Again, the graphic representation of the of *Pull-Up Method* rule in Figure 10.7 does not include all necessary preconditions but rather covers a simplified version for convenience. However, the missing parts may be represented similarly. For example, as illustrated by the case of an infeasible *Pull-Up Method* in Listing 10.4 (Figure 10.9, respectively), the superclass may inherit a method with a similar signature as the one being pull-upped. This may also lead to altered program behavior if the inherited method is called from another class. As this inherited method is mapped to a different signature object within the program model, we have to explicitly handle this case by an additional graph pattern. The example in Listing 10.4 shows that additional AST-crossing edges for representing static semantic dependencies among program entities are necessary to neglect unsound refactorings.

Figure 10.10 shows a Henshin rule for the *Pull-Up Method* refactoring including such additional application conditions:

libraries: As for the *Create Superclass* refactoring, only classes that do not come from a library can be modified (tLib = false).

accesses: The preserved method definition is not allowed to access any other member of the class it is defined in before the refactoring («forbid#1»). This NAC is necessary as these members are not accessible from the superclass.

overriding: The violating access from the example is prevented by NAC «forbid#2». In the end, we can get this violation every time a superclass of parent defines a method with the same signature (signature) as the one to be pulled upwards (definition0). Due to polymorphism, the child's superclass (parent) could always be used in the context of its own superclasses. Thereby, this usage might contain an invocation of the overridden method realizing signature. As polymorphism is not statically analyzable, we forbid all *Pull-Up Method* refactorings in which the method to be pulled upwards overrides an implementation from a superclass of parent. As this is semantically equivalent to overriding a method with the same signature, we can avoid specifying a type-hierarchy in the rule.

already implemented: The third NAC in the rule is the one already considered in Figure 10.7. This NAC is expressed identically in NAC «forbid#3».

When applying the *Pull-Up Method* refactoring, it is not sufficient only to delete all implementations of the child classes except one. For every deleted implementation, the incoming accesses have to be redirected to the preserved method definition. This redirect is expressed on the lower right of the rule.

Comparable to the *Pull-Up Method* refactoring, a *Pull-Up Field* refactoring can be specified. As in Java fields hide fields of superclasses instead of overriding these as methods do, this refactoring would require fewer preconditions. To be more precise, «forbid#2» would not be necessary, as the original field would still be accessible by using the super qualifier of Java.

Move Method Refactoring

The last refactoring considered by us is the *Move Method* refactoring [18]. We conceive this refactoring as an essential refactoring, as it has been shown that *Move Method* refactorings are considerably effective in improving class responsibility assignment (CRA) [263] in flawed object-oriented program designs [264].

An example application context for a *Move Method* refactoring on iTrust is given in Figure 10.11. This figure shows a program model excerpt focusing on the iTrust source code shown in Listings 10.5, 10.6, and 10.7. These source code fragments show relevant parts of the implementation of consistency checks at storing an office visit in the iTrust system.

```
1   package edu.ncsu.csc.itrust.model.officeVisit;
2
3   public class OfficeVisitValidator extends POJOValidator {
4
5       public void validate(OfficeVisit obj) throws FormValidationException
        {
6           String patientMID = obj.getPatientMID();
7           ...
8           errorList.addIfNotNull(checkFormat("Patient MID", patientMID,
                ValidationFormat.NPMID, false));
9           ...
10      }
11  }
```

Listing 10.5 Source code excerpt from the iTrust class `OfficeVisitValidator`

As soon as an office visit should be stored, the `validate` method of the `OfficeVisitValidator` is executed to check the validity of the office visit entry. An excerpt of the relevant source code is shown in Listing 10.5. Among others, this method contains a check whether the MID of the patient meets the expected format. For this check the method `checkFormat`, defined in the super-class of the class `OfficeVisitValidator`, is called. Among others, in this

call, the office visit object and the expected format as defined in the enumeration
ValidationFormat are passed to the method.

```
 1   package edu.ncsu.csc.itrust.model;
 2
 3   public class POJOValidator {
 4
 5       abstract public void validate(T obj) throws FormValidationException;
 6
 7       protected String checkFormat(String name, String value,
             ValidationFormat format, boolean isNullable) {
 8           String errorMessage = name + ": " + format.getDescription();
 9           if (value == null || "".equals(value))
10               return isNullable ? "" : errorMessage;
11           else if (format.getRegex().matcher(value).matches())
12               return "";
13           else
14               return errorMessage;
15       }
16   }
```

Listing 10.6 Source code excerpt from the iTrust class POJOValidator

The implementation of the method checkFormat is shown in Listing 10.6.
This method reads a regular expression specifying the expected format and an error
message from the given instance of ValidationFormat. If the regular expression does not match, the error message is returned otherwise an empty string is
returned. The implementation of the enumeration ValidationFormat is shown
in Listing 10.7.

As the method checkFormat accesses besides methods from the Java standard library only members from the enumeration ValidationFormat and even
not a single member from its own class, considering the CRA problem, moving
this method to the enumeration could be a good idea. The conditions for such a
move operation to be behavior preserving are specified as part of a *Move Method*
refactoring.

Figure 10.12 shows the essential parts of a rule for *Move Method* refactorings
defined on our type graph, using the same notation as for the previous refactorings.
The rule takes a source class source, a target class target, a method signature
signature, and a method definition realizing the signature, deletes the containment arrow between source class and the pair of definition and signature (red arrows
annotated with --) and creates new containment arrows from the target class (green
arrow annotated with ++), only if such an arrow to the signature not already
exists before rule application. The latter precondition is expressed by a *forbidden*

```
1     package edu.ncsu.csc.itrust.model;
2
3     public enum ValidationFormat {
4
5         NPMID("[0-8][0-9]{0,9}", "1-10 digit number not beginning with 9"),
6
7
8         private Pattern regex;
9         private String description;
10
11        ValidationFormat(String regex, String errorMessage) {
12            this.regex = Pattern.compile(regex);
13            this.description = errorMessage;
14        }
15
16        public Pattern getRegex() {
17            return regex;
18        }
19
20        public String getDescription() {
21            return description;
22        }
23    }
```

Listing 10.7 Source code excerpt from the iTrust class `ValidationFormat`

(crossed-out) arrow. For a comprehensive list of all necessary preconditions, we refer to [69].

Besides preconditions, for refactoring operations to yield a correct result, it must satisfy further postconditions to be evaluated after rule application, especially concerning accessibility constraints as declared in the original program, i.e., member accesses like method calls in the original program must be preserved after refactoring [24]. As an example, Listing 10.8 shows a (simplified) postcondition for the *Move Method* rule using the OCL notation. The postcondition is applied to every class member (`TMember`) in the program and checks whether the declared accessibility of the member is at least as generous as required, based on the canonical ordering `private < default < protected < public`. For the calculation of a class member's required access modifier, it utilizes the helper-function `requiredAccessibility(TMember)` [69].

context TMember
  post: **self**.tModifier.tVisibility >= requiredAccessibility(**self**)

Listing 10.8 Postcondition of a *Move Method* refactoring concerning the suitability of member visibilities

For instance, if the *Move Method* refactoring is applied to POJOValidator, the method checkFormat violates this postcondition, as the call originating from the method validate, that is defined in a class from another package, requires accessibility public, whereas the declared accessibility is protected. Instead of immediately rejecting refactorings like this *Move Method* refactoring, we can

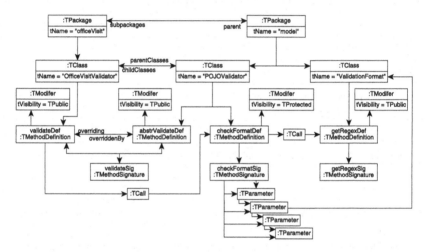

Figure 10.11 Excerpt from the program model focusing on the iTrust source code excerpts in Listings 10.6, 10.7, and 10.5

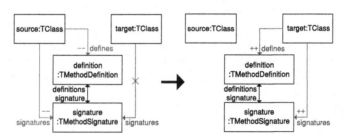

Figure 10.12 Model-transformation rule for a *Move Method* refactoring

use an accessibility-repair operation for each member violating the postcondition which therefore causes a relaxation of the visibilities [146]. Such a repair operation sets the violating visibility to the lowest required visibility. However, this repair is not always possible as relaxations may lead to incorrect refactorings altering the original program semantics, e.g., due to method overriding/overloading [69].

In contrast, imagine a refactoring that moves a method only having accesses from members defined in one single class to this specific class. This refactoring would satisfy the postcondition for any original visibility as the required accessibility becomes `private`, whereas it had to be at least the `default` visibility before to allow access. In those cases, we may also apply the repair operation, now leading to a reduction of the visibility.

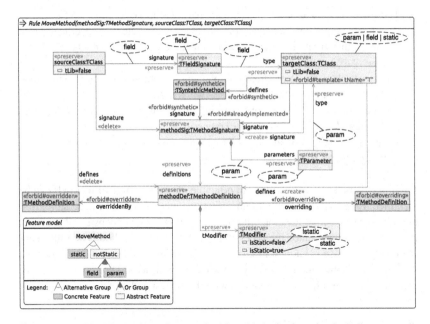

Figure 10.13 Model-transformation rule for *Move Method* refactoring including preconditions

Besides the refactoring being behavior preserving, the refactoring has to be possible, meaning that all information accessed has to be accessible from the target class, too. This is not given for every target of a move operation. Figure 10.13 shows a Henshin VB rule of a *Move Method* refactoring that includes both, behavior-preserving constraints and constraints ensuring the move to be possible in terms of compatible target classes.

The rule's central part is the method definition (`methodDef`) and method signature (`methodSig`) pair in the rule's center. The definition represents the implementation of the method that should be moved to a different class. The node `sourceClass` represents the class currently defining the method and the node `targetClass` the class the method should be moved to. The movement is expressed by deleting the references between the `sourceClass` and the method (`methodSig`/`methodDef`) and adding these references for the `targetClass`.

For the movement of a method to be possible (but not necessarily behavior-preserving), some conditions have to hold:

1. The source class and target class are not part of a library (`tLib = false`).
2. As template types only serve as a placeholder for concrete type specifications in variables, the target class cannot be a template type («`forbid`»#`template tName="T"`).
3. The target class does not already implement a method with the same method signature («`forbid`»#`alreadyImplemented`).
4. The method is not overridden or overriding another method («`forbid`»#`overridden` and «`forbid`»#`overriding`).
5. There is no call from another class to the method through a sub-class of `sourceClass` («`forbid`»#`synthetic`).

Based on the presented conditions, in principle, possible moves of methods can be identified. However, for a correct refactoring, the method has to be accessible from the scope of its original location after the refactoring [18]. We consider three cases in which we can guarantee the accessibility of the moved method. The fulfillment of already one case is enough to guarantee reachability. We assign one feature of the VB rule's feature model to every of the considered cases. The patterns of every case in the rule are the ones annotated with the corresponding features. The cases considered by us are:

static: Static methods do not have an object as execution context. For this reason, static methods can be moved to every class.
param: Parameters specify parts of a method's execution context. For this reason, the instances of the method's parameters are accessible from the source class and the method can be moved to the types of parameters.
field: As for parameters, through fields, the method stays accessible in its original context as the method can be invoked on the field.

In this section, we have shown the formalization of three refactoring operations on the type graph used in this thesis. Next, we discuss the application of these refactorings to Java programs as part of the GRaViTY framework.

10.2.3 Co-Evolution due to Refactoring Application

While tailoring the graph-based representation of Java programs, one of the central questions is how to determine an appropriate level of abstraction for the program model to meet the particular program transformation scenario. In some cases, it may be even convenient to directly use the original AST as a program representation. ASTs have the advantage that they contain a complete representation of the syntactic elements of the program at any level of granularity. Moreover, numerous tools provide out-of-the-box solutions to modify programs at the AST level [265, 266]. Furthermore, Eclipse and Java compilers have their own Java AST representation, too [267]. Using these tools, it is possible to synchronize the Java source code and its AST representation without the risk of losing information.

Nevertheless, in application scenarios where the program modifications involve the analysis of complex inter-dependencies, as shown in our refactoring examples, AST may suffer from being too detailed for an efficient transformation specification. In those cases, a custom-tailored program model representation such as the type graph presented in Chapter 5 is desirable. However, transforming programs into abstract representations necessarily involves the loss of program information which obstructs the backpropagation of changes corresponding to program model transformations into the affected part of the source code and, vice versa, in case of source code edits. Hence, an appropriate synchronization mechanism is required to incrementally ensure consistency between both the source code and the program representation of Java programs. As described in Section 6.2, bidirectional graph transformation provides such techniques.

In what follows, we discuss the suitability of this bidirectional graph transformation for propagating the changes made by the three refactoring operations into the source code. The suitability to update the program model in case of changes in the implementation has already been discussed in Chapter 6.

Create Superclass Refactoring Changes made by a *Create Superclass* refactoring can be propagated by our synchronization approach as packages, classes, and inheritance relations are expressed on the same level of abstraction in the implementation and the program model. As no elements with abstractions, e.g., method definitions, are touched by this refactoring, there is no risk for the loss of information. Accordingly, we can always propagate *Create Superclass* refac-torings from the program model into the implementation.

Pull-Up Method Refactoring For the *Pull-Up Method* refactoring, there is a risk that the body of the method definition that has been pulled up is lost. However, the presented TGG has been designed to preserve the bodies of method and field definitions. This property has been discussed in detail in Section 6.2.2. Accord-ingly, the synchronization of changes made by a *Pull-Up Method* refactoring is possible without issues.

Move Method Refactoring As for the *Pull-Up Method* refactoring, there is the risk for the *Move Method* refactorings that the information about the body of the method definition that will be moved is lost. For the same reasons as before, this risk is mitigated in the TGG used for synchronization.

The next risk is that the implementation of the method cannot be adapted to the new location, meaning that there can be errors in the way how the data used in the method is accessed. Here, we have to consider two cases, static methods, and non-static methods. As static methods cannot access data specific to objects, an adaption of the accesses is not necessary and the propagation of these is possible. For non-static methods there might be the need to adapt the method, e.g., if the method is moved to a parameter type, this parameter has to be replaced by a parameter providing access to the previous owning class. Such adaptions on the statement level cannot be specified on the program model and therefore not be propagated by the TGG. The method would be propagated with an unchanged method body, which eventually has to be adapted by a developer.

Such cases can be handled by refactoring implementations working on an AST or model having similar granularity, e.g., the Eclipse refactoring implementation. By combining such an implementation with our approach, we can benefit from both approaches. We can have the detailed preconditions and postconditions of our approach together with the possibility of detailed adaptions on the statement level.

To conclude, we can propagate all refactorings to the implementation without the loss of information. However, for the *Move Method* refactoring there might be situations that require additional changes by developers after the synchronization. For all other refactorings, no manual changes are required.

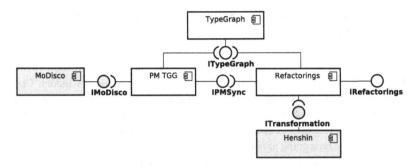

Figure 10.14 Component diagram of the refactoring implementation and integration into GRaViTY

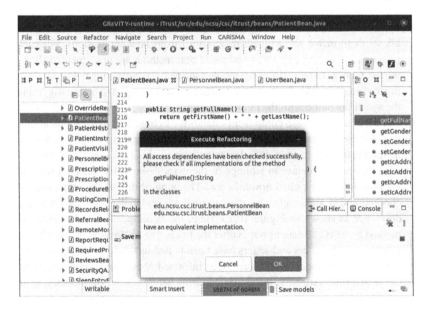

Figure 10.15 Presentation of a refactoring in the GRaViTY refactoring UI

10.2.4 Tool Support for the Application of Formalized Refactorings

Our implementation of the refactorings relies on the graph-transformation engine Henshin [26] for the execution of the refactoring on the program model. Currently we support the refactorings *Pull-Up Method*, *Create Superclass*, and *Move Method*. Figure 10.14 shows a component diagram of our refactoring implementation. The refactorings are specified within the `Refactorings` component as Henshin rules on the type graph of our program model. The `Refactoring` component uses the Henshin transformation engine (`Henshin` component) to match possible refactoring opportunities and to execute refactorings. After the execution of a refactoring on the program model, implementation of our synchronization in the `PM TGG` component is used to propagate the changes into the MoDisco model and to generate the refactored source code from this model. The refactoring implementation can be used in two ways:

API: The `Refactorings` component exports an API (`IRefactorings`), that allows us to match and execute refactorings from Java applications. For each refactoring a `isApplicible` and `perform` methods are implemented allowing us to check if a refactoring is possible and behavior-preserving before modifying the program model. Afterward, the change can be inspected before triggering the synchronization with the implementation.

UI: The `Refactorings` component extends the Eclipse IDE with graphical support for executing refactorings. A developer can for example right-click on a method in the source code and select to pull this method upwards. Then methods with the same signature in siblings of the class defining the selected method are proposed to be pulled upwards, too. The applicability of the refactoring is checked and if applicable, the affected methods and classes are shown to the developer as shown in Figure 10.15. Here, the developer selected to pull the method `getFullName` upwards after the fields `firstName` and `lastName` as well as their getters and setters have been pulled upwards to the parent. Otherwise, the developer would have been informed about the inapplicability of the refactoring. After the developer confirms her selection, the refactoring is executed.

The presented tool support allows developers to effectively refactor software systems as part of the GRaViTY development approach.

Table 10.1 Evaluation results for the refactorings

Test Case		Eclipse	GRaViTY Refactorings	
Refactoring	Elements	Success	Success	Duration in ms
1	csc	8	yes	yes	48
2	csc	8	yes	yes	46
3	pum	10	yes	yes	211
4	pum	7	yes	yes	44
5	pum	5	yes	yes	45
6	pum	5	yes	yes	44
7	csc	8	yes	yes	50
8	csc	8	yes	yes	46
9	pum	8	yes	yes	46
10	pum	8	yes	yes	45
11	csc	10	yes	yes	26
12	pum	10	yes	yes	289
13	pum	10	yes	yes	46
14	csc+pum	5	yes	yes	260
15	csc+pum	5	yes	yes	286
16	csc	146	yes	yes	149
17	csc	146	yes	yes	960
18	23csc+24pum	48	yes	yes	3185
19	pum	11	**no**	yes	63

10.2.5 Evaluation of the Refactoring Technique

To demonstrate the feasibility of our technique, we created an evaluation framework called *Automated Refactoring Test Environment* (ARTE) [131]. ARTE provides test cases consisting of

(i)   input Java source code to be transformed into an equivalent program model,
(ii) one or more refactorings to be performed on the program model, and
(iii) the output Java program expected after performing the refactorings.

ARTE also supports negative test cases, where the given refactoring or chain of refactorings should not be applied to the input program. In those cases, the refactoring implementation under test should is supposed to detect some precondition to fail and to deliver a corresponding message to the user.

Based on ARTE, we empirically studied the correctness of the refactoring application. Here, we used a version of our tool prototype that has been presented in [130]. Technically, this version differs in two aspects from the one presented in this chapter. First, JaMoPP [143] has been used for parsing Java source code and was replaced by MoDisco to support newer Java versions. Second, the presented graph patterns had been specified using the SDM notation of eMoflon [162, 268] that has been replaced by Henshin rules. These are visually closer to the patterns introduced in this chapter. Besides the readability of the rule specification, the SDM's run time performance in 2015th transformation tool contest on refactorings was rather weak [145], while Henshin performed in the comparable class responsibility assignment case of 2018 rather good [269]. As both, Henshin and eMoflon built upon the formalism of algebraic graph transformations, the evaluation of the application's correctness is transferable. In what follows, we first introduce the setup of our experiment and discuss the results of the experiments afterward.

Setup. We manually specified our test input programs to cover the most interesting cases regarding the refactoring operations *Pull-Up Method* (pum) and *Create Superclass* (csc). Most of the test programs contain only a few classes and methods, representing a minimal positive or negative example for a particular (set of) precondition(s) under investigation. In this way, we mainly focused our experiments on assessing correctness as a refactoring implementation is only practically relevant if it complies with a considerable amount of correctness criteria. In this regard, we considered scalability and performance measures to be of secondary importance in our setting. Although the test programs have been specified manually, they already existed before we implemented our approach. In particular, our test cases cover all crucial preconditions known from the literature. Those test cases constitute executable Java programs, although they merely perform basic console output operations.

Results Table 10.1 summarizes the results for the test cases in ARTE and includes a comparison to Eclipse regarding the correctness of the refactoring specifications. (Eclipse offers *Pull-Up Method* for Java and *Create Superclass* can also be simulated by performing *Extract Superclass* with no extracted elements.)

The current version of ARTE contains 9 test cases for Pull Up Method, 7 test cases for *Create Superclass* and 3 test cases combining both refactorings. Each row in Table 10.1 represents one test case, identified by its number. The first column shows the kind of refactoring(s) being tested by that particular test case. Multiple executions of refactorings of the same kind are represented by corresponding numbers, e.g., Test Case 18. The second column, Elements, represents the size of the test case concerning the number of classes, constructors, methods, and fields of the input program. The third and fourth columns represent the correctness of the refactorings specified by Eclipse and our approach, respectively, by showing if the test cases have been successfully executed. Note that Test Case 19 contains our example scenario introduced in Section 10.2.1. Thus, results regarding correctness underpin the relevance of our approach. Eclipse does not check for external method accesses and, as a consequence, fails at Test Case 19. In our approach, we have made this check convenient by adding access edges to the program model and succeed in this test case as well. The fifth column contains our execution times for each test case, given in milliseconds. Unfortunately, we were not able to provide time measurements for Eclipse as we could not separate the actual methods performing the refactoring from other Eclipse tasks and the overhead caused by the graphical interface. Based on manual time measurements, we assume that the Eclipse execution times are comparable to ours, thus indicating the practical relevance of our technique.

The test cases 15 and 16 in ARTE also determine if synchronization de facto happens incrementally, i.e., the unaffected program parts remain untouched and are not regenerated – this is ensured by including program parts in the test input that are behaviorally equivalent to the original ones, but having different code being generated by the transformation.

Concluding the evaluation results, we found that our implementation prototype fulfills the requirements of all our test cases, i.e., our refactoring specifications are proven to be correct for typical cases of the respective refactoring operation. Moreover, multiple refactorings can be applied sequentially to the program model before synchronizing it with the source code. The synchronization has proven to be incremental according to the notion above.

10.2.6 Threats to Validity

In this section, we discuss threats to the internal and external validity of the evaluation of our refactoring approach.

Internal Validity

We evaluated our refactoring approach based on synthetic examples that have been specified by ourselves. Here, lies a risk that we did not consider all relevant cases. To mitigate this threat, we discussed among the authors of [130] the considered cases until we have not been able to find any uncovered case.

External Validity
The evaluation based on synthetic examples might limit the generalization of the results. The systematic specification of examples indicates the possibility of generalization.

Also, due to the short run-time of the refactorings, effects like the Java garbage collection might have a high impact on the measured run times. To mitigate this threat, we reported the median run time of multiple executions.

10.2.7 Conclusion on Formalizing Refactorings

In this section, we have shown how OO refactorings can be formalized using graph transformation rules and how the changes made by these rules on the program model can be propagated into the implementation. While graph transformation rules have only been suitable to check the applicability of an OO refactoring before, using our approach also their application is possible. Furthermore, our evaluation has shown the effectiveness of our refactoring implementation to detect behavior-changing refactorings upfront. However, while we consider visibilities at checking and executing refactorings, we currently only consider these from the perspective of correctness.

10.3   Security-aware Refactorings

The validity of proposed refactorings is mostly concerned with purely *functional* behavior preservation [24], whereas their impact on extra-functional properties like program security has received little attention so far [270]. However, applying elaborated information-flow metrics for identifying security-preserving refactorings is computationally too expensive in practice [271].

In what follows, we first summarize an experiment on the interplay between refactorings and visibilities in Section 10.3.1. Afterward, based on the insights from this experiment, we introduce possible security-preserving extensions to the *Move Method* refactoring in Section 10.3.2. Thereby we use the formalization as introduced in Section 3 and extend it with additional security-preserving constraints. Finally, we conclude in Section 10.3.3.

10.3.1 Controlling the Attack Surface of Object-Oriented Refactorings

For studying the interplay between refactorings and security, as an alternative to elaborated information-flow metrics, we consider *attack-surface metrics* as a sufficiently reliable, yet easy-to-compute indicator for the preservation of program security [214, 215]. *Attack surfaces* of programs comprise all conventional ways of entering a software system by users/attackers, e.g., invoking API methods or inheriting from super-classes, such that an unnecessarily large surface increases the danger of exploiting vulnerabilities. Hence, the goal of a secure program design should be to grant the least privileges to class members to reduce the extent to which data and operations are exposed to the world [215]. In *Java*-like languages, accessibility constraints by means of modifiers `public`, `private` and `protected` provide a built-in low-level mechanism for controlling and restricting information flow within and across classes, sub-classes and packages [69]. Accessibility constraints introduce compile-time security barriers protecting trusted system code from untrusted mobile code [272]. As a downside, restricted accessibility privileges naturally obstruct possibilities for refactorings, as CRA updates (e.g., moving members [264]) may be either rejected by those constraints, or they require to relax accessibility privileges, thus increasing the attack surface [273].

Considering the attack surface of an object-oriented program, the refactoring of moving `checkFormat`, discussed in Section 10.2.2, should be definitely blamed as harmful. The enforced relaxations of accessibility constraints for ending in a compiling state unnecessarily widen the attack surface of the original program. This especially applies to those refactorings widening the visibility of security-critical methods. In contrast, the imaginary refactoring allowing to reduce the visibility of the moved method should be appreciated as it even narrows the attack surface.

Ruland et al. presented a search-based technique to find optimal sequences of refactorings for object-oriented *Java*-like programs regarding sets of optimization objectives [146]. Their model-based tool implementation, called *GOBLIN*, represents individuals, i.e., intermediate refactoring results, as program-model instances complying with the program model introduced in Chapter 5. Hence, instead of regenerating source code after every single refactoring step, they apply and evaluate sequences of refactoring operations, specified as model-transformation rules in *Henshin* [218], to the program model. To this end, they apply *MOMoT* [274], a generic framework for search-based model transformations.

To deal with the discussed interaction between class member's visibilities and design quality, together with Ruland et al., we investigated this relation, by explicitly taking accessibility constraints into account in *GOBLIN* [146]. We apply *Move*

Method refactorings as introduced in combination with operations for on-demand strengthening and relaxing of accessibility declarations [69] and control their impact on attack-surface metrics. As objectives, we consider

1. *elimination of design flaws*, particularly,

    (a) optimization of object-oriented coupling/cohesion metrics [275, 276] and
    (b) avoidance of anti-patterns, namely *The Blob* [21],

2. *preservation of original program design*, i.e., minimizing the number of changes, and
3. *attack-surface minimization* in terms of class member visibilities.

Our experimental results gained from applying refactorings to real-world Java programs provide us with detailed insights into the impact of attack-surface metrics on fitness values of refactorings and the resulting trade-off with competing design-quality objectives. To ensure the functional validity of the applied refactorings, we specified them as graph transformation rules and included some preconditions and postconditions as shown in Section 10.2.2 [130, 131, 145]. Our experimental results demonstrate that attack-surface impacts of refactorings deserve more attention in the context of refactoring recommendations, revealing a practically relevant trade-off (or, even contradiction) between traditional design-improvement efforts and extra-functional (particularly, security) aspects. Also, Ruland et al. uncover in the experiment that existing tools are mostly unaware of attack-surface impacts of recommended refactorings [146]. As a consequence of these observations, in the next section, we investigate the specification of security-preserving refactorings by enriching our refactoring specifications with security-preserving constraints.

10.3.2 Security Preserving Refactorings

By applying the UMLsec secure dependency check at the design phase, the implementation will be structured into security-critical parts and non-security-critical parts. This architecture allows to encapsulate security-critical parts and to lower the attack surface. At refactoring, we have to ensure that we not only preserve this design but also do not open new attack vectors that might result in new attacks.

Critical Class Member Visibilities
Considering the attack surface discussed in the previous experiment, one example

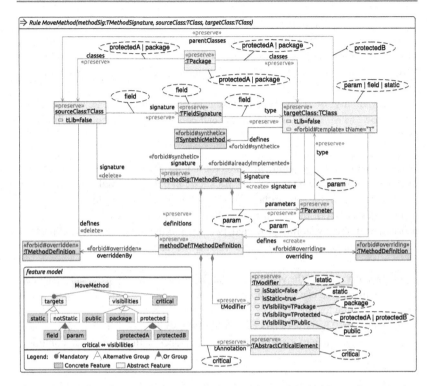

Figure 10.16 Specification of a *Move Method* refactoring enriched with security constraints

that makes attacks easier is to give a classified member wider visibility. This change might allow an attacker to directly access a classified member, e.g., from injected code, which was not possible before.

In Figure 10.13 of Section 10.2.2, we showed the formalization of the *Move Method* refactoring as Henshin rule. However, in this VB rule, we did not consider visibilities as a security-critical element but added a postprocessing step that sets the visibility of the moved member to the narrowest visibility possible for the program to compile. In Figure 10.16, we show a variation of this rule that includes constraints on the visibilities of members that are critical according to the UMLsec security requirements.

For critical members, we prevent refactorings that would increase their visibility. Accordingly, we extended the rule's feature model with a feature `critical` indicating critical versions of the rule. In these critical versions, the method to be moved is annotated with a security requirement, captured by instances of the node type `TAbstractCriticalElement`. Iff `critical` is selected, `visibilities` have to be selected in the feature model, containing features associated with constraints on visibilities.

The visibility of a method is given in the attribute `tVisibility` of the `:TModifier` node. Java programs can contain four different visibilities we have to consider:

public: The first case is public methods for that no additional restrictions apply.

package: Methods with the visibility package can only be moved to classes in the same package as the source class. This condition is expressed by the `:TPackage` node that is part of the rule if the feature `package` is selected.

protected: For the visibility protected, two possibilities allow the move, expressed by the features `protectedA` and `protectedB`.

>   **protectedA:** As for the visibility package, the target class is in the same package as the source class. For this reason, the `TPackage` node is also part of the rule if the feature `protectedA` is selected.
>
>   **protectedB:** The target class is a child of the source class. This is represented by an instance of a `parentClass` reference with the presence condition `protectedB`.

private: Private methods cannot be moved to another class. Since the method's visibility is part of all rule products, no explicit handling of private methods is required.

Every rule product containing `critical` either moves a method with public, package, or protected visibility. For the protected visibility, there are two non-exclusive options. As we did it for possible targets of the move, we explicitly include case `protectedA ∧ protectedB` as we expect these refactorings to be more beneficial due to the close distance between the source and target class. For methods that are not critical, no restrictions for moving these apply.

Critical Class Member Target Class

While class visibilities can be an indicator of a software system's security standard, these are no strong security mechanisms. Usually, a software system's security design combines security levels with authentication mechanisms at the borders of the security levels. Here, UMLsec's secure dependency allows specifying which class members belong to which security level.

A weakening of the security design can happen if a classified member is relocated into a class that did not contain classified members before. In this case, we increase the size of the security-critical code and may open new attack vectors through the original members of the class the member has been relocated to. After the refactoring, code that had been developed applying strong security standards is combined with code that has been treated less critically. Also, security mechanisms might not apply to the non-critical code. For example, the Java security manager can be configured to treat specific locations in the software system differently. Considering the run-time verification of secure dependency presented in Chapter 9, by definition, accesses to critical members within the class defining the critical members are treated as secure. Accordingly, additional members get access to classified information that has not been considered to have this access. This additional access might cause security violations.

To prevent such *Move Method* refactorings, in Figure 10.17, we present additional application conditions preventing moves of critical members into non-critical classes. In the figure, for simplicity, we only show the conditions for the *secrecy* case. However, the conditions for the other cases, e.g., the *integrity* case, are defined analogously.

The idea of these application conditions is that the member to be moved either has no security annotations («`forbid#secrecy`») or if the member has a security annotation («`require#secrecy`») additional conditions have to be fulfilled. These additional application conditions capture that the target class of the move (`targetClass`) is already on the considered security level, in this case, the security level *secrecy*. A class is on the security level of *secrecy* if it defines a member on this security level or accesses a member on the security level. On the program model, this can be expressed in two ways.

First, similarly to UMLsec in the UML models, using the `critical` annotation. Application condition «`require#secrecy1`» captures this case. A move to the target class for a method classified with `secrecy` is allowed, if `targetClass` is annotated with `TCritical` and this annotation has a `secrecy` reference to a method or field (`TMember`). Where this member is defined is not relevant in this case as the `targetClass` is on the security level of *secrecy* regardless of defining a member on this level itself or having a member that accesses a member on this security level.

The second case is that the `TSecrecy` annotation is used to put a member of `targetClass` on the security level of *secrecy*. This case is shown in application condition «`require#secrecy2`». For the move to be allowed, it is suf-

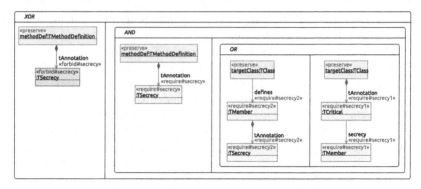

Figure 10.17 Security extension to the *Move Method* refactoring regarding allowed targets for critical methods

ficient that one of the two application conditions «require#secrecy1» and «require#secrecy2» is fulfilled.

10.3.3 Conclusion on the Security Preserving Refactorings

In this section, we have shown that there is a significant interplay between refactorings and security specifications such as visibilities. However, it is possible to optimize a software system's design and these security requirements at the same time. From a security perspective, the considered metrics like the attack surface measured in terms of visibilities are only a minor indicator of a software system's security. We showcased how the formal refactoring specifications can be extended to preserve security constraints, e.g., specified using UMLsec's security requirements.

10.4   Conclusion on the Refactoring of Security-Critical Software Systems

While the refactoring of a software system is already challenging, this challenge even gets greater on security-critical software systems. In this chapter, we have shown how refactorings can be formalized using graph transformation languages. Existing works show that such formalizations allow reasoning about the correctness of the refactorings regarding them not changing a software system's behavior [24]. Also, such formalization allows checking the applicability of the refactorings upfront [24,

37]. However, the correctness of the refactored implementation could not be guaranteed as the refactorings had to be performed manually on the implementation. Here, we showed how this gap can be overcome using the program model and synchronization mechanism introduced in this thesis. Finally, we have shown how the formalized refactorings can be extended with security constraints, leveraging design-time security requirements.

In summary, the presented solution allows the restructuring of security-critical software systems as part of the GRaViTY development approach. During this task, the discusses security extensions allow to automatically prevent security-violating refactorings.

Part V
Variants

Specification of Variability throughout Variant-rich Software Systems

This chapter shares material with the GPCE'2018 publication „Model-Based Security Analysis of Feature-Oriented Software Product Lines" [277].

Software product line engineering [278] enables the systematic reuse of software artifacts through the explicit management of variants in terms of variability. A *Software Product Line* (SPL) is a family of software product variants sharing a set of core assets and differing in a set of *features*, that is, increments of functionality only present in some of the product variants. Representing an SPL in terms of *features*, and mapping these features to development artifacts such as design-time models and source code allows generating individually-tailored product variants on-demand by retrieving the corresponding artifacts for a given feature selection. Since SPLs are useful for tailoring products to diverse customer needs, companies such as Boeing, Bosch, Hewlett Packard, Toshiba, and General Motors use SPLs to develop business-critical software [279].

Individually tailored variants of software systems have made our everyday lives considerably easier, and yet they give rise to a rapidly growing multitude of security threats. To allow dealing with these threats but also to allow traceability of security requirements on different system representations, we need an appropriate notation for security assumptions as well as for variability points. These requirements have to allow automated security analysis, e.g., by detecting instances of security violation patterns and traceability in case of changes. Figure 11.1 shows the integration of variability into the GRaViTY approach. Comparable to security requirements, the variability specifications correspond to each other. The required notations for security assumptions and variability points are represented by the *Variability* and *Security* extensions on the UML models, the source code, and the program model.

While the specification of security requirements on UML models and the source code has been introduced by us in Chapters 3.6.1 and 6.4, the interaction of these with variability has not been considered until now. Given these circumstances, the

© The Author(s), under exclusive license to Springer Fachmedien Wiesbaden GmbH, part of Springer Nature 2022
S. M. Peldszus, *Security Compliance in Model-driven Development of Software Systems in Presence of Long-Term Evolution and Variants*,
https://doi.org/10.1007/978-3-658-37665-9_11

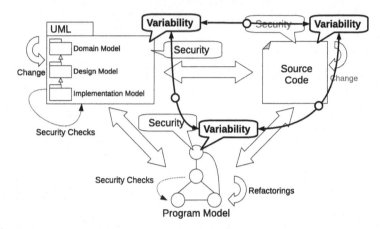

Figure 11.1 Variant-rich software systems in the concept of the GRaViTY approach

question is how we can apply the developed techniques for security compliance
checks and maintenance to software product lines as considered in the fifth research
question of this thesis:

RQ5: How can we verify and preserve security compliance in variant-rich software
systems?

For answering this research question, first, we have to find a suitable notation for
variability. This notation has to allow efficient ways to detect security violations
on software product lines and to support developers in restructuring them. In this
regard, we aim at representing variability similarly across all artifacts considered
by GRaViTY. Furthermore, we must be able to keep the variability specifications
consistent. Accordingly, in this chapter, we answer RQ5.1 regarding the specification
of structural variability on Java source code, UML models, and the program model:

RQ5.1: How can we specify variability throughout a software system, including
design-time models and security requirements?

In this chapter, we assume that implementation-level variability is specified using
Antenna [25] preprocessor statements. For supporting the consistent specification
of variability across the artifacts considered in GRaViTY, as shown in Figure 11.1,
we make the following contributions:

1. Two variability extensions oriented on Antenna for specifying variability throughout all artifacts considered in GRaViTY:

    (a) The SecPL profile to specify variability in UML models.
    (b) An extension to GRaViTY's type graph to allow explicit reasoning about variability in program models.

2. An approach for parsing Antenna variability annotations in the implementation and mapping these to the two proposed variability extensions for preserving the consistency of the variability specifications.

For demonstrating the variability-related approaches of this thesis, we converted the iTrust system into a software product line. As shown in Chapter 2, the iTrust system has been developed based on use case descriptions. In the iTrust product line, it is possible to configure the software system to only contain selected kinds of users and selected use cases. For example, a version of the iTrust system can be deployed that does not allow patients to access the software system and therefore also does not contain the use cases describing activities performed by patients.

In this chapter, we discuss how to support developers in the model-driven development and maintenance of secure software product lines supporting design-time UML models, source code, and our program model. First, we introduce background on variability engineering in Section 11.1 and our addition of variability to the iTrust example in detail. In Section 11.2, we discuss how we can specify variability on UML models and the program model considering the existing Antenna notation for variability on Java source code [25]. We present our prototypical tool support for variability across all artifacts in Section 11.3 and evaluate the suitability of the introduced variability notations in Section 11.4. Finally, we discuss threats to validity in Section 11.5 and conclude on our variability extensions and their integration into GRaViTY in Section 11.6.

11.1 Background on Variability Engineering

Variability engineering is concerned with variability in arbitrary kinds of systems. In this chapter, we focus on software systems and variability within their software. A software product line constitutes a configurable software system built upon a common core platform [280]. Product implementation variants are derivable from those generic implementations in an automated way by selecting a set of domain features, i.e., user-visible product characteristics, to be assembled into a customized

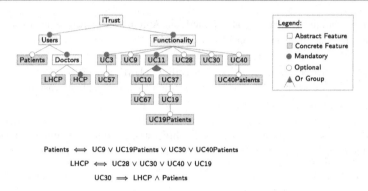

Patients ⟺ UC9 ∨ UC19Patients ∨ UC30 ∨ UC40Patients

LHCP ⟺ UC28 ∨ UC30 ∨ UC40 ∨ UC19

UC30 ⟹ LHCP ∧ Patients

Figure 11.2 Feature model excerpt of a software product line version of the iTrust system

product variant. Software product line engineering defines a comprehensive process for building and maintaining a product line. During domain engineering, a product line is designed by

(1) identifying the set of relevant domain features within the problem space and
(2) by developing corresponding engineering artifacts within the solution space associated with a feature (combination) for assembling implementation variants for feature selections.

In what follows, first, we discuss the concept of features in an SPL in detail. Afterward, we discuss how variability is implemented, and finally, we discuss how to deploy an executable product from an SPL.

11.1.1 Feature Identification and Specification

Technically, a feature is a unit of functionality that can be configured, that is, switching features on or off [279]. During domain engineering, logical dependencies between features further refine the valid configuration space by restricting combinations of features. For instance, domain feature models provide an intuitive, visual modeling language for specifying the configuration space of a product line [281]. Feature models comprise a tree-based representation of feature dependencies. In a feature model, a feature can only be selected if its parent feature has been selected. Besides, there are constraints on the child features of a parent feature, such as mandatory features or group constraints for all child features.

There are various tools and notations for specifying feature models [281–284]. In this thesis, we use FeatureIDE [284, 285] and its notation. Figure 11.2 shows an excerpt of a particular feature model created from the use cases of the iTrust system and their dependencies, complying with Figure 2.1 and the corresponding description of Chapter 2.

In our iTrust product line, we consider every use case and its realization in the software system to be a feature of the software system. In addition, the users supported by the system are considered as features of the software system. In the feature model, these are concrete features, meaning that they are directly used in the implementation or specification of the software system. Besides these concrete features, there are abstract features that allow structuring in the feature model. For example, the abstract feature Users is used to group the roles that can be supported by the product line. Among others, these are Patients and, grouped under another abstract feature, LHCPs, and HCPs.

In the context of iTrust system, the feature HCP has always to be selected while Patients and LHCP are optional. If a feature is mandatory or optional, this is denoted by a filled or empty circle. As a mandatory use case, we specified UC11 (Document office visit). The feature corresponding with this use case has two child features (UC10 and UC37) that are grouped in an *or*-group which means that at least one of the two features has to be selected. Besides *or*-groups there are *alternative*-groups in FeatureIDE, stating that exactly one feature has to be selected. As we reverse engineered our iTrust product line from a single product, there are no use cases that exclude each other in this case.

Last, there are crosstree constraints stated below the feature model that are constraints over the features that have to hold in addition to the constraints in the tree representation. Crosstree constraints are logical constraints over the features of the feature model. In FeatureIDE, besides primitive logical operators like and, or, and not, complex logical operators like implication and bi-implication are supported. For example, if the feature UC30 has been selected, this implies that LHCP and Patients have to be selected, too.

The shown feature model comprises 16 concrete features, of which at least four features have to be selected. The features HCP, UC3, and UC11 have to be selected in all cases. In addition, UC10 or UC37 has to be selected. All in all, there are 528 possible configurations of our reverse-engineered iTrust feature model.

11.1.2 Implementation of Variability

After the identification and specification of features, the next step is implementing the SPL. To establish traceability, features can be mapped directly to source code and to design-time models:

- Preprocessor directives can be used to annotate feature-specific code portions, and the entire code-base can be divided into modules [279].
- Design models can be annotated with presence conditions over a set of features [286].

In GRaViTY, we use preprocessor directives specified using Antenna [25] for specifying variability on Java source code. Antenna provides C-like preprocessor directives for Java. As the directives are not part of the Java language, in Antenna these are specified in comments. Originally, Antenna has been developed for JavaME apps but can also be used with standard Java applications. FeatureIDE provides support for Antenna preprocessor directives and allows using features from FeatureIDE feature models in the directives.

Listing 11.1 shows an excerpt of the iTrust implementation of use case UC10 of doctors entering or editing personal health records of patients. The whole class should only be part of the deployed iTrust system if the feature assigned to this use case (UC10) has been selected. This variability is realized by an Antenna preprocessor directive in line 1. This directive states that everything behind this directive is only part of the software system if the condition of the directive evaluates to true. Such #if directives have always to be followed by a #endif directive that states where the conditional part ends. In line 33, this specific directive corresponding to the #if from line 1 is shown. Nesting of preprocessor directives is possible, for example, the editing of health records can interact with the management of allergies if feature UC67 is selected. In this case, the class contains a field allergyDAO and an method updateAllergies for managing allergies (lines 4–6 and 9–31). The implementation of the updateAllergies method checks among others if the allergy has already been added to the patient and if there are interactions with prescriptions of the patient but only if the management of allergies as considered in use case UC37 is part of the software system.

11.1.3 Product Deployment

After implementing a software product line, we have to deploy executable products of our software product line. Here, features not only correspond to configuration parameters within the problem space of a product line but also refer (to assemblies of) engineering artifacts within the solution space at any level of abstraction. For instance, concerning the behavioral specification of variable software systems at the component level, modeling approaches such as state machines are equipped with feature parameters denoting well-defined variation points within a generic product line specification including any possible model variant [287]. This way, explicit specifications of common and variable parts among product variants within the solution space allow for systematic reuse of engineering artifacts among the members of a product family.

Variability comes in two flavors, depending on the time when features are configured to get a product configuration:

static: Variability that is resolved at the deployment of the software system, e.g., by compiling a version of iTrust that only contains the selected use cases.

dynamic: Variability that is present at run-time and dynamically resolved according to the circumstances of the execution. For example, extensions of iTrust that are not part of the bought product but can be dynamically enabled or disabled at run-time if a more expensive version of the product is bought or expired.

While static variability does not allow to change the product configuration after deployment, for dynamic variability, it is possible to reduce the configuration space available after deployment by statically configuring a subset of the available features.

For the development of an SPL using Antenna and FeatureIDE, FeatureIDE allows developers to statically select a (partial) feature configuration and comments out all the source code that is not part of the selected configuration. Accordingly, if a complete feature configuration has been selected, the remaining code comprises a compilable and deployable product of the SPL. Reconsidering the SPL shown in Listing 11.1, we selected in FeatureIDE a configuration that contains UC10 and UC67 but in which UC37 is deselected. For this reason, the implementation belonging to UC37 has been commented out by FeatureIDE (lines 20–27).

```
 1  //#if UC10
 2  public class EditPHRAction extends PatientBaseAction {
 3      private final PatientDAO patientDAO;
 4      //#if UC67
 5      private final AllergyDAO allergyDAO;
 6      //#endif
 7      private final HealthRecordsDAO hrDAO;
 8      ...
 9      //#if UC67
10      public String updateAllergies(long pid, String description) {
11          ...
12          String patientName = this.patientDAO.getName(pid);
13          List<AllergyBean> allergies = allergyDAO.getAllergies(pid);
14          for(AllergyBean cur : allergies){
15              if(cur.getDescription().equals(bean.getDescription())) {
16                  return "Allergy "+bean.getNDCode()+" has already been added
                        for "+patientName+".";
17              }
18          }
19          ...
20          //#if UC37
21          //@List<PrescriptionBean> beansRx = this.patientDAO.
                  getCurrentPrescriptions(pid);
22          //@for(PrescriptionBean element : beansRx) {
23          //@  if(element.getMedication().getNDCode().equals(bean.getNDCode()))
                  {
24          //@     return "Medication "+element.getMedication().getNDCode()+"
                  is currently prescribed to "+patientName+".";
25          //@ }
26          //@}
27          //#endif
28          ...
29          return "Allergy Added";
30      }
31      //#endif
32  }
33  //#endif
```

Listing 11.1 Excerpt of the Java class EditPHRAction of the iTrust SPL using Antenna preprocessor directives

11.2   UML and PM Variability Extension

Comparable to Antenna for the specification of variability in Java source code, we need mechanisms for specifying variability on UML models and the program model. For this purpose, we introduce a variability extension to the type graph and for variability within UML models the *SecPL profile*, allowing users to specify variability in the program model and respectively UML models. To annotate structural and behavioral elements that only exist in some products, model elements can have presence conditions, that is propositional expressions over a set of features. The set of features is defined using a feature model, a standard SPL representation. We aim at using the same feature model as for the source code throughout all artifacts considered within GRaViTY, including source code, UML models, and program models.

Within this thesis, we assume that SPLs were originally developed at the implementation level using *Antenna*, a widely-spread preprocessor mechanism for annotating Java source code with variability [25]. However, other preprocessor mechanisms with similar annotations could be potentially supported without much additional effort. On top of that, developers might use custom annotations such as @Secrecy to specify security requirements on fields and methods that will be extracted and added to the output model as discussed in Chapter 6.

In what follows, first, we introduce our variability extensions to the program model and UML models. Afterward, discuss how these extensions can be integrated into the GRaViTY synchronization mechanism to support Java SPLs specified using Antenna.

11.2.1 Variability Notations in GRaViTY

To specify variability on all artifacts considered within the GRaViTY approach, we need mechanisms comparable to Antenna to reflect the variability annotations on these artifacts. In this section, first, we introduce our variability extension to the type graph of our program model, and afterward, a profile for specifying variability within UML models.

Program Model Variability Annotations
The program model is an abstract view on the implementation abstracting all information from the statement level. Accordingly, we have to reflect the Antenna preprocessor statements in the same manner. Figure 11.3a shows our variability extension to GRaViTY's type graph. We define a new annotation type TPresenceCondition

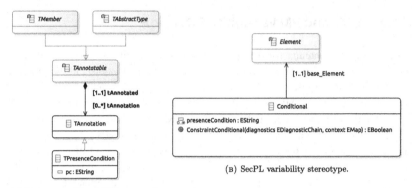

(A) Program model variability annotation.

(B) SecPL variability stereotype.

Figure 11.3 Metamodels of the GRaViTY variability extensions

generalizing `TAnnotation`. This new annotation type contains a presence condition (`pc`) under which the annotated program model element is part of a product. This `TAnnotation` can be applied to any `TAnnotatable` element from the type graph, e.g., `TMember` or `TAbstractType` covering methods and fields as well as all kinds of types. This allows for covering variability on the class-method-field level. However, Antenna allows also variability on the statement-level of methods and fields. As the program model does not contain this information in detail, we have to cover this variability differently. The visible effects of statements in the program model are accesses between members (`TAccess` and its child types). Depending on the variability at the statement level some accesses might be present in a product or not. As these are also `TAnnotatable`, we can reflect this information by annotating accesses with a corresponding instance of `TPresenceCondition`.

Figure 11.4 shows an excerpt of the iTrust program model including the proposed variability extension. The shown excerpt focuses on the statements in lines 12 and 21 of the iTrust source code shown in Listing 11.1. These statements belong to the method `updateAllergies` of the class `EditPHRAction`. This class itself is wrapped by the preprocessor statements `//#if UC10 ... //#endif`. This is reflected by the `TClass` representing `EditPHRAction` being annotated with a `TPresenceConditon`, as shown in the top left side of Figure 11.4. The `TMethodDefinition` representing `updateAllergies` is again wrapped by additional Antenna preprocessor statements. In the end, this method is part of the software system if $UC11 \land UC67$ are part of the feature configuration. As the existence of the `TMethodDefinition` depends on the existence of the defining

TClass, this method is only annotated with a TPresenceCondition whose
pc is set to UC67. In the statements in lines 12 and 21, both times the field
patientDAO is accessed. This field is only part of the software system if the feature UC10 is selected. Again, the corresponding presence condition already applies
to the defining TClass. Accordingly, the node of the type TFieldDefinition
is not annotated with an additional presence condition. All additional Antenna preprocessor statements relevant for the considered excerpt are at the statement level of
the method updateAllergies. For the statements in line 12, no additional presence conditions apply. Accordingly, the two resulting accesses, a TRead of the field
patientDAO and a TCall of the method getName, are not annotated with any
additional presence conditions. In contrast to this, the statements in line 21 are only
part of the method if the following presence condition holds: UC10 ∧ UC67 ∧ UC37.
Again, we do not have to repeat conditions that are derived from owning elements.
Accordingly, the two accesses are only annotated with TPresenceConditions
whose pc is set to UC37. The called method getCurrentPrescriptions is
conditional itself.

SecPL Variability Stereotype
Our variability extension for UML models works similarly to the one presented for
the program model. Figure 11.3b shows the UML profile specification of this variability extension. We specified a «Conditional» stereotype that is applicable

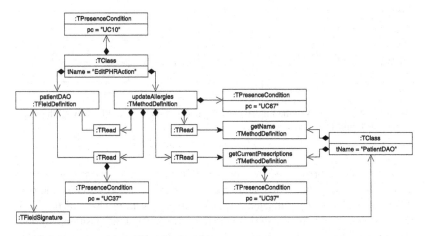

Figure 11.4 Program model excerpt showing the application GRaViTY's variability extension

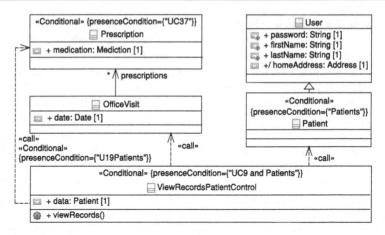

Figure 11.5 Excerpt from the iTrust SPL's design model showing the usage of the SecPL profile

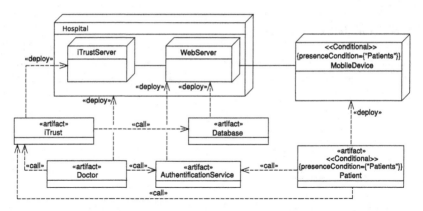

Figure 11.6 Excerpt from the implementation model of the iTrust SPL showing the usage of the SecPL profile

to every UML Element and has a presence condition (presenceCondition) as a tagged value. The tagged value presenceCondition specifies the condition under which the annotated Element is present in products of the UML model product line. In presence conditions, we support propositional formulas with negations, conjunctions, and disjunctions over the set of features. In addition, to ease the development of UML product lines, we specified a constraint `ConstraintConditional` that evaluates the syntactical correctness of `presenceCondition` within a UML editor. While the process of managing presence conditions can be complicated, adequate tool support is a promising strategy to support users during such tasks [288].

For the demonstration of the application of «`Conditional`», we applied the stereotype to two excerpts of iTrust SPL's design-time models. In Figure 11.5, an excerpt of the design model is shown, that is focusing on UC9 of the iTrust system of providing a patient with access to her health records. As an example for health records, we show the recorded office visits of a patient. For accessing health records, a `ViewRecordsPatientsControl` has been specified, that checks which health records are visible to a `Patient` user and provides them. As the `LoginControl` used to introduce *Secure Dependency* in Figure 3.6 of Section 3.6.1, the `ViewRecordsPatientsControl` has access to the attributes of the class `User`, and therefore, has to be on the security level of secrecy for the signature of the attribute `password:String`. In Figure 11.6, we show the same excerpt of the implementation model as in Figure 3.4 from the introduction of model-driven development in Section 3.3.

Variability on UML models can be specified using the SecPL «`Conditional`» stereotype. For instance, the class *Prescription* in Figure 11.5 is present if the feature UC37 is selected and the class `ViewRecordsPatientControl` is present if the features UC9 and `Patients` are selected.

If a conditional element owns other elements, these owned elements are only part of the model if the owning element is part of the model. For example, the attribute `medication:Medication` is only part of the software system if `Prescription` is part of the software system. While it is possible to annotate associations with «`Conditional`» often their precedence condition can be derived from the presence conditions of the elements at the ends of the association. For example, *office visits* have an association with the prescriptions made during the visit. As the association end `prescriptions` has only a value if the feature UC37 is selected and the class `Prescription` is present, this association is also only present if the feature UC37 is selected. The «`call`» dependency between `ViewRecordsPatientControl` and `Prescriptions` is only present if it's own presence condition is fulfilled and the presence conditions at all ends. In this case, the features UC9, UC19`Patients`, and UC37 have to be selected.

Using GRaViTY's two presented variability extensions, variability can be specified on UML models and the program model in a consistent way. Also, the underlying mechanism is directly oriented on Antenna, allowing to synchronize the variability annotations among all three artifacts. We discuss this synchronization in the next section.

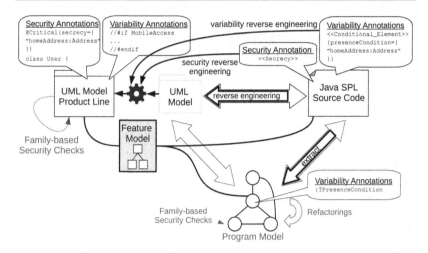

Figure 11.7 Concept of GRaViTY's reverse engineering mechanism for SPLs

11.2.2 Parsing of Antenna Annotations and Mapping to Models

To integrate variability on all artifacts supported within the GRaViTY approach, we have to be able to parse the Antenna annotations in the source code and to synchronize these with the variability annotations in the program model and UML models. However, despite our primary intention to support *security by design*, in practice, security concerns often need to be addressed in codebases long after they were initially deployed. Apart from poor planning, a root cause are migration scenarios where the original application was developed for an offline context [289]. In this section, besides the integration into the synchronization mechanism of GRaViTY, we study the application of our methodology to situations where the goal is to *harden* an existing software system. To this end, we provide a mechanism for the reverse engineering of SecPL models from existing codebases. Our mechanism extends the state-of-the-art methodology for *model-based reverse engineering*, which is concerned with the process of obtaining useful higher-level representations of legacy systems [4].

The key idea is to let the developers annotate security-critical parts of the source code of the input SPL. We can then generate a UML class model product line that is amenable to the analysis capabilities to be introduced in Chapter 12. However, an application as part of the synchronization mechanism discussed in Chapter 6 is also possible. In principle, the proposed TGGs could be extended with additional rules comparable to those for synchronizing security requirements. However, as Antenna preprocessor statements are defined in comments, detailed information about the lines in which these are specified is not present in the MoDisco model used by GRaViTY as intermediate source code representation. While in most cases the comments are related to the expected model elements, this is not always the case. For example, an `//#endif` directive after the closing brace of a method definition might be associated in the MoDisco model to the next method definition in the source code. For this reason, supporting variability annotations as part of the TGGs is currently not feasible.

Figure 11.7 gives an overview of our mechanism's internal workings. We use the TGG transformation introduced in Section 6.2.2 to extract a UML model or program model from the existing Java codebase. In addition, we parse the Antenna preprocessor annotations from the source code to add corresponding «`Conditional`» stereotypes in the UML model and `@TPresenceCondition` annotations in the program model.

In the following, we show a regular expression used during our parsing process, which simultaneously acts as a lightweight specification of possible annotations. *Ifdef directives* respecting the following expression are represented as presence conditions of elements in the class diagram.

$$//\backslash s * \#if(def)?. * (n|r) \tag{11.1}$$

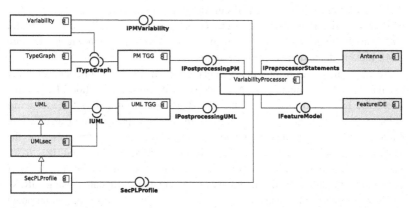

Figure 11.8 Component diagram showing the integration of the variability processing into GRaViTY's synchronization mechanism

This expression matches every line comment starting from the beginning specified by the // to the end of the line which has the keyword if or ifdef directly after the start characters, ignoring white space. The rest of the line contains the presence condition.

Listing 11.2 shows a source code excerpt illustrating the use of our variability annotations. The given regular expression matches lines 1 and 5 of the source code excerpt. Based on the position of those matches in the source code and the positions of the *endif directives* we can calculate which Java elements are covered by such an annotation. This also covers GRaViTY's security annotations. The positions of Java elements are again determined by matching regular expressions.

```
1   //#ifdef UC37
2   @Critical(secrecy={"medication:Medication"})
3   public class Prescription {
4       ...
5       //#if U19Patients
6       ... // #endif
7   } //#endif
```

Listing 11.2 Source code with Antenna and GRaViTY's security annotations

11.3   Tool Support for the Synchronization of Variability Annotations

Figure 11.8 shows a component diagram of our implementation of GRaViTY's variability extension. We specified our variability extension to the type graph as EMF metamodel in the Variability component. Comparably, we specified our UML variability profile in the component SecPLProfile extending the standard UML metamodel and the UMLsec profile.

To create instances of program models and UML models using our variability extensions, we implemented the Antenna parser discussed in Section 11.2.2 in the VariabilityProcessor component. This component parses the Antenna preprocessor statements and relates these to the features specified in FeatureIDE feature models. Also, this component is registered as a postprocessor at the TGG-based synchronizations realized in the components PM TGG and UML TGG. These two components have been discussed in detail in Section 6.2.3. After a program model or UML model has been created or updated using GRaViTY's synchronization mechanism, the VariabilityProcessor component searches the locations of all model elements in the source code and checks which Antenna preprocessor statements apply to these. If one ore more Antenna prepro-

cessor statements apply, corresponding instances of `TPresenceCondition` or
«`Conditional`» are created.

11.4   Evaluation of the Variability Extension

In the previous section, we introduced a prototypical implementation of GRaViTY's
variability extension. Based on this implementation, we evaluate the feasibility to
represent SPLs using GRaViTY on the levels of UML models and program models.

Setup. In our evaluation, we applied our reverse engineering mechanism to multiple
large open-source projects. By doing this, we produced SecPL models and program
models by applying our reverse engineering mechanism to the available codebases.
While most selected projects featured Antenna annotations specifying variability on
the source code level, this was not the case for OpenJDK's[1] implementation of the
Java Secure Socket Extension (*JSSE*) and iTrust. Comparable to iTrust, we extended
JSSE's codebase with variability, by assigning features to the different supported
protocols. As simple existing product lines, we considered the text editor called
Notepad [290]. As real-world examples, that have already been subject to earlier
SPL research [291], we considered *MobilePhoto* and *Lampiro*. *MobilePhoto* [292]
is a mobile multi-media platform with academic background. *Lampiro* [293] is an
instant messaging client which has been naively developed as a software product
line with Antenna and therefore of special interest for applicability of our approach
to real examples. Our Lampiro model is the largest one considered, comprising 29K
elements in the reverse-engineered UML model, including classes, dependencies,
and operations.

Results. We have been able to successfully generate UML class diagrams and program models for all examples and to add the expected variability annotations to these.
After generating the models, we randomly checked whether the models are annotated as expected with `TPresenceConditon` and «`Conditional`». Thereby,
we tried to focus on the most complicated Antenna preprocessor statements, e.g.,
multiple levels of nesting or complicated conditions. During this inspection, we did
not find any missing or dislocated presence conditions.

---

[1] OpenJDK: http://openjdk.java.net/

11.5   Threats to Validity

In this section, we discuss threats to the validity of the experiment showing the practical applicability of our proposed variability extensions.

11.5.1 Construct Validity

The main threats to validity concern the construction of our tool prototype. For the support of Antenna preprocessor statements, we implemented an ad-hoc solution that has major drawbacks that may threaten validity: The ad-hoc implementation based on regular expressions cannot guarantee scalability and completeness. For this reason, we did not consider scalability or performance in our evaluation. Regarding completeness, we currently do not support variability at the statement level of methods. However, we discussed the principle suitability of our variability extensions to express this variability on the program model and in UML models. Nevertheless, we have shown the feasibility to express variability in the program model and on UML models as well as the possibility to create a solution for synchronization.

11.5.2 Internal Validity

The main concern regarding internal validity is the manual inspection of the generated models by us. This inspection comes with two threats. First, we did not inspect all variability annotations in the implementation and the generated models and might have overseen divergences. However, as our focus was on the suitability to express variability and not to evaluate our synchronization mechanism in detail, the results indicate, in combination with our discussion, the suitability to express variability on the program model and in the UML models. Second, we might have been biased by our knowledge about the strength and weaknesses of our implementation. To lower this threat, the authors of [277] performed the review in a pair-programming manner.

11.5.3 External Validity

We considered only a limited number of SPLs in our experiments which might limit the generalization of our observations to other SPLs. To mitigate this threat, we tried to consider SPLs from different domains and of different sizes.

11.6   Conclusion on GRaViTY's Variability Extension

In this chapter, we presented variability extensions for UML models and the program model. Also, we discussed the synchronization of UML models and program models containing variability with their implementation and presented a reverse engineering approach. While the proposed parsing and mapping mechanism works in an ad-hoc manner it has been shown to be suitable for practical problems. However, currently, only the propagation of variability annotations in the implementation into the program model and UML models is possible. When models and code may be subject to evolution, keeping security requirements synchronized on both levels is challenging. To also support these two opposite directions, in the future, one can extend the MoDisco parser to allow the explicit parsing of Antenna preprocessor statements and the synchronization of these using TGGs. By improving this synchronization between the different artifacts of SPLs, one can provide a full integration as part of the GRaViTY approach. Nonetheless, we have successfully shown the possibility to represent variability consistently across the artifacts of variant-rich software systems.

Security in UML Product Lines

12

This chapter shares material with the GPCE'2018 publication "Model-Based Security Analysis of Feature-Oriented Software Product Lines" [277].

As discussed in the previous chapters of this thesis, security is a business-critical factor in enterprises, since each security issue implies a potential loss of customer trust. Since security concerns permeate the entire software system, the system design needs to treat them as first-class citizens. To this end, model-based techniques, such as UMLsec [73], can be used to specify and analyze the consistency of security requirements in early phases, such as in architecture models at design time. Considering this, we have shown in the previous chapters of this thesis how security requirements that were specified at design time can be traced throughout the development process and how compliance with these security requirements can be verified.

However, security becomes yet more challenging during the development of *Software Product Lines* (SPLs, [279]). For the management of security requirements, developing an SPL is challenging due to the complexity arising from *variability*: an SPL with n features can include up to 2^n individual products. In domains like automotive engineering, where SPLs can have thousands of features [294], the resulting software engineering problems can be of astronomical scale.

In many cases, practical solutions for handling variability involve trade-offs between precision and traceability. For instance, during testing of SPLs, developers use *sampling* techniques [38, 295, 296], in which a selection of all products is considered to uncover implementation defects. However, in the case of security, sampling is problematic: a vulnerability affecting any of the products represents a potential leakage of secrets and, therefore, a business risk. Worse, a remarkable research result indicates that focusing on a selection of an SPL's products for security engineering might be *harmful*: security measures implemented in a subset of all products can be used by attackers to automatically generate exploits for the remaining products [297, 298]. For these reasons, we need an efficient way to specify and

S. M. Peldszus, *Security Compliance in Model-driven Development of Software Systems in Presence of Long-Term Evolution and Variants*, https://doi.org/10.1007/978-3-658-37665-9_12

analyze the security requirements of *all* products in an SPL as considered in the fifth research question of this thesis.

RQ5:   How can we verify and preserve security compliance in variant-rich software systems?

When developing SPLs, comparable to security by design, variability should be considered from the very beginning. For this purpose, developers can use the SecPL profile introduced in the previous chapter (Section 11.2) to specify variability already on design-time models. Here lies a significant challenge in the interaction of design-time security and variability. Due to variability, it can be the case that the presence of a security violation depends on some variable part of the product line and is not contained in every single product. Also, it can be that specific security requirements are variable parts themselves, e.g., only apply if the software system is deployed for a specific country. We need means to specify variability interacting with security and to verify the compliance of this specification. For this reason, this chapter extends Chapter 11's answer to RQ5.1 to also support detailed specification of variability within security requirements and answers RQ5.2 regarding verification of security requirements in UML model product lines:

RQ5.1:   How can we specify variability throughout a software system, including design-time models and security requirements?
RQ5.2:   How can security violations be detected on SPLs?

To address the need for specification and analysis of security requirements on the level of UML models, we propose a comprehensive methodology for managing security in SPLs systematically as an extension of the GRaViTY development approach on software product lines [277]. Specifically, as shown in Figure 12.1, we make the following contributions:

1. An extension of the *SecPL profile* presented in Section 11.2, allowing users to specify variability in security requirements besides variability on structural model elements. For this purpose, SecPL refines UMLsec's stereotypes for the specification of security requirements and extends these with presence conditions. (RQ5.1)
2. A *family-based security analysis* approach for the efficient checking of the security requirements expressed using our UML profile. The key idea is to express security checks as OCL constraints [299]. We provide such encodings for the most prominent UMLsec checks; additional ones may be created by experts.

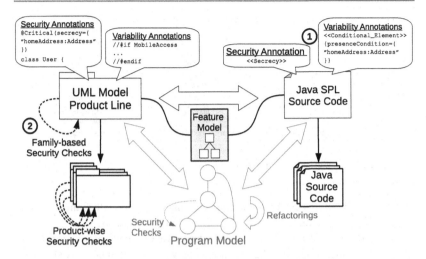

Figure 12.1 The SecPL approach's concept to security in UML product lines

To avoid the combinatorial explosion arising when each product is generated and analyzed separately, we evaluate these OCL constraints using a method for constraint checking on feature-annotated models based on SAT solvers [300]. Here, we either obtain a counterexample, that is, a subset of features giving rise to an insecure product, or proof that all products are secure. (RQ5.2)

To our knowledge, our work is the first to support a model-based security analysis of all products in a software product line. While our analysis relies on template interpretation [300], one of our key contributions is to provide suitable encodings of security constraints that we feed as input to template interpretation, similar to other analysis techniques that rely on a backend SAT solver. Moreover, to the best of our knowledge, our evaluation is the first to assess the benefit of a template-interpretation-based technique on a set of realistic models.

Our methodology uses UML-based system models for capturing the system design and annotating it with security requirements. In industry, system models are used for various purposes, including informal communication, documentation, learning, and code generation; UML is the most widely applied modeling language in many software domains [185]. We rely on UMLsec, introduced in Section 3.6.1, and combine it with feature-based variability engineering. However, our approach is

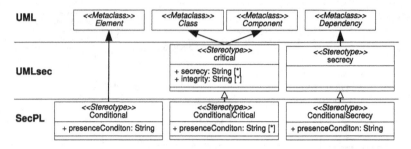

Figure 12.2 SecPL profile excerpt showing variability and security stereotype specification

not limited to UML but can be adapted to modeling languages with similar diagram types as well, for example, SysML [301] for automation systems.

First, in Section 12.1, we introduce our extension to the SecPL profile from Chapter 11. Afterward, in Section 12.2, we discuss how products can be derived considering the variability within security requirements. In Section 12.3, we introduce our family-based security analysis supporting variability within structural UML elements and security requirements. We introduce a prototypical implementation of this security analysis in Section 12.4 and evaluate the approach in Section 12.5. Finally, we discuss threats to validity in Section 12.6 and conclude in Section 12.7.

12.1   Security and Variability Profile

We provide a UML extension to support the specification of security requirements, product-line variability, and security variability. The *SecPL profile* extends UML with 17 security and variability stereotypes and tagged values. The security-specific concepts of SecPL are built atop of those of UMLsec [73]; annotating elements with variability-specific presence conditions is inspired by solutions such as *model templates* [286].

To support variability we extended the stereotypes of UMLsec with presence conditions. Figure 12.2 shows an excerpt with three of SecPL's stereotypes and their relationship to UML and UMLsec. Besides the stereotype «Conditional» that extends the UML meta-class *Element*, already introduced in Section 11.2, we show the two security-specific stereotypes «ConditionalCritical» and «ConditionalSecrecy» that generalize their non-conditional counterparts from UMLsec. All in all the SecPL profile consists out of 17 stereotypes similar to the presented ones and includes validation rules for the well-formedness of the presence conditions.

12.1.1 «ConditionalCritical»

The «ConditionalCritical» generalizes UMLsec's «critical» to specify security requirements. In this thesis, we mainly focus on the security requirements of protection from unauthorized view access (*secrecy*) and unauthorized modification *(integrity)*. However, we also cover the other security requirements provided by the UMLsec profile. To this end, «ConditionalCritical» inherits «critical»'s tagged values for these requirement kinds. Each of these tagged values stores a list of operation signatures and property signatures. Variability of security requirements is specified using a list of presence conditions, which are mapped to the corresponding signatures based on their position in the list.

For example, in Figure 12.3, if prescriptions are part of the software system, access to the prescriptions of an office visit should only be allowed for legitimate entities. For this reason, the member end prescriptions of the association between OfficeVisit and Prescription must be on the security level of secrecy. As this member end is only part of the software system if the feature UC37 is selected, this security requirement is only meaningful in this case. Accordingly, a «ConditionalCritical» with the presence condition UC37 is applied to the class OfficeVisit.

Multiple requirements on the same element are supported by leaving certain positions in the lists of the tagged values empty so that each presence condition is mapped to precisely one entry. For example, the class ViewRecordsPatientController has a second conditional security requirement regarding the property medication of the class Prescription. While for the first security requirement only the feature UC37 has to be selected, this security requirement is only relevant and present when UC37 ∧ UC19Patients have been selected. This is the case as the class Prescription and the dependency to it have to be part of the model for this security requirement to be meaningful.

12.1.2 «ConditionalSecrecy», «ConditionalIntegrity», etc.

These stereotypes control the existence of their non-variable counterparts from the standard UMLsec profile in products of the SPL. A «ConditionalSecrecy»

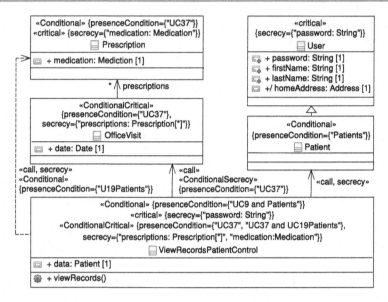

Figure 12.3 Excerpt from the iTrust SPL's design model showing the usage of the SecPL profile including variability and security stereotypes

functions as an instance of «secrecy» with a presence condition specifying under which constraint the «secrecy» is present in the product models of the SPL.

For example, in Figure 12.3, the OfficeVisit has only a member end prescriptions if the feature UC37 is selected. If this feature is selected, the signature of the member end is put to the security level of secrecy. Accordingly, a «secrecy» stereotype is required on the dependency between ViewRecords UserAction and OfficeVisit but only if the feature UC37 is selected. This is represented by an instance of «ConditionalSecrecy» with the presence condition UC37.

As its non-variable counterpart, «ConditionalSecrecy» plays an important role also on dependencies in deployment diagrams as considered in the UMLsec *Secure Links* check. For example, Figure 12.4 shows an excerpt from iTrust's implementation model including variability. Patients are communicating with the iTrust system, e.g., performing the actions discussed before. Until now, we did not consider a patient that has not authenticated herself at the system but is only accessing the public pages provided by the iTrust system. In this case, less restrictive security requirements apply. If a patient is logged in or not can be represented with a dynamic feature loggedIn. If the patient is logged in, all information communicated with the iTrust system has to be treated as confidential while this is not the case for the information transferred on the public pages on which no sensitive information can be entered. This is represented by an instance of «ConditionalSecrecy» on the dependency between the artifacts Patient and iTrust at the bottom of the figure.

12.1.3 «ConditionalEncrypted», «ConditionalLAN», etc.

Similar to the «ConditionalSecrecy», these stereotypes control the existence of their non-variable counterparts and can be applied to communication paths in UML models. The deployment diagram in Figure 12.4, shows a usage of the «ConditionalEncrypted» stereotype on a communication path in the iTrust UML product line. Over the communication between the iTrust web application and patients only publicly available information is communicated as long as no user authenticated herself at the iTrust system. Accordingly, we assume, that information has only to be threatened on the security level of secrecy if the user authenticated herself at the system. For guaranteeing *secrecy* for patients that should be able to access the software system from the Internet, in UMLsec an encrypted

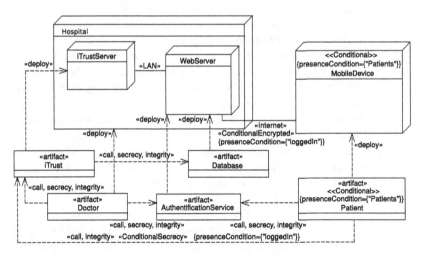

Figure 12.4 Excerpt from the implementation model of the iTrust SPL showing the usage of the SecPL profile

communication path is a suitable measure. For cost reasons, we only want to use encrypted communication if we have to. Accordingly, we make the use of the encryption, specified by «encrypted» in the non-variable UMLsec profile, dependent on the fact whether the patient authenticated herself. For identifying if the authentication took place, we use the dynamic feature loggedIn as presence condition but this time on an instance of «ConditionalEncrypted» at the communication path between the WebServer and the MobileDevice of the patient. The communication path between the WebServer and iTrustServer represents a LAN connection specified by the non-variable «LAN» stereotype of UMLsec. This communication path type is suitable for both, with no explicit security requirement on the data communicated along with it and the security requirement of secrecy. As the type of this connection is not dependent on the state of the Patient's authentication, here we do not use the variable counterpart «ConditionalLAN».

12.2   Deriving Products

When it comes to deployment of the software system products have to be derived for the SPL to get an executable product. Products of the SPL are derived by configuring the features, that is, selecting a specific subset of features. On the implementation, using Antenna with FeatureIDE, this is realized by commenting out all source code parts whose presence condition does not evaluate to true. Similarly, there is the need to derive products from the model product lines including security requirements, e.g., to investigate a security violation that has been detected in a specific product. As for the implementation, products of the model product line are derived by configuring the features. As a result, model elements and security requirements whose presence conditions evaluate to false are removed from the model, yielding a regular UML model annotated with UMLsec security requirements.

As an example, we configure a product that only contains the use cases shown in the use case diagram in Figure 12.5. Doctors can only document office visits, make prescriptions and view the prescriptions of patients for whose they are a LHCP. Patients can view their general records but not the fully detailed prescription reports. The corresponding feature configuration is {HCP, LHCP, Patients, UC3, UC9, UC11, UC19, UC37}.

Figure 12.6 shows the result of deriving a product for this configuration of our example SPL from Figure 12.3. Inactive elements such as the call-dependency from ViewRecordsPatientControl to Prescription have been removed. Also, all conditional security stereotypes have been removed or replaced by the

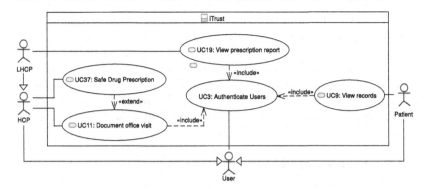

Figure 12.5 Use case diagram showing the use cases supported in a product of the iTrust product line

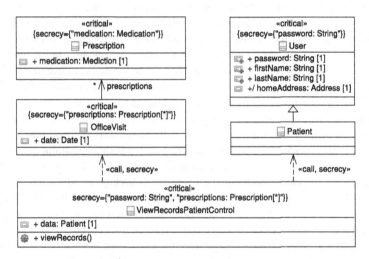

Figure 12.6 Design model product of the iTrust product line with UMLsec security requirements

corresponding standard UMLsec stereotypes. For example, the «Condition-alCritical» on the class OfficeVisit has been replaced with an non-variable «critical» as the feature UC37 is part of the configuration. The «ConditionalCritical» on the class ViewRecordsPatientAction has been partly merged with the already existing «critical» stereotype on this class. The «ConditionalCritical» specifies security levels for two signatures but with different presence conditions. The first presence condition UC37 evaluates to true as the feature UC37 is part of the configuration. Accordingly, the signature prescriptions:Prescription[*] is added to the «critical» stereotype. In contrast to this, the second presence condition UC37 and UC19Patients evaluates to false as the feature UC19Patients is not part of the configuration. For this reason, the specification of the security level for the signature medication:Medication is not part of the derived product.

12.3   Family-based Security Analysis

A prime benefit of model-based security approaches is the possibility to perform a security analysis on design-time models, allowing the implementation of security by design practices. For example, using the *Secure Dependency* check, we can determine if objects in the software system respect the security requirements of the data they send and receive. In the product line setting addressed by SecPL, performing such analysis on each product of an SPL separately is infeasible since the number of products can grow exponentially with the number of features. To deal with this challenge, we propose a family-based security analysis, which lifts checks such as *Secure Dependency* from the level of individual products to the entire SPL.

Our analysis assumes an encoding of the to-be-performed check as an OCL constraint. We provide such encodings for two widely used UMLsec checks; additional ones may be provided by an expert user. To evaluate such a constraint against the design-time model at hand, we use a method called *template interpretation* [300]. Template interpretation was originally designed for checking well-formedness properties, such as *"each association has at least two member ends"*, in unstereotyped UML models with variability. To address our security setting, our OCL constraints also take stereotypes into account. Template interpretation generates a certain propositional formula that can be evaluated using an SAT solver. In the formula, features are represented as variables. If the formula is satisfiable, the SAT solver returns a satisfying example, that is, a subset of features giving rise to an insecure product. Else, we have proof that the security requirement is fulfilled in each product.

In the remainder of this section, we present our security checks with their OCL encodings, we illustrate the generation of a certain formula via template interpretation, and we wrap up.

12.3.1 UMLsec Checks as OCL Constraints

We focus on UMLsec's *Secure Links* and *Secure Dependency* checks [73]. In combination, these checks support the analysis of security requirements on the physical and logical system levels. We consider the security requirements *secrecy* and *integrity* from Section 3.6.1.

As defined in Section 3.6.1, for the *Secure Dependency* check two properties have to hold in a compliant software system:

(i) for all $s \in S.members$: $s \in C.secrecy \Leftrightarrow s \in S.secrecy$,

(ii) for all $s \in S.members$: $s \in C.secrecy \Rightarrow d$ is stereotyped «secrecy», where C and S refer to the client and supplier of a «call» or «send» dependency and s refers to the signature of a member.

We specified an OCL version of the *Secure Dependency* check. For brevity, the illustration in Listing 12.1 focuses on an excerpt, capturing the "$\Rightarrow$" direction of property (i) and the full property (ii) of the *Secure Dependency* check. Also, we show only the *secrecy* case of this check. In the full constraint, the opposite direction and the *integrity* case are considered analogously.

Dependencies representing a potential dependency d are aggregated on lines 1–9. On lines 1–3, we consider both models and packages, since both concepts may represent subsystems. On lines 10–13, we check whether the dependency's target class has a «critical» stereotype so that the set of secrecy members exists. Note that we use the function *has* as a shortcut to check if an element has a particular stereotype. Interfaces do not need to have this stereotype, since their implementing classes do. On lines 14–27, we iterate over the secrecy-stereotyped members of the source class to check if the dependency has the required «secrecy» stereotype (line 17), and if the operation in question is tagged with secrecy in the «critical» stereotype of the target class, in case it exists. As a simplification of the shown OCL constraint we show instead of iterating over both getOperations() and getProperties() a method getMembers().

Similar to the *Secure Dependency* check, we encoded the *Secure Links* check as an OCL constraint. The *Secure Links* is a check concerning the physical deployment of a software system. It analyses whether the network of nodes with their communication paths respects the user-specified security requirements concerning a given attacker model. In what follows, we recall a definition [73] for the security requirement «integrity». A corresponding definition for «secrecy» is obtained by replacing the considered threat with *read*. The *Secure Links* check has been introduced in detail in Section 3.6.1.

```
 1   context Model inv:
 2   let callSendRelations = self.allOwnedElements()→select(e|
 3    e→oclIsKindOf(Package) and (
 4     e.has(securedependencies) or self.has(securedependencies)
 5    )
 6   )
 7   →collect(p|p.allOwnedElements()
 8    →select(d|d→oclIsKindOf(Dependency)) and (d.has(call) or d.has(send))
 9   )
10   in callSendRelations→forAll(cs|
11    cs.target→forAll(trg |
12     trg→oclIsKindOf(Interface) or (trg→oclIsKindOf(Class) and trg.has(critical
              ))
13   )
14   and cs.source→forAll(src |
15    src.getStereotypeApplications(critical)→forAll(srcCritical |
16     srcCritical.getSecrecy()→forAll(srcSecrecy |
17      cs.has(secrecy) and
18      cs.target→select(trg|trg→oclIsKindOf(Class))→forAll(trg |
19       trg.getMembers()→forAll(mem |mem.getName() <> srcSecrecy)
20       or
21       trg.getStereotypeApplications(critical)→exists(trgCritical |
22        trgCritical.getSecrecy()→exists(trgSecrecy | trgSecrecy = srcSecrecy)
23       )
24      )
25     )
26    )
27   )
28  )
```

Listing 12.1 *Secure Dependency* OCL constraint (*secrecy* case, excerpt)

A subsystem fulfills *Secure Links* iff for all «integrity» dependencies d between objects on different nodes n, m, ∃ communication path p between n and m with a stereotype s so that write ∉ Threats(s), where Threats(s) is a set of threats posed by an outside attacker to s-stereotyped communication paths.

We specify the *Secure Links* check using the OCL constraint in Listing 12.2. The check is formulated for the UML element model, but we also consider the contained packages on line 3, since both concepts can be used to represent subsystems. Note that we use the function has as a shortcut to check if an element has a particular stereotype. In UML, deployment is based on the notion of artifacts being deployed to a node. On line 7, we assume that artifacts aggregating some objects and their

```
1   context Model inv:
2   let callSendRelations = self.allOwnedElements()→select(e |
3   e→oclIsKindOf(Package) and e.has(securelinks) or self.has(secureLinks)
4   )→collect(p | p.allOwnedElements())→select(d |
5   d→oclIsKindOf(Dependency) and (
6     (d.has(call) or d.has(send))
7     and d.source→oclIsKindOf(Artifact) and d.target→oclIsKindOf(Artifact)
8   )
9   )
10  in let pathsBetween(srcNode:Node,trgNode:Node):Set(ComminicationPath) =
          srcNode.getCommunicationPaths()→select(comm |
11  comm.getMemberEnds()→select(end | end.getType() = trgNode)→size() > 1
12  )
13  in callSendRelations→ forAll(cs |
14  cs.source→forAll(src |
15    src.getDeploymentRelationships()→forAll(srcDep |
16    srcDeployment.getLocationNodes()→forAll(srcNode |
17      cs.target→forAll(trg |
18      trg.getDeploymentRelationships()→forAll(trgDep |
19      trgDep.getLocationNode()→forAll(trgNode |
20      pathsBetween(srcNode,trgNode)→exists(comm |
21        not callSend.has(integrity)
22          or comm.has(LAN) or comm.has(wire) or comm.has(encrypted)
23        )
24        )
25      )
26      )
27    )
28    )
29  )
30  )
```

Listing 12.2 *Secure Links* OCL constraint (*integrity* case)

security requirements have been specified. The set of `callSendRelations`
computed on lines 2–9 represents the dependencies d of the *Secure Links* definition.
We check the condition by iterating over node pairs n, m on lines 13–20 and checking
if permitted kinds of communication paths are in place on lines 21–25. Specifically,
for «integrity»-stereotyped dependencies, these kinds include precisely LAN,
wire, and encrypted. A variant of this constraint exists for the *secrecy* case.

For example, an «Internet»-typed communication path signifies the use of
an unencrypted connection, allowing an outside attacker to perform man-in-the-

middle attacks. An «encryption»-stereotyped communication indicates the use of encryption, shielding from the write attack by an outside attacker.

12.3.2 Template Interpretation

Template interpretation [300] supports the evaluation of OCL constraints on models in which model elements are annotated with presence conditions (such models are called *model templates* in [300]). The key idea is to replace the standard OCL semantics with a variability-aware one: The result of evaluating a constraint is not a plain value, but a set of value-formula pairs, where the formulas specify the condition under which each of the values occurs. This condition, in turn, depends on the presence conditions of the model elements involved in the constraint. Based on this set, to find out if a particular value can actually occur, we combine its formula with the constraints specified in the feature model. We feed the result to an SAT solver to efficiently check whether the formula can be satisfied.

Since we aim to establish if a particular constraint, representing a security check, holds in all configurations, we feed the negation of the condition under which it evaluates to true to the SAT solver. Note that we do not translate OCL constraints into SAT problems, but calculate all possible outcomes of the OCL constraint execution and the conditions under which they can occur concerning the feature model.

For instance, to check if a particular class is stereotyped with the stereotype «critical», we can evaluate the constraint class.has(critical) on the class. Assuming standard OCL semantics, the result of this check is true or false. But with template interpretation, we take presence conditions into account. For the class Prescription in Figure 12.3, the following result is obtained: {(true, UC37), (false, ¬UC37)}. Similarly, for the class OfficeVisit {(true, UC37), (false, ¬UC37)} but this time due to the «ConditinalCritical». The paper [300] explains how to generate such sets of value-formula pairs for arbitrary OCL constraints, including those with complex operators such as forAll() and size().

We need to answer the question if an OCL constraint c representing a security check sec, such as *Secure Links*, on an element e holds in all products of a considered SPL. This question can be represented as the following SAT problem:

$$s = f \wedge (p^*(e) \Rightarrow \neg c_{true}) \tag{12.1}$$

Here, f is the conjunction of the feature constraints in the feature model, $p^*(e)$ is e's extended presence condition, and c_{true} is the condition under which c evaluates to `true`. The extended presence condition of the element e is taken into account as the constraint can only be evaluated if the element is part of the software system. For example, considering the constraint `self.getClientDependencies()` $\rightarrow$`size()>1` for the class `ViewRecordsPatientAction` in Figure 12.3, we would obtain for the constraint locally on the class that $c_{true} =$ `U19Patients` $\vee$ `Patients`. Please note, that the dependency to the class `Patient` is implicit conditional as the class `Patient` is conditional. However, for the existence of the dependencies the presence condition of class `ViewRecordsPatientAction` is also a dependency, leading to $c_{true} =$ (`U19Patients` $\vee$ `Patients`) $\wedge$ `UC9` $\wedge$ `UC9` $=$ `UC9` $\wedge$ `Patients`. The feature constraints are taken into account because they determine the allowed set of configurations. For example, the feature model in Figure 11.2 contains the constraint `Patients` $\iff$ (`UC9` $\vee$ `UC19Patients` $\vee$ `UC30` $\vee$ `UC40Patients`). Due to this constraint, we can know that all products that contain the feature `UC9` have more than one outgoing dependency at the class `ViewRecordsPatientAction`.

The implication allows neglecting irrelevant configurations in which e is absent and thus, cannot violate the constraint. The extended presence condition $p^*(e)$ accounts for the containment hierarchy: The presence of an element depends on the presence of its container objects. Therefore, $p^*(e)$ is obtained via the conjunction of $e's$ presence condition with the presence conditions of its container elements.

The output of evaluating s with a SAT solver is either the result that c is `true` in all configurations, that is, `sec` holds in e for all products, or a *witness*, that is, a configuration leading to a product in which `sec` is not fulfilled in e.

12.3.3 Discussion of Correctness and Performance

In this section, first, we discuss the correctness of the presented approach, and second, factors impacting its performance.

Correctness of the Security Checks: The correctness of template interpretation relies on the argumentation in [300]. The correctness of our implementation, including the OCL constraints, was studied by systematic testing. Specifically, we systematically extended the test cases of the existing implementation with variability: We considered all possible combinations of annotating the involved elements with variability. The resulting test suite comprises 54 test cases. As test oracle, we used the existing Java-based implementation of UMLsec's checks in CARiSMA, the standard implementation of UMLsec. For a given SecPL-based test model, we enumerated all products, producing a set of UMLsec models on which we performed the CARiSMA check. The results of the variability-aware security check and the single CARiSMA checks were equivalent in all cases, yielding confidence in the correctness of our analysis.

Performance of the Security Checks: The performance of the overall security analysis depends on the generation of the formula as well as the SAT check. As argued in [300], the generation procedure has polynomial complexity concerning the size of the input model. For most of OCL's operators, the generation is linear; however, in the case of $size$, it requires quadratic time, since it considers the cross-product of model elements. SAT solving is NP-complete in general, but state-of-the-art SAT solvers can handle a million variables and several millions of constraints efficiently [302], which is more than sufficient for typical product line scenarios.

12.3.4 Extensibility of the Approach

In the previous sections, we introduced a security and variability profile and constraints for two UMLsec checks on UML product lines. The approach has been designed to allow flexible extension according to the needs of a software project. For the extension of the approach, we identified two dimensions:

Support of Additional Security Checks: We provide OCL encodings for the widely used UMLsec checks: *Secure Links* and *Secure Dependency* [105, 106, 303–305]. As illustrated in the example, in combination, these checks aim to protect secrecy and integrity on the physical and the logical level. Our solution is extensible in the sense that expert users can define additional checks by providing additional stereotypes with a corresponding OCL encoding. These checks can be used by end-users for annotating and checking UML models transparently, without using or understanding OCL.

Adaptation to Domain-Specific Languages: Our profile, but also extended profiles, can be applied in combination with domain-specific languages that are based on UML profiles. For example, a central diagram type in SysML models is block diagrams. The blocks in block diagrams are elements of the UML type Class with the stereotype «Block». Accordingly, SysML blocks can own properties, just like classes in class diagrams can do. The properties in SysML are more fine-grained, reflected in additional SysML-specific stereotypes such as «AdjunctProperty» or «DistributedProperty». Since the categorization of properties in these stereotypes is orthogonal to the included security requirements, the *Secure Dependency* check can be applied to block diagrams straightforwardly, by applying both the SysML and the SecPL stereotypes to the underlying UML model.

As shown in this section, SecPL can easily be extended to cover additional security checks and to be applicable to different domains.

12.4   Tool Support for Family-based Security Checks of UML Product Lines

The analysis is implemented as a prototypical plugin for the Eclipse IDE using the Papyrus UML editor for creating and annotating UML models. During the task of annotating UML models, the user is supported with well-formedness checks of presence conditions, an overview of feature usages in the UML model as well as the option to execute our check on all products. Figure 12.7 shows a screenshot of the Papyrus UML editor in the Eclipse IDE and the SecPL tool support for specifying UML product lines. In the center of the figure, the iTrust model excerpt from Figure 12.3 is shown in the Papyrus editor. At the bottom of the figure, the SecPL extension is shown. The *SecPL Features* view contains a list of all features defined in the FeatureIDE model of the project. In this case, this is the feature model from Figure 11.2 used as an example in this chapter. The view shows for every feature if it is currently used in the UML product line or not. Also, for every feature, the location of the usage and the corresponding presence condition can be shown. For example, the feature `Patients` is used in two locations. Both times in a «`Conditional`» stereotype on the classes `Patient` and `ViewRecordsPatientControl`. On top of the view, the number of possible configurations and whether security violations have been found using the SecPL checks. When introducing the feature model, we mentioned that there are 528 possible configurations of the feature model but in Figure 12.7 it is stated that there are 464 possible configurations. This is due to the feature of analyzing partial configurations. In this case, the feature `Patients` is selected by a checkmark meaning that only the configurations containing the feature `Patients` are considered. This allows to first only focus only on partial configurations at the development and broaden the scope afterward.

To allow developers to actively trigger the SecPL checks or to integrate them into a continuous integration pipeline we integrated the SecPL checks into the CARiSMA tool. Figure 12.8 shows the integration of SecPL into CARiSMA. In the figure's center, we can see a CARISMA analysis configuration file. In this file, besides the *fair exchange* of the classic CARiSMA implementation, the two SecPL checks are added to the configuration. For the current execution, which can be triggered

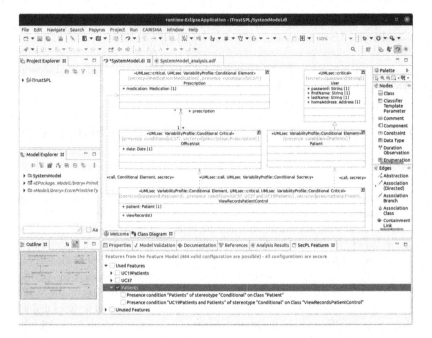

Figure 12.7 Papyrus UML editor with *SecPL Features View* showing usages of features in UML product lines

by clicking on the RUN button, only the SecPL *Secure Links* check is selected. The results of this execution are shown in the *Analysis Results* view at the figure's bottom.

Since our OCL constraints are formulated in a rather coarse-grained fashion, based on the model- and package-level, determining the root cause of a failed check can be a non-trivial task for developers. However, for debugging purposes, developers can use the produced witnesses to inspect a single product where the issue occurs, rather than the full SPL representation. During this task, she can use full-fledged tool support, e.g., as provided by CARiSMA [229], for the analysis of the detected insecure product. If a product with security violations is detected, the standard UMLsec check is automatically executed on this product to generate detailed error messages, using the standard implementation of UMLsec by the CARiSMA tool. The user interface for this task is shown in Figure 12.9. To produce a security violation, we changed to presence condition of the «ConditionalCritical»

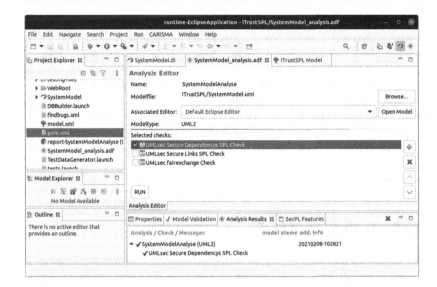

Figure 12.8 Integration of SecPL into CARiSMA

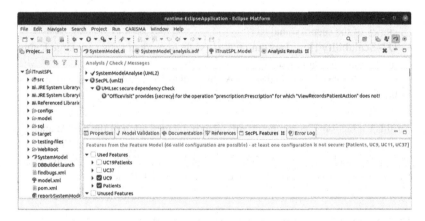

Figure 12.9 Detection of a Security Violation using SecPL

on the class `ViewRecordsPatientControl` to be more restrictive for the signature `prescription:Prescription` on the security level secrecy. As we can see in the *SecPL Features* view, the iTrust UML product line now contains at least one security violation and one configuration containing a violation is stated ($Patients \land UC9 \land UC11 \land UC37$). The UML product for this configuration is automatically generated and the default CARiSMA *Secure Dependency* check is executed on this product. Details on the violation in the product are shown as before in the *Analysis Results* view of CARiSMA. In this case, the changed presence condition lead to the class `ViewRecordsPatientControl` not specifying `prescription:Prescription` on the security level of secrecy in this product.

12.5   Evaluation of SecPL

We designed a methodology for specifying and analyzing security requirements in software product lines. In this section, we evaluate the following aspects of our methodology:

- **O1–Efficiency** To what extent does our family-based analysis improve the efficiency of the security analysis?
- **O2–Scalability** How does our analysis scale to product lines with large feature models and domain models?
- **O3–Usefulness** Is our methodology easily understandable, usable, and applicable to realistic software engineering projects?

For this evaluation, we use the prototypical implementation of the SecPL analysis presented in the previous section. We performed all experiments on a Windows 10 PC with an Intel i5-3570K, 8 GB of RAM, and Oracle JDK 8 inside of an Eclipse Neon.3 instance which was allowed to allocate up to 6 GB memory.

12.5.1 O1–Efficiency of the Security Checks

To evaluate our methodology based on realistic subjects, we collected a suite of models suitable for our security- and variability-oriented setting. The collection was performed based on convenience sampling, in most cases by reusing evaluation samples from the existing literature on software product lines and model-based security. We give an overview of our subjects in Table 12.1 with relevant information,

Table 12.1 Subjects of the efficiency evaluation of the variability-aware security checks

Project name	Input artifacts	#Elements	#*Call*	#Features	#Products
BMW	Magazine article	116	13	16	54
E2E	UMLsec models	130	14	7	94
BCMS	UML models	3,034	4	8	254
JSSE	Java	24,077	28	6	64
Notepad	Java + Antenna	252	4	13	512
MobilePhoto	Java + Antenna	4,069	35	13	3,072
Lampiro	Java + Antenna	29,045	24	20	5,892

including the number of dependencies with «call» and «send» stereotypes, since they are a key part in both considered checks. The models stem from a variety of sources that can be divided into two groups.

The first group represents original modeling examples. First, we created a model based on the description of the in-car system of *BMW*. Second, we used a UMLsec scenario obtained from the CARiSMA developers from their prior collaboration with an industry partner and extended it with variability: *EndToEndEncryption* (E2E) is based on a set of system models specifying different versions of *Munich Re*'s IT infrastructure [306]. For our evaluation, we refactored those models into a product line. Third, the *Barbados Car Crash Management System* (bCMS) [307] is based on a requirements specification of the car crash management system SPL. For our evaluation, we used an available UML implementation in the form of enumerated products [308] and manually refactored it into a SecPL model. While the bCMS model is relatively large, only a small part of the model required security annotations, resulting in four relevant calls.

The second group is made up of projects from the open-source Java context. As discussed in Section 11.4, we produced SecPL models by applying our reverse engineering mechanism to the available codebases. We consider OpenJDK's implementation of the *Java Secure Socket Extension* (*JSSE*), a particularly interesting security-critical scenario. Besides variability annotations, we added security annotations based on security-critical keywords like "keystore". *Notepad* [290] is a text editor in which the opening and writing of files are security-critical. For example, many iOS apps have been infected by a corrupted editor [309]. *MobilePhoto* [292] is a mobile multi-media platform supporting for sharing media over an Internet connection. *Lampiro* [293] is an instant messaging client which has been naively developed as a software product line. In these cases, we added security annotations to the codebase and propagated these into the models at reverse engineering.

Setup. We experimentally evaluated the efficiency of our analysis using the models described above, using the state-of-the-art tool, CARiSMA, as a baseline. For each model, we compared the execution time for checking the SecPL model using our analysis (SecPL check) to the sum of the execution times for checking all products using CARiSMA, which supports regular UMLsec checks on single products (product-wise check). In both cases, we measure the timespan from loading a UML model with SecPL stereotypes to the delivery of the analysis results for all products. Our analysis is more efficient if the execution times of the SecPL implementation are significantly lower than those of CARiSMA.

Results. The product-wise check produced a result for five out of seven subjects, *BMW*, *E2E*, *BCMS*, *JSSE*, and *Notepad*. In these cases, the SecPL checks were between one and three orders of magnitude faster (Figure 12.10). For the subjects *MobilePhoto* and *Lampiro*, the product-wise check terminated with a garbage collection (GC) overhead exception after 700 to 1,000 checked products and 3 to 5 hours of run time, whereas the SecPL checks took below 100 seconds. On average, the product-wise check spent 91.6% of the time generating the products, and the remaining 8.4% performing the checks. We observed that the run time of the product-wise check mainly depends on the number of products, whereas the SecPL check is mainly influenced by the model size and the number of relevant calls. In sum, SecPL outperformed the product-wise check constantly.

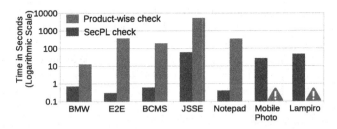

Figure 12.10 Execution times of the family-based SecPL check and the product-wise check with CARiSMA

O2–Scalability of the Security Checks

For our scalability evaluation, we needed to freely control the size of our test models. To this end, we generated synthetic models. Our rationale was to create models being representative of realistic examples, which we address as follows.

To study the effect of the model size, we generated large class models, being amenable to the *Secure Dependency* check. Based on typical cases in the security-critical portions of the realistic examples, we incrementally added classes with on average four operations and three dependencies. Our initial model contained two classes with one call dependency between them and one operation each. In each iteration, we added a class with a «critical» stereotype and a normally distributed number of operations, on average four, and a normally distributed number of dependencies, on average three. We added all member signatures of classes reachable over a dependency to the *secrecy* tag of the class's «critical» stereotype. The resulting model is potentially expensive to check:

(i) it comprises many involved dependencies and operations, and
(ii) since it fulfills *Secure Dependency*, every class treats all relevant signatures with *secrecy*, the check does not terminate early with a counterexample.

To study the effect of the feature model size, we took a randomly generated UML model from the model-size experiment with 4K classes, incrementally added independent features to the feature model successively, and assigned each feature to one class in the model via a suitable «conditional» stereotype. We checked models annotated with between zero and 4K features, adding 50 features in each iteration.

Setup. To experimentally evaluate scalability, we measure the execution times of our SecPL implementation on different synthetic models with a growing number of model elements and features as described above. Our analysis is scalable if the execution time avoids exponential growth for increasingly larger domain models and feature models.

Results. In our scalability experiment regarding model size, the largest generated model we checked had 524K UML elements, including 66K classes with an average number of four operations and three call dependencies to other classes. As shown in the upper part of Figure 12.11 the execution of this test case took 97.3 minutes. The regression function we calculated from these measurements is a second-order polynomial and fits the measured data with a coefficient of determination (R^2) of nearly one (0.999985). This observation is in line with the performance considerations

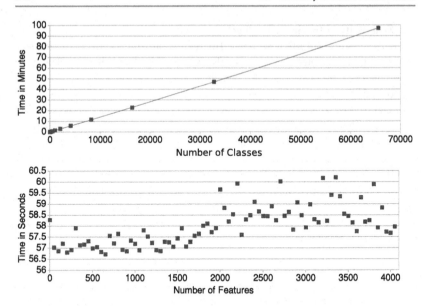

Figure 12.11 Scalability results of SecPL regarding *Number of Classes* and *Number of Features*

for template interpretation. For our scalability experiment regarding the number of features, we used a randomly generated model with 4K UML classes (32K UML elements) and successively added up to 4K independent features ($1.04 \cdot 10^{1233}$ products). The measured data points as illustrated in Figure 12.11 show a higher variance compared to those from the previous experiment. The analysis took between 57 and 58 seconds up to 1.7K features and started oscillating between 58 and 60 seconds until around 4K features. In sum, our analysis showed scalable behavior up to thousands of features, the magnitude of large product lines in automotive engineering [294].

12.5.2 O3–Usefulness of the Tool Support and Security Checks

To evaluate the usefulness of our methodology, we conducted a user experiment with participants from academia and industry.

Setup.   We recruited nine participants from academia, two of them with a significant industrial background, and one representative of an industry partner. The participants from academia came from three universities and one private research institute and had their focus on security, SPL, and modeling domains. The industry-experienced academics had long-running backgrounds as IT freelancers. Moreover, one of them was employed at a large steel-based technology group at the time of the experiment. The industry partner, SinnerSchrader, is Germany's fourth-largest digital marketing company and cooperates with many major international companies.

After a short introduction to SecPL, we asked the participants to perform a development task based on an in-car system oriented on a BMW system described in the literature [310]. This software system allows users to unlock their BMW car using a mobile application. It has been shown that sensitive data is released in error messages if a specific modem has been selected in the car product line. The task was to extend a provided UML model of this software system with a new alternative modem type by using our tool prototype while addressing the included security requirements. Afterward, the participants filled in a questionnaire in which they rated their subjective experience in eight questions based on a five-point Likert scale. Five questions addressed usability concerns, such as the difficulty of specifying a new security requirement; three questions were concerned with understandability, such as the certainty that the participant's understanding of the used stereotypes was correct. We provide a replication package including the task, questions, and results together with the submission.

After the experiment, we conducted informal interviews with all participants, in which we asked for feedback concerning usability and understandability. In the interviews with the industry-based and -experienced participants, we additionally asked them to comment on the applicability of our methodology to their business segments and those of their customers.

Results.   In what follows, we discuss the results of our evaluation regarding the usefulness of the proposed approach. First, we discuss the approach's usability and understandability. Next, we discuss the practical applicability of the approach.

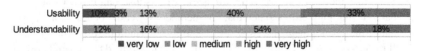

Figure 12.12 Aggregated answers from the user study regarding the usability and understandability of SecPL

Usability and Understandability: The answers to our questions indicate that our methodology is easily usable and understandable. According to Figure 12.12 in both categories, more than 70 percent of the answers suggest a high or very high usability and understandability, an impression confirmed by the feedback in the interviews. On the downside, some participants perceived the editing of annotations through Papyrus's user interface as cumbersome, as reflected by some of the negative scores for usability. Moreover, some participants were worried that a larger model "cluttered" with annotations may become hard to read. A promising strategy to deal with these issues is by providing improved tool support, for example, to support the editing of large models based on custom-tailored views [311], including views on individual products of the product line [312]. A further question raised by participants was where to start when annotating the model with security requirements. To this end, approaches analyzing higher-level security specifications and suggesting SecPL security annotations can be helpful [74]. Moreover, a textual UML notation may further help to improve usability. Despite the mostly positive understandability ratings, one participant reported considerable problems while understanding the stereotypes. An interactive help system may help to further improve understandability.

Practical Applicability: According to our industry partner's representative, our notation for specification and analysis of security requirements on product lines is an accurate fit for their business needs. As an example for a possible application, they mentioned a current collaboration in the automotive domain on real-time car software upgrades based on changing customer needs. They want to dynamically advertise and sell upgrades according to customers' needs by dynamically reconfiguring the car, e.g., to sell the usage of the trailer hitch for some days when the customer is relocating. The specification and analysis of security requirements on software product lines are essential for this concept. The participant deemed our graphical notation on UML models as a possibility to realize the specification in a user-friendly way.

One of the industry-experienced participants conjectured that our approach might be very helpful for developers familiar with modeling, but felt that he was not proficient enough in this topic to really judge applicability.

The other industry-experienced participant, who is also employed for a steel-based technology group, stated that our methodology could be used for coordinating the development of security-critical software in multiple distributed teams. If the project has been planned using UML, specially trained team members can easily annotate the models with required and provided security levels of class members. However, for direct use in industry, the tool support has to be improved; distributed and parallel editing of UML models has to be supported. Nevertheless, he pointed out that these are general issues with model-based development, and that they are by no means necessarily aggravated by incorporating SecPL.

To conclude, these first impressions give a promising outlook on the applicability of our methodology in the industry. Since we do not require any artifacts beyond those involved in typical software development processes, our participants found that an alignment of our methodology with these processes seems generally possible.

12.6 Threats to Validity

In this section, we discuss threats to validity according to four categories of threats.

12.6.1 External Validity

External validity is threatened by our limited selection of models that may not be representative of all realistic models. While our suite of test subjects selected for **O1** represents a broad variety of use cases, we cannot generalize our findings to arbitrary models. The models generated for our scalability measurements in **O2** were inspired by the realistic ones used to evaluate **O1**; their purpose was to illustrate the effect of increased model size and feature number. The model in **O3** is by no means representative for all possible usage contexts; however, it was chosen as a critical example inspired by a real case. Also, we performed the experiment only with a limited number of expert users.

12.6.2 Internal Validity

Regarding internal validity, a potential threat concerns the correctness of our implementation. In Section 12.3, we argued for the correctness of our OCL implementations of the considered UMLsec checks by using CARiSMA as a test oracle. Since both implementations were developed independently from another, the identical results from the test suite give us a high level of confidence in the correctness of our implementation. For additional user-specified constraints, correctness has to be ensured as well, for example, by providing a similar test suite. Moreover, while we aimed to systematically specify all security requirements in the considered examples, we cannot guarantee the completeness of our security annotations.

12.6.3 Conclusion Validity

Concerning conclusion validity, a more definitive verdict on the practical applicability of our methodology requires the involvement of a larger sample of practitioners. To this end, the conduction of a broader developer survey in the future could help to prove or disprove our conclusion. In particular, we did not evaluate if users can work with our reverse-engineered models effectively, which depends on the employed model editor's usability during the editing of larger models.

12.6.4 Construct Validity

Regarding construct validity, our methodology is based on existing technology, such as template interpretation and the Papyrus UML editor, which also impact its applicability. Our evaluation assesses the applicability of these techniques *in the domain of software security*, which has not been done in previous work. Moreover, to the best of our knowledge, we also provide the first evaluation of a template-interpretation-based technique on a set of realistic models.

12.7   Conclusion on Security in UML Product Lines

Security is one of the hardest properties of software to accomplish in practice. With this work, we provide a comprehensive methodology for the model-based security analysis of software product lines. We extended our UML variability extension to also support variability within UMLsec security requirements. Using the SecPL profile, users specify security requirements as well as variability information as part of the design-time system models. Furthermore, we investigated how we can detect security violations on the UML product lines without iterating over all products. For this purpose, we specified UMLsec checks as OCL constraints and evaluated these using a template interpretation technique of Czarnecki et al. [300]. This way, our analysis addresses the scalability issues encountered in this setting by lifting the analysis to the level of the entire product line rather than individual products. In our evaluation, this solution enabled the analysis of realistic product lines in realistic cases where the naive approach terminated without a result; a user study indicates the usefulness of our methodology.

In the future, our work can mainly be extended in two directions. First, our methodology can be applied to a broader selection of use cases. Since UMLsec has been used in protocol engineering [104], a promising application involves protocol families. Second, an extended form of our analysis could inform the automated configuration of a product line, e.g., by considering the established security degree and the cost for security measures to assess solutions.

Security Compliance and Restructuring in Variant-rich Software Systems

13

This chapter shares material with the FASE'2018 publication "Taming Multi-Variability of Software Product Line Transformation" [313] and "A Staged Technique for Software Product Line Transformations" submitted for publication.

In the previous chapter, we discussed the specification and verification of security requirements on UML model product lines. With this contribution, we reached the state at which we started at the beginning of this thesis for single-product software systems. We have the means to specify and verify UMLsec security requirements in product lines but the verification of these requirements on the implementation is missing. Also, the maintenance support of GRaViTY, e.g., security-preserving refactorings, has not been transferred to software product lines, yet.

In general, despite the benefits of software product lines, a growing amount of variability leads to combinatorial explosions of the product space and, consequently, to severe challenges. Notably, this applies to software engineering tasks such as refactorings [314], refinements [315], and evolution steps [316], which, to support systematic management, are often expressed as model transformations. In this thesis, we used model transformations for security-preserving refactorings in Chapter 10 and to specify security violation patterns in Section 8.6. The open challenge is the application of these model transformation rules to software product lines as part of the GRaViTY development approach. In this chapter, we provide an approach that allows the application of the security violation patterns and security-preserving refactorings to variant-rich software systems. By doing this, in combination with the previous chapters' contributions, we answer RQ5 to its full extend.

RQ5: How can we verify and preserve security compliance in variant-rich software systems?

S. M. Peldszus, *Security Compliance in Model-driven Development of Software Systems in Presence of Long-Term Evolution and Variants*, https://doi.org/10.1007/978-3-658-37665-9_13

To be more precise, following Figure 13.1, by applying the security violation patterns to software product lines, in addition to Chapter 12's answer concerning UML product lines, we answer RQ5.2 for the program model. As the program model is a representation for analyzing the source code, we also answer this research question for the implementation. Together with the UML model-level security check from Chapter 12, we answer RQ5.2, entirely covering design-time models and the implementation of variant-rich software systems. Using the same approach, we can apply the security-preserving refactorings to software product lines and answer RQ5.3.

RQ5.2: How can security violations be detected on SPLs?
RQ5.3: How can we apply security-aware refactorings to SPLs?

To be more precise, our answers to RQ5.2, in terms of applying security violation patterns to SPLs, and RQ5.3, of how to apply refactorings to SPLs, are specific instances of the general problem of applying multi-variant transformation rules to SPLs. In this chapter, we provide a generic solution to this problem and demonstrate this solution on the two examples.

Generally, when applying a given model transformation to a software product line, a key challenge is to avoid enumerating and considering all possible products individually. To this end, Salay et al. [317] have proposed an algorithm that "*lifts*"

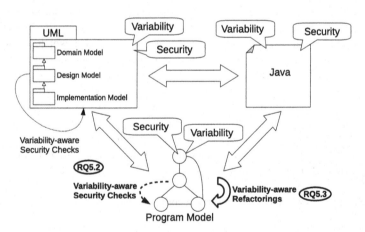

Figure 13.1 Concept including security-compliance checks and restructurings in variant-rich systems

regular transformation rules to a whole product line. The algorithm transforms the SPL, represented as a variability-annotated model, e.g., using SecPL or the variability annotations for the program model, in such a way as if each product had been considered individually.

Yet, in complex transformation scenarios as increasingly found in practice [318], not only the considered models include variations but the transformation system can contain variability as well, for example, due to desired optional behavior of rules, or for rule variants arising from the sheer complexity of the involved meta-models. While several works [319–321] support systematic reuse to improve maintainability, *variability-based model transformation* (VB) [322, 323] also aims to improve the performance when a transformation system with many similar rules is executed. To this end, these rules are represented as a single rule with variability annotations, called *VB rule*. During rule applications, a special *VB rule application* technique [262] saves redundant effort by considering common rule parts only once. In Chapter 10, we used these VB rules to specify variability in refactorings, e.g., regarding possible targets of *Move Method* refactorings. In summary, for cases where either the model or the transformation system alone contains variability, solid approaches are available.

However, a more challenging case occurs when a variability-intensive transformation is applied to an SPL, e.g., the refactorings formalized using graph transformation in Section 10.2. In this *multi-variability* setting, where *both* the input model and the specification of a transformation contain variability, the existing approaches fall short to deal with the resulting complexity: One can either consider all rules, so they can be "lifted" to the product line, or consider all products, so they become amenable to VB model transformation. Both approaches are undesirable, as they require enumerating an exponentially growing number of artifacts and, therefore, threaten the feasibility of the transformation.

In this chapter, we introduce a methodology for SPL transformations inspired by the *uniformity principle* [324], a tenet that suggests handling variability consistently throughout all software artifacts. We propose to capture the variability of SPLs and transformations using variability-annotated models and rules. Model and rule elements are annotated with *presence conditions*, specifying the conditions under which the annotated elements are present. The presence conditions of model and rule elements are specified over two separate sets of features, representing SPL and rule variability. Annotated models and rules can be created manually using available editor support [325, 326], or automatically from existing products and rules by using merge-refactoring techniques [327, 328].

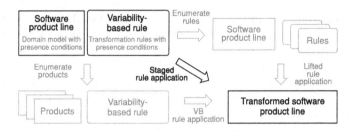

Figure 13.2 Overview of the multi-variant model transformation

Given an SPL and a VB rule, as shown in Figure 13.2, we provide a *staged* rule application technique (black arrow) for applying a VB rule to an SPL. In contrast to the state of the art (shown in gray), enumerating products or rules upfront is not required. By adopting this technique, existing tools that use transformation technology, such as refactoring engines, may benefit from improved performance. Specifically, we make the following contributions:

- We introduce a staged technique for applying a VB rule to an SPL. Our technique combines core principles of VB rule applications and lifting while avoiding their drawbacks regarding enumerating all products or rules upfront.
- We present an algorithm for implementing the rule application technique, which supports efficient rule applications by relying on state-of-the-art SAT solvers.
- We evaluate the usefulness of our technique by studying its performance in a substantial number of cases within two software engineering scenarios including the refactorings introduced in Chapter 10.

Our work builds on the underlying framework of algebraic graph transformation (AGT) [144]. AGT is one of the standard model transformation language paradigms [329]; in addition, it has recently gained momentum as an analysis paradigm for other widespread paradigms and languages such as ATL [330]. We focus on the annotative paradigm to variability. Suitable converters to and from alternative paradigms, such as the composition-based one [312], may allow our technique to be used in other cases as well.

In what follows, first, we introduce our application scenario in terms of a state machine from the iTrust SPL as well as a UML refactoring rule in Section 13.1. Afterward, in Section 13.2, we introduce our multi-variant transformation approach.

In Section 13.3, we introduce our implementation of the multi-variant transformation as an extension of the Henshin transformation engine. We evaluate this approach in Section 13.4 regarding performance in two realistic scenarios including the refactorings introduced in Chapter 10. Finally, we discuss threats in Section 13.5 and conclude in Section 13.6.

13.1 Application Scenario

In this section, first, we introduce an exemplary product line within our iTrust running example, and second, a refactoring product line for UML models.

13.1.1 iTrust example SPL

As the iTrust application scenario for this chapter, we consider a state machine from iTrust's design-time models. This state machine specifies the states during the treatment of a patient within a hospital using iTrust. The core states are oriented on an example from [331] but have been simplified and adapted to iTrust. Generally, the treatment of a patient involves four states. First, the patient is admitted to the hospital. Afterward, the patient is in the state of diagnosis in which doctors inspect the patient to find the reasons for her health issues. After the patient has been diagnosed, the treatment starts. Finally, when the patient has recovered, she is discharged.

Figure 13.3 shows a simplified state machine product line for the treatment of a patient using iTrust. Unlike the example in [331], we do not consider cases of

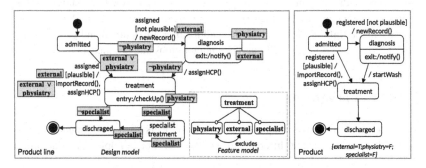

Figure 13.3 State machine showing the states of a patient's treatment

patients deploying additional symptoms or detailed triggers for state changes. In our example, we included variations of the state machine depending on how the iTrust SPL is deployed. To be more precise, we considered the following three optional features:

physiatry: A custom-tailored version of iTrust has been developed for a customer operating a physical medicine and rehabilitation clinic, also known as physiatry. This physiatry is integrated into a bigger hospital and therefore does not the ability to create diagnoses but relies on the diagnoses created by the hospital. To keep the system's user interface simple and reduce the attack surface, iTrust can be deployed without the functionality to edit diagnoses. Instead, the functionality to import diagnoses from an external source, e.g., the hospital into that the physiatry is integrated, has been added.

external: The functionality to import diagnoses from external sources, that has been developed for the physiatry, has been used to support the general import of diagnoses from other hospitals. If the imported diagnosis is plausible, the `diagnosis` state can be bypassed and the treatment can be started immediately. Whenever a patient enters the `treatment` state, a checkup has to be performed. As diagnoses are necessary in case the imported diagnosis is not plausible, this feature cannot be combined with the `physiatry` feature.

specialist: The third optional feature allows treatment by external specialists as part of the treatment. If treatment by external specialists is supported, after the regular treatment, patients can be handed over to a specialist. In this case, patients enter an additional state before being discharged.

Concrete products can be obtained from *configurations* in that each optional feature is either set to `true` or `false`. A product arises by removing those elements whose presence condition evaluates to false in the given configuration. For instance, selecting `external` and deselecting `physiatry` and `specialist` yields the product shown in the right of Figure 13.3. Since all features are optional and `physiatry` excludes `external`, the SPL has six configurations and products in total.

13.1.2 Rule Variants

In complex model transformation scenarios, developers often create transformation rules that are similar but different from each other. For example, the refactorings introduced in Chapter 10 had similar base parts but different variations, e.g., regarding possible target classes of *Move Method* refactorings or security constraints.

As a simpler example, consider the two refactoring rules `foldEntryActions` and `foldExitActions` (Figure 13.4), called A and B in short. These rules express a "fold" refactoring for state machine diagrams: if a state has two incoming or outgoing transitions with the same action, these actions are to be replaced by an entry or exit action of the state. The rules have a left- and a right-hand side (LHS, RHS). The LHS specifies a pattern to be matched to an input graph, and the difference between the LHS and the RHS specifies a change to be performed for each match, like the removing of transition actions, and the adding of exit and entry actions.

In addition, both rules each contain two *Negative Application Conditions* (NACs, [333]). Intuitively, a NAC specifies a particular pattern whose presence is *forbidden*, yielding a precondition that needs to be fulfilled to render the rule applicable at a given place in the model. NAC1 of rule A specifies that the state receiving the entry action, identified with x, may not already have an entry action. NAC1 of rule B specifies the equivalent condition for exit instead of entry actions. These NACs are required in state machine diagrams that only support one entry and exit action per state. In both rules, NAC2 specifies that the target state may not be a complex state, which is a state nesting sub-states. These NACs are required to enforce a general policy that such complex states may not have entry or exit actions since the actual entry and exit action would be performed within the nested states. NACs

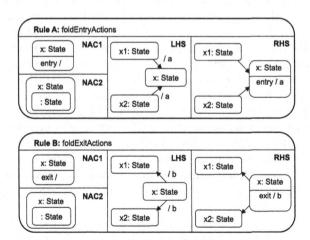

Figure 13.4 Two rules for refactoring state machines (adapted from [332])

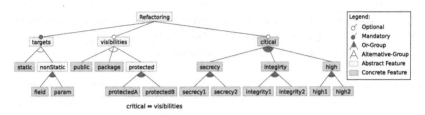

Figure 13.5 Feature model of the *Move Method* refactoring rule, including all security constraints

are considered in conjunction, that is, the rule is only applicable if both NACs are satisfied.

13.1.3 Variability-based Model Transformation

Rules A and B are simple; however, in a realistic transformation system, the number of required rules can grow exponentially with the number of variation points in the rules. An example of these is the security constraints for refactorings discussed in Section 10.3.2. Figure 13.5 shows the *Move Method* refactoring's feature model, including all security constraints introduced in Section 10.3. Only the application conditions avoiding the increase of a method's visibility when moving the method to another class (feature `visibilities` and its child features) and the semantic-preserving features (`targets` and its child features) already result in 20 variants of this refactoring rule. The four additional security constraints for moving methods only to critical classes introduced in Section 10.3.2 are not included yet. For these, we have four additional application conditions per considered UMLsec security level. As two of these conditions are exclusive, these can be represented by one feature, e.g., `secrecy` for the secrecy case of the conditions. In the end, these can be compared to three possible configurations for each security level. Assuming the three security levels *secrecy*, *integrity*, and *high* of UMLsec, there are 64 variants of these constraints. In combination with the visibility constraints, we get 1,264 variants of the *Move Method* refactoring. To avoid such a combinatorial explosion, a set of variability-intensive rules can be encoded into a single representation using a *VB rule* [323, 328].

A VB rule consists of an LHS, a RHS, a `feature model` specifying a set of interrelated rule features, and *presence conditions* annotating LHS and RHS

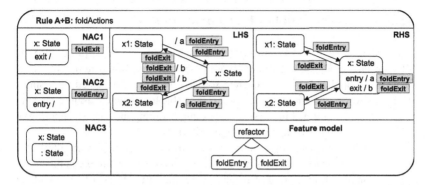

Figure 13.6 Variability-based rule encoding the two example rules

Table 13.1 Approaches for dealing with multi-variability

	Independent combinations	
Approach	*Example*	*General case*
Naive	12	$2^{\#F_P} * 2^{\#F_r}$
VB transformation [323]	6	$2^{\#F_P}$
Lifting [317]	2	$2^{\#F_r}$
Staged application (new)	1	1

elements with a condition under which they are present. Individual "flat" rules are obtained via configuration, i.e., binding each feature to either `true` or `false`.

The VB rule A+B, shown in Figure 13.6, is equivalent to the individual rules A and B. Notably, nodes, edges, and the negative application conditions NAC1 and NAC2 each have a presence condition. The scope of these presence conditions is generally the entire NAC. (A possible design alternative would be to annotate individual NAC elements with presence conditions. However, this option's practical usefulness is limited by semantic complications related to the notion of "subrule", which we will discuss later.) The feature model specifies a root feature `refactor` with alternative child features `foldEntry` and `foldExit`. Since exactly one child feature has to be active at one time, two possible configurations exist. The two rules arising from these configurations are isomorphic to rules A and B.

13.2   Multi-Variant Model Transformation

Usually, we design model transformations such as `foldActions` but also the refactorings introduced in Chapter 10 or the security violation patterns from Section 8.6 for applications to a concrete software product represented by a single model. However, in various situations, it is desirable to extend the usage context to a *set* of models collected in an SPL. For example, during the batch refactoring of an SPL, all products should be refactored uniformly.

Variability is challenging for model transformation technologies. As illustrated in Table 13.1, products and rules need to be considered in manifold combinations. In our example of refactoring of the state machine from the iTrust SPL, without dedicated variability support, the user needs to specify 6 products and 2 rules individually and trigger a rule application for each of the 12 combinations. A better strategy is enabled by VB model transformation: by applying the VB rule A+B, only 6 combinations need to be considered. Another strategy is to apply rules A and B to the SPL by *lifting* [317] them, leading to 2 combinations and the biggest improvement so far. Still, in more complex cases, all of these strategies are insufficient. Since none of them avoids exponential growth along with the number of optional SPL features ($\#F_P$) or optional rule features ($\#F_r$), the feasibility of the transformation is threatened.

13.2.1 Solution Overview

A variability-based rule, e.g., the specification of a refactoring, represents a set of similar transformation rules, while a product line represents a set of similar models. Variability-based rule application allows us to save matching effort by considering shared parts of rules to a graph only once. We can show that the sets of partially and fully flattened rule applications are equivalent.

For every fully flattened (FF) rule application, we can find a corresponding partially flattened (PF) one, and vice versa: Given a FF rule application at a base-match, we compose the base-match with the product inclusion into the model to obtain a match into the model. Per Theorem 2 in [323], a match induces a VB match and rule application. From a diagram chase, we see that the base-match is the morphism arising from rerouting m_c onto the product P_i. Consequently, the rule application is PF. Conversely, a PF variability-based rule application induces a corresponding FF rule application by its definition.

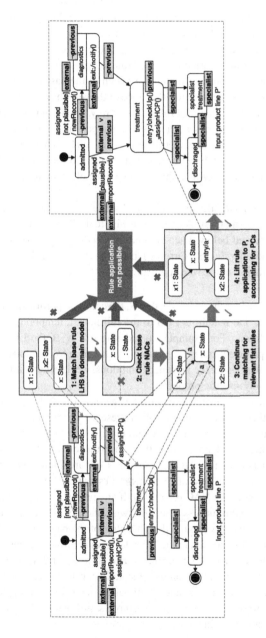

Figure 13.7 Staged rule application of a VB rule to a product line

Lifting takes a single rule and applies it to a model and its presence conditions in such a way as if the rule had been applied to each product individually. The considered rule in our case is a flat rule with a match to the model.

The key idea of lifting a variability-based rule to a product line is as follows: each match of a flat rule to a product includes a match of the base rule into the model. The absence of such a match implies that none of the rules has a match, allowing us to stop without considering any flat rule in its entirety. Such exit point is particularly beneficial if the VB rule represents a subset of a larger rule set in which only a few rules can be matched at one time. Conversely, if a match for a base rule exists, a rule application arises if the match can be rerouted onto one of the products. In this case, we consider the flat rules, saving redundant matching effort by reusing the matches of the base rule.

We propose a *staged* rule application technique for applying a VB rule to an SPL to address this situation. As shown in Figure 13.7, this technique proceeds in four steps discussed below. Each step has a *success* case (arrows labeled with a checkmark) and an *exit* case (arrows labeled with a cross). Exit cases lead to immediate termination of the rule application.

- In step 1, we consider the base rule, that is, the common portion of rules encoded in the VB rule, and match its LHS to the full model, temporarily ignoring its presence conditions. For example, considering rule A+B, the LHS of the base rule contains precisely states x1, x2, and x. A match to the model is indicated by dashed arrows. Using the presence conditions, we determine if the match can be mapped to any specific product.

- In step 2, for each prematch, we consider the base rule NACs, that is, the VB rule's NACs that do not have an explicit presence condition, equivalent to the presence condition true. For a given prematch, we check a subset of the base rule NACs (which we characterize in this paper) that can be checked at this point. Prematches that do not fulfill these base rule NACs are filtered out. Our example prematch fulfills the one relevant NAC (NAC3) since treatment does not nest any substates; hence the NAC is fulfilled. If any prematches are remaining after filtering, we are in the success case; otherwise, the exit case is reached.

- In step 3, we extend the identified prematches of the base rule to identify pre-matches of the rules encoded in the VB rule again ignoring presence conditions. In the example, we would derive rules A and B; in general, to avoid fully flat-tening all involved rules, one can incrementally consider common subrules. An example prematch is denoted in terms of dashed lines for the mappings of tran-sitions and actions. If we obtain a non-empty set of prematches, we are in the success case, otherwise in the exit case.

- In step 4, to perform rule applications based on identified prematches, we use *lifting* to apply the rule for which the match was found. Lifting transforms the model and its presence condition in such a way as if each product was considered individually. In the process, it also checks a remaining condition that renders the prematches proper matches (discussed later). In the example, only products for the configuration {`external=true; previous=false`} are amenable to the `foldAction` refactoring. Consequently, the new entry action `assignHCP` has the presence condition `external` $\land$ `¬physiatry`, and other presence conditions are adjusted accordingly. During lifting, a certain condition is checked. The condition determines if the match can be mapped to any specific product (based on the model's presence conditions) so that all NACs of the flattened rule are satisfied. If none of the considered matches fulfills these conditions, the exit case is reached. Otherwise, we are in the success case.

Performance-wise, the main benefit of this technique is twofold: First, using the termination criteria, we can exit the matching process early without considering the specifics of products and rule variants. This early termination is particularly beneficial in situations where none or only a few rules of a larger rule set are applicable most of the time, which is typically the case, for example, in translators. Second, even if we have to enumerate some rules in step 2, we do not have to start the matching process from scratch, since we can save redundant effort by extending the available base matches. Consequently, Table 13.1 gives the number of independent combinations (in the sense that rule applications are started from scratch) as 1.

13.2.2 Multi-Variant Transformation Algorithm

We present an algorithm for implementing the VB rule $\check{r}$'s staged application to a product line P. The main idea is to proceed in four steps:

1. First, we match the base rule of $\check{r}$ to the model, ignoring presence conditions, obtaining a set of prematches.
2. Second, we check certain NACs of the base rule on the prematches to filter out those prematches with violations.
3. Third, we consider individual rules as far as necessary to obtain prematches to the model.
4. Fourth, based on the matches, we perform the actual rule application using the lifting algorithm from [317] in a black-box manner.

Algorithm 4 shows the computation in more detail. Our formalization so far supports the checking of NACs as part of the lifting phase. In that phase, we consider an individual flattened rule r_c to which we apply Sayal et al.'s lifting operator, which is geared for dealing with NACs, including those of r_c. In our multi-variability scenario, relying on lifting leads to a sound, but not necessarily efficient solution: it might lead to considering many flat rules arising from the VB rule individually, only to discover late in the process that none of these rules is applicable, due to NACs being not fulfilled.

Algorithm 4: Staged application of a VB rule to a product line.

Input : Product line P, VB rule $\check{r}$
Output: Transformed product line P

1 $precheckBaseNACs :=$ precheckBaseNACs($\check{r}$);
2 $BMatches :=$ findPreMatches($Model_P$, r_0);
3 **foreach** $m_{base} \in$ BMatches **do**
4 | $BNACMatches :=$ findNACMatches($Model_P$, m_{base}, $precheckBaseNACs$);
5 | $\Phi_{pc} := \bigwedge \{ pc \in \text{pcs}(m_{base}) \}$;
6 | $\Phi_{nac} := \bigvee \{ \bigwedge \{ pc \in \text{pcs}(m_{bNac}) \} \mid m_{bNac} \in BNACMatches \}$;
7 | **if** $\Phi_P \wedge \Phi_{pc} \wedge \neg\Phi_{nac}$ is *SAT* **then**
8 | | **foreach** $c \in configs(\check{r})$ **do**
9 | | | $flatRule := r_{\check{r}}.$removeAllElements($e \mid c \not\models pc_e$);
10 | | | $flatRule := flatRule.$removeAllNACs($n \mid c \not\models pc_n$);
11 | | | $PreMatches :=$ findPreMatches($Model_P$, $flatRule$, m);
12 | | | **foreach** $m_{pre} \in$ PreMatches **do**
13 | | | | $NACMatches :=$ findNACMatches($Model_P$, m_{pre}, nacs($\check{r}$) /
   | | | | precheckBaseNACs);
14 | | | | lift(P, $flatRule$, m_{pre}, $NACMatches$);
15 | | | **end**
16 | | **end**
17 | **end**
18 **end**

As a performance optimization, we allow certain NACs to be checked early. We consider the base rule NACs, that is, the set of NACs that are shared by all subrules of the considered VB rule. In general, not every base rule NAC can be checked early in the way we do it. This is because the additions that a subrule performs to the base rule might render a NAC fulfilled that is *not* fulfilled when considering just the base rule. Elements that matched the NAC's pattern for the base rule, match the additions of the subrule and cannot be matched by the NAC's pattern anymore. Hence, checking the involved NAC for the base rule only would lead to some prematches being prematurely discarded.

To determine if a given NAC can indeed be checked early, we define a property called *precheck-NAC* and provide a sufficient criterion to check it. The intuition behind *precheck-NAC* is to determine those NACs that, when fulfilled in the larger context of an extended rule, are also fulfilled in the smaller context of the base rule.

First, in line 1, we compute the set of base rule NACs for which a precheck is possible. To this end, we apply the *precheck-NAC* criterion to all base rule NACs and collect those that fulfill the criterion. Afterward, in line 2, $\check{r}$'s base rule r_0 is matched to the model $Model_P$, leading to a set of prematches for the base rule. If this set is empty, we have reached an exit criterion and can stop directly, as the following part is skipped. Otherwise, given a match m_{base}, in line 7, we check if at least one product P_i exists onto that m can be rerouted.

To this end, in lines 4–7, we use an SAT solver to check if there is a valid configuration of P's feature model for which all presence conditions of matched elements evaluate to `true`, and at the same time, no NAC can be matched in all valid configurations of P's feature model. In line 4, we match all base NACs on the model $Model_P$ using the match m_{base} as the context for each NAC. For the match of the base rule, we calculate the conjunction of the presence conditions of the nodes matched by the base rule, giving the condition under which the match is part of the model. In line 6, we calculate the disjunction over the conditions for being part of the model of all NAC matches. The condition for a NAC match to be present in a product of the model is again the disjunction over the matched elements' presence conditions. The formula considered in line 7 checks whether a base match m_{base} is liftable: this is the case if there exists a product that includes all matched elements, and there exist no NAC matches extending m_{base}.

If there is a valid configuration fulfilling the condition, we iterate over the valid configurations of $\check{r}$ in line 8 (we may proceed more fine-grained using partial configurations; this optimization is omitted for simplicity). A flat rule is obtained in lines 9 and 10 by removing all elements and NACs from the rule whose presence condition evaluates to `false`. We match this rule to the model in line 11; to save redundant effort, we restrict the search to prematches that extend the current prematch. The absence of such a prematch is a further exit criterion for the current rule configuration c. Otherwise, we match for every prematch all NACs of the *flatRule* that have not been matched yet. Afterward, in line 14, we feed the flat rule, the prematch, and the matches of the NACs to lifting in line 13. The evaluation of final NAC and dangling conditions is left to lifting; in the positive case, P is transformed afterward.

For illustration, consider the prematch m_1 = {admitted, diagnostics, treatment} for the rule *foldActions* from Figure 13.7. In line 1, we consider the rule's NACs. Based on the previous descriptions, we know that NAC3 is a base NAC and fulfills the precheck condition, and thus, is stored in precheckBaseNACs. Then we calculate Φ_{pc}. As none of the states involved in the prematch has a presence condition, Φ_{pc} is set to true. Similarly, Φ_{nac} is set to false because the prematch m_1 fulfills the only considered (*NAC3*). Altogether, the constraint is satisfiable and the prematch liftable. Therefore we consider the VB rule's configurations. Two valid configurations exist, c_1 = {foldEntry=true, foldExit=false} and c_2 = {foldEntry= false, foldExit=true}. Considering c_1, the presence condition *foldExit* evaluates to false; removing the corresponding elements yield a rule isomorphic to Rule A in Figure 13.6. Now, prematch m_1 is extended using this rule, leading to a prematch as shown in step 3 of Figure 13.7, and then lifted, as discussed in the earlier explanation of the example. Step 3 is repeated for configuration c_2; yet, as no suitable prematch in c_2 exists, the shown transformation is the only possible one.

This algorithm benefits from the correctness results shown in [313]. The effect of the rule application to the products is the same as if each product had been considered individually. In terms of performance, two limiting factors are the use of a graph matcher and an SAT solver; both of them perform an NP-complete task. Still, we expect practical improvements from our strategy of reusing shared portions of the involved rules and graphs, and from the availability of efficient SAT solvers that

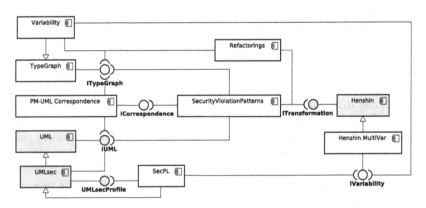

Figure 13.8 Component diagram of the Multi-Variant Henshin implementation and its integration into GRaViTY

scale up to millions of variables [302]. This hypothesis is studied in our evaluation in Section 13.4.

13.3 Tool Support for Multi-Variant Model Transformation

We implemented our technique for Henshin [218, 228], a graph-based model transformation language. Henshin itself is not part of the GRaViTY framework but is insensitively used by the framework for applying transformation rules.

Figure 13.8 shows a component diagram focusing on the multi-variant extension of Henhsin and its integration into GRaViTY. The multi-variant transformation algorithm presented in Section 13.2.2 is implemented in the component `Henshin MultiVar` that extends the default Henshin implementation from the component `Henshin`. The implementation of the multi-variant transformation is based on a mapping from EMF elements to their presence conditions. To support arbitrary meta-models, `Henshin MultiVar` defines an interface `IVariability` that is used to request the presence conditions for the model a transformation is applied to. This interface specifies method signatures for requesting the presence conditions of model elements and updating their presence conditions as well as loading the used feature model. We implemented this interface as well for our variability extension to the type graph as for SecPL. When the `Refactorings` component is used to apply a refactoring to an SPL or the `SecurityViolationPatterns` component is used to check an SPL for security violations, these can use the standard interface provided by the `Henshin` transformation tool.

13.4 Evaluation of the Multi-Variant Model Transformation

To evaluate our technique, we applied our implementation to two transformation scenarios with product lines and transformation variability. In the first scenario, we applied a large set of relatively small edit detection rules to UML product lines in the first application scenario. In the second scenario, we calculated all possible *Move Method* refactorings on Java software product lines, including various conditions for their applicability. Our evaluation's goal was to study if our technique indeed produces the expected performance benefits in these scenarios. The implementation of our evaluation and the considered subjects and rules are available in our GitHub repository[1].

13.4.1 Detection of Edit Operations

The first experiment's goal is to study the performance of the stage rule application on a large set of relatively small detection rules, of which only a few match on the models.

Setup. The transformation is concerned with the detection of applied editing operations during model differencing [334]. This setting is particularly interesting for a performance evaluation: Since differencing is a routine software development task, low latency of the used tools is a prerequisite for developer effectiveness. The rule set, called *UmlRecog*, is tailored to the detection of UML edit operations. Each rule detects a specific edit operation, such as "move method to superclass", based on a pair of model versions and a low-level difference trace. *UmlRecog* comprises 1404 rules, which, as shown in Table 13.2, fall into three main categories: *Create/Set*, *Change/Move*, and *Delete/Unset*. To study the effect of our technique on performance, an encoding of the rules into VB rules was required. We obtained this encoding using RuleMerger [328], a tool for generating VB rules from classic ones based on clustering and clone detection [335]. We obtained 504 VB rules; each of them representing between 1 and 71 classic rules. *UmlRecog* is publicly available as part of a benchmark transformation set [308].

We applied this transformation to the 6 UML-based product lines specified in Table 13.3. The product lines came from diverse sources and include manually designed ones (1–2), and reverse-engineered ones from open-source projects (3–6).

Table 13.2 Subject refactoring rule set used in the evaluation of the staged rule application

Category	#Rules	#VBRules
Create/Set	274	171
Delete/Unset	164	121
Change/Move	966	212
Total	1404	504

---

[1] GitHub repository containing the implemented tool and evaluation data: https://github.com/SvenPeldszus/henshin-multivar

Each product line was available as a UML model annotated with presence conditions over a feature model. To produce the model version pairs used by *UmlRecog*, we automatically simulated development steps by non-deterministically applying rules from a set of edit rules to the product lines, using the lifting algorithm to account for presence conditions during the simulated editing step.

As a baseline for comparison, we considered the lifted application of each rule in *UmlRecog*. An alternative baseline of applying VB rules to the flattened set of products was not considered: The SPL variability in our setting is much greater than the rule variability, which implies a high performance penalty when enumerating products. Since we currently do not support besides negative application conditions any advanced transformation features, e.g., amalgamation, we used variants of the flat and the VB rules without these concepts. We used a Ubuntu 20.04 system (Oracle JDK 1.8, Intel Core i5-6200U, 8GB RAM) for all experiments.

Results. Table 13.4 gives an overview of the results of our experiments. The total execution times for our technique were between 7.14 and 13.58 seconds, compared

Table 13.3 Subject product lines of the staged rule application's evaluation

SPL	#Elements	#Products
1: InCar	116	54
2: E2E	130	94
3: JSSE	24,077	64
4: Notepad	252	512
5: Mobile	4,069	3,072
6: Lampiro	29,045	5,892

Table 13.4 Execution times (in Seconds) of the lifting and the staged transformation approach

	Create/Set			Delete/Unset			Change/Move			TOTAL		
	lift	stage	factor	lift	stage	factor	lift	stage	factor	lift	stage	factor
InCar	2.83	2.29	**1.24**	0.94	0.66	**1.43**	32.35	4.73	**6.84**	36.12	7.68	**4.70**
E2E	3.42	2.77	**1.24**	1.00	0.65	**1.54**	25.48	4.81	**5.30**	29.90	8.22	**3.64**
JSSE	3.92	3.44	**1.14**	1.07	1.01	**1.06**	25.71	9.13	**2.82**	30.70	13.58	**2.26**
Notepad	2.04	2.04	**1.00**	0.69	0.75	**0.92**	23.96	4.34	**5.52**	26.69	7.14	**3.74**
Mobile	3.08	2.17	**1.42**	0.74	1.05	**0.71**	24.86	4.54	**5.47**	28.69	7.76	**3.70**
Lampiro	3.39	2.41	**1.41**	0.73	0.63	**1.15**	25.49	7.76	**3.28**	29.60	10.80	**2.74**

to 26.69 and 36.12 seconds for lifting, yielding a speedup by factors between 2.26 and 4.7. For both techniques, all execution times are in the same order of magnitude across product lines. A possible explanation is that the number of applicable rules was small: if the vast majority of rules can be discarded early in the matching process, the execution time is constant with the number of rules.

The greatest speedups were observed for the *Change/Move* category, in which rule variability was the greatest as well, indicated by the ratio between rules and VB rules in Table 13.2. This observation is in line with our rationale for reusing shared matches between rules. Regarding the number of products, a trend regarding better scalability is not apparent, thus demonstrating that lifting is sufficient for controlling product-line variability. Still, based on the overall results, the hypothesis that our technique improves performance in situations with significant product-line and transformation variability can be confirmed.

13.4.2 Move Method Refactorings

Refactorings have been proposed as an efficient measure for optimizing the object-oriented structure of programs [18]. Practically, as discussed in Chapter 10, refactorings are often performed in an ad-hoc manner. However, to allow the demonstration of correctness, they can be specified using graph transformation rules [130, 131, 145]. In contrast to the change detection rules for UML diagrams, considered for the evaluation of the performance, the refactorings introduced in Section 10.2, are more complicated.

Setup. In this experiment, we study the application of a complicated refactorings operation, including various application conditions. Computationally, the detection of possible refactorings is the most expensive part of applying a refactoring specified as graph transformation rule. Also, the matches found for VB rules are always matches for specific rule products. There is no difference between applying the rule using only lifting or applying a VB rule product. For this reason, in this experiment, we calculate all possible *Move Method* refactorings on each subject system of the experiment. For this purpose, we use a variant of the visibility-preserving *Move Method* refactoring introduced in Section 10.2 that is not restricted to only critical members. In total, the considered *Move Method* refactoring has 20 variants.

As subject systems, we use the Java-based subjects from the previous evaluation part as well as an SPL created from the iTrust Electronics Health Records Application, introduced at the beginning of this chapter. For the iTrust application, various use cases have been defined. Based on these use cases, we create an SPL by

Table 13.5 Subject product lines for the application of *Move Method* refactorings and execution times

SPL	Code Metrics			SPL Metrics		Results		Measurements		
	LLOC	#Classes	#Methods	#Features	#Products	#Matches	#Refactorings	Lift	Stage	Speedup
Notepad	894	41	92	15	512	256	126	0.5s	0.1s	4.68
Mobile	5,919	100	536	13	3,072	305	215	0.3s	0.3s	1.30
JSSE	20,900	220	1,876	6	64	18,628	17,723	6.5s	3.7s	1.75
iTrust	32,553	443	3,106	20	548	26,287	26,164	137.3s	11.2s	12.23
Lampiro	34,550	258	2,037	20	5,892	36,475	33,592	16.2s	10.1s	1.60

assigning features to use cases and actors related to the use cases. A summary of the considered subject systems and metrics regarding their size are shown in Table 13.5 ordered by logical lines of code (LLOC).

Results. Table 13.5 gives an overview of the experiment's results. For every subject, we show the median value of 10 runs. On average, the matching is 4.31 times faster using our staged application than lifting the rule products. The median speedup is 1.75. All in all, there is a high variance between the different subject's speedups. Furthermore, as expected, there are matches of rule products representing the same refactoring, e.g., for the rule product $field \wedge param$ also the products containing only one of the two features match. For this reason, we show for every subject both numbers, the number of rule matches, and the number of refactorings resulting from these matches.

If we investigate the results in more detail, we can identify some factors influencing the speedup. As Lampiro and iTrust are approximately the same sizes in terms of LLOC and numbers of features, we inspect them closer. Remarkably, the iTrust feature model has much more restricting constraints than the Lampiro one, as there are only 548 possible configurations with the same number of features. However, as both approaches evaluate these constraints in the same way and there tend to be more evaluations in the staged application (of base-match and pre-match), this cannot be the reason for the considerable difference in speedup. With 443 classes and 3106 methods, there are 1.37 million moves to check for iTrust and 523 thousand for Lampiro, with 258 classes and 2,037 methods. Of these possible moves, 2% are possible refactoring matches for iTrust and 7% are possible refactoring matches for Lampiro. These refactoring matches are calculated from 3020 and 1575 base matches. Here, we can see the reason for the considerable speedup on iTrust. While the number of moves to check nearly triples (2.6x), the number of matches only slightly increases (1.4x), and the rejections are to a significant amount due to the base rule.

This evaluation shows that the staged application of VB rules results in a significant speedup for both many small rules and large, complicated rules on real-world-sized models. Furthermore, in the refactoring experiment, we have seen that base NACs have a significant influence on the execution time of VB rules. Finally, the experiment demonstrates the application of GRaViTY's security-preserving refactorings to software product lines.

13.5   Threats to Validity

In this section, we discuss threats to validity. First, we discuss the external threats we identified, and second, we discuss threats to construct validity.

13.5.1 External Validity

We only considered a limited set of scenarios, based on six product lines and one large-scale transformation. We aim to apply our technique to a broader class of cases in the future. The version pairs were obtained in a synthetic process, arguably one that produces pessimistic cases. Our treatment so far is also limited to a particular transformation paradigm, AGT, and one variability paradigm, the annotative one. Still, AGT and annotative variability are the underlying paradigms of many state-of-the-art tools. Finally, while we now consider advanced AGT concepts in the form of negative application conditions, there are still other concepts not addressed by our work. Specifically, we do not address amalgamation, a feature enabling a "for all" operator in rules [336]. However, studying the interaction between amalgamation and variability is worthwhile future research.

13.5.2 Construct Validity

While the observed performance improvements make a clear case for the practical usefulness of our technique, it has some assumptions with implications concerning usefulness. Specifically, we rely on annotative representations, which might be challenging to work with for developers due to the use of embedded presence conditions. While there is first empirical evidence suggesting that annotative representations of model-based software product lines do not impair model comprehension [337], there is currently no user study of the usability of VB rules.

13.6   Conclusion on Multi-Variant Model Transformation

To allow the application of refactorings and security violation patterns to SPLs we introduced a multi-variant model transformation approach allowing applying variability-based transformation rules to software product lines. To be more precise, we propose a methodology for software product line transformations in which not only the input product line but also the transformation system contains variability.

At the heart of our methodology, a staged rule application technique exploits reuse potential concerning shared portions of the involved products and rules. We present a formalization of our technique, including an optimization that supports an efficient checking of negative application conditions, an advanced transformation feature. We demonstrated practical benefit by applying our technique to two scenarios from a software evolution context. We observed speedups in all considered cases, in some of them by one order of magnitude. As part of this evaluation, we have shown how our methodology can be used for refactoring software product lines using the security-preserving refactorings presented in Chapter 10. The application of security violation patterns introduced in Section 8.6 to SPLs works analogously.

The proposed multi-variant transformation approach is not only applicable to our two scenarios but to every variability-based transformation rule and product line. For example, the UML product line UMLsec checks, currently expressed by us using OCL constraints, could also be implemented using this technique.

In the future, further variability dimensions, e.g., meta-model variability as considered in [338], can be explored to widen the applicability of the proposed approach. Also, the application of VB rules to product lines using different variability concepts such as feature-oriented programming (FOP) [279, 339] is a worthwhile extension. In feature-oriented model-driven design, the ideas of FOP have been combined with model-driven design [340]. The open question is how we can support the models created using this development approach.

While we offer a sufficient criterion for the preponing of NAC checks, further improvements could be made by strengthening this criterion, ideally by complementing it with a necessary one. Finding such a criterion presents a potential use case for conflict and dependency analysis [341]. Also, one can study the support of sophisticated graph transformation concepts such as amalgamation and path expressions, potentially allowing us to express more sophisticated security checks on software product lines.

Furthermore, there is potential in static rule analysis allowing run-time optimizations of the rule matching. For example, consider a VB with a rule product that is entirely contained in another rule product. Comparable to base rules, first matching the contained rule product and extending the match could be more efficient than calculating entirely new matches for both rule products. While in this scenario, the one rule is a kind of base rule for the other, there can also be situations where multiple rule products are similar in more than the base rule of the VB rule, and it is beneficial to consider a second level base rule. As all these considerations do not take run-time information into account, statically calculating such situations and building an application strategy is very promising for optimizing the VB rule application.

To conclude, using the presented approach, we can verify security requirements not only throughout the life-cycle of a single software product but also at the development of SPLs. Also, the maintenance of a software system in terms of refactorings is supported in this scenario. This allows the application of the GRaViTY approach to software product lines.

Part VI

Tool Support and Application

The GRaViTY Framework

14

Throughout this thesis, we presented prototypical implementations of the discussed approaches. At implementing the single tool prototypes for evaluation, we frequently reused implementations of tool prototypes implemented as part of other chapters. Our GitHub repository [1] provides an integration of all tool prototypes into the overall GRaViTY framework. The implementation of the GRaViTY framework is licensed under the open-source *Eclipse Public License* (EPL)[2].

In this chapter, we discuss the integration of the presented tool prototypes, resulting in the holistic GRaViTY framework for supporting the model-driven development and maintenance of secure software systems. For this purpose, first, we discuss the structuring of GRaViTY into Eclipse plugins. Afterward, we consider GRaViTY as SPL and discuss its configuration space. Finally, we discuss the extensibility of the GRaViTY framework and conclude.

14.1   Structuring into Eclipse Plugins

GRaViTY extends the Eclipse IDE with functionalities for the model-driven development of secure variant-rich software systems. For implementing such extensions, Eclipse supports a plugin mechanism based on OSGi[3]. For installation, plugins are bundled into features that are deployed to Eclipse update sites. For GRaViTY, we deployed 27 plugins in 14 features on our update site[4]. Figure 14.1 shows a screenshot of the GRaViTY update site in the Eclipse *Install New Software* view. In this

---

[1] GRaViTY's GitHub Repository: https://github.com/GRaViTY-Tool/gravity-tool

[2] Eclipse Public License (EPL). https://www.eclipse.org/legal/epl-2.0/

[3] OSGi Working Group Website: https://www.osgi.org/

[4] GRaViTY Update Site: https://www.gravity-tool.org/updatesite/

S. M. Peldszus, *Security Compliance in Model-driven Development of Software Systems in Presence of Long-Term Evolution and Variants*, https://doi.org/10.1007/978-3-658-37665-9_14

view, the features of GRaViTY are shown and can be selected for installation into Eclipse.

All tool parts presented in the previous chapters are integrated with each other according to Figure 14.2 building the GRaViTY framework. This figure shows only the components of GRaViTY but no external dependencies, e.g., dependencies to Henshin, eMoflon, CARiSMA respectively UMLsec, or SecDFDs. Such dependencies are already mentioned in previous chapters, in corresponding sections describing the tool support in detail. To allow a head-less usage of GRaViTY, e.g., as part of a continuous integration framework, in almost all tool prototypes, the UI is separated from the backend. In what follows, we introduce the components shown in Figure 14.2 in detail.

core-feature: The `core-feature` bundles basic functionality for interacting with the Eclipse API and the general logic for managing tasks of GRaViTY. Thereby, the plugin `org.gravity.eclipse.ui` contains functionality executed in the UI, e.g., adding a `GRaViTY` menu to Eclipse. The `org.gravity.eclipse` plugin contains interactions with the Eclipse

Figure 14.1 Screenshot of GRaViTY's update site

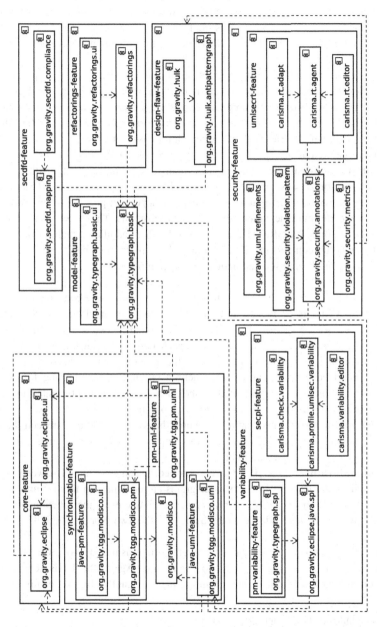

Figure 14.2 Component diagram of GRaViTY's implementation

backend. For example, in this plugin, a resolver between the Java model of Eclipse JDT and the type graph is implemented. Given an element from one of the two models, the resolver allows retrieving the corresponding element in the other model.

model-feature: GRaViTY's type graph itself and the visualization of program models presented in Section 5.3 are realized by the plugins `org.eclipse.typegraph.basic` and `org.eclipse.typegraph.basic.ui`. Also, the implementation of `org.eclipse.typegraph.basic` enriches the type graph with queries such as the search for a type in a program model by its fully-qualified name. These two plugins are bundled as the `model-feature`.

synchronization-feature: This feature contains shared helper functionalities for the synchronizations supported by GRaViTY. Currently, this is only the `org.gravity.modisco` plugin, providing a wrapper and processing support for the concrete implementations of the synchronizations. The three synchronizations supported by GRaViTY are bundled by three additional features that are shown as sub-components of this feature. The implementation of these synchronizations has been discussed in detail in Section 6.2.3.

> **java-pm-feature:** The synchronization between Java source code, represented by a MoDisco[5] model, and GRaViTY's program model is bundled into the `java-pm-feature`. This feature bundles two plugins. First, the `org.gravity.tgg.modisco.pm` feature containing the TGG for synchronizing MoDisco models with the program model. Second, a user interface for configuring the synchronization, e.g., configuring for how many projects program models should be cached, is implemented in the `org.gravity.tgg.modisco.ui` plugin.
>
> **java-uml-feature:** This feature contains the synchronization between Java source code and UML class diagrams, implemented in the `org.gravity.tgg.modisco.uml` plugin.
>
> **pm-uml-feature:** The synchronization and correspondence model between program models and UML class diagrams are contained in this feature. The plugin `org.gravity.tgg.pm.uml` implements the functionality to create a correspondence model using the other two synchronizations.

refactoring-feature: The security-aware refactorings as introduced in Chapter 10 represented by the `refactoring-feature`. Again, the UI is separated from the backend implementation in the plugins bundled by the feature. The

---

[5] Eclipse MoDisco Project: https://www.eclipse.org/MoDisco/

plugin `org.gravity.refactorings` implements the backend and `org.gravity.refactorings.ui` the UI.

design-flaw-feature: The `design-flaw-feature` bundles the implementation of the design-flaw detection tool *Hulk* [21, 34]. Among others, this feature contains two plugins that are of primary interest for this thesis. First, the `org.gravity.hulk.antipatterngraph` plugin defines an extension to the type graph allowing annotating program models with design-flaw information. Second, the main logic of *Hulk* but also various OO metrics, code-smells, and anti-pattern detections are implemented in the `org.gravity.hulk` plugin. Both plugins are used in this thesis for the realization of the security metrics (`org.gravity.security.metrics`).

security-feature: Most security-related implementation parts are bundled into the `security-feature`. The `org.gravity.uml.refinements` plugin contains the implementation of the UMLsec extension for tracing between UML models with different abstraction levels, introduced in detail in Section 6.3.6. The Java security annotations and their counterparts in the program model, discussed in detail in Section 6.4.1, are contained in the `org.gravity.security.annotations` plugin. From this plugin, we also export a library only containing the Java annotations. The `org.gravity.security.violation.patterns` plugin implements tool support for the security violation patterns, introduced in Section 8.6. The security metrics discussed in Section 8.3 are realized as an extension to the *Hulk* design-flaw detection tool in the `org.gravity.security.metrics` plugin.
Security-related implementation parts of GRaViTY focusing on run-time security are bundled into a separate feature deeply coupled with this feature.

umlsecrt-feature: This feature bundles the tool support for the run-time monitor introduced in Chapter 9. The run-time agent (`carisma.rt.agenet`), discussed in detail in Section 9.4, is the only component of GRaViTY that is not an Eclipse plugin but a standalone Java project. The tool support for specifying countermeasures for the run-time agent and adapting UML models based on observations by the agent is integrated into the Eclipse IDE as plugins again. These features are realized by the plugins `carisma.rt.editor` and `carisma.rt.adapt`, also discussed in detail in Section 9.4.

secdfd-feature: All implementation parts related to SecDFDs [111] are bundled in this feature. First, these are the semi-automated mappings between DFDs and source code as introduced in Section 7.2. These are realized in the `org.gravity.secdfd.mapping` plugin. Second, the static compliance checks discussed in Sections 8.2, 8.4, and 8.5, are realized in the `org.gravity.secdfd.compliance` plugin.

variability-feature: The support for SPLs is bundled in the `variability-feature`. This feature bundles the shared parts of the owned more specific variability features. To be more precise, this is the parsing of Antenna preprocessor statements based on regular expressions as discussed in Section 11.3 and realized in the `org.garvity.eclipse.java.spl` plugin. The two owned features bundle plugins for supporting variability on the program model and UML model level.

> **pm-variability-feature:** This feature bundles the plugin `org.gravity.typegraph.spl`, providing variability support on the program model. This implementation has been discussed in detail in Section 11.3.
>
> **secpl-feature:** Plugins providing support for variability on the UML model level are bundled in the `secpl-feature`. First, this is the plugin `carisma.profile.umlsec.variability` allowing to annotate UML models with presence conditions and creating these annotations from Antenna preprocessor statements as discussed in Section 11.3. Second, the security checks for UML product lines are implemented in the plugin `carisma.check.variability`. Third, the `carisma.variability.editor` plugin provides editor support for variability on UML models. The implementation of the last two plugins has been discussed in detail in Section 12.4.

Figure 14.2 also shows the dependencies between the different plugins. For example, the TGG-based synchronization between Java source code and the program model, realized in the plugin `org.gravity.tgg.modisco.pm`, requires the plugins that define the type graph of the program model (`org.gravity.typegraph.basic`), GRaViTY's MoDisco wrapper (`org.gravity.modisco`), and the `org.gravity.eclipse` plugin. These dependencies are discussed in detail in the sections discussing the single parts of GRaViTY's implementation.

In total, the GRaViTY's implementation comprises 37k lines of handwritten code. Including generated code, e.g., from the specification of the TGGs or the metamodels, the whole GRaViTY tool has 574k lines of code. With up to 574k lines of code, GRaViTY comprises a medium up to large software project when generated code is considered. Due to this size, there is a considerable risk for errors that must be mitigated through appropriate quality assurance. Furthermore, the GRaViTY framework has been developed and maintained over the past 6 years, building upon a tool prototype for the transformation tool contest (TTC) 2015 [131, 145]. Frequently, implemented functionality had to be adapted to be more general, cover new cases or better fit new contributions to GRaViTY. Among others, GRaViTY has been adapted to new frameworks multiple times, e.g., new versions of Java, Eclipse, or eMoflon. All of this requires the implementation of systematic quality assurance. To build the foundation for systematic quality assurance, we implemented the continuous integration principle. For this purpose, besides the deployment technology of Eclipse, we use Maven in combination with Eclipse Tycho[6] for building the GRaViTY framework. Eclipse Tycho is a Maven extension providing support to build Eclipse plugins using Maven. Also, our continuous integration pipeline includes regression tests and static analysis using SonarQube. In total, we implemented 205 regression tests.

14.2 GRaViTY as Software Product Line

GRaViTY's implementation as 27 Eclipse plugins allows a flexible deployment tailored to the needs of a developer that wants to apply the GRaViTY approach. In the end, GRaViTY can be seen as a software product line that allows developers to use the desired parts of GRaViTY without overloading the Eclipse IDE with unused functionality.

In the GRaViTY SPL, each plugin is represented by one of the 27 concrete features of the feature model in Figure 14.3. This feature model also includes constraints expressing the dependencies between the single plugins. All in all, there are 15.755 possible configurations of GRaViTY. While in principle, 15.755 configurations are possible, not all of these combinations are meaningful for an installation in Eclipse. For example, GRaViTY can widely be deployed without a user interface which reduces the dependencies at usage by other plugins but does not allow the usage by developers. However, considering the integration of GRaViTY into a third-party application this might be a useful configuration, e.g., as discussed in Section 10.3.1, GOBLIN uses the refactorings and design-flaw detection of GRaViTY but comes with its own user interface. Nevertheless, such configurations are unlikely to be useful in an installation over GRaViTY's update site for manual use by developers.

To avoid such installations and to reduce the variability to an amount suitable for developers, the features of GRaViTY aggregate the plugins that are likely to be used together. Figure 14.4 shows an extension of GRaViTY's feature model with features representing the deployment information captures in the update site features. The features from Figure 14.3, representing GRaViTY's plugins, are shown collapsed. The features on GRaViTY's update site are assigned to categories, repre-

---

[6] Eclipse Tycho: https://projects.eclipse.org/projects/technology.tycho

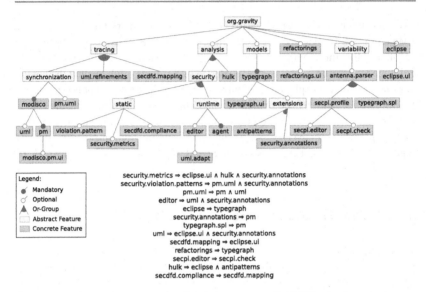

Figure 14.3 Feature model showing the relations among GRaViTY's plugins

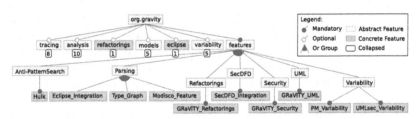

Figure 14.4 Extension to GRaViTY's feature model including the features provided at the update site

sented by abstract features in the feature model. The installable update site features are represented by concrete features in the feature model. These concrete features are coupled by constraints with the collapsed features representing plugins. For simplicity, these constraints are not shown in the feature model. For example, the `Type_Graph` feature contains the `org.gravity.typegraph.basic` and `org.gravity.typegraph.basic.ui` plugins. These two plugins are represented by the `typegraph` and `typegraph.ui` features in the feature model. This inclusion in the `Type_Graph` feature can be expressed by an inclusion constraint: `Type_Graph` ⇒ `typegraph` ∧ `typegraph.ui`. In this context, plugins can only be installed as part of an update site's features which has to be expressed as two additional implications: `typegraph` $\Rightarrow$ `Type_Graph` and `typegraph.ui` $\Rightarrow$ `Type_Graph`. Considering these three constraints, there are two valid configurations. Either all three considered features are selected or none of them. In the same way, we expressed all relations between the update site features and their contained plugins. In summary, this leads to a significant reduction of variants. The number of variants is reduced to 66 variants of GRaViTY that can be installed from the GRaViTY update site.

14.3   Conclusion on the Implementation of GRaViTY

In this chapter, we outlined the technical integration of the single tool prototypes to a modular overall tool framework called GRaViTY. This tool framework has been implemented as a prototype to demonstrate and evaluate the approaches developed and presented within this thesis. Altogether, the GRaViTY framework reached a significant size. The modular architecture allows a deployment suitable to the needs of developers using the GRaViTY approach without overloading their IDE with unused functionality. Also, the modularity supports the reuse of GRaViTY in future research projects. For example, the GOBLIN tool has shown how single components of GRaViTY can be reused in other tools. In this regard, throughout this thesis, we discussed various possible extensions to GRaViTY. Also, the single parts of GRaViTY can be reused as part of other research approaches.

First, the fine-grained structuring of GRaViTY into plugins allows efficient reuse in other projects without including too many new dependencies. Due to this structuring, clear interfaces have been defined for accessing the single plugin's functionalities. We discussed most of these interfaces in the implementation sections of this thesis.

On the downside, the integration of GRaViTY into Eclipse might hinder the reuse in contexts outside of Eclipse. In this regard, the used *MoDisco* plugin for parsing Java source code has the tightest coupling with Eclipse as it requires a running Eclipse workspace. While this can be achieved by deploying GRaViTY together with a headless Eclipse, this is no efficient solution.

Second, it can be beneficial to extend GRaViTY itself, e.g., to provide new analyses. In this scenario, GRaViTY's fine-grained structure is beneficial, too. It is most likely, that such an extension will be implemented as an additional plugin. However, this plugin will not only use the existing functionalities of GRaViTY but also extend and influence GRaViTY's functionality. For example, additional preprocessing or postprocessing steps for GRaViTY's synchronization step could be necessary. As discussed in Section 6.2.3, for this purpose, we export interfaces using Eclipse's extension points. The feasibility of these exported extension points has been demonstrated in the Master's thesis of Mebus that extended GRaViTY's program model with data flow and had to register additional processing steps for this purpose [150].

All together, GRaViTY can easily be extended to cover additional functionalities but also be reused in additional contexts. One major drawback of GRaViTY's implementation is the tight coupling with Eclipse. This coupling hinders the reuse of GRaViTY outside the Eclipse ecosystem. Here, the used *MoDisco* plugin for parsing Java source code has the tightest coupling with Eclipse as it requires a running Eclipse workspace. In future versions of GRaViTY, this coupling should be reduced to allow even better use of GRaViTY also in additional contexts. Here, we mainly see the integration of GRaViTY into additional IDEs but also continuous integration frameworks such as Maven or Gradle.

Case Studies 15

In the previous chapters, we applied the locally restricted contributions of this thesis to the iTrust running example. However, we did not discuss and evaluate the integration of these single contributions to the overall GRaViTY approach outlined in Chapter 4. In Chapter 14, we presented the technical integration of the single tool prototypes presented throughout this thesis into the GRaViTY tool.

In this chapter, we evaluate whether the GRaViTY tool is suitable to support the development of secure software systems as intended. In this regard, we identified two objectives we focus on. First, we investigate whether the technical integration of GRaViTY allows an application of the GRaViTY approach throughout software development processes. Second, we focus on the perspective of developers and security experts working with GRaViTY. Here, we are interested in the practical usability of GRaViTY when applied to software development. Thereby, we focus more on usability as part of software development than on detailed usability in terms of software ergonomics, e.g., regarding the realized user interface. In the end, we investigate if GRaViTY can be applied to model-driven development, as outlined in Chapter 3, without changing the performed procedures as a measure for usability.

O1–Technical Feasibility: Is the integration of the tool prototypes technically feasible to support the development of secure software systems?

O2–Practical Usability: Can the GRaViTY approach be practically applied to develop secure software systems without changing MDD procedures?

In the previous chapters, we performed controlled experiments for evaluating the presented approaches. As both objectives of this chapter target qualitative real-world experiences, case studies provide suitable means to investigate the objectives [342]. Accordingly, to study the two objectives, we demonstrate and discuss the application of the overall GRaViTY development approach to two real-world case studies.

© The Author(s), under exclusive license to Springer Fachmedien Wiesbaden GmbH, part of Springer Nature 2022
S. M. Peldszus, *Security Compliance in Model-driven Development of Software Systems in Presence of Long-Term Evolution and Variants*,
https://doi.org/10.1007/978-3-658-37665-9_15

The first case study is *iTrust* that has already been used as the running example. The second case study is the *Eclipse Secure Storage* of the Eclipse IDE. As the developers of iTrust provide complete documentation and there are models available in existing research [23, 49–51], we use iTrust to demonstrate the feasibility of the GRaViTY approach for developing a new software system taking security into account in Section 15.1. While Eclipse also provides good documentation of the implementation, there are no requirements or models available. For this reason, in Section 15.2, we apply the GRaViTY approach to Eclipse Secure Storage to demonstrate the feasibility of using GRaViTY on legacy projects.

The description of both case studies is structured into multiple development steps. For each step, first, we generally introduce the step. Then we describe the *execution* of the development step by applying GRaViTY, and afterward, we present a *discussion* of our observations in this step. After all steps of a case study, we generally discuss our observations in this case study.

15.1   Case Study 1: iTrust

As introduced in Section 2.2, iTrust comprises an *Electronic Health Records* system developed as a class project over 25 semesters [47, 50]. The main documentation is provided as requirements describing use cases of the iTrust system. The software system itself has been implemented in Java using Java Server Pages (JSP). Also, design-time models have been created as part of various research [54, 343].

15.1.1 Description of the Case Study Execution

In this case study, we simulate the implementation of the iTrust system using GRaViTY from the very beginning, starting with requirements engineering. After the initial development of the software system, we focus on the restructuring of iTrust as part of the maintenance. Finally, we showcase the conversion of iTrust into an SPL. In all steps, we reuse the existing iTrust artifacts and create all required artifacts following the GRaViTY development approach.

Requirements Engineering

As discussed in Section 3.3.1, usually the development of a software system starts with an analysis of the domain as part of the requirements engineering. The knowledge about entities and relations within the software system's domain is captured in a domain model. The domain model elements are then used to specify their realiza-

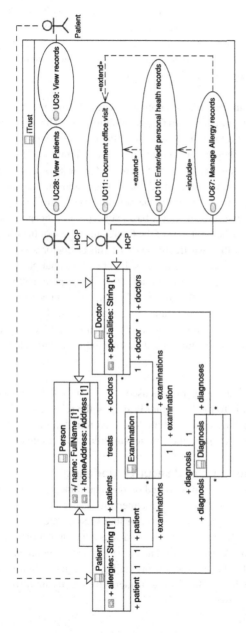

Figure 15.1 Use case diagram refining iTrust's domain model

tion in the software system. Here, the specification of the software system's intended functionality is one of the first steps of requirements engineering. For this purpose, the UML provides the notation of use case diagrams. A detailed use case diagram for iTrust has been discussed in Section 2.2. In this section, we focus on the relation of this use case diagram with the domain model.

Execution. To simulate the requirements engineering, we manually recreated iTrust's use case diagram based on iTrust's requirements. Thereby, we took a domain model as given and refined it by specifying the use case diagram. Whenever there was a refinement relation between the use case diagram and the domain model, we explicitly modeled this relation. Figure 15.1 shows some of these refinement relations between entities from the domain model and the use case diagram elements. On the left side of the figure, the domain model introduced in Section 3.3.1 is shown. The domain model shows basic concepts in a hospital such as doctors treating patients. On the right side of the figure, an excerpt of the use cases of iTrust is shown focusing on the basic treatment of patients by doctors. As use case diagrams do not specify data or structures of the software system but basic tasks performed in a software system, only domain model entities corresponding to actors in the use case diagram are refined. In the concrete diagram, two kinds of doctors (LHCP and HCP) are defined that perform treatment-related tasks such as documenting office visits (UC11). In the next step, the domain model and use case diagrams are refined further to specify an architecture that allows the implementation of the specified use cases.

Discussion. Considering the models used in this part of the case study, refinement relations are suitable to model explicitly specify the relations and come only with a low overhead for the considered models. Accordingly, we can assume both, the technical feasibility (**O1**) and the practical usability (**O2**) as given.

Software Architecture and Security Modeling

After requirements engineering, based on the requirements models and the textual requirements, the software system's architecture is specified. Following the principle of security by design, we have to consider security requirements explicitly in this step. Accordingly, in this section, we discuss the simulation of the architecture specification for the iTrust system. The model-driven development of iTrust's software architecture has been discussed in detail in Section 3.3. In this part of the case study, we focus on the feasibility of refinements for specifying software architecture and security engineering.

Execution. In what follows, we do not focus on the architecture itself but a simulated incremental growth of the architecture until the state described in Section 3.3 is reached. Thereby, we consider interleaving steps of extending the architecture and security engineering.

Starting from the models developed at requirements engineering, we iteratively refine these models until we reach a detailed specification of the iTrust system. After every extension step, comprising the addition of a coherent set of model elements, a security engineering step takes place. Here, we considered the security engineering using UMLsec and SecDFDs as presented in Section 3.6. As the SecDFD and UMLsec specifications and checks are known from the literature, we do not focus on their usage but the *Secure Realization* security-refinement mechanism introduced in Section 6.3.5. As part of our case study, we simulated these steps by selecting parts of the design and implementation models introduced in Section 3.3 and iteratively rebuilding the models. Whenever we added a new part to the models, we also created the corresponding refinement relations as discussed in Section 6.3.

We started our simulation with a domain model already containing fundamental security requirements, such as that personal data has to be classified at the security level of secrecy as introduced in Section 3.6.1. Based on this model, we simulated three evolution steps:

1. In the first step, we defined classes in the design model refining persons and actors of the domain model and use case diagram.
2. Afterward, we added the data classes for storing medical information about patients.
3. Finally, we added classes and operations for implementing the functionality of the use cases.

Discussion. As we only used technology provided by standard UML and no extensions of GRaViTY, these non-security-related refinements have been labor some but straightforward. Also, the specification of *Secure Realization* was straightforward but often triggered security-related follow-up tasks.

After every extension step, we have been provided with a list of missing security realizations for fulfilling the *Secure Realization* security requirement. As we did not specify security requirements as part of extending the design model but considered their specification as a separate task performed after the extension, these security violations are expected. Practically, these lists of security violations served as todo-lists for the abstract domain model level security requirements to consider in the design model.

The same applies to the security violations detected by default UMLsec checks, such as secure dependency, executed each time after specifying new security refinements. At the explicit specification of realizations, additional security requirements necessary due to dependency were obviously and added by us. However, there have cases we did not immediately recognize. These cases have been reported to us by CARiSMA at checking secure dependency. Here, as intended by the check, we have been thinking about whether a security level should be extended to a new class or if we should overthink the dependency. However, as the given design of iTrust is required for the subsequent steps of the case study, we fixed all reported security issues by adding the required UMLsec stereotypes.

Nevertheless, this demonstrates not only the technical feasibility (**O1**) of the GRaViTY approach but also the effectiveness of UMLsec and *Secure Realization* in detecting potential security issues and positively influencing the security design of a software system. Also, from our perspective, GRaViTY's security reporting naturally integrated into the development process.

Implementation

After reaching a state in which the design-time models are detailed enough, we have to start implementing the software system. Thereby, tracing is required from the first written line of code for applying the GRaViTY approach. For this reason, we focus on the integration of GRaViTY's tracing approach into software development.

Execution. Using the synchronization mechanism of GRaViTY, we generated an early class layout from the implementation model. Afterward, we filled this layout manually with functionality. During this step, the implementation model has been kept synchronized by GRaViTY with the manual changes. We performed this manual extension by copying and pasting implementation fragments of the iTrust implementation into the generated class layout. However, as the MoDisco parser is not incremental, in addition, we had to simulate these changes on the MoDisco model by manually copying the corresponding changes into this model. After every set of source code changes, we generated a MoDisco model and copied the changes into the MoDisco model used by GRaViTY, making the changes processable for the used TGG.

Discussion. In this case study, we have been able to successfully generate an initial code skeleton that is connected with the design-time models through GRaViTY's correspondence model. From a user perspective, there was no difference compared to code generation using other modeling tools such as Enterprise Architect[1] or Astah[2].

Furthermore, we have been able to continuously synchronize the growing source code with the design-time models. However, while in a final product this should be performed automatically at suitable points of time, e.g., whenever a build is triggered in the IDE or a change is committed to a repository, this synchronization had to be simulated in this case study. As already mentioned, the reason for this was the non-incremental implementation of the MoDisco parser that did not allow feeding changes directly into the TGGs for synchronization. Nevertheless, we demonstrated the principle feasibility of continuous synchronization from a technical point of view (**O1**). The practical feasibility from a viewpoint of a developer (**O2**) seems reasonable but suitable execution points have to be identified in future works.

Security Compliance

The continuous verification of the planned and implemented security is an essential contribution of GRaViTY. As part of this case study, we investigate how these verification steps integrate into the software development process.

Execution. Comparable to the incremental specification of the software system's architecture, we also interleaved security verification steps with the implementation steps. These implementation steps have been discussed as the subject of the previous part of this case study. After synchronizing every change made on the implementation with the design models, we manually executed all security compliance checks.

Discussion. As in the generated class design and the first pasted code fragments no security mechanisms have been contained, all have been reported as absent. For this reason, initially, we faced a long list of absences regarding the planned security design. However, as we incrementally added more functionality from iTrust's implementation, the size of the lists of absences reduced until we got rid of all absences. Thereby, the absences functioned as a kind of todo-lists for security-related tasks and as selection criteria for the next code fragments to paste. As the inserted source code was security compliant, no other violations have been reported. The violating case has been considered in the evaluations of the static security compliance approaches in Chapter 8. Nevertheless, this demonstrated the technical feasibility (**O1**) of GRaViTY's security compliance checks. From the perspective of usability (**O1**), using GRaViTY's security compliance checks is comparable to other

---

[1] Enterprise Architect: https://www.sparxsystems.com/products/ea/index.html

[2] Astah: https://astah.net/

static analyses, e.g., PMD[3] or Checkstyle[4]. However, the automated execution after changes, which static analysis tools often offer, should also be added to GRaViTY for increasing its usability.

Restructuring

After reaching the state in which our case study system's implementation was identical to the original iTrust implementation, we investigated this implementation regarding possibilities for restructuring the software system. Thereby, we only focused on restructuring in terms of refactorings. Concrete possibilities for refactoring iTrust have been discussed in Chapter 10.

Execution. To find' additional refactoring opportunities, we executed the search-based optimization tool GOBLIN [146], discussed in Section 10.3.1, on iTrust. Thereby, we added all three refactorings introduced in Section 10.2 (*Create Superclass, Pull-Up Method,* and *Move Method*) to GOBLIN. Besides, the optimization criteria considered in the summarized experiment of Ruland et al. (design-flaws, coupling/cohesion, visibilities, and the number of changes), we also added the *Critical Design Proportion* metric discussed in Section 8.3 as an optimization criterion.

Discussion. Due to iTrust's architecture along with the Java server pages, most times the implemented functionality was already well-located, and we only rarely found additional beneficial refactoring opportunities. Applying the refactorings we found, did not differ much from applying the refactorings integrated into the Eclipse IDE. For this reason, we consider the technical feasibility (**O1**) and the usability (**O2**) as given.

Variability Engineering

As the last part of this case study, we considered the re-engineering of iTrust into an SPL. In this case study, we mainly focus on the specification of an SPL in terms of the variability within all artifacts of the software system. However, we also consider the security checks for SPLs.

Execution. As described in Section 11.1, we started on the use case diagrams with the identification of possible features. Finally, we ended in assigning individual use cases to features. Afterward, we investigated two different approaches for realizing the identified features in the software system. First, a top-down approach by speci-

---

[3] Website of the PMD analyzer: https://pmd.github.io/
[4] Website of Checkstyle: https://checkstyle.org/

fying variability on the models and propagating it to code, and second, a bottom-up approach in which we specified variability on the source code and propagated it into the design-time models. After realizing the variability in the iTrust system, we executed the SecPL checks to verify the security of the iTrust SPL.

Discussion. While annotating the use case diagrams with presence conditions was straightforward, issues emerged within this model-based re-engineering method. Mainly, the design-time models considered by us rarely contained detailed behavior specifications allowing us to judge the side effects of presence conditions. For the re-engineering, it turned out to be more efficient in adding Antenna preprocessor statements into the implementation using FeatureIDE. Here, we have been able to adjust the presence conditions until we achieved compiling source code. Afterward, we propagated these presence conditions into the UML models using GRaViTY's tool support introduced in Section 11.3.

As our restructuring of iTrust into an SPL ended in the state described in Chapter 11, we expected no security violations regarding the SecPL checks when executing these on the entirely restructured SPL. This expectation was fulfilled in this case study. The GRaViTY approach is technically feasible (**O1**) to specify variability on UML models and the Implementation as well as to propagate the Antenna annotations into the design-time models. Regarding usability (**O2**), additional support is needed for the re-engineering of a software system into an SPL on the model level. In contrast to this, the bottom-up re-engineering was very usable. To this end, it seems likely that the forward engineering of an SPL from the beginning comes with good usability as fewer implementation level dependencies have to be considered at specifying variability. However, this should be studied in more detail in future works.

15.1.2 Discussion of the Observations

In this case study, we have shown that the integration of the single approaches works for the considered case study. Only triggering the propagation of implementation-level changes had to be simulated by providing changes on the MoDisco model level. This limitation can be overcome by incremental parsers [344] such as Tree-Sitter[5]. Altogether, we consider the technical feasibility of the GRaViTY for supporting the development of secure software systems (**O1**) as given for the considered waterfall-like case.

---

[5] Tree-Sitter: https://tree-sitter.github.io/tree-sitter/

Considering the usability and the integration into the development process (**O2**), we never had the impression that we were using the tool only for the purpose of using the tool. There was always a benefit in using the tool and it only rarely impacted the development process. However, more seamless integration and more automation in the execution of the tool would be beneficial and interrupt the development process less. Especially in the context of security checks, huge lists are presented when a developer decides to execute the security checks. Instead of executing all security checks on the whole software system after finishing a coherent set of changes, these checks should be extended to support near real-time notifications when modeling or implementing a specific part of the software system. Also, only information relevant to the part of the software system a developer is currently working on should be shown.

15.2   Case Study 2: Eclipse Secure Storage

Our second case study focuses on applying GRaViTY to a security-critical part of the Eclipse IDE. *Eclipse Secure Storage* [203] is used by Eclipse plugins such as the Eclipse git client to store confidential data like passwords. The Eclipse Secure Storage is implemented as an Eclipse plugin itself using Java. How exactly the secure storage works is described in the help document of Eclipse [203]. However, this description is rather high-level and complemented by the low-level API documentation. We consider Eclipse Secure Storage due to its security-criticality, good documentation, and wide usage in practice.

15.2.1 Discussion of the Case Study Execution

In this case study, we focus on migrating legacy projects to GRaViTY. In what follows, we first discuss the reverse engineering of the Eclipse Secure Storage to create a state in which the application of the GRaViTY approach is possible. Next, we discuss security engineering, aiming at making security requirements explicit and checking the software system regarding compliance with them. Finally, we discuss the run-time monitoring of the Eclipse Secure Storage based on a fictive malicious Eclipse plugin and the adaption of the reverse-engineered models.

Reverse Engineering of Models
The first essential step for applying GRaViTY to legacy projects is to reconstruct trace links between design-time models and the implementation. If no design-time

models are available, models suitable for developers or security experts to work with must be reverse-engineered. This reverse engineering can be performed both manually or by automated tool support.

Execution. As there are no models available for Eclipse Secure Storage, the first step of this case study was the reverse engineering of models. For the reverse engineering of models, we followed a three-step approach. First, we manually created data flow diagrams and UML activity diagrams based on the documentation of Eclipse Secure Storage. Afterward, we automatically reverse-engineered a detailed UML class diagram from the source code of Eclipse Secure Storage using GRaV-iTY. Finally, we used the semi-automated mapping approach to establish refinements between the manually created diagrams, the automatically reverse-engineered class diagram, and the software system's implementation.

Data Flow Diagrams and Activity Diagrams: To get a better understanding of Eclipse Secure Storage, in a first step we manually reverse engineered Data Flow Diagrams showing essential processes of Eclipse Secure Storage. As discussed in Section 3.6.2, UML activity diagrams can be specified analogously. After specifying the first DFD, we applied the semi-automated mapping approach introduced in Chapter 7 for creating a correspondence model between design-time models and source code as well as the structural compliance checks discussed in Section 8.2. Based on these compliance checks, we have been able to adapt our DFD to reflect the implementation better. Whenever we detected a structural divergence, we investigated this divergence and adapted the DFD. Also, the semi-automated mapping proposed classes we did not consider to be involved in the scenario but are involved in the scenario and have been accepted by us as correct suggestions. In summary, the reverse engineering approaches and compliance checking made it easier to get a detailed understanding of Eclipse Secure Storage in detail by putting our focus on detected divergences or unexpected correspondences.

Figure 15.2 depicts the final DFD of the Eclipse Secure Storage. An arbitrary plugin attempts to access a secret by sending a request including path information of where to look for the secret, e.g., a password request for a user name of a Git account. The secure storage queries an internal tree-like data structure to find the corresponding node containing the requested secret. Next, the cache is queried for the secret value, which can be in clear text, i.e., *secret* on flow 6 in Figure 15.2, or encrypted, i.e., `encr. data.` on flow 7. If the value is in clear text, the secret is sent to the plugin. In the case of an encrypted value, a decrypt operation either fetches the root password from the operating system or prompts the user to provide it. Upon successful decryption, the secret is sent to the requesting plugin in flow 10 of Figure 15.4.

Implementation-level Class Diagram: In Figure 15.3, we present an excerpt from the reverse-engineered UML model of Eclipse Secure Storage. For showing the internal working of Eclipse Secure Storage, we included classes from Eclipse's Git implementation to represent a concrete plugin accessing the Eclipse Secure Storage. The class *SecurePreferences*, at the bottom left of Figure 15.3, represents mappings between secrets and keys to access them internally. The field *name* holds the name of the context under which a secret is stored. If a secret is requested using the *get* method of this class, the secret is loaded from the key store and the user may have to provide her master password to unlock the keyring. The interface *ISecurePreferences* specifies public methods over which secret data of different plugins can be accessed. Stored secrets can be requested using the method *get* and written using *put*. This interface is implemented by the class *SecurePreferencesWrapper* that wraps the internal instances of the class *SecurePreferences* using container objects.

The two classes of the Eclipse Git implementation responsible for storing passwords are shown at the top of the figure (*Activator* and *EGitSecureStore*). These are initialized by *Activator* at the startup of the application. For this initialization, the *SecurePreferencesFactory* of the Eclipse Secure Storage is used to get the default password store and initialize the class *EGitSecureStore*. Then, this class provides a mapping between Git repositories and associated user names and passwords using the *ISecurePreferences* interface.

Creation of Refinements: To allow the security tracing between the SecDFDs and the UML class diagrams, we replaced every SecDFD with a UML activity diagram as shown in Section 3.6.2. When in the correspondence model between the DFDs and the source code, a DFD element had a correspondence with a source code element that corresponds to an element from the UML class diagram, we created a refinement reference from the class diagram element to the activity diagram element corresponding with the DFD element.

Discussion. In this case study, we noticed that the semi-automated mapping approach proposed within this thesis is not only suitable for restoring a correspondence model between DFDs and source code but assists in defining a DFD for a given implementation of a software system. As we did not transfer the semi-automated mappings to UML activity diagrams, we had to manually perform this transition by first reverse engineering DFDs and corresponding activity diagrams, mapping the DFDs to the implementation, and then transferring the mappings from the DFD

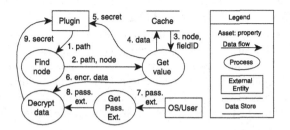

Figure 15.2 DFD for reading a secret from the Eclipse Secure Storage

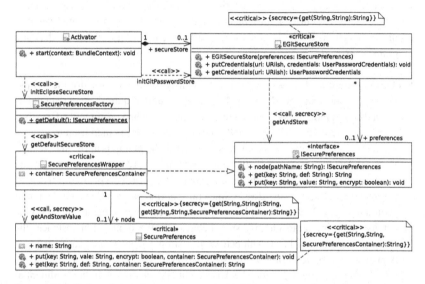

Figure 15.3 Eclipse Secure Storage annotated with UMLsec *Secure Dependency* stereotypes

to the UML activity diagram. However, as this process is straightforward, there seems to be no reason to object to the technical realizability of this task. Accordingly, we consider the technical suitability of the reverse-engineering (**O1**) as given. Regarding the usability and benefits for the developers (**O2**), the application of our approach gave us more detailed insights into the implementation than only studying the implementation and its documentation.

Static Security Specification and Checks

One of the two main goals of applying GRaViTY to legacy projects is to create artifacts that allow an easier specification of security requirements, comparing to their specification on the implementation, and the security compliance checks with these security requirements. The other main goal is to continue with the continuous verification of the software system's security after the initial state has been proven to be secure. In this part of the case study, we focus on creating such an initial secure state using GRaViTY.

Execution. After the reverse engineering of design-time models, we started annotating these with security requirements. Here, we started with essential security requirements on the SecDFDs and more detailed security requirements on the class diagram, afterward.

SecDFD: Figure 15.4 shows an excerpt (for clarity) of the SecDFD for the Eclipse Secure Storage example discussed before. If a plugin requires secret data that is cached encrypted, the user must enter a `password` when prompted, c.f. `pass. ext.` in Figure 15.4. The externally provided password is then used to decrypt the cached secret data, and if this was successful, the plugin is allowed to read it. First, the designer must specify that the external password is confidential. Second, the designer needs to specify the process contract, e.g., a decrypt contract (`DECR`) for the process `Decrypt_data`. Since the external password is confidential, it should not be leaked to other plugins running in the environment. These simple extensions allow us to identify such behavior in the model. For instance, the extended notation [111] is shipped with a simple label propagation (using a dept-first search) according to the specified process contracts. Once the labels have been propagated, a static check is executed to determine if any confidential information flows to an attacker zone. In Figure 15.4, the Plugin is not a malicious entity, i.e., it is not part of an attacker zone. The developer can manipulate the elements of attacker zones to change the design model and improve security.

UMLsec: As part of the design phase, we extended the reverse-engineered UML model (Figure 15.3) with annotations according to UMLsec *Secure Dependency*. For example, as Eclipse Secure Storage intends to provide secure storage of secrets, all objects representing secrets and methods for accessing secrets should be put on the *secrecy* security level. Accordingly, the class `SecurePreferences` is annotated «`critical`» and the `secrecy` list holds the signature `get(String, String,SecurePreferencesContainer):String` (visualized in the comment linked to the class), all classes with a dependency to this class that is stereotyped with «`call`» have to respect this secrecy security level. This is represented by a «secrecy» stereotype on the dependency and «critical» containing this signature, as on the class SecurePreferencesWrapper.

```
1   @Critical(secrecy={"get(String,String,SecurePreferencesContainer):
        String"})
2   public class SecurePreferencesWrapper implements ISecurePreferences {
3       private SecurePreferences node;
4
5       @Secrecy
6       public String get(String key, String def) {
7           return node.get(key, def, container);
8       }
9   }
```

Listing 15.1 Source code of the password store with security annotations

Listing 15.1 shows the Java security annotations that have been automatically propagated to the Java source code from the SecurePreferencesWrapper shown in Figure 15.3. The value secrecy={get(String, String): String} of «critical» is represented by a @Secrecy annotation on the get method in line 5 of the example. Additionally, the security requirement secrecy is specified for a member with the signature get(String, String, SecurePreferencesContainer):String in the @Critical annotation in line 1. This method is called in line 7 of the source code fragment.

Discussion.   Annotating the reverse engineered-models with security requirements was straightforward. Unlike the iTrust case study, there is only one level of inheritance simplifying this step. Technically, we demonstrated the feasibility of the tools for annotating the models and especially of GRaViTY's synchronization mechanism

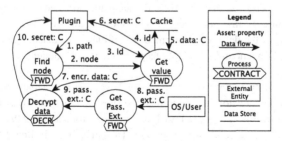

Figure 15.4 SecDFD for reading a aecret from the Eclipse Secure Storage

for propagating the security requirements into the implementation. Accordingly, the technical feasibility (**O1**) is given. From a developer's perspective, the main struggles in annotating the models lie in the used UML editors. The handling of the relatively large UML class diagram is not as fluently as the navigation through the Java source files. However, once a suitable view had been created, for us, this graphical representation was easier to follow than the source code files. To conclude, regarding **O2** the approach is usable in principle but there could be improvements. First, by better editor support and second by an automated creation of views on UML models.

Run-Time Monitoring

In the last part of this case study, we focus on leveraging the specified security requirements to enforce these at run-time using UMLsecRT. In the implementation of a software system specified by a UML model, the dependencies stereotyped with «call» are usually implemented as method calls and field accesses. Even if a model does not contain violations, at run-time it has to be guaranteed that the security requirements specified at design time are not violated. Furthermore, detecting all dependencies which can occur at run-time is statically undecidable, e.g., due to the use of Java reflection [122, 240]. What can also not be foreseen from a static perspective are violations caused by an exchanged library or malicious code. In Eclipse, for example, every installed plugin can access the password store. Which plugins a developer installs into her Eclipse IDE is not predictable. However, considering the discussed security annotations, only plugins that comply with the *secrecy* security level should be allowed to access the password store.

Execution. To execute this part of the case study, we implemented a malicious plugin trying to illegally access passwords stored in the Eclipse Secure Storage. Moreover, we extended the Eclipse Secure Storage implementation with countermeasures for actively preventing such illegal accesses. After these two extensions, we monitored Eclipse with the UMLsecRT agent and executed the malicious plugin. In what follows, we first introduce the malicious plugin. Afterward, we exemplary introduce one of the defined countermeasures. Finally, we discuss the execution of the UMLsecRT agent and the adaptions performed by the agent.

Example Security Violation: In Listing 15.2, we show how a malicious plugin can exploit the secure storage API to read the stored passwords. To avoid detection by static analyses, it uses the Java-Reflection API for accessing the `get` method of the class `ISecurePreferences`. To achieve this, in line 2 the malware navigates to the *ISecurePreferences* instance holding the desired passwords and then accesses them in lines 3 to 5. First, a `Method` object is requested, set to *accessible*, and finally the value of this method is requested and passed to a method `sendPassword`.

Counter measures: Listing 15.3 exemplifies the usage of calling an additional method to determine an early return value: `secure():String` will be called if a security violation of the secrecy property of the method `get` occurs at runtime. This method generates a random password that is returned instead of the real one.

```
1    public String readPassword(ISecurePreferences s) {
2        ISecurePreferences git = s.node("git/gitlab");
3        Method m = git.getClass().getMethod("get", ...);
4        m.setAccessible(true);
5        return (String) m.invoke(git);
6    }
```

Listing 15.2 Source code of a malicious Eclipse plugin

Monitoring and adaption: Figure 15.5 shows a deployment diagram of the Eclipse Secure Storage we reverse engineered before the execution of the security monitoring. The shapes with white background resemble the elements coming from the (reverse-engineered) model. On top is the call between the class `EGitSecureStore` and the interface `ISecurePreferences` from Figure 15.3. Below those two types, we can see on which artifacts those are deployed and on which execution environment they are manifested. The shapes with a gray background on the right were automatically added as an evolution step by a UMLsecRT guarded execution. These show actions of the malware introduced in Listing 9.4 that have not been considered by the system's developers.

Figure 15.6 is a sequence diagram generated by UMLsecRT during monitoring execution of the Eclipse IDE including the Eclipse Secure Storage and the malicious plugin (see Listing 15.2). It outlines a call sequence leading to a security violation and the mitigation carried out against it. The source of the security violation is the call of the method `get(String, String):String`, commented with *Violation of Secrecy* in the diagram, that has been called by the method `readPassword`. While this call is obfuscated by the use of Java reflection in the implementation, we can show the effective calls in the generated sequence diagrams. Which countermeasure has been executed is also shown in a comment. In this case, the method `secure()` has been called as specified in Listing 15.3. After the violating call, the attacker called `sendPassword(String)` but due to the countermeasure not with the secret value. As discussed in Chapter 9, due to efficiency reasons, only beginning with a security violation all future accesses

```
1   public class SecurePreferencesWrapper implements ISecurePreferences {
2       @Secrecy(earlyReturn = "secure")
3       public String get(String key, String def) {
4           return node.get(key, def, container);
5       }
6
7       @CounterMeasure
8       public String secure() {
9           StringBuilder s = new StringBuilder();
10          Random random = new SecureRandom();
11          for(int i = 0; i < 10 + random.nextInt(10); i++) {
12              s.append((char) random.nextInt('z' - 'a') + 'a');
13          }
14          return s.toString();
15      }
16  }
```

Listing 15.3 Specification of a countermeasure

are recorded and will be visualized. In this case, this is just one additional call of `sendPassword`.

Discussion. As showcased, we successfully applied the run-time monitoring for detecting and mitigating the security violation based on the security requirements specified on the reverse-engineered models. Also, the models have been adapted to investigate the security violation in detail. As shown in Figures 15.5 and 15.6, detailed models have been generated allowing us to get a deeper understanding. However, as we might be biased, this part of the case study should be repeated with independent developers and security experts. Nevertheless, the technical feasibility (**O1**) has been demonstrated in the context of a legacy project, and from our side, there are also strong indications for good usability for developers and security experts (**O2**).

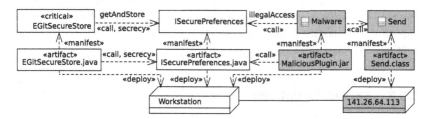

Figure 15.5 Deployment and manifestation of classes with adaptions

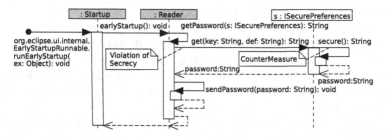

Figure 15.6 Sequence diagram automatically generated by UMLsecRT

15.2.2 Discussion of the Observations

Similar to the first case study, we have been able to use GRaViTY throughout the whole considered scenario. However, there are two limitations. First, the propagation of security requirements from the SecDFDs into the class diagrams and the implementation required manual workarounds. However, overcoming this limitation by additional tool support seems reasonable. Second, we did not consider continuous security checks at maintenance and extension of Eclipse Secure Storage. Nevertheless, as we reached a state comparable to an intermediate state of the iTrust case study, synchronizing future changes is theocratically possible. That we have been able to use the created correspondence model to propagate security requirements from the design-time models into the implementation is also an indication in this regard. Accordingly, we can assume the technical feasibility of GRaViTY (**O1**) for the application on legacy projects to be given. Regarding the usability from the perspective of developers and security experts, we had the goal of verifying the security of Eclipse Secure Storage statically and at run-time. Considering this goal, all actions have been straightforward. Especially, we did not have to care about the synchronization between the reverse-engineered models and the implementation as intended by GRaViTY. However, annotating the UML models using Papyrus has been somewhat cumbersome and could be improved. Nevertheless, as software ergonomics are not the focus of **O2** and GRaViTY did not extend Papyrus to the UMLsec stereotypes, we assume good usability.

15.3   Threats to Validity

The validity of the two case studies discussed in this chapter is subject to multiple threats. In this section, we discuss possible threats to validity and our mitigation for lowering the impact of the identified threats.

The main treat identified by us is that the case studies have mainly been performed by the author of this thesis. This might give rise to a threat to internal validity as the author could be biased. To clearly outline this threat, we described the case studies and the performed development activities and our conclusions in detail. Additional case studies with independent developers and security experts should be performed in future works.

The generalization of our observations and conclusions might be limited as we only considered two subject systems. To lower this threat, we selected the subject systems from two different domains, namely healthcare and storage of secrets. Also, both subject systems have been selected to use as different technologies as possible. The iTrust system is a web application based on JSP while Eclipse Secure Storage is based on Eclipse plugins.

In every case study, we simulated one development scenario. Here, we have not been able to cover every possible scenario. For example, we have no scenario explicitly focusing on the application of GRaViTY in agile software development. Nevertheless, the two considered scenarios are fundamentally different allowing us to increase our coverage as far as possible within the available resources. Also, we descriptively outlined the principle suitability of GRaViTY to cover additional development scenarios. Nevertheless, additional development scenarios should be considered in the future.

15.4   Conclusion on the Case Studies

We successfully applied GRaViTY as part of the two case studies considered in this chapter. Thereby, we demonstrated the technical suitability of the developed approach (**O1**) for developing secure software systems. As some parts of the case studies required manual simulations of parts of the approach, additional tool support can make the development more effective. Nevertheless, our case studies revealed that the current implementation of the GRaViTY approach already provides much support for effectively and efficiently aiding the development of secure software systems. Altogether, the case studies demonstrated the technical feasibility (**O1**) of GRaViTY.

Considering the key assumptions on users of the GRaViTY approach introduced in Section 4.1, we can also assume good usability from the perspective of developers and security experts (**O2**). In what follows, we discuss our observations regarding the four key assumptions.

Suitable Views: As part of the case studies, we specified security requirements mainly on design models. While it was necessary to specify some security requirements on a very detailed version of these models, often it was possible to specify security requirements on abstract models and to propagate these into more detailed models and the implementation.

Side effects: While performing the case studies, we never had to care about the side effects of our actions. However, there still have been some situations in which we had to resolve conflicts caused by side effects. But these have always been presented to us prominently by the tool support, e.g., by an additional dependency causing security issues revealed by the continuous security checks.

Synchronization: In the case study, we have always been able to synchronize our changes without facing issues. As our case studies only partly contained the situation in which larger changes on the UML models had to be propagated into the implementation there might be cases in which issues with the synchronization can arise. However, such cases have explicitly been discussed in Section 6.2.

Continious Security: Throughout the whole case study, the primary goal of continuous security compliance checks has been reached. After specifying the first security requirements we have always been able to check the software system for security violations.

While the principle usability has been demonstrated, the case studies also revealed space for future improvements. The software ergonomics not explicitly considered in the case studies should yield more attention in future works. Also, additional automatization should be considered in the future. This mainly targets the automated execution of synchronization steps and security verifications. Regarding security verifications, more incremental execution of the checks should be considered to allow near real-time feedback and focusing only on parts currently in the scope of a developer. Last but not least, reverse engineering of more abstract models and automated extraction of views should also be targeted.

Part VII
Closing Chapters

Related Work

16

In this chapter, we discuss works related to the GRaViTY approach introduced in this thesis. To the latest of our knowledge, GRaViTY is one of the first approaches allowing continuous and integrated model-based security engineering covering the whole software development life cycle. Therefore, most related works target single parts of GRaViTY. Accordingly, we structured this chapter along with the main areas considered in GRaViTY. First, in Section 16.1, we discuss related works regarding tracing and synchronization of changes. In Section 16.2, we discuss related approaches for ensuring the security compliance of software systems. Afterward, we discuss related works aiming at the refactoring of software systems in Section 16.3. Last, in Section 16.4, we discuss related works in the domain of software product lines.·

16.1   Tracing between Models and Code

In GRaViTY, the tracing between models and code plays an essential role in the approach. Both, the management and leveraging of traces are also an essential part of other works.

Winkler and Pilgrim performed a survey on traceability in requirements engineering and model-driven development [345]. While traceability in both domains has much in common, they are still separated. In requirements engineering traceability mainly means to follow requirements throughout the development process and in model-driven engineering traceability mainly means to explicitly create trace links between corresponding artifacts. While we consider security requirements and follow them in case of security context knowledge changes, our approach tracing mainly takes place in the area of model-driven development.

In the single underlying model approach (SUM), Atkinson et al. define a single model, that can express all information about the software system [346]. Suitable views according to the current task are extracted from this model. The SUM is comparable to the different connected UML models of our approach, in which we integrate all design-time information. SUM supports an automated extraction of views that could be helpful in GRaViTY for manual edits of the generated parts of the implementation model. While we support well-known plain UML, SUM made many modifications to the UML to support all those kinds of different abstractions. Also, SUM does not provide an integration with the concrete implementation.

With VITRUVIUS Kramer et al. developed a SUM approach that also integrates Java source code [347]. Unlike our approach, the trace links to the model are written into the source code as annotations and might lead to unreadable source code, as discussed in Chapter 6.

On a very similar technical basis as our framework is the Codeling tool of Konersmann [348]. The idea of Codeling is the integration of architecture model information into the program code. Like our approach, Konersmann uses TGGs for the model to model transformations at architecture extraction. In contrast to us, he does not continuously keep the extracted models up to date but always writes all changes, made on an extracted model, back to the source code. Every time an architectural view on the software system is needed, Codeling extracts it again. By doing so, Konersmann circumvents the challenge of incremental updates required by our TGG-based synchronization, presented in Section 6.2.2, at the cost of massively increasing the code base with additional information.

Combinations of models, metamodels, and transformations, such as those used in GRaViTY for keeping all artifacts synchronized and allowing tracing, are often referred to as *megamodels* [349]. When developers work in parallel on different artifacts, issues regarding restoring consistency can arise [350]. In GRaViTY, this can be the case if there are conflicting structural changes in the UML models and the source code. Stevens presents an approach for resolving such conflicts based on build-time information [351].

Commercial tools like Enterprise Architect (EA) also provide round-trip engineering for UML models and Code [352]. The main limitation of these tools is the restriction to UML models very close to the code which eases the synchronization. While EA allows a translation from UML stereotypes to Java annotations, which could be used for transferring UMLsec annotations into the code, they do not support more complex information transfers.

While all approaches are dealing with the same challenges as us in similar ways, none of them provides the support to maintain security requirements on different artifacts in a sophisticated way and to check those security requirements in between the different artifacts.

Explicitly designed for the tracing of the security structure and properties is the SecSTAR approach of Fang et al. [353]. SecSTAR monitors the software system execution and traces security-related information throughout the software system. Based on the recorded diagrams for security analysis are generated. These diagrams can be seen as part of the system model considered by us. Nhlabatsi et al. present an approach to monitor assumptions about security requirements, such as the location of devices, at run time [354]. Thereby, security requirements are specified upfront and might be subject to knowledge changes as considered by us.

Similar to our considered problem of mapping DFD elements to code, *feature location* techniques aim to find the code assets that contribute to the implementation of a given feature. Two existing surveys [355, 356] summarize the variety of available techniques, which largely differ in their assumed input, program representation, and required degree of user interaction. Most closely related to ours are those works that derive an initial mapping based on name similarities and use it as input for a structural search. Zhao et al.'s approach [357] assumes as input a set of features provided in one textual description for each feature. They use an information retrieval technique called *Latent Semantic Analysis* (LSA) to identify a set of seed elements deemed as relevant for each feature. They then filter a call graph representation of the input program to remove those branches that do not include a relevant element. Strüber et al.'s approach [358] uses LSA in the same way, then scores all elements based on topology measures and assigns each element to the feature it is deemed most relevant for. Font et al.'s approach [359] assumes user-specific input seeds that they extend with a genetic algorithm to generate a candidate for the implementation of the given feature; a textual description of the input feature is then used to judge the relevance of the identified fragment. In contrast to feature location techniques, which use textual descriptions and manually specified correspondences as input, we rely on a different source of information. Our heuristics exploit the rich structural information given by the input DFDs to guide the search of the program model; that is, we exploit an assumed correspondence between the two models being available in our scenario.

16.2   Security Compliance of Models and Code

In this section, we discuss works related to the continuous security compliance checks between models and code presented in this thesis. First, we focus on model-based works for the specification and analysis of security. Afterward, we discuss works explicitly focusing on security compliance among different artifacts. Finally, we discuss works for monitoring or enforcing security at run-time.

16.2.1 Model-Based Security Analysis

An overview of model-based security analysis can be found in [360], which reviews existing approaches for security analysis of model-based object-oriented software designs, and identifies ways in which these approaches can be improved and made more rigorous. A newer systematic literature review on model-driven security in general can be found in [361]. Most security specifications of the considered works provide a DSL based on UML's profile mechanism.

UMLsec [6] provides a model-based approach to develop and analyze security-critical software systems, in which security requirements such as secrecy, integrity, and availability are expressed in UML diagrams [5]. UMLsec is provided as a UML profile, containing different stereotypes and tagged values to annotate UML diagrams with security requirements of which only a few have been considered in this thesis. The CARiSMA tool performs the corresponding security analysis [362]; it has been applied to various industrial applications, e.g., to investigate the security of the *Common Electronic Purse Specifications* [363]). Furthermore, UMLsec and CARiSMA are the foundation for various other works. Ahmadian et al. extended CARiSMA to support privacy-related security requirements and checks regarding their consistency [364–367]. Also, they provide support for selecting suitable measures for preventing the identified privacy threats. Similarly, Ramadan et al. extend CARiSMA with fairness checks for preventing systematic discrimination by the developed software system already at design time [368–370].

Siveroni et al. [371] researched supporting the design and verification of secure software systems, emphasizing the early stages of development like requirements elicitation. The proposed approach realizes static verification of properties and enables to reason about temporal and general properties of a UML subset, e.g. UML state machines. Formal verification carried out using the SPIN model checker. The approach focuses solely on the early stages of software design and thus only properties that can be checked statically.

Other work addresses the model-based use of security patterns [372–374]. Further research makes use of aspect-oriented modeling for model-based security [375]. [376] proposes an approach for model-based security verification.

16.2.2 Security Compliance

Existing works on maintaining security consistently in different development stages focus on *forward* and *reverse engineering*, that is, the automated transformation of a more high-level to a more technical representation, and back. Considering forward engineering, Ramadan et al. [377] use model transformation to automatically generate security-annotated UML class models [6] from security-annotated BPMN models. Ahmadian et al. use security requirements (SecBPMN [378]) to provide suggestions to developers which elements in UML diagrams might correspond to the annotated BPMN elements [74, 367].

Most closely related to ours is the approach of Nguyen et al. [379, 380]. Comparable to us, they propose a model-driven security approach. While we focus on data security, they focus on authorization in the software system under development. Security requirements defined at design-time, are enforced in later phases of software development and their enforcement is tested. Concerning security tests, Schieferdecker et al. provide a survey on model-based security testing techniques [381]. Besides architectural models, as considered in our approach, also threat, fault, and risk models, as well as weakness and vulnerabilities models, are used for deriving security tests. Usually, security tests can be automatically generated based on test generation criteria.

Abi-Antoun et al. [382], which is concerned with DFD-to-code conformance checks. They automatically reverse engineer a DFD from the given implementation, calling it the *source DFD*. The user has to specify a mapping between a manually created *high-level DFD* and the source DFD, which is then used to uncover inconsistencies. In contrast to this manual approach to mapping, our approach is semi-automated: It automatically proposes an initial set of mappings, which is iteratively refined based on user feedback.

Some research addresses linking the model to the code level within model-based security through model-driven reverse engineering [383, 384]; similar to our work, Martínez et al. [384] use OCL to specify security policies.

Considering evolving software systems, Anisetti et al. present a security certification scheme for evolving services [385].

Beyond the security scope of this paper, conformance checking is generally a well-studied topic in model-driven engineering. Paige et al. [386] use metamodels as the common reference point to enable conformance checks between diagrams representing different views on a software system. Diskin et al. [387] present a framework for global consistency checks of heterogeneous models based on constraints. By supporting the explicit specification of overlaps between the considered models, they avoid the need for a global metamodel. Expanding on this work, König and

Diskin [388] improve the efficiency of this approach by supporting an early local-
ization of relevant parts of the models whose consistency is to be checked. Reder
and Egyed [389] propose an efficient approach to consistency checking based on
predefined consistency rules. However, none of these works address security, and
an application to data flow-related threats as addressed by DFDs is not obvious.

The problem of measuring attack surfaces serving as a metric for evaluating
secure object-oriented programming policies has been investigated by Zoller and
Schmolitzky [215] and Manadhata and Wing [214], respectively.

Closely related to the specification of security checks is the specification of design
flaws, such as code smells or anti-patterns. A common method to detect code smells
and anti-patterns through software metrics. Simon et al. define a generic distance
measure that can be applied to identify anomalies inducing certain refactorings in an
underlying language [390]. Mäntylä makes use of atomic metrics to evaluate their
applicability for code smell detection compared to human intuition, concluding that
metric-based detection often contradicts human perception [391]. Munro proposes
to capture informal code smell descriptions by means of a set of metrics and to
identify possible occurrences in Java programs based on those metrics [392].

16.2.3 Run-time Security Monitoring

Lee et al. focused on inter-app communication in Android that may enable an
attacker to inject arbitrary activities [393]. Ultimately, user interaction can be
hijacked to break the Android sandbox mechanism. Thus, they propose a static
analysis tool using operational semantics of the activity life-cycle, unveiling potential vulnerabilities. In contrast to that, UMLsecRT aims at providing the developer
a lightweight model extension to cover up security risks in early design phases,
coupled with the source code and run-time.

Ion et al. [394] investigated the security policy architecture of J2ME (Java for
mobile devices), which in contrast to Java Standard Edition does not provide an
extensible security architecture. They modified the J2ME VM to be able to deal
with custom security policies at run-time with no considerable overhead. In contrast, UMLsecRT uses a Java agent and thus does not require changes to the VM.
By incorporating model-based design, we support developers in gaining additional
knowledge about how the code behaves at run-time.

Costa et al. present a more fine-grained and flexible policy-based security mechanism for J2ME and implemented it in two variants [115]. First, similar to [394],
by adapting the J2ME VM, facing the issue that keywords in policies are restricted
to the methods that can be intercepted at fixed enforcement points. Second, based

on byte-code manipulation, preceding and succeeding every call to the J2ME API. They noticed a performance overhead below 5, while we achieve a similar overhead, supporting full Java and monitoring all accesses.

Hiet et. al propose to secure Java Web applications by monitoring information flows [243]. They extend Blare, an intrusion detection tool on OS level, to realize a policy-based intrusion detection by tracing inter-method flows in Java applications, supported by the JRE calling an internal security manager before every I/O access. They encountered a slow down of factor 12 for loading and factor 4 for execution. Blare requires a modified Linux kernel to run on, while JBlare requires a modified JRE, which are heavy-weight assumptions against the target environment. Reacting to breaches or preventing them as well as round-trip engineering is not discussed.

Bodden et al. present an approach to reduce the time to invest in run-time verification of large programs [259]. Given a sufficient number of users, parts of the run-time verification are distributed among the users. Instead of instrumenting the whole program, only a partition is instrumented at a time. Using regular expressions, traces for unwanted behavior are specified. The authors implemented two variants, noticing generally a high instrumentation overhead.

Staicu et al. performed a large-scale study of 235,850 Node.js applications, identifying two APIs giving direct system access [395]. They tackle this issue by first building templates for all values passed to injection APIs. After that, a run-time policy is synthesized to support monitoring, which is integrated into the code by code rewriting. Checking also is supported at design time by static checks.

Ognawala et al. propose a mixture of concrete and symbolic execution to detect non-trivial vulnerabilities [396]. They let the user interactively investigate calls in-depth and assess possible vulnerabilities on a graphical representation. While the authors focus on other types of vulnerabilities than we do, they also conclude that an interactive, graphical vulnerability report supports developers to prioritize bug fixing activities.

16.3 (Security-aware) Refactorings

Various techniques have been proposed for both, graph-based program transformation and object-oriented program refactoring. In this section, we mention the most important work and relate it to the technique proposed in Chapter 10 of this thesis. Also, we discuss existing works regarding their relation to security aspects of the refactored software systems.

While general work on representing programs as graphs has been proposed decades ago [397], recent work particularly focuses on graph transformation for the purpose of reengineering (e.g., refactoring). Initially, Eetvelde et al. proposed the application of graph rewriting rules to typed program graphs for program refactorings [135, 136]. Based on this work, the notion of rule refinement to treat hierarchical program substructures as a whole, as well as the notion of rule cloning are introduced for multiple instantiations of rewriting rules [398]. Thereupon, Mens et al. developed a foundation for refactoring Java-like programs based on algebraic graph transformations that comprises object-oriented standard refactorings such as Pull Up Method and Extract Field [24, 140]. Moreover, Ferenc et al. propose Columbus, a tool that applies metamodeling techniques to support graph transformations on C++ programs [9]. With a particular focus on Java, Corradini et al. proposed a graph transformation system for Java programs [137]. Moreover, mature tools, such as JaMoPP [143] and MoDisco [141, 161] exist that provide modeling techniques to translate Java programs into a graph-based representation.

While all of the aforementioned approaches partially overlap with our proposed technique (in fact, our refactorings are very similar to those proposed by Mens et al.), we extend existing work by proposing a systematic and formalized method for bidirectional, graph-based program transformation for the first time.

Program refactoring is a fundamental concept in software reengineering for specifying allowed changes in a software system. It has been proposed more than 15 years ago as a means to improve the structure of source code in a behavior-preserving fashion [18, 64]. However, while the concept and the technique have been shown to be valid and useful, many existing implementations, such as in the Eclipse IDE, are limited (or even erroneous) due to their informal nature [66, 69]. Hence, various methods have been proposed to formally specify refactorings and, thus, to allow for verifying behavior preservation. For instance, Schaefer et al. formulate refactoring as a dependency preservation problem that, amongst others, preserves name bindings after refactorings [67]. Moreover, they extend the idea of decomposing refactorings by considering micro-refactorings as very basic blocks of macro-refactorings, being easier to implement and verify [63]. Thereupon, chained refactorings are built by applying macro-refactorings in a predefined order. Further works on making refactorings more reliable use constraint checking [69] and type checking [62]. We extend these methods by a) proposing a graph-based method for refactoring and b) by supporting the co-evolution of the textual and graph-based representation of the program utilizing bidirectional program transformation.

To test the correctness of performed refactoring operations, Mongiovi et al. propose *SafeRefactorImpacthas* [399] that analyzes a refactoring operation and generates test cases for the impacted methods.

Steimann and Thies were the first to propose a comprehensive set of accessibility constraints for refactorings covering full Java [69]. Although their constraints are formally founded, they do not consider software metrics to quantify the attack surface impact of (sequences of) refactorings. Alshammari et al. propose an extensive catalog of software metrics for evaluating the impact of refactorings on program security of object-oriented programs [212]. Similarly, Maruyama and Omori propose a technique [270] and tool [31] for checking if a refactoring operation raises security issues. However, all these approaches are concerned with general security and accessibility constraints of specific refactorings, but they do not consider explicit security requirements.

Ghaith and Ó Cinnéide consider a catalog of security-relevant metrics to recommend refactorings using CODE-IMP [400]. Finally, Abid et al. propose to prioritize refactoring operations to improve the quality of security-critical code first for preventing future security violations [401]. Security-critical files that should be prioritized at refactoring are identified by the history of vulnerabilities, security bug reports, and a set of keywords.

16.4 Software Product Lines

We consider related works regarding software product lines in two directions. First, we generally consider the transformation of product lines. Here, we mainly relate other works to our variability extension of Henshin introduced in Chapter 13. Second, we consider approaches targeting the security of software product lines.

16.4.1 Product Line Transformations

During an SPL's lifecycle, not only the domain model but also the feature model evolves [402, 403]. To support the combined transformation of domain and feature models, Taentzer et al. [404] propose a unifying formal framework that generalizes Salay et al.'s notion of lifting [317], yet in a different direction than us: focusing on combined changes, this approach is not geared for internal variability of rules; similar rules are considered separately. Both works could be combined using a rule concept with separate feature models for rule and SPL variability.

Beyond transformations of SPLs, transformations have been used to *implement* SPLs. Feature-oriented development [340] supports the implementation of features as additive changes to a base product. Delta-oriented programming [405] adds flexibility to this approach: changes are specified using *deltas* that support deletions and modifications as well. Impact analysis in an evolving SPL can be performed by transforming deltas using higher-order deltas that encapsulate certain evolution operators [316]. For increased flexibility regarding inter-product reuse, deltas can be combined with traits [406]. Sijtema [319] introduced the concept of variability rules to develop SPLs using ATL. Conversely, SPL techniques have been applied to certain problems in transformation development. Xiao et al. [407] et al. propose to capture variability in the backward propagation of bidirectional transformations by turning the left-hand-side model into an SPL. Hussein et al. [321] present a notion of rule templates for generating groups of similar rules based on a data provenance model. These works address only one dimension of variability, either of an SPL or a transformation system.

In the domain of graph transformation reuse, rule refinement [320] and amalgamation [336] focus on reuse at the rule level; graph variability is not in their scope. Rensink and Ghamarian propose a solution for rule and graph decomposition based on a certain accommodation condition, under which the effect of the original rule application is preserved [408]. In our approach, by matching against the full domain model rather than decomposing it, we trade off compositionality for the benefit of imposing fewer restrictions on graphs and rules.

16.4.2 Security of Software Product Lines

Sion et al. [409] present a research agenda towards systematically addressing security concerns in software product lines in a way that considers security separate from other variability dimensions by allowing to express security and its variability, select the right solution, properly instantiate a solution, and verify and validate it. This research agenda seems certainly relevant and worthwhile, but there do not seem to be results published to date.

Myllärniemi et al. [410] propose a kind of modeling language for specifying security and functional variability at the architectural level of a software system. Their solution allows the user to select among multiple countermeasures; however, security analysis in the style of our work is not possible in this solution, since security requirements on the level of threats and assets are deliberately left outside the scope of this work.

Nadi and Krüger [411] use the modeling language Clafer, which combines feature modeling and metamodeling, for modeling cryptographic components. In comparison, their work could be considered a specific product line of security-relevant software products, whereas our goal is to apply security concepts to harden arbitrary software product lines.

Mellado et al. [412, 413] present approaches which deal with security requirements from the early stages of the product line life cycle systematically and intuitively way especially adapted for product line based development. These works do neither address the system design nor the implementation, as we do in this thesis.

Fægri and Hallsteinsen [414] present a software product line reference architecture for security. This work does not use a model-based design approach, as we do.

General scalability issues arising due to variability have motivated a variety of software analyses for SPLs; for an overview, see the comprehensive survey by Thüm et al. [415]. A key distinction is that between *product-based* approaches that operate on a selection of all products, and *family-based* ones that lift the analysis to a representation of the overall SPL. Product-based approaches are useful in scenarios where the result does not need to be complete, a prime example being testing.

Model-based testing of SPLs [287, 416–418] focuses on the use of dedicated test models for this purpose. To improve test coverage, Cichos et al. [287] derive test cases from a "150%" test model for the SPL, and Johansen et al. [416] use a certain notion of covering arrays that can be derived from the feature model. Ali et al. [417] propose a methodology for reducing the specification effort during model-based testing of SPLs. Lachmann et al. prioritize products by their risk for failures for integration tests of SPLs [419]. These approaches do not aim to ensure a complete analysis of all products of the product line.

The SecPL security analysis and security checks based on the multi-variant model transformation, introduced by us, fall into the category of family-based analysis, which aims at completeness w.r.t. all products. Most works in this category focus on program analyses, such as syntax and type checking [420], static program analysis [421], or model checking [421]. A seminal model-level work is the well-formedness analysis for model templates by Czarnecki and Pietroszek [300] that we used as a foundation for our analysis (see Section 12.3). While this work operates on vanilla UML models to validate well-formedness constraints, our analysis works on stereotyped UML models for checking security requirements. Salay et al's [317] work on the lifting of transformation rules to model-based SPLs includes a matching step that can be considered a family-based analysis. However, none of these works addresses security.

Conclusion

17

This thesis aimed at investigating the state of the art of security compliance in model-driven development and maintenance of variant-rich software systems, the identification of open problems in realizing. As motivated in the introduction to this thesis, considering security at the development and maintenance of software systems is as challenging and important as never before. While software systems are becoming more complex, they also process more sensitive information, and new attack vectors constantly emerge. Among others, this especially applies for the sector of health care, considered throughout this thesis in terms of the iTrust EHR system as the running example. In recent research, following the principle of security by design [28], various approaches for eliciting suitable measures within a software system's design have been developed [6, 111, 361]. However, the compliance of a software system's implementation with the planned security stayed an open issue tackled in this thesis.

As discusses in Chapter 3, besides design-time security approaches, there are various approaches for supporting the development of secure software systems in all stages of software development. However, mostly these approaches are limited to their local specialties and are not integrated as required for the effective development of secure software systems. One reason for this lack of integration is missing traceability among the development artifacts of software systems. Furthermore, often, this causes inconsistencies, e.g., between the planned and implemented design. To be more precise, such inconsistencies, potentially leading to security violations, are often caused by continuous changes as part of the development process. Often, such changes are not reflected in all artifacts. Regarding security, not only structural consistency is essential but also security preservation. For this reason, practitioners frequently claim that they cannot apply simple refactorings without requiring a full re-certification of the whole software system. Finally, the significant reuse among

S. M. Peldszus, *Security Compliance in Model-driven Development of Software Systems in Presence of Long-Term Evolution and Variants*, https://doi.org/10.1007/978-3-658-37665-9_17

software systems, e.g., in terms of variants of a product, makes all of this even more complicated.

To overcome these problems, in this thesis, we presented an integrated approach for continuous security compliance checks at the model-driven development of software systems. The proposed GRaViTY approach addresses the five challenges, identified at problem discussion in Section 1.1, for supporting security compliance at the development and maintenance of variant-rich secure software systems as follows:

Inconsistency and missing traceability: In Chapter 6, we introduced a combination of tracing within UML models and correspondence model-based tracing between UML models and their implementation. While we use standard UML technologies for tracing among UML models with different abstraction, we employ TGGs [422], a bidirectional graph transformation technology, for tracing between models and code. Based on transformation rules, TGGs build a correspondence model between two models and allow to automatically synchronize changes between the two models. This allows us to prevent inconsistencies throughout the software development automatically. Furthermore, in Chapter 7, we discussed semi-automated restoring of traceability and the reverse engineering of UML models.

Non-integrated solutions: To overcome non-integrated solutions, GRaViTY connects design-time security with implementation-level security. In this regard, the presented automation allows us to effectively check security at low costs by allowing security experts to only specify security requirements once in combination with an automated propagation based on our tracing mechanism. In Chapter 8, we discussed the leveraging of design-time security requirements for implementation-level security checks. Based on the design-time security specifications, we execute implementation-level security checks. Besides newly developed checks, specifically tailored for verifying considered design-time security requirements, we also discussed how state-of-the-art taint analysis can be improved by connecting design-time security with the data flow analyzer. Finally, in Chapter 9, we presented a run-time monitor for detecting and mitigating violations of design-time security requirements. Furthermore, we support an adaption of the design-time models to allow an inspection of observed security violations.

Security-aware restructuring: For supporting the security-aware restructuring of software systems, in Chapter 8, we introduced incremental security violation patterns that can be used for detecting security violations after changes. Especially, we discuss their incremental execution for efficiently verifying the security compliance of single changes instead of full security compliance checks.

In addition, we provide security-preserving refactorings for ensuring security compliance at implementation-level restructuring in Chapter 10. The security-preserving refactorings allow checking security compliance of changes before modifying the implementation.

Variant-rich systems: Finally, in Chapter 11, we investigated the application of the proposed approach to variant-rich software systems. For the verification of the consistency of UMLsec security requirements in model product lines, we encoded the checks as OCL constraints and applied a state-of-the-art template interpretation approach. For the application of arbitrary pattern-based checks, e.g., the security violation patterns or our security-preserving refactorings, we extended the Henshin graph transformation engine to support variability in two dimensions. First, we support variability within transformation rules, and second, the models the rules are applied to.

Besides evaluations of the single contributions within the proposed approach, we successfully evaluated the feasibility of the overall approach on two real-world case studies in Chapter 15.

17.1 Research Outcomes

At the beginning of this thesis, in Section 1.3, we identified five research questions regarding the development of secure software systems based on the identified problems. In this section, we summarize our research outcomes and give answers o the research questions.

RQ1: How can security requirements be traced among different system representations throughout a software system's development process?
We investigated the suitability of refinement relations for tracing among UML models. In this regard, UML already comes with sufficient language elements for the specification of trace links among UML models with different abstractions. However, the creation and maintenance of trace links among UML models is laborsome but can be assisted by tool support. For the tracing of security requirements among UML models more sophisticated refinement rules have to be defined. For this purpose, we extended the UMLsec profile for tracing security refinements. For the tracing between UML models and the implementation, we identified TGGs as a suitable solution that not only provides trace links but also a mechanism for change propagation.

RQ2: How can we apply model-based security engineering to legacy projects that have no or disconnected design-time models?
We identified the creation of suitable tracing structures between models and code as the main challenge in applying the GRaViTY approach to legacy projects. For this reason, we investigated the suitability of the TGG approach for reverse engineering UML class diagrams including correspondence models for tracing. We successfully demonstrated the application for reverse engineering UML class diagrams. For supporting early design-time models, we proposed a semi-automated mapping approach for restoring a correspondence model between the design-time models and the implementation.

RQ3: How can developers be supported in realizing, preserving, and enforcing design-time security requirements in software systems?
We discussed leveraging the created trace links for security compliance checks among models and the implementation. Based on these trace links, structural compliance can be verified in terms of correspondence, divergence, and absence. Regarding explicit security compliance, we identified two possibilities for security tracing, namely the propagation of security requirements and dynamic security tracing. Using the provided security tracing, developers can be supported by security checks in implementing a security-compliant software system. First, security checks tailored to single design-time security requirements can be executed on the implementation parts corresponding with relevant model elements for checking the presence of security measures in the implementation. Here, we demonstrated the feasibility of static checks and dynamic checks at run-time. Second, the configuration of state-of-the-art security analyses can be optimized to be more precise and effective. Altogether, developers can be supported by automatically reporting security violations in the implementation concerning design-time security requirements. Furthermore, the adaption of design-time models based on observations at run-time allows developers to investigate security violations and improving software systems.

RQ4: How do changes within a software system affect its security compliance, and how can these effects be handled?
Changes in a software system can affect security in manifold directions. For handling the effects of changes, we investigated two approaches. First, an automated propagation of changes to all artifacts of a software system in combination with an incremental re-execution of security compliance checks on the parts of the software system affected by the change. The TGGs used for tracing allows the

propagation of changes between the UML models and the implementation followed by an automated security verification. Here, the security violation patterns allow an incremental verification of the implemented security. Second, the prevention of violating changes by enriching change specifications with security-preserving constraints. Taking OO refactorings as change specifications, we investigated how security-preserving refactorings can be specified and executed. Such security-preserving refactorings allow the restructuring of a software system by preserving its security. In combination, both approaches allow to effectively handle the impact of changes on a software system's security.

RQ5: How can we verify and preserve security compliance in variant-rich software systems?
The main challenge in supporting software product lines is the practical infeasibility of applying the developed security checks and security-preserving refactorings to all products of an SPL. Also, for allowing tracing within a software product line, variability has to be supported on all artifacts of the software system. However, when specifying variability similarly on all products, structural and security tracing using our approaches does not differ from a single product software system. For supporting security compliance within SPLs, we investigated the application of security checks and security-preserving refactorings to SPLs by specifying formally these and utilizing application technologies that take care of the variability. This way, variability has not to be considered in the specification of the security checks and refactorings, allowing the application to both single product software systems and SPLs. For verifying security on model product lines, we demonstrated the suitability of the interpretation of OCL constraints to verify UMLsec security requirements. For the application of security-preserving refactorings and security violation patterns, we introduced multi-variant model transformations.

17.2 Assumptions and Limitations

Throughout the thesis, we outlined assumptions on the application of the single parts of our approach and discussed its limitations. In this section, based on the discussed assumptions and limitations, we discuss assumptions and limitations for the overall GRaViTY approach.

17.2.1 Required Artifacts

Our main assumption is that our approach will be applied to software systems developed using a model-driven development approach. The presence of design-time models as a prerequisite for using our approach might lead to limitations of its applicability. In this regard, we consider two factors that might limit the practical applicability of our approach.

First, the required model-driven development approach might not be applicable in the context of agile project development. However, considering the legal requirements in many security-critical domains, standards such as the ISO/EC 62304 for the development of medical device software [7], the development, and maintenance of the artifacts required by our approach is a prerequisite in most cases. Such standards do not require specific development processes as long as the required artifacts are provided. The same applies to our approach. For example, Rumpe demonstrates how software systems can be developed agile using model-based development [423].

Second, our approach may not be able to reimburse the costs incurred to create the required models. However, as our approach's main scope is large software systems developed for strongly regulated areas, these artifacts are likely required by standards, with which the software systems have to comply. In this case, there are no additional costs for using our approach. For all other software systems, the application of our approach might require additional effort to create those artifacts. From this perspective, the only reason standing against our approach might be that, up to some size, manually keeping the security context knowledge up to date and manually selecting measures in case of changes might be more cost-efficient than using our approach for (semi-)automating these activities. In comparison with this, the automated reverse-engineering of UML models can be a cost-efficient solution to apply our approach. Either way, if developers want to apply our approach, they have to implement model-driven development practices.

17.2.2 Tracing and Synchronization

The application of the TGGs for realizing the tracing and synchronization gives rise to multiple limitations. These limitations mainly consider the detailedness of the used models and transformations as well as concurrent change handling. As a consequence, these have an effect on the application of the approach and might limit its application or extension.

First, the specification of the transformation is laborsome and sometimes needs preprocessing for being realizable. This high effort might limit the approach's applicability to other programming languages than Java.

Second, as well the TGGs of our approach as the semi-automated mappings require detailed models of a software system. The synchronization between models and code, needs a UML class diagram on the same level of abstraction as the implementation. The semi-automated mappings need less detailed models but the considered DFDs might still be more detailed than practitioners would specify them, e.g., as a part of STRIDE [110].

Third, conflicting concurrent changes is not only a problem concerned with the TGGs used by us, but generally this problem is relevant for the synchronization of multiple artifacts that may change independently of each other. In the context of megamodels, this problem has been discussed in detail for transformations comparable to the ones considered by us [349].

17.2.3 Security Requirements and Checks

In this thesis, we only considered a limited set of security requirements. We focus on data security in terms of security levels and processing contracts. However, for capturing security at its full extend, additional security requirements have to be considered. Such additional security requirements could not only require additional ways to specify them on all relevant artifacts but could also open new challenges in tracing and synchronization.

As a consequence of the selected security requirements, currently, we only verify the structural properties and the presence of security measures. Consequently, we do not verify the completeness of enforcing design-time security requirements. While this still allows to detect a wide variety of security compliance issues, additional security checks might be required to reach a state of completeness that would allow an automated security certification.

For specifying security checks, besides hand-written code, we inspected the suitability of graph transformation rules and OCL constraints. However, security checks are often based on path expressions or detailed analysis on statement level currently not supported within GRaViTY. Although specifying security checks based on such concepts can simply be supported by using additional tools, e.g., the *Graph Repository Query Language* (GReQL) of *JGraLab* for path expressions [424, 425], more foundational research is necessary for applying path expressions to software product lines.

17.2.4 Security Preservation and Re-Certification

Although one of the motivations of this thesis was to allow the preservation of security in case of changes as an step towards supporting incremental re-certifications, the support for this is still limited. The proposed security-preserving refactorings allow including certification preserving constraints but possibly limit the applicability of the refactorings to non security critical cases. As a consequence, when a security-critical part of a software system has to be refactored, it is likely that changes are necessary that require an re-certification. In such cases, incremental security verification approaches such as the proposed security violation patterns can help in efficiently detecting security violations caused by changes but are not in a state in which guarantees can be given. For this purpose, additional security requirements have to be covered.

Nevertheless, the proposed approaches are still a significant step towards automated re-certifications in case of minor changes. Our approach gives a framework that allows the specification and execution of incremental security compliance checks between an accepted security design and its implementation. For automated re-certifications, a sufficient set of security requirements and corresponding security compliance checks have to be defined.

17.2.5 Software Product Lines

Within our approach, we assumed a one to one representation of variability on all artifacts of a variant-rich software system. However, in practice, there might be the case that variability is expressed with different abstraction among the different artifacts, e.g., more detailed variability specifications on the implementation level than in the design models. This might lead to side effects not captured by our approach and limiting the applicability. However, only different variability specifications on corresponding elements can cause problems, e.g., more detailed variability specifications at the level of method bodies can be handled by our approach.

In this thesis, we assumed that it is essential to always verify the security of all products of an SPL. Although there is evidence that security fixes applied to single products can be exploited for attacking other products [297, 298], the underlying assumption is that there are products on the market that have not been checked. In this regard, there might also be product lines that have theoretically very many variants but only a few are released. In such cases, it might be more cost effective to check only released variants for security.

17.3 Outlook

Although the proposed GRaViTY approach is a significant step towards effective continuous model-based security engineering, multiple research directions have potential for further improvements and research. In this section, we discuss potential future improvements considering three principles for improvement:

Extension: Possible extensions to the approach for improving continuous model-based security engineering, e.g., by widening the scope of the GRaViTY approach or providing new levels of automatization.

Combination: Possible combinations with other approaches for providing additional advantages to continuous model-based security engineering.

Actualization: New approaches or optimizations that overcome parts of the proposed approach for improving the overall GRaViTY approach.

Based on these three principles, in what follows, we discuss possible future research directions.

17.3.1 Automated Trace Creation

As discussed in the limitations of the approach, the creation of trace links is currently entirely manual among UML models and based on strict rules between UML and the implementation. Furthermore, these detailed rules require very detailed design-times models. An automated tracing at model-refinement and between models and code that is not based on strict rules would be a substantial actualization of the approach. Monitoring of artifacts touched by developers could be a suitable source for automatically deriving trace links. This way, tracing would be more flexible and could cover additional software development artifacts, e.g., textual requirements, without special treatment.

Also, the used MoDisco parser currently prevents GRaViTY from practically synchronizing UML models and their implementation in case of implementation-level changes. To overcome this issue, other parsers that support incremental parsing should be investigated and our implementation should be actualized accordingly. Similarly, one can actualize the implementation of our semi-automated mappings to support UML activity diagrams.

17.3.2 Continuous Integration

Automated security compliance checks in case of changes are also one main characteristic of popular security approaches such as SecDevOps [127]. If our approach is deployed within a continuous integration framework, it can be integrated into SecDevOps, complementary to other vulnerability detection techniques such as penetration testing or static code analysis. In this case, the combination with our approach adds a new level of automatization beyond local security checks on single artifacts. Our approach will be executed together with other automated security tests that focus on fine-grained local security requirements while our approach contributes the tracing and compliance checks between security requirements.

17.3.3 Multi-Language Software Systems

The key idea of the program model, presented in Chapter 5 of this thesis, is to be suitable for giving a high-level representation of arbitrary OO program. In this thesis, we only demonstrated the suitability for Java programs. The evaluation of the suitability for representing program written in other languages will be investigated in future works. However, assuming this suitability, we are not limited to program models for software systems written in a single programming language but can represent the whole implementation of multi-language software systems in a single program model. In such a program model, all dependencies between the different parts of the software system would be explicit which would allow more comprehensive security analyses and would reduce the reliance on assumptions at the borders of the single parts. This future research is likely to require an actualization of our program model's type graph and an extension to create program models for other programming languages. Here, one should investigate the combination with other state of the art parsers, such as Eclipse CDT for C/C++ code[1].

17.3.4 Security Requirements and Checks

The most potential for future research is in the area of covered security requirements and security checks. In this regard, the approach could be extended to cover additional security requirements. In this thesis, we mainly focused on data security in terms of security levels, data flows, and basic data processing contracts.

---

[1] Eclipse CDT (C/C++ Development Tooling): https://www.eclipse.org/cdt/

Additional security requirements can be research regarding data security but also regarding other security requirements. Regarding data security, concepts such as authorization could be considered for improving the approach. Additional security requirements could comprise availability or authentication. Future works can cover both the extension in terms of new security profiles and checks or the combination with existing additional security profiles.

17.3.5 Customization

The ultimate goal is to support security requirements that cover all aspects of security. As security is subject to continuous change [426], suitable interfaces for adjusting the supported security requirements are needed. Furthermore, relevant security requirements and according security checks for verifying the security compliance of a software system are likely to be system specific. In this regard, CARiSMA provides an interface for registering new security profiles and model-level checks and Hulk provides an interface for registering program model level analyses that are inherited by GRaViTY. However, for entirely supporting customization, additional logic for orchestration of the checks is required. In the best case, all extensions are centrally managed by GRaViTY and can be specified using a simple domain specific language (DSL).

17.3.6 Expressiveness of Languages

In this thesis, we used multiple languages to express security checks. For expressing incremental security violation patterns, we used the notation of graph transformation rules. For applying UMLsec checks to software product lines, we expressed these as OCL constraints. However, we identified limitations in these languages in expressing all kinds of security checks. For example, currently, no path expressions are supported. Furthermore, comparable to the customization of the security checks, a single DSL for specifying all kinds of security checks would be desirable. Accordingly, in future works, one should explore which concepts are required for expressing security checks to its full extend and will provide a DSL for specifying these. The execution of the specified security checks can be realized by extending used tools or combining GRaViTY with additional tools for execution.

17.3.7 Distributed System Analysis

For tailoring taint analysis to the security specifics of a software system, we leveraged security information captured in design-time models. A case very often covered in design-time models but never in a software system's implementation is information about entities the software system is interacting with. From a security perspective, this information is among the most valuable security information as it directly specifies parts of a software system's attack surface, namely the intended surface of the software system. In future works, this information can be leveraged to optimize implementation-level security analysis or to even provide analyses not possible before. Ultimately, the leveraging of this design-time information can allow performing holistic security analyses considering all implementations of distributed systems.

17.3.8 Code Generation

In this thesis, we considered code generation only for generating the foundational structure of a software system's implementation. As the design-time models used in our approach contain detailed security requirements, these requirements could be leveraged for automatically generating suitable security mechanisms into the implementation. This way, we could tackle two problems. First, we can reduce the cost of implementing these security mechanisms. Second, often security mechanisms are implemented insecurely due to wrong usage of APIs [118]. To avoid such cases, correct code, e.g., for opening a secure socket, could be generated that is connected with the manual implementation afterward.

17.3.9 Software Product Lines

Regarding software product lines, the most obvious future work is the application of all parts of GRaViTY that currently only support single products, e.g., structural and contract compliance checks. The same applies for all future extensions already discusses in this section. Of special interest in this regard, are the support of path expressions on software product lines as these allow to specify an additional category of security checks.

Entirely out of scope for this thesis are effects on security caused by the specification of variability itself. Although we considered variability of design-time security requirements impacting the run-time security behavior of a software system, e.g., under which run-time circumstances an encrypted communication path is required, we did not investigate this further on the implementation or run-time level. Here, the variable parts of a software system immediately interact with the software system's security. In most cases, unlike the explicit variability specification at the model level, such variability is likely to be realized in terms of variables. In future works, this can be investigated in more detail. Furthermore, GRaViTY can be extended with static and dynamic support for security compliance analysis targeting on such cases.

17.4 Summary

In this thesis, we discussed continuous model-based security engineering. For ensuring the security of contentiously evolving variant-rich software systems it is essential to support the implementation with continuous automated security compliance checks. For this purpose, suitable trace links among models and with the implementation have to be maintained. In the best case, these trace links are automatically updated and utilized to keep the models structurally consistent with a changing implementation. Finally, for avoiding insecure products, security compliance checks should not only cover single variant of a software system, e.g., executed at release of the product, but always consider the whole software product line. In this regard, the approaches presented in this thesis, substantially contribute to realizing continuous model-based security engineering.

Bibliography

[1] R. Eikenberg, "Samsung Galaxy S3 als Merkelphone zugelassen," *heise online*, 2013. [Online]. Available: https://heise.de/-1953029

[2] M. Christakis and C. Bird, "What Developers Want and Need from Program Analysis: An Empirical Study," in *Proceedings of the 31ˢᵗ International Conference of Automated Software Engineering (ASE)*. IEEE Computer Society, 2016, pp. 332–343. https://doi.org/10.1145/2970276.2970347

[3] R. France and B. Rumpe, "Model-driven Development of Complex Software: A Research Roadmap," in *Proceedings of the Conference on the Future of Software Engineering (FOSE)*. IEEE Computer Society, 2007, pp. 37–54. https://doi.org/10.1109/FOSE.2007.14

[4] M. Brambilla, J. Cabot, and M. Wimmer, "Model-driven Software Engineering in Practice," *Synthesis Lectures on Software Engineering*, vol. 1, no. 1, pp. 1–182, 2012.

[5] S. Cook, C. Bock, P. Rivett, T. Rutt, E. Seidewitz, B. Selic, and D. Tolbert, "UML Superstructure Specification," Object Management Group (OMG), OMG Standard formal/2017-12-05, 2017, version 2.5.1. [Online]. Available: http://www.omg.org/spec/UML/

[6] J. Jürjens, *Secure Systems Development with UML*. Springer, 2005.

[7] International Organization for Standardization (ISO), "Medical Device Software — Software Life Cycle Processes," International Standard IEC 62304:2006, 2007.

[8] B. Hailpern and P. Tarr, "Model-driven Development: The Good, the Bad, and the Ugly," *IBM Systems Journal*, vol. 45, no. 3, 2006.

[9] T. Gorschek, E. Tempero, and L. Angelis, "On the Use of Software Design Models in Software Development Practice: An Empirical Investigation," *Journal of Systems and Software (JSS)*, vol. 95, pp. 176–193, 2014. https://doi.org/10.1016/j.jss.2014.03.082

[10] M. H. Hamilton, "The Apollo On-Board Flight Software," 2019.

[11] V. Rajlich and P. Gosavi, "Incremental Change in Object-Oriented Programming," *IEEE Software*, vol. 21, no. 4, pp. 62–69, 2004.

[12] M. M. Lehman, "Programs, Life Cycles, and Laws of Software Evolution," *Proceedings of the IEEE*, vol. 68, no. 9, pp. 1060–1076, 1980. https://doi.org/10.1109/PROC.1980.11805

[13] D. L. Parnas, "Software Aging," in *Proceedings of the 16ᵗʰ International Conference on Software Engineering (ICSE)*. IEEE Computer Society, 1994, pp. 279–287.

S. M. Peldszus, *Security Compliance in Model-driven Development of Software Systems in Presence of Long-Term Evolution and Variants*, https://doi.org/10.1007/978-3-658-37665-9

[14] "HLASM Language Reference – Assembler Language," IBM Corporation, Tech. Rep. SC26-4940-06, 1990.

[15] TIOBE Software BV, "TIOBE Programming Community Index," 2021. [Online]. Available: https://www.tiobe.com/tiobe-index/

[16] E. Gamma, R. Helm, R. Johnson, and J. Vlissides, *Design Patterns: Elements of Reusable Object-oriented Software*. Pearson Education, 1994.

[17] W. Opdyke, "Refactoring Object-Oriented Frameworks," Ph.D. dissertation, University of Illinois, 1992.

[18] M. Fowler, *Refactoring: Improving the Design of Existing Code*, ser. Object Technology Series, J. C. Shanklin, Ed. Addison-Wesley, 1999.

[19] L. Northrop, "Software Product Lines: Reuse That Makes Business Sense," in *Proceedings of the Australian Software Engineering Conference (ASWEC)*. IEEE Computer Society, 2006, p. 1. https://doi.org/10.1109/ASWEC.2006.45

[20] C. Wohlin and P. Runeson, "Certification of Software Components," *Transactions on Software Engineering (TSE)*, vol. 20, no. 6, pp. 494–499, 1994. https://doi.org/10.1109/32.295896

[21] S. Peldszus, G. Kulcsár, M. Lochau, and S. Schulze, "Continuous Detection of Design Flaws in Evolving Object-Oriented Programs using Incremental Multi-pattern Matching," in *Proceedings of the 31st International Conference on Automated Software Engineering (ASE)*, 2016. https://doi.org/10.1145/2970276.2970338

[22] D. Sondhi, "Testing for Implicit Inconsistencies in Documentation and Implementation," in *Proceedings of the 12th Conference on Software Testing, Validation and Verification (ICST)*. IEEE Computer Society, 2019, pp. 483–485. https://doi.org/10.1109/ICST.2019.00059

[23] S. Peldszus, K. Tuma, D. Strüber, J. Jürjens, and R. Scandariato, "Secure Data-Flow Compliance Checks between Models and Code based on Automated Mappings," in *Proceedings of the 22nd International Conference on Model-driven Engineering Languages and Systems (MODELS)*. IEEE Computer Society, 2019, pp. 23–33. https://doi.org/10.1109/MODELS.2019.00-18

[24] T. Mens, S. Demeyer, and D. Janssens, "Formalising Behaviour Preserving Program Transformations," in *Proceedings of the 1st International Conference on Graph Transformation (ICGT)*, ser. Lecture Notes in Computer Science (LNCS), A. Corradini, H. Ehrig, H. J. Kreowski, and G. Rozenberg, Eds., vol. 2505. Springer, 2002, pp. 286–301. https://doi.org/10.1007/3-540-45832-8_22

[25] J. Pleumann, O. Yadan, and E. Wetterberg, "Antenna Preprocessor." [Online]. Available: http://antenna.sourceforge.net/

[26] D. Strüber, K. Born, F. Hermann, T. Kehrer, C. Krause, M. Tichy *et al.*, "Henshin," 2011. [Online]. Available: https://www.eclipse.org/henshin/

[27] eMoflon Developer Team, "eMoflon – A Tool for Building Tools," 2019. [Online]. Available: http://www.emoflon.org/

[28] J. C. S. Santos, K. Tarrit, and M. Mirakhorli, "A Catalog of Security Architecture Weaknesses," in *Proceedings of the International Conference on Software Architecture Workshops (ICSAW)*. IEEE Computer Society, 2017, pp. 220–223. https://doi.org/10.1109/ICSAW.2017.25

[29] W. J. Brown, R. C. Malveau, H. W. McCormick, III, and T. J. Mowbray, *AntiPatterns: Refactoring Software, Architectures, and Projects in Crisis.* John Wiley & Sons, Inc., 1998.

[30] C. Hammer and G. Snelting, "Flow-sensitive, Context-sensitive, and Object-sensitive Information Flow Control Based on Program Dependence Graphs," *International Journal of Information Security*, vol. 8, no. 6, pp. 399–422, 2009. https://doi.org/10.1007/s10207-009-0086-1

[31] K. Mauyama and T. Omori, "A Security-Aware Refactoring Tool for Java Programs," in *Proceedings of the 4th Workshop on Refactoring Tools (WRT)*. Association for Computing Machinery (ACM), 2011, pp. 22–28. https://doi.org/10.1145/1984732.1984737

[32] M. Kessentini, W. Kessentini, H. Sahraoui, M. Boukadoum, and A. Ouni, "Design Defects Detection and Correction by Example," in *Proceedings of the 19th International Conference on Program Comprehension (ICPC)*. IEEE Computer Society, 2011, pp. 81–90. https://doi.org/10.1109/ICPC.2011.22

[33] S. Arzt, S. Rasthofer, C. Fritz, E. Bodden, A. Bartel, J. Klein, Y. Le Traon, D. Octeau, and P. McDaniel, "FlowDroid: Precise Context, Flow, Field, Object-sensitive and Lifecycle-aware Taint Analysis for Android Apps," in *Proceedings of the 35th Conference on Programming Language Design and Implementation*, ser. ACM SIGPLAN Notices, vol. 49, no. 6. Association for Computing Machinery (ACM), 2014, pp. 259–269. https://doi.org/10.1145/2666356.2594299

[34] S. Peldszus, "Graph-based Anti-Pattern Detection for Java Programs," Master's thesis, University of Darmstadt, 2015.

[35] S. Peldszus and J. Jürjens, "Werkzeuggestützte Sicherheitszertifizierung – Anwendung auf den Industrial Data Space," in *Proceedings of the Software Quality Days*. Software Quality Lab GmbH, 2017, pp. 10–14.

[36] S. Peldszus, J. Cirullies, and J. Jürjens, "Sicherheitszertifizierung für die Digitale Transformation – Anwendung auf den Industrial Data Space," in *Software-QS-Tag*, 2017.

[37] T. Mens and P. Van Gorp, "A Taxonomy of Model Transformation," *Electronic Notes in Theoretical Computer Science (ENTCS)*, vol. 152, pp. 125–142, 2006. https://doi.org/10.1016/j.entcs.2005.10.021

[38] S. Oster, F. Markert, and P. Ritter, "Automated Incremental Pairwise Testing of Software Product Lines," in *Proceedings of the 14th International Conference on Software Product Lines (SPLC)*, ser. Lecture Notes in Computer Science (LNCS), J. Bosch and J. Lee, Eds., vol. 6287. Springer, 2010, pp. 196–210. https://doi.org/10.1007/978-3-642-15579-6_14

[39] A. R. Hevner, S. T. March, J. Park, and S. Ram, "Design Science in Information Systems Research," *MIS Quaterly*, vol. 28, no. 1, pp. 75–105, 2004.

[40] K. Peffers, T. Tuunanen, C. E. Gengler, M. Rossi, W. Hui, V. Virtanen, and J. Bragge, "The Design Science Research Process: A Model for Producing and Presenting Information Systems Research," in *Design Science Research in Information Systems and Technology*, 2006, pp. 83–106.

[41] G. D. Crnkovic, "Constructive Research and Info-computational Knowledge Generation," in *Proceedings of the International Conference on Model-based Reasoning in Science and Technology (MBR)*, ser. Studies in Computational Intelligence, L. Magnani, W. Carnielli, and C. Pizzi, Eds., vol. 314. Springer, 2010, pp. 359–380. https://doi.org/10.1007/978-3-642-15223-8_20

[42] S. Rasthofer, S. Arzt, and E. Bodden, "A Machine-learning Approach for Classifying and Categorizing Android Sources and Sinks," in *Proceedings of the Network and Distributed System Security Symposium (NDSS)*, 2014. https://doi.org/10.14722/ndss.2014.23039

[43] X. Wang, X. Qin, M. B. Hosseini, R. Slavin, T. D. Breaux, and J. Niu, "GUILeak: Tracing Privacy Policy Claims on User Input Data for Android Applications," in *Proceedings of the 40th International Conference on Software Engineering (ICSE)*. Association for Computing Machinery (ACM), 2018, pp. 37–47. https://doi.org/10.1145/3180155.3180196

[44] R. Eikenberg, "Warum eine komplette Arztpraxis offen im Netz stand," *c't*, vol. 2019, no. 25, pp. 16–17, 2019.

[45] R. Eikenberg, "Nachholbedarf bei der IT-Sicherheit deutscher Arztpraxen," *c't*, vol. 2019, no. 26, pp. 38–39, 2019.

[46] F. Aminpour, F. Sadoughi, and M. Ahamdi, "Utilization of Open Source Electronic Health Record Around the World: A Systematic Review," *Journal of Research in Medical Sciences*, vol. 19, no. 1, pp. 57–64, 2014. [Online]. Available: http://www.ncbi.nlm.nih.gov/pmc/articles/pmc3963324/

[47] A. Meneely, B. Smith, and L. Williams, "iTrust Electronic Health Care System Case Study." [Online]. Available: https://github.com/ncsu-csc326/iTrust2

[48] International Organization for Standardization (ISO), "Medical Devices – Part 1: Application of Usability Engineering to Medical Devices," International Standard IEC 62366-1:2015, 2007.

[49] A. K. Massey, P. N. Otto, L. J. Hayward, and A. I. Antón, "Evaluating Existing Security and Privacy Requirements for Legal Compliance," *Requirements Engineering Journal (RE)*, vol. 15, pp. 119–137, 2010, Special Issue—Security Requirements Engineering. https://doi.org/10.1007/s00766-009-0089-5

[50] S. Heckman, K. T. Stolee, and C. Parnin, "10+ Years of Teaching Software Engineering with iTrust: the Good, the Bad, and the Ugly," in *Proceedings of the 40th International Conference on Software Engineering: Software Engineering Education and Training*. Association for Computing Machinery (ACM), 2018, pp. 1–4. https://doi.org/10.1145/3183377.3183393

[51] J. Bürger, D. Strüber, S. Gärtner, T. Ruhroth, J. Jürjens, and K. Schneider, "A Framework for Semi-automated Co-evolution of Security Knowledge and System Models," *Journal of Systems and Software (JSS)*, vol. 139, pp. 142–160, 2018. https://doi.org/10.1016/j.jss.2018.02.003

[52] S. S. Heckman and K. Presler-Marshall, "Requirements of the iTrust Electronic Health Care System." [Online]. Available: https://github.com/ncsu-csc326/iTrust2/wiki/requirements

[53] European Parliament and Council of the European Uninon, "Regulation (EU) 2016/679 – General Data Protection Regulation (GDPR)," in *Official Journal of the European Union*, 2016.

[54] J. Bürger, "Recovering Security in Model-Based Software Engineering by Context-Driven Co-Evolution," Ph.D. dissertation, University of Koblenz-Landau, 2019.

[55] J. Bürger, T. Kehrer, and J. Jürjens, "Ontology Evolution in the Context of Model-Based Secure Software Engineering," in *Proceedings of the 14th International Conference on Research Challenges in Information Science (RCIS)*, ser. Lecture Notes in Busi-

ness Information Processing (LNBIP), F. Dalpiaz, J. Zdravkovic, and P. Loucopoulos, Eds., vol. 385. Springer, 2020, pp. 437–454. https://doi.org/10.1007/978-3-030-50316-1_26

[56] C. W. Krueger, "Easing the Transition to Software Mass Customization," in *Proceedings of the Workshop on Software Product-family Engineering (PFE)*, ser. Lecture Notes in Computer Science (LNCS), F. van der Linden, Ed., vol. 2290. Springer, 2002, pp. 282–293. https://doi.org/10.1007/3-540-47833-7_25

[57] G. Booch, "Object-oriented Development," *Transactions on Software Engineering (TSE)*, no. 2, pp. 211–221, 1986.

[58] A. C. Kay, "The Early History of Smalltalk," in *History of Programming Languages—ii*. Association for Computing Machinery (ACM), 1996, pp. 511–598. https://doi.org/10.1145/234286.1057828

[59] G. McGraw, *Software Security: Building Security In*, 4th ed., ser. Addison-Wesley Software Security Series. Addision-Wesley, 2008.

[60] E. Bertino, "Data Hiding and Security in Object-oriented Databases," in *Proceedings of the 8th International Conference on Data Engineering (icde)*. IEEE Computer Society, 1992. https://doi.org/10.1109/ICDE.1992.213176

[61] J. Gosling, B. Joy, G. Steele, G. Bracha, and A. Buckley, *The Java Language Specification – Java SE 8 Edition*. Addison-Wesley, 2015.

[62] F. Tip, R. M. Fuhrer, A. Kieżun, M. D. Ernst, I. Balaban, and B. D. Sutter, "Refactoring Using Type Constraints," *Transactions on Programming Languages and Systems (TOPLAS)*, vol. 33, no. 3, pp. 9:1–9:47, 2011. https://doi.org/10.1145/1961204.1961205

[63] M. Schäfer, M. Verbaere, T. Ekman, and O. de Moor, "Stepping Stones Over the Refactoring Rubicon," in *Proceedings of the 23rd European Conference on Object-oriented Programming (ECOOP)*, S. Drossopoulou, Ed. Springer, 2009, pp. 369–393. https://doi.org/10.1007/978-3-642-03013-0_17

[64] D. B. Roberts, "Practical Analysis for Refactoring," Ph.D. dissertation, University of Illinois, 1999.

[65] A. Garrido and J. Meseguer, "Formal Specification and Verification of Java Refactorings," in *Proceedings of the 6th International Workshop on Source Code Analysis and Manipulation (SCAM)*. IEEE Computer Society, 2006, pp. 165–174. https://doi.org/10.1109/SCAM.2006.16

[66] M. Schäfer, T. Ekman, and O. de Moor, "Sound and Extensible Renaming for Java," in *Proceedings of the 23rd Annual Conference on Object-oriented Programming, Systems, Languages, and Applications (OOPSLA)*, ser. ACM SIGPLAN Notices, vol. 43, no. 10. Association for Computing Machinery (ACM), 2008, pp. 277–294. https://doi.org/10.1145/1449955.1449787

[67] M. Schäfer and O. de Moor, "Specifying and Implementing Refactorings," in *Proceedings of the International Conference on Object Oriented Programming Systems Languages and Applications (OOPSLA)*, ser. ACM SIGPLAN Notices, vol. 45, no. 10. Association for Computing Machinery (ACM), 2010, pp. 286–301. https://doi.org/10.1145/1869459.1869485

[68] G. Soares, R. Gheyi, D. Serey, and T. Massoni, "Making Program Refactoring Safer," *IEEE Software*, vol. 27, no. 4, pp. 52–57, 2010. https://doi.org/10.1109/MS.2010.63

[69] F. Steimann and A. Thies, "From Public to Private to Absent: Refactoring Java Programs under Constrained Accessibility," in *Proceedings of the 23rd European Conference on Object-oriented Programming (ECOOP)*, ser. Lecture Notes in Computer Science (LNCS), D. S., Ed., vol. 5653. Springer, 2009, pp. 419–443. https://doi.org/10.1007/978-3-642-03013-0_19

[70] R. Straeten, V. Jonckers, and T. Mens, "A Formal Approach to Model Refactoring and Model Refinement," *Software & Systems Modeling (SoSyM)*, vol. 6, no. 2, pp. 139–162, 2007. https://doi.org/10.1007/s10270-006-0025-9

[71] M. Vittek, "Refactoring Browser with Preprocessor," in *Proceedings of the 7th European Conference Onsoftware Maintenance and Reengineering (CSMR)*. IEEE Computer Society, 2003, https://doi.org/10.1109/CSMR.2003.1192417

[72] J. A. Estefan et al., "Survey of Model-based Systems Engineering (MBSE) Methodologies," *Incose MBSE Focus Group*, vol. 25, no. 8, pp. 1–12, 2007.

[73] J. Jürjens, "UMLsec: Extending UML for Secure Systems Development," in *Proceedings of the 5th International Conference on the Unified Modeling Language (UML)*, ser. Lecture Notes in Computer Science (LNCS), J.-M. Jézéquel, H. Hussmann, and S. Cook, Eds., vol. 2460. Springer, 2002, pp. 412–425. https://doi.org/10.1007/3-540-45800-X_32

[74] A. S. Ahmadian, S. Peldszus, Q. Ramadan, and J. Jürjens, "Model-based Privacy and Security Analysis with CARiSMA," in *Proceedings of the 11th Joint Meeting on Foundations of Software Engineering (FSE)*. Association for Computing Machinery (ACM), 2017, pp. 989–993. https://doi.org/10.1145/3106237.3122823

[75] Y. Zheng and R. N. Taylor, "A Classification and Rationalization of Model-based Software Development," *Software & Systems Modeling (SoSyM)*, vol. 12, pp. 559–678, 2013. https://doi.org/10.1007/s10270-013-0355-3

[76] T. Stahl, M. Voelter, and K. Czarnecki, *Model-driven Software Development: Technology, Engineering, Management*. John Wiley & Sons, 2006.

[77] G. Wagner, *Information Management - An Introduction to Information Modeling and Databases*. web-engineering.info, 2019.

[78] K. Fakhroutdinov, "Hospital Management – UML Class Diagram Example," UML-Diagrams Website, last accessed April, 2020. [Online]. Available: https://www.UML-diagrams.org/examples/hospital-domain-diagram.html

[79] I. Christantoni, C. Biffi, and D. B. A. C. Sanz, "VisiOn Pilots Report," VisiOn EU Project, Tech. Rep., 2017.

[80] "VisiOn Project," 2016. [Online]. Available: http://www.visioneuproject.eu/

[81] W. W. Royce, "Managing the Development of Large Software Systems: Concepts and Techniques," in *Proceedings of the 9th International Conference on Software Engineering (ICSE)*. IEEE Computer Society, 1987, pp. 328–338.

[82] T. E. Bell and T. A. Thayer, "Software Requirements: Are They Really a Problem?" in *Proceedings of the 2nd International Conference on Software Engineering (ICSE)*. IEEE Computer Society, 1976, pp. 61–68.

[83] R. S. Pressman and B. R. Maxim, *Software Engineering: A Practitioner's Approach*, 8th ed., V. Bradshaw, Ed. McGraw-Hill Education, 2015.

[84] D. Angermeier, C. Bartelt, O. Bauer, G. Beneken, K. Bergner, U. Birowicz, T. Bliß, C. Breitenstrom, N. Cordes, D. Cruz, P. Dohrmann, J. Friedrich, M. Gnatz, U. Hammerschall, I. Hidvegi-Barstorfer, H. Hummel, D. Israel, T. Klingenberg, K. Klugseder,

I. Küffer, M. Kuhrmann, M. Kranz, W. Kranz, H.-J. Meinhardt, M. Meisinger, S. Mittrach, H.-J. Neußer, D. Niebuhr, K. Plögert, D. Rauh, A. Rausch, T. Rittel, W. Rösch, E. Saas, J. Schramm, M. Sihling, T. Ternité, S. Vogel, B. Weber, and M. Wittmann, "V-Modell XT – Das deutsche Referenzmodell für Systementwicklungsprojekte," Verein zur Weiterentwicklung des V-Modell XT e.V. c/o 4Soft GmbH, Tech. Rep. 2.3, 2019.

[85] M. McHugh, F. McCaffery, and V. Casey, "Barriers to Adopting Agile Practices When Developing Medical Device Software," in *Proceedings of the 12th International Conference on Software Process Improvement and Capability Determination (SPICE)*, ser. Communications in Computer and Information Science (CCIS), A. Mas, A. Mesquida, T. Rout, R. V. O'Connor, and A. Dorling, Eds., vol. 290. Springer, 2012, pp. 141–147. https://doi.org/10.1007/978-3-642-30439-2_13

[86] K. Beck, M. Beedle, A. van Bennekum, A. Cockburn, W. Cunningham, M. Fowler, J. Grenning, J. Highsmith, A. Hunt, R. Jeffries, J. Kern, B. Marick, R. C. Martin, S. Mellor, K. Schwaber, J. Sutherland, and D. Thomas, "Manifesto for Agile Software Development," 2001. [Online]. Available: https://agilemanifesto.org/

[87] digital.ai, "14th Annual State of Agile Report," digital.ai, Tech. Rep., 2020.

[88] K. Schwaber and M. Beedle, *Agile Software Development with Scrum*. Pearson Prentice Hall, 2002.

[89] S. Vaupel, D. Strüber, F. Rieger, and G. Taentzer, "Agile Bottom-Up Development of Domain-Specific IDEs for Model-Driven Development," in *Proceedings of the Workshop on Flexible Model Driven Engineering (FlexMDE)*, ser. CEUR Workshop Proceedings, D. D. Ruscio, J. de Lara, and A. Pierantonio, Eds., vol. 1470. CEUR-WS, 2015, pp. 12–21. [Online]. Available: http://ceur-ws.org/Vol-1470/FlexMDE15_paper_4.pdf

[90] P. Lous, M. Kuhrmann, and P. Tell, "Is Scrum Fit for Global Software Engineering?" in *Proceedings of the 12th International Conference on Global Software Engineering (ICGSE)*. IEEE Computer Society, 2017, pp. 1–10. https://doi.org/10.1109/ICGSE. 2017.13

[91] J. Knodel and D. Popescu, "A Comparison of Static Architecture Compliance Checking Approaches," in *Proceedings of the 6th Working Conference on Software Architecture (WICSA)*. IEEE Computer Society, 2007, pp. 12–12. https://doi.org/10.1109/WICSA. 2007.1

[92] D. Ganesan, T. Keuler, and Y. Nishimura, "Architecture Compliance Checking at Runtime," *Information and Software Technology (IST)*, vol. 51, no. 11, pp. 1586–1600, 2009. https://doi.org/10.1016/j.infsof.2009.06.007

[93] L. De Silva and D. Balasubramaniam, "Controlling Software Architecture Erosion: A Survey," *Journal of Systems and Software (JSS)*, vol. 85, no. 1, pp. 132–151, 2012. https://doi.org/10.1016/j.jss.2011.07.036

[94] Software Reviews Working Group and IEEE-SA Standards Board, "Standard for Software Reviews and Audits," Institute of Electrical and Electronics Engineers (IEEE), International Standard IEEE 1028, 2008. https://doi.org/10.1109/IEEESTD. 2008.4601584

[95] S. McIntosh, Y. Kamei, B. Adams, and A. E. Hassan, "The Impact of Code Review Coverage and Code Review Participation on Software Quality: A Case Study of the Qt, Vtk, and Itk Projects," in *Proceedings of the 11th Working Conference on Mining*

Software Repositories (MSR). Association for Computing Machinery (ACM), 2014, pp. 192–201. https://doi.org/10.1145/2597073.2597076

[96] A. Bacchelli and C. Bird, "Expectations, Outcomes, and Challenges of Modern Code Review," in *Proceedings of the 35th International Conference on Software Engineering (ICSE)*. IEEE Computer Society, 2013, pp. 712–721. https://doi.org/10.1109/ICSE.2013.6606617

[97] N. Carroll and I. Richardson, "Software-as-a-Medical Device: Demystifying Connected Health Regulations," *Systems and Information Technology*, vol. 18, no. 2, pp. 186–215, 2016. https://doi.org/10.1108/JSIT-07-2015-0061

[98] International Organization for Standardization (ISO), "Systems and Software Engineering – Systems and Software Quality Requirements and Evaluation (SQuaRE) – Guide to SQuaRE," International Standard ISO/IEC 25000:2014, 2005.

[99] D. Bertram, A. Voida, S. Greenberg, and R. Walker, "Communication, Collaboration, and Bugs: The Social Nature of Issue Tracking in Small, Collocated Teams," in *Proceedings of the Conference on Computer Supported Cooperative Work*. Association for Computing Machinery (ACM), 2010, pp. 291–300. https://doi.org/10.1145/1718918.1718972

[100] T. F. Bissyandé, D. Lo, L. Jiang, L. Réveillère, J. Klein, and Y. L. Traon, "Got Issues? Who Cares About It? A Large Scale Investigation of Issue Trackers from GitHub," in *Proceedings of the 24th International Engineering (ISSRE)*. IEEE Computer Society, 2013, pp. 188–197. https://doi.org/10.1109/ISSRE.2013.6698918

[101] Common Criteria Implementation Board (CCIB), "Common Criteria for Information Technology Security Evaluation (CC 3.1)," International Standardization Organization (ISO), International Standard ISO/IEC 15408, 2017.

[102] W. Jackson, "Under Attack: Common Criteria has Loads of Critics, but is it Getting a Bum Rap," *Government Computer News*, 2007.

[103] S. Türpe, "The Trouble with Security Requirements," in *Proceedings of the 25th International Requirements Engineering Conference (RE)*. IEEE Computer Society, 2017, pp. 122–133. https://doi.org/10.1109/RE.2017.13

[104] A. Bauer and J. Jürjens, "Runtime Verification of Cryptographic Protocols," *Computers & Security (COSE)*, vol. 29, no. 3, pp. 315–330, 2010. https://doi.org/10.1016/j.cose.2009.09.003

[105] B. Best, J. Jürjens, and B. Nuseibeh, "Model-based Security Engineering of Distributed Information Systems using UMLsec," in *Proceedings of the 29th International Conference on Software Engineering (ICSE)*. IEEE Computer Society, 2007, pp. 581–590. https://doi.org/10.1109/ICSE.2007.55

[106] J. Jürjens, J. Schreck, and P. Bartmann, "Model-based Security Analysis for Mobile Communications," in *Proceedings of the 30th International Conference on Software Engineering (ICSE)*. Association for Computing Machinery (ACM), 2008, pp. 683–692. https://doi.org/10.1145/1368088.1368186

[107] Axway Software, BizAgi Ltd., Bruce Silver Associates, IDS Scheer, International Business Machinesand MEGA International, Model Driven Solutions, Object Management Group, Oracle, SAP AG, Software AG Inc., TIBCO, and Unisys, "Business Process Model And Notation (BPMN)," Object Management Group (OMG), OMG Standard formal/13-12-09, 2014, version 2.0.2. [Online]. Available: http://www.omg.org/spec/BPMN

[108] T. DeMarco, "Structure Analysis and System Specification," in *Pioneers and Their Contributions to Software Engineering*, M. Broy and E. Denert, Eds. Springer, 1979, pp. 255–288. https://doi.org/10.1007/978-3-642-48354-7_9

[109] G. Macher, E. Armengaud, E. Brenner, and C. Kreiner, "A Review of Threat Analysis and Risk Assessment Methods in the Automotive Context," in *Proceedings of the 35th International Conference on Computer Safety, Reliability, and Security (SafeComp)*, ser. Lecture Notes in Computer Science (LNCS), A. Skavhaug, J. Guiochet, and F. Bitsch, Eds., vol. 9922. Springer, 2016, pp. 130–141. https://doi.org/10.1007/978-3-319-45477-1_11

[110] A. Shostack, *Threat Modeling: Designing for Security*. John Wiley & Sons, 2014.

[111] K. Tuma, R. Scandariato, and M. Balliu, "Flaws in Flows: Unveiling Design Flaws via Information Flow Analysis," in *Proceedings of the International Conference on Software Architecture (ICSA)*. IEEE Computer Society, 2019, pp. 191–200. https://doi.org/10.1109/ICSA.2019.00028

[112] K. Tuma, "Efficiency and Automation in Threat Analysis of Software Systems," Ph.D. dissertation, University of Gothenburg, 2021.

[113] B. Potter and G. McGraw, "Software Security Testing," *IEEE Security & Privacy*, vol. 2, no. 5, pp. 81–85, 2004. https://doi.org/10.1109/MSP.2004.84

[114] D. Xu, M. Tu, M. Sanford, L. Thomas, D. Woodraska, and W. Xu, "Automated Security Test Generation with Formal Threat Models," *Transactions on Dependable and Secure Computing (TDSC)*, vol. 9, no. 4, pp. 526–540, 2012. https://doi.org/10.1109/TDSC.2012.24

[115] G. Costa, F. Martinelli, P. Mori, C. Schaefer, and T. Walter, "Runtime Monitoring for Next Generation Java ME Platform," *Computers & Security (COSE)*, vol. 29, no. 1, pp. 74–87, 2010. https://doi.org/10.1016/j.cose.2009.07.005

[116] M. Kim, S. Kannan, I. Lee, O. Sokolsky, and M. Viswanathan, "Java-MaC: A Run-time Assurance Tool for Java Programs," *Electronic Notes in Theoretical Computer Science*, vol. 55, no. 2, pp. 218–235, 2001. https://doi.org/10.1016/S1571-0661(04)00254-3

[117] K. Rindell, J. Ruohonen, and S. Hyrynsalmi, "Surveying Secure Software Development Practices in Finland," in *Proceedings of the 13th International Conference on Availability, Reliability and Security (ARES)*, ser. International Conference Proceeding Series (ICPS). Association for Computing Machinery (ACM), 2018. https://doi.org/10.1145/3230833.3233274

[118] S. Krüger, S. Nadi, M. Reif, K. Ali, M. Mezini, E. Bodden, F. Göpfert, F. Günther, C. Weinert, D. Demmler, and R. Kamath, "CogniCrypt: Supporting Developers in using Cryptography," in *Proceedings of the 32nd International Conference of Automated Software Engineering (ASE)*, 2017, pp. 931–936. https://doi.org/10.1109/ASE.2017.8115707

[119] X. Fu, X. Lu, B. Peltsverger, S. Chen, K. Qian, and L. Tao, "A Static Analysis Framework For Detecting SQL Injection Vulnerabilities," in *Proceedings of the 31st Annual Computer Software and Applications Conference (COMPSAC)*. IEEE Computer Society, 2007, pp. 87–96. https://doi.org/10.1109/COMPSAC.2007.43

[120] E. J. Schwartz, T. Avgerinos, and D. BrUMLey, "All You Ever Wanted to Know about Dynamic Taint Analysis and Forward Symbolic Execution (But Might Have Been Afraid to Ask)," in *Proceedings of the Symposium on Security and Privacy (SP)*. IEEE Computer Society, 2010, pp. 317–331. https://doi.org/10.1109/SP.2010.26

[121] J. Lerch, B. Hermann, E. Bodden, and M. Mezini, "FlowTwist: Efficient Context-sensitive Inside-out Taint Analysis for Large Codebases," in *Proceedings of the 22nd international Symposium on Foundations of Software Engineering (FSE)*. Association for Computing Machinery (ACM), 2014, pp. 98–108. https://doi.org/10.1145/2635868.2635878

[122] B. Livshits, J. Whaley, and M. S. Lam, "Reflection Analysis for Java," in *Proceedings of the 3rd Asian Symposium on Programming Languages and Systems (APLAS)*, ser. Lecture Notes in Computer Science (LNCS), K. Yi, Ed., vol. 3780. Springer, 2005, pp. 139–160. https://doi.org/10.1007/11575467_11

[123] E. Bodden, A. Sewe, J. Sinschek, H. Oueslati, and M. Mezini, " Static Analysis in the Presence of Reflection and Custom Class Loaders," in *Proceedings of the 33rd International Conference on Software Engineering (ICSE)*. Association for Computing Machinery (ACM), 2011, pp. 241–250. https://doi.org/10.1145/1985793.1985827

[124] J. Williams and A. Dabirsiaghi, "The Unfortunate Reality of Insecure Libraries," Contrast Security, Tech. Rep., 2012.

[125] J. Long et al., "OWASP Dependency Check," 2016. [Online]. Available: https://www.owasp.org/index.php/OWASP_Dependency_Check

[126] "GitHub Security Features." [Online]. Available: https://github.com/features/security

[127] V. Mohan and L. B. Othmane, "SecDevOps: Is It a Marketing Buzzword? - Mapping Research on Security in DevOps," in *Proceedings of the 11th International Conference on Availability, Reliability and Security (ARES)*, J. E. Guerrero, Ed. IEEE Computer Society, 2016, pp. 542–547. https://doi.org/10.1109/ARES.2016.92

[128] A. Lanusse, Y. Tanguy, H. Espinoza, C. Mraidha, S. Gerard, P. Tessier, R. Schnekenburger, H. Dubois, and F. Terrier, "Papyrus UML: An Open Source Toolset for MDA," in *Proceedings of the 5th European Conference on Model-driven Architecture Foundations and Applications (ECMDA-FA)*, 2009, pp. 1–4.

[129] The Eclipse Foundation, "Papyrus Modeling Environment," 2019. [Online]. Available: https://www.eclipse.org/papyrus/

[130] S. Peldszus, G. Kulcsár, M. Lochau, and S. Schulze, "Incremental Co-Evolution of Java Programs based on Bidirectional Graph Transformation," in *Proceedings of the 12th Principles and Practices of Programming on the Java Platform (PPPJ)*. Association for Computing Machinery (ACM), 2015, pp. 138–151. https://doi.org/10.1145/2807426.2807438

[131] G. Kulcsár, S. Peldszus, and M. Lochau, "Object-oriented Refactoring of Java Programs using Graph Transformation," in *Proceedings of the 8th Transformation Tool Contest (TTC)*, ser. CEUR Workshop Proceedings, T. Horn, F. Krikava, and L. Rose, Eds., vol. 1524. CEUR-WS, 2015, pp. 53–82. [Online]. Available: http://ceur-ws.org/Vol-1524/paper3.pdf

[132] A. V. Aho, M. S. Lam, R. Sethi, and J. D. Ullman, *Compilers – Principles, Techniques, & Tools*, 2nd ed. Pearson International Education, 2007.

[133] C. Click and K. D. Cooper, "Combining Analyses, Combining Optimizations," *Transactions on Programming Languages and Systems (TOPLAS)*, vol. 17, no. 2, pp. 181–196, 1995. https://doi.org/10.1145/201059.201061

[134] F. E. Allen, "Control Flow Analysis," in *Proceedings of a Symposium on Compiler Optimization*. Association for Computing Machinery (ACM), 1970, pp. 1–19. Control Flow

[135] N. V. Eetvelde and D. Janssens, "A Hierarchical Program Representation for Refactoring," *Electronic Notes in Theoretical Computer Science (ENTCS)*, vol. 82, no. 7, pp. 91–104, 2003. https://doi.org/10.1016/S1571-0661(04)80749-7

[136] N. V. Eetvelde and D. Janssens, "Extending Graph Rewriting for Refactoring," in *Proceedings of the 2nd International Conference on Graph Transformation (ICGT)*, ser. Lecture Notes in Computer Science (LNCS), H. Ehrig, G. Engels, F. Parisi-Presicce, and G. Rozenberg, Eds., vol. 3256. Springer, 2004, pp. 399–415. https://doi.org/10.1007/978-3-540-30203-2_28

[137] A. Corradini, F. L. Dotti, L. Foss, and L. Ribeiro, "Translating Java Code to Graph Transformation Systems," in *Proceedings of the 2nd International Conference on Graph Transformation (ICGT)*, ser. Lecture Notes in Computer Science (LNCS), H. Ehrig, G. Engels, F. Parisi-Presicce, and G. Rozenberg, Eds., vol. 3256. Springer, 2004, pp. 383–398. https://doi.org/10.1007/978-3-540-30203-2_27

[138] T. Mens, G. Taentzer, and O. Runge, "Analysing Refactoring Dependencies using Graph Transformation," *Software & Systems Modeling (SoSyM)*, vol. 6, no. 3, pp. 269–285, 2007. https://doi.org/10.1007/s10270-006-0044-6

[139] R. Ferenc, A. Beszedes, M. Tarkiainen, and T. Gyimothy, "Columbus - Reverse Engineering Tool and Schema for C++," in *Proceedings of the International Conference on Software Maintenance (ICSM)*. IEEE Computer Society, 2002, pp. 172–181. https://doi.org/10.1109/ICSM.2002.1167764

[140] T. Mens, N. Van Eetvelde, S. Demeyer, and D. Janssens, "Formalizing Refactorings with Graph Transformations," *Journal of Software Maintenance and Evolution: Research and Practice (SME)*, vol. 17, no. 4, pp. 247–276, 2005. https://doi.org/10.1002/smr.316

[141] H. Bruneliere, J. Cabot, F. Jouault, and F. Madiot, "MoDisco: A Generic and Extensible Framework for Model Driven Reverse Engineering," in *Proceedings of the 25th International Conference of Automated Software Engineering (ASE)*. Association for Computing Machinery (ACM), 2010, pp. 173–174. https://doi.org/10.1145/1858996.1859032

[142] The Eclipse Foundation, "MoDisco Website," 2018. [Online]. Available: https://www.eclipse.org/MoDisco/

[143] F. Heidenreich, J. Johannes, M. Seifert, and C. Wende, "Closing the Gap between Modelling and Java," in *Proceedings of the 2nd International Conference on Software Language Engineering (SLE)*, ser. Lecture Notes in Computer Science (LNCS), M. van den Brand, D. Gašević, and J. Gray, Eds., vol. 5969. Springer, 2010, pp. 374–383. https://doi.org/10.1007/978-3-642-12107-4_25

[144] H. Ehrig, K. Ehrig, U. Prange, and G. Taentzer, *Fundamentals of Algebraic Graph Transformation*, 1st ed., ser. Monographs in Theoretical Computer Science. An EATCS Series, W. Brauer, G. Rozenberg, and A. Salomaa, Eds. Springer, 2006.

[145] S. Peldszus, G. Kulcsár, and M. Lochau, "A Solution to the Java Refactoring Case Study using eMoflon," in *Proceedings of the 8th Transformation Tool Contest (TTC)*, ser. CEUR Workshop Proceedings, T. Horn, F. Krikava, and L. Rose, Eds., vol. 1524. CEUR-WS, 2015, pp. 118–122. [Online]. Available: http://ceur-ws.org/Vol-1524/paper20.pdf

[146] S. Ruland, G. Kulcsár, E. Leblebici, S. Peldszus, and M. Lochau, "Controlling the Attack Surface of Object-Oriented Refactorings," in *Proceedings of the 21st Interna-

tional Conference on Fundamental Approaches to Software Engineering (FASE), ser. Lecture Notes in Computer Science (LNCS), A. Russo and A. Schürr, Eds., vol. 10802. Springer, 2018, pp. 38–55. https://doi.org/10.1007/978-3-319-89363-1_3

[147] C. Brun and E. Merks, "EcoreTools 2.0," 2014. [Online]. Available: http://www.eclipse.org/ecoretools/

[148] D. Steinberg, F. Budinsky, M. Patenostro, and E. Merks, *EMF: Eclipse Modeling Framework*, 2nd ed., E. Gamma, L. Nackman, and J. Wiegand, Eds. Addison Wesley, 2008. [Online]. Available: http://www.eclipse.org/emf

[149] The Eclipse Foundation, "Sirius," 2021. [Online]. Available: http://www.eclipse.org/sirius/

[150] D. Mebus, "Objektorientierte High-Level Datenflussanalyse," Master's thesis, University of Koblenz-Landau, 2019.

[151] B. Wiebe, "Eine empirische Studie über die Korrelation zwischen Sicherheitsschwachstellen und Qualitätseigenschaften von Software-Designs," Bachelor's thesis, University of Koblenz-Landau, 2017.

[152] A. Ivanova, "On Correlations between Vulnerabilities, Quality-, and Design-Metrics," Bachelor's thesis, University of Koblenz-Landau, 2019.

[153] Eclipse Foundation, "Eclipse Java Development Tools (JDT)." [Online]. Available: https://www.eclipse.org/jdt/

[154] S. Peldszus, "Model-driven Development of Evolving Secure Software Systems," in *Proceedings of the 7th Collaborative Workshop on Evolution and Maintenance of Long-living Software Systems (EMLS)*, ser. CEUR Workshop Proceedings, R. Hebig and R. Heinrich, Eds., vol. 2581. CEUR-WS, 2020. [Online]. Available: http://ceur-ws.org/Vol-2581/emls2020paper1.pdf

[155] International Organization for Standardization, International Electrotechnical Commission, and IEEE Standards Association (IEEE-SA) Standards Board, "Systems and Software Engineering – Vocabulary," International Standard ISO/IEC/IEEE 2476524765:2017, 2017. https://doi.org/10.1109/IEEESTD.2017.8016712 Systems and Software Engineering – Vocabulary

[156] G. Spanoudakis and A. Zisman, "Software Traceability: A Roadmap," in *Handbook of Software Engineering and Knowledge Engineering*. World Scientific, 2005, pp. 395–428. https://doi.org/10.1142/9789812775245_0014

[157] F. A. C. Pinheiro, "Requirements Traceability," in *Perspectives on Software Requirements*, ser. Springer International Series in Engineering and Computer Science (SECS), J. C. S. do Prado Leite and J. H. Doorn, Eds. Springer, 2004, vol. 753, pp. 91–113.https://doi.org/10.1007/978-1-4615-0465-8_5

[158] H. Schwarz, J. Ebert, and A. Winter, "Graph-based Traceability: A Comprehensive Approach," *Software & Systems Modeling (SoSyM)*, vol. 9, pp. 473–492, 2010. https://doi.org/10.1007/s10270-009-0141-4

[159] A. Espinoza, P. P. Alarcon, and J. Garbajosa, "Analyzing and Systematizing Current Traceability Schemas," in *Proceedings of the 30th Annual Workshop on Software Engineering*. IEEE Computer Society, 2006, pp. 21–32. https://doi.org/10.1109/SEW.2006.12

[160] A. Schürr, "Specification of Graph Translators with Triple Graph Grammars," in *Proceedings of the International Workshop on Graph-theoretic Concepts in Computer*

Science (WG), ser. Lecture Notes in Computer Science (LNCS), vol. 903. Springer, 1995, pp. 151–163. https://doi.org/10.1007/3-540-59071-4_45

[161] H. Brunelière, J. Cabot, G. Dupé, and F. Madiot, "MoDisco: A Model Driven Reverse Engineering Framework," *Information and Software Technology (IST)*, vol. 56, no. 8, pp. 1012–1032, 2014. https://doi.org/10.1016/j.infsof.2014.04.007

[162] E. Leblebici, A. Anjorin, and A. Schürr, "Developing eMoflon with eMoflon," in *Proceedings of the 7th International Conference on Theory and Practice of Model Transformations (ICMT)*, ser. Lecture Notes in Computer Science (LNCS), D. D. Ruscio and D. Varró, Eds., vol. 8568. Springer, 2014, pp. 138–145. https://doi.org/10.1007/978-3-319-08789-4_10

[163] E. Leblebici, A. Anjorin, and A. Schürr, "Inter-model Consistency Checking Using Triple Graph Grammars and Linear Optimization Techniques," in *Proceedings of the 20th International Conference on Fundamental Approaches to Software Engineering (FASE)*, ser. Lecture Notes in Computer Science (LNCS), M. Huisman and J. Rubin, Eds., vol. 10202. Springer, 2017, pp. 191–207. https://doi.org/10.1007/978-3-662-54494-5_11

[164] N. Moha, Y.-G. Guéhéneuc, L. Duchien, and A.-F. Le Meur, "DECOR: A Method for the Specification and Detection of Code and Design Smells," *Transactions on Software Engineering (TSE)*, vol. 36, no. 1, pp. 20–36, 2010. https://doi.org/10.1109/TSE.2009.50

[165] F. Khomh, S. Vaucher, Y.-G. Guéhéneuc, and H. Sahraoui, "BDTEX: A GQM-based Bayesian Approach for the Detection of Antipatterns," *Journal of Systems and Software (JSS)*, vol. 84, no. 4, pp. 559–572, 2011. https://doi.org/10.1016/j.jss.2010.11.921

[166] Z. Ujhelyi, A. Horváth, D. Varró, N. I. Csiszár, G. Szőke, L. Vidács, and R. Ferenc, "Anti-pattern Detection with Model Queries: A Comparison of Approaches," in *Proceedings of the Conference on Software Maintenance, Reengineering, and Reverse Engineering and Working Conference on Reverse Engineering (CSMR-WCRE)*. IEEE Computer Society, 2014, pp. 293–302. https://doi.org/10.1109/CSMR-WCRE.2014.6747181

[167] E. Tempero, C. Anslow, J. Dietrich, T. Han, J. Li, M. Lumpe, H. Melton, and J. Noble, "The Qualitas Corpus: A Curated Collection of Java Code for Empirical Studies," in *Proceedings of the 17th Asia Pacific Software Engineering Conference (APSEC)*. IEEE Computer Society, 2010, pp. 336–345. https://doi.org/10.1109/APSEC.2010.46

[168] C. Alphonce and P. Ventura, "QuickUML: A Tool to Support Iterative Design and Code Development," in *Companion of the 18th Annual Acm Sigplan Conference on Object-oriented Programming, Systems, Languages, and Applications (OOPSLA)*. Association for Computing Machinery (ACM), 2003, pp. 80–81. https://doi.org/10.1145/949344.949359

[169] G. Johnson, "QuickUML." [Online]. Available: https://quj.sourceforge.io/

[170] J. D. Lamb, "Java Scientific Calculator (JSciCalc)." [Online]. Available: http://jscicalc.sourceforge.net/

[171] E. Gamma, K. Beck *et al.*, "JUnit." [Online]. Available: https://junit.org/

[172] A. Thomas, D. Barashev *et al.*, "GanttProject." [Online]. Available: https://www.ganttproject.biz/

[173] Apache Foundation, "Nutch." [Online]. Available: http://nutch.apache.org/

[174] Apache Foundation, "Lucene." [Online]. Available: https://lucene.apache.org/

[175] Apache Foundation, "Log4j." [Online]. Available: https://logging.apache.org/log4j/

[176] IFA Informatik and E. Gamma, "JHotDraw." [Online]. Available: https://sourceforge. net/projects/jhotdraw/

[177] A. Dangel, J. Sotuyo *et al.*, "PMD Source Code Analyzer." [Online]. Available: https:// sourceforge.net/projects/pmd/

[178] S. Pestov *et al.*, "JEdit." [Online]. Available: http://www.jedit.org/

[179] P. Wendykier, "JTransforms." [Online]. Available: https://sites.google.com/site/ piotrwendykier/software/jtransforms

[180] Apache Foundation, "Xerces." [Online]. Available: http://xerces.apache.org/

[181] Azureus Software Inc., "Azureus/Vuze." [Online]. Available: http://www.vuze.com/

[182] F. Büttner and M. Gogolla, "On Generalization and Overriding in UML 2.0," in *Proceedings of the Workshop on OCL and Model Driven Engineering*, 2004, pp. 1–15.

[183] M. Fockel, J. Holtmann, and J. Meyer, "Semi-automatic Establishment and Maintenance of Valid Traceability in Automotive Development Processes," in *Proceedings of the 2nd International Workshop on Software Engineering for Embedded Systems (sees)*. IEEE Computer Society, 2012, pp. 37–43. https://doi.org/10.1109/SEES.2012. 6225489

[184] P. Tonella, "Reverse Engineering of Object Oriented Code," in *Proceedings of the 27th International Conference on Software Engineering (ICSE)*. IEEE Computer Society, 2005, pp. 724–725. https://doi.org/10.1109/ICSE.2005.1553682

[185] H. Störrle, "How are Conceptual Models Used in Industrial Software Development?: A Descriptive Survey," in *Proceedings of the 21st International Conference on Evaluation and Assessment in Software Engineering (EASE)*, ser. International Conference Proceeding Series (ICPS), E. Mendes, S. J. Counsell, and K. Petersen, Eds. Association for Computing Machinery (ACM), 2017, pp. 160–169. https://doi.org/10.1145/ 3084226.3084256

[186] J. T. Lallchandani and R. Mall, "A Dynamic Slicing Technique for UML Architectural Models," *Transactions on Software Engineering (TSE)*, vol. 37, no. 6, pp. 737–771, 2011. https://doi.org/10.1109/TSE.2010.112

[187] G. Taentzer, T. Kehrer, C. Pietsch, and U. Kelter, "A Formal Framework for Incremental Model Slicing," in *Proceedings of the 21st International Conference on Fundamental Approaches to Software Engineering (FASE)*, ser. Lecture Notes in Computer Science (LNCS), A. Russo and A. Schürr, Eds., vol. 10802. Springer, 2018, pp. 3–20. https:// doi.org/10.1007/978-3-319-89363-1_1

[188] R. Xu, D. Wunsch *et al.*, "Survey of Clustering Algorithms," *IEEE Transactions on Neural Networks*, vol. 16, no. 3, pp. 645–678, 2005. https://doi.org/10.1109/TNN. 2005.845141

[189] A. Elkamel, M. Gzara, and H. Ben-Abdallah, "An UML Class Recommender System for Software Design," in *Proceedings of the 13th International Conference of Computer Systems and Applications (AICCSA)*. IEEE Computer Society, 2016, pp. 1–8. https:// doi.org/10.1109/AICCSA.2016.7945659

[190] C. Dougherty, K. Sayre, R. C. Seacord, D. Svoboda, and K. Togashi, "Secure Design Patterns," Carnegie-Mellon University Pittsburgh, Software Engineering Institute, Tech. Rep., 2009.

[191] V. Saini, Q. Duan, and V. Paruchuri, "Threat Modeling Using Attack Trees," *Journal of Computing Sciences in Colleges (CCSC)*, vol. 23, no. 4, pp. 124–131, 2008.

[192] M. S. Lund, B. Solhaug, and K. Stølen, *Model-driven Risk Analysis: The CORAS Approach*, 1st ed. Springer, 2011. https://doi.org/10.1007/978-3-642-12323-8

[193] T. Abe, S. Hayashi, and M. Saeki, "Modeling Security Threat Patterns to Derive Negative Scenarios," in *Proceedings of the 20th Asia-pacific Software Engineering Conference (APSEC)*, R. Bilof, Ed. IEEE Computer Society, 2013, pp. 58–66. https://doi.org/10.1109/APSEC.2013.19

[194] R. Scandariato, K. Wuyts, and W. Joosen, "A Descriptive Study of Microsoft's Threat Modeling Technique," *Requirements Engineering Journal (RE)*, vol. 20, no. 2, pp. 163–180, 2015. https://doi.org/10.1007/s00766-013-0195-2

[195] K. Tuma, G. Calikli, and R. Scandariato, "Threat Analysis of Software Systems: A Systematic Literature Review," *Journal of Systems and Software (JSS)*, vol. 144, pp. 275–294, 2018. https://doi.org/10.1016/j.jss.2018.06.073

[196] M. Deng, K. Wuyts, R. Scandariato, B. Preneel, and W. Joosen, "A Privacy Threat Analysis Framework: Supporting the Elicitation and Fulfillment of Privacy Requirements," *Requirements Engineering Journal (RE)*, vol. 16, no. 1, pp. 3–32, 2011. https://doi.org/10.1007/s00766-010-0115-7

[197] L. Sion, K. Yskout, D. Van Landuyt, and W. Joosen, "Solution-aware Data Flow Diagrams for Security Threat Modeling," in *Proceedings of the 33rd Annual Symposium on Applied Computing (SAC)*. Association for Computing Machinery (ACM), 2018, pp. 1425–1432. https://doi.org/10.1145/3167132.3167285

[198] B. J. Berger, K. Sohr, and R. Koschke, "Extracting and Analyzing the Implemented Security Architecture of Business Applications," in *Proceedings of the 17th European Conference on Software Maintenance and Reengineering (CSMR)*. IEEE Computer Society, 2013, pp. 285–294. https://doi.org/10.1109/CSMR.2013.37

[199] H. Ehrig, G. Rozenberg, and H.-J. Kreowski, *Handbook of Graph Grammars and Computing by Graph Transformation*. World Scientific, 1999, vol. 3.

[200] V. I. Levenshtein, "Binary Codes Capable of Correcting Deletions, Insertions, and Reversals," *Soviet Physics Doklady*, vol. 10, pp. 707–710, 1966.

[201] "JPetStore." [Online]. Available: http://www.mybatis.org/jpetstore-6/

[202] "ATMExample." [Online]. Available: http://www.math-cs.gordon.edu/local/courses/cs211/ATMExample/

[203] Eclipse contributors, "Workbench User Guide – Secure Storage – How secure storage works," The Eclipse Foundation, Tech. Rep., 2013. [Online]. Available: https://help.eclipse.org/oxygen/index.jsp?topic=%2Forg.eclipse.platform.doc.user%2Freference%2Fref-43.htm

[204] "CoCoME." [Online]. Available: https://github.com/cocome-community-case-study

[205] R. Heinrich, K. Rostami, and R. Reussner, *The Cocome Platform for Collaborative Empirical Research on Information System Evolution*. KIT Scientific Publishing, 2016.

[206] S. Peldszus, J. Bürger, T. Kehrer, and J. Jürjens, "Ontology-Driven Evolution of Software Security," *Data & Knowledge Engineering (DKE)*, vol. 134, 2021. https://doi.org/10.1016/j.datak.2021.101907

[207] K. Tuma, S. Peldszus, D. Strüber, R. Scandariato, and J. Jürjens, "Checking Security Compliance between Models and Code," *International Journal on Software and Systems Modeling (SoSyM)*, 2022. https://doi.org/10.1007/s10270-022-00991-5

[208] P. H. Meland and J. Jensen, "Secure Software Design in Practice," in *Proceedings of the 3rd International Conference on Availability, Reliability and Security (ARES)*. IEEE Computer Society, 2008, pp. 1164–1171. https://doi.org/10.1109/ARES.2008.48

[209] S. R. Chidamber and C. F. Kemerer, "A Metrics Suite for Object Oriented Design," *Transactions on Software Engineering (TSE)*, vol. 20, no. 6, pp. 476–493, 1994. https://doi.org/10.1109/32.295895

[210] K. Sultan, A. En-Nouaary, and A. Hamou-Lhadj, "Catalog of Metrics for Assessing Security Risks of Software Throughout the Software Development Life Cycle," in *Proceedings of the International Conference on Information Security and Assurance (ISA)*, B. Werner, Ed. IEEE Computer Society, 2008, pp. 461–465. https://doi.org/10.1109/ISA.2008.104

[211] J. A. Wang, H. Wang, M. Guo, and M. Xia, "Security Metrics for Software Systems," in *Proceedings of the 47th Annual Southeast Regional Conference*. New York, NY, USA: Association for Computing Machinery (ACM), 2009. https://doi.org/10.1145/1566445.1566509

[212] B. Alshammari, C. Fidge, and D. Corney, "Assessing the Impact of Refactoring on Security-critical Object-oriented Designs," in *Proceedings of the Asia Pacific Software Engineering Conference (APSEC)*. IEEE Computer Society, 2010, pp. 186–195. https://doi.org/10.1109/APSEC.2010.30

[213] NIST, "Common Vulnerability Scoring System (CVSS)." [Online]. Available: https://nvd.nist.gov/vuln-metrics/cvss

[214] P. K. Manadhata and J. M. Wing, "An Attack Surface Metric," *Transactions on Software Engineering (TSE)*, vol. 37, no. 3, pp. 371–386, 2011.https://doi.org/10.1109/TSE.2010.60

[215] C. Zoller and A. Schmolitzky, "Measuring Inappropriate Generosity with Access Modifiers in Java Systems," in *Proceedings of the Joint Conference of the 22nd International Workshop on Software Measurement and the 7th International Conference on Software Process and Product Measurement (IWSM/MENSURA)*. IEEE Computer Society, 2012, pp. 43–52. https://doi.org/10.1109/IWSM-MENSURA.2012.15

[216] B. Alshammari, C. Fidge, and D. Corney, "Security Metrics for Object-oriented Class Designs," in *Proceedings of the 9th International Conference on Quality Software (ICSQ)*. IEEE Computer Society, 2009, pp. 11–20. https://doi.org/10.1109/QSIC.2009.11

[217] I. Chowdhury, B. Chan, and M. Zulkernine, "Security Metrics for Source Code Structures," in *Proceedings of the 4th International Workshop on Software Engineering for Secure Systems (SESS)*. Association for Computing Machinery (ACM), 2008, pp. 57–64. https://doi.org/10.1145/1370905.1370913

[218] T. Arendt, E. Biermann, S. Jurack, C. Krause, and G. Taentzer, "Henshin: Advanced Concepts and Tools for In-place Emf Model Transformations," in *Proceedings of the International Conference on Model-driven Engineering Languages and Systems (MODELS)*, ser. Lecture Notes in Computer Science (LNCS), D. C. Petriu, N. Rouquette, and Ø. Haugen, Eds., vol. 6394. Springer, 2010, pp. 121–135. https://doi.org/10.1007/978-3-642-16145-2_9

[219] A. Sabelfeld and A. C. Myers, "Language-based Information-flow Security," *Journal on Selected Areas in Communications (JSAC)*, vol. 21, no. 1, pp. 5–19, 2003. https://doi.org/10.1109/JSAC.2002.806121

[220] J. Bacon, D. Eyers, T. F.-M. Pasquier, J. Singh, I. Papagiannis, and P. Pietzuch, "Information Flow Control for Secure Cloud Computing," *Transactions on Network and Service Management (TNSM)*, vol. 11, no. 1, pp. 76–89, 2014. https://doi.org/10.1109/TNSM.2013.122313.130423

[221] L. Li, T. F. Bissyandé, M. Papadakis, S. Rasthofer, A. Bartel, D. Octeau, J. Klein, and L. Traon, "Static Analysis of Android Apps: A Systematic Literature Review," *Information and Software Technology (IST)*, vol. 88, pp. 67–95, 2017. https://doi.org/10.1016/j.infsof.2017.04.001

[222] Perl::DOC, "Perl Language Reference," 2020. [Online]. Available: https://perldoc.perl.org/index-language.html

[223] S. Arzt, S. Rasthofer, and E. Bodden, "SuSi: A Tool for the Fully Automated Classification and Categorization of Android Sources and Sinks," University of Darmstadt, Tech. Rep. TUDCS-2013-0114, 2013.

[224] W. Klieber, L. Flynn, A. Bhosale, L. Jia, and L. Bauer, "Android Taint Flow Analysis for App Sets," in *Proceedings of the 3rd International Workshop on the State of the Art in Java Program Analysis (soap)*. Association for Computing Machinery (ACM), 2014, pp. 1–6. https://doi.org/10.1145/2614628.2614633

[225] R. Vallee-Rai and L. J. Hendren, "Jimple: Simplifying Java Bytecode for Analyses and Transformations," McGill University, Tech. Rep., 1998.

[226] P. Ferrara, L. Olivieri, and F. Spoto, "Tailoring Taint Analysis to GDPR," in *Proceedings of the 6th Annual Privacy Forum (APF)*, ser. Lecture Notes in Computer Science (LNCS), M. Medina, A. Mitrakas, K. Rannenberg, E. Schweighofer, and N. Tsouroulas, Eds., vol. 11079, Springer. Springer, 2018, pp. 63–76. https://doi.org/10.1007/978-3-030-02547-2_4

[227] S. Arzt, "Static Data Flow Analysis for Android Applications," Ph.D. dissertation, Technische Universität Darmstadt, 2017.

[228] D. Strüber, K. Born, K. D. Gill, R. Groner, T. Kehrer, M. Ohrndorf, and M. Tichy, "Henshin: A Usability-Focused Framework for EMF Model Transformation Development," in *Proceedings of the 10th International Conference on Graph Transformation (ICGT)*, ser. Lecture Notes in Computer Science (LNCS), J. de Lara and D. Plump, Eds., vol. 10373. Springer, 2017, pp. 196–208. https://doi.org/10.1007/978-3-319-61470-0_12

[229] J. Jürjens *et al.*, "CARiSMA," 2018. [Online]. Available: http://carisma.UMLsec.de/

[230] M. Gegick and L. Williams, "On the Design of More Secure Software-intensive Systems by Use of Attack Patterns," *Information and Software Technology (IST)*, vol. 49, no. 4, pp. 381–397, 2007. https://doi.org/10.1016/j.infsof.2006.06.002

[231] J. P. Near and D. Jackson, "Derailer: Interactive Security Analysis for Web Applications," in *Proceedings of the 29th International Conference on Automated Software Engineering (ASE)*. Association for Computing Machinery (ACM), 2014, pp. 587–598. https://doi.org/10.1145/2642937.2643012

[232] V. B. Livshits and M. S. Lam, "Finding Security Vulnerabilities in Java Applications with Static Analysis," in *Proceedings of the 14th Usenix Security Symposium (USENIX Security)*, vol. 14, 2005.

[233] L. Li, A. Bartel, T. F. Bissyandé, J. Klein, Y. Le Traon, S. Arzt, S. Rasthofer, E. Bodden, D. Octeau, and P. McDaniel, "IccTA: Detecting Inter-component Privacy Leaks in Android Apps," in *Proceedings of the 37th International Conference on Software*

Engineering (ICSE). IEEE Computer Society, 2015, pp. 280–291. https://doi.org/10. 1109/ICSE.2015.48

[234] B. Morin, T. Mouelhi, F. Fleurey, Y. Le Traon, O. Barais, and J.-M. Jézéquel, "Security-driven Model-based Dynamic Adaptation," in *Proceedings of the 25th International Conference on Automated Software Engineering (ASE)*. Association for Computing Machinery (ACM), 2010, pp. 205–214. https://doi.org/10.1145/1858996.1859040

[235] L. Xiao, "An Adaptive Security Model Using Agent-oriented MDA," *Information and Software Technology (IST)*, vol. 51, no. 5, pp. 933–955, 2009. https://doi.org/10.1016/ j.infsof.2008.05.005

[236] M. Almorsy, J. Grundy, and A. S. Ibrahim, "MDSE@R: Model-driven Security Engineering at Runtime," in *Proceedings of the 4th International Symposium on Cyberspace Safety and Security (CSS)*, ser. Lecture Notes in Computer Science (LNCS), Y. Xiang, J. Lopez, C.-C. J. Kuo, and W. Zhou, Eds., vol. 7672, 2012, pp. 279–295. https://doi. org/10.1007/978-3-642-35362-8_22

[237] Y.-W. Huang, F. Yu, C. Hang, C.-H. Tsai, D.-T. Lee, and S.-Y. Kuo, "Securing Web Application Code by Static Analysis and Runtime Protection," in *Proceedings of the 13th International Conference on World Wide Web (WWW)*. Association for Computing Machinery (ACM), 2004, pp. 40–52. https://doi.org/10.1145/988672.988679

[238] T. Hettel, M. Lawley, and K. Raymond, "Model Synchronisation: Definitions for Round-Trip Engineering," in *Proceedings of the 1st International Conference on Theory and Practice of Model Transformations (ICMT)*, ser. Lecture Notes in Computer Science (LNCS), A. Vallecillo, J. Gray, and A. Pierantonio, Eds., vol. 5063. Springer, 2008, pp. 31–45. https://doi.org/10.1007/978-3-540-69927-9_3

[239] L. Ben Othmane, G. Chehrazi, E. Bodden, P. Tsalovski, and A. D. Brucker, "Time for Addressing Software Security Issues: Prediction Models and Impacting Factors," *Data Science and Engineering (DSE)*, vol. 2, no. 2, pp. 107–124, 2017. https://doi.org/10. 1007/s41019-016-0019-8

[240] G. C. Murphy, D. Notkin, W. G. Griswold, and E. S. Lan, "An Empirical Study of Static Call Graph Extractors," *Transactions on Software Engineering and Methodology (TOSEM)*, vol. 7, no. 2, pp. 158–191, 1998. https://doi.org/10.1145/279310.279314

[241] D. Evans and D. Larochelle, "Improving Security using Extensible Lightweight Static Analysis," *IEEE Software*, vol. 19, no. 1, pp. 42–51, 2002. https://doi.org/10.1109/52. 976940

[242] B. Chess and G. McGraw, "Static Analysis for Security," *IEEE Security & Privacy*, vol. 2, no. 6, pp. 76–79, 2004. https://doi.org/10.1109/MSP.2004.111

[243] G. Hiet, V. V. T. Tong, L. Me, and B. Morin, "Policy-based Intrusion Detection in Web Applications by Monitoring Java Information Flows," in *Proceedings of the 3rd International Conference on Risks and Security of Internet and Systems (CRISIS)*. IEEE Computer Society, 2008, pp. 53–60. https://doi.org/10.1109/CRISIS.2008.4757463

[244] S. Chiba, "Javassist," 2019. [Online]. Available: http://www.javassist.org

[245] S. Chiba, "Load-time Structural Reflection in Java," in *Proceedings of the 14th European Conference on Object-oriented Programming (ECOOP)*, ser. Lecture Notes in Computer Science (LNCS), E. Bertino, Ed., vol. 1850. Springer, 2000, pp. 313–336. https://doi.org/10.1007/3-540-45102-1_16

[246] T. Lindholm, F. Yellin, G. Bracha, and A. Buckley, "The Java® Virtual Machine Specification," Oracle, Tech. Rep., 2015.

[247] M. Eddy and N. Perlroth, "Cyber Attack Suspected in German Woman's Death," *The New York Times*, Sep. 2020. [Online]. Available: https://www.nytimes.com/2020/09/18/world/europe/cyber-attack-germany-ransomeware-death.html

[248] Oracle, "Java Agent API," 2019. [Online]. Available: https://docs.oracle.com/javase/8/docs/api/java/lang/instrument/package-summary.html

[249] MITRE Corporation, "Common Weakness Enumeration," 2019. [Online]. Available: https://cwe.mitre.org

[250] Center for Assured Software, "Juliet Test Suite v1.2 for Java – User Guide," National Security Agency, Tech. Rep., 2012.

[251] P. E. Black, "Juliet 1.3 Test Suite: Changes From 1.2," National Institute of Standards and Technology (NIST), Tech. Rep., 2018.

[252] S. Peldszus, J. Bürger, and J. Jürjens, "UMLsecRT Repository." [Online]. Available: https://github.com/carisma-tool/UMLsecrt

[253] S. M. Blackburn, R. Garner, C. Hoffmann, A. M. Khang, K. S. McKinley, R. Bentzur, A. Diwan, D. Feinberg, D. Frampton, S. Z. Guyer *et al.*, "The DaCapo Benchmarks: Java Benchmarking Development and Analysis," in *Proceedings of the 21st Annual Conference on Object-oriented Programming Systems, Languages, and Applications (OOPSLA)*, ser. SIGPLAN Notices, vol. 41, no. 10. Association for Computing Machinery (ACM), 2006, pp. 169–190. https://doi.org/10.1145/1167515.1167488

[254] Webbug Group, "OpenJDK Issue 8155588," 2016. [Online]. Available: https://bugs.openjdk.java.net/browse/JDK-8155588

[255] DaCapo Project, "DaCapo Website," 2018. [Online]. Available: http://dacapobench.sourceforge.net/

[256] Pivotal Software, "Spring Framework," 2019. [Online]. Available: http://spring.io

[257] FasterXML, "Jackson," 2019. [Online]. Available: https://github.com/FasterXML/jackson

[258] P. Dewitte, K. Wuyts, L. Sion, D. V. Landuyt, I. Emanuilov, P. Valcke, and W. Joosen, "A Comparison of System Description Models for Data Protection by Design," in *Proceedings of the 34th Symposium on Applied Computing (SAC)*, C.-C. Hung and G. A. Papadopoulos, Eds. Association for Computing Machinery (ACM), 2019, pp. 1512–1515. https://doi.org/10.1145/3297280.3297595

[259] E. Bodden, L. Hendren, P. Lam, O. Lhoták, and N. A. Naeem, "Collaborative Runtime Verification with Tracematches," in *Proceedings of the 7th International Workshop on Runtime Verification (RV)*, ser. Lecture Notes in Computer Science (LNCS), O. Sokolsky and S. Taşıran, Eds. Springer, 2007, pp. 22–37. https://doi.org/10.1007/978-3-540-77395-5_3

[260] G. Kiczales, J. Lamping, A. Mendhekar, C. Maeda, C. Lopes, J. M. Loingtier, and J. Irwin, "Aspect-Oriented Programming," in *Proceedings of the 11th European Conference on Object-oriented Programming (ECOOP)*, ser. Lecture Notes in Computer Science (LNCS), S. Demeyer, Ed., vol. 1743. Springer, 1997, pp. 220–242. https://doi.org/10.1007/3-540-46589-8_17

[261] M. Y. Liu and I. Traore, "Empirical Relation between Coupling and Attackability in Software Systems: A Case Study on DOS," in *Proceedings of the Workshop on Programming Languages and Snalysis for Security (PLAS)*, V. C. Shreedhar and S. Zdancewic, Eds. Association for Computing Machinery (ACM), 2006, pp. 57–64. https://doi.org/10.1145/1134744.1134756

[262] D. Strüber, J. Rubin, M. Chechik, and G. Taentzer, "A Variability-Based Approach to Reusable and Efficient Model Transformations," in *Proceedings of the International Conference on Fundamental Approaches to Software Engineering (FASE)*, ser. Lecture Notes in Computer Science (LNCS), A. Egyed and I. Schaefer, Eds., vol. 9033. Springer, 2015, pp. 283–298. https://doi.org/10.1007/978-3-662-46675-9_19

[263] M. Bowman, L. C. Briand, and Y. Labiche, "Solving the Class Responsibility Assignment Problem in ObjectOriented Analysis with Multi-Objective Genetic Algorithms," *Transactions on Software Engineering (TSE)*, vol. 36, no. 6, pp. 817–837, 2010. https://doi.org/10.1109/TSE.2010.70

[264] O. Seng, J. Stammel, and D. Burkhart, "Search-based Determination of Refactorings for Improving the Class Structure of Object-oriented Systems," in *Proceedings of the 8th Annual Conference on Genetic and Evolutionary Computation (GECCO)*, M. Cattolico, Ed. Association for Computing Machinery (ACM), 2006, pp. 1909–1916. https://doi.org/10.1145/1143997.1144315

[265] T. Parr, *The Definitive ANTLR Reference: Building Domain-specific Languages*. Pragmatic Bookshelf Raleigh, 2007.

[266] R. Pawlak, C. Noguera *et al.*, "Spoon: Program Analysis and Transformation in Java," Inria, Tech. Rep., 2006.

[267] M. Aeschlimann, D. Baumer, and J. Lanneluc, "Java Tool Smithing Extending the Eclipse Java Development Tools," *Proceedings of the 2nd EclipseCon*, 2005.

[268] U. Norbisrath, R. Jubeh, and A. Zündorf, *Story Driven Modeling*. CreateSpace Independent Publishing Platform, 2013.

[269] K. Born, S. Schulz, D. Strüber, and S. John, "Solving the Class Responsibility Assignment Case with Henshin and a Genetic Algorithm," in *Proceedings of the 9th Transformation Tool Contest (TTC)*, ser. CEUR Workshop Proceedings, A. Garcia-Dominguez, F. Křikava, and L. M. Rose, Eds., vol. 1758. CEUR-WS, 2018, pp. 45–54. [Online]. Available: http://WWW.ceur-ws.org/Vol-1758/paper8.pdf

[270] K. Maruyama and T. Omori, "Security-aware Refactoring Alerting Its Impact on Code Vulnerabilities," in *Proceedings of the 15th Asia-pacific Software Engineering Conference (APSEC)*. IEEE Computer Society, 2008, pp. 445–451. https://doi.org/10.1109/APSEC.2008.57

[271] S. F. Smith and M. Thober, "Refactoring Programs to Secure Information Flows," in *Proceedings of the Workshop on Programming Languages and Analysis for Security (PLAS)*. Association for Computing Machinery (ACM), 2006, pp. 75–83. https://doi.org/10.1145/1134744.1134758

[272] F. Long, D. Mohindra, R. C. Seacord, D. F. Sutherland, and D. Svoboda, *The CERT Oracle Secure Coding Standard for Java*, 1st ed., ser. SEI Series in Software Engineering. Addison-Wesley Professional, 2011.

[273] Y. Shin and L. Williams, "Is Complexity Really the Enemy of Software Security?" in *Proceedings of the 4th Workshop on Quality of Protection (QOP)*. Association for Computing Machinery (ACM), 2008, pp. 47–50. https://doi.org/10.1145/1456362.1456372

[274] M. Fleck, J. Troya, and M. Wimmer, "Search-Based Model Transformations with MOMoT," in *Proceedings of the 9th International Conference on Theory and Practice of Model Transformations (ICMT)*, ser. Lecture Notes in Computer Science (LNCS),

P. V. Gorp and G. Engels, Eds., vol. 9765. Springer, 2016, pp. 79–87. https://doi.org/10.1007/978-3-319-42064-6_6

[275] L. C. Briand, J. W. Daly, and J. Wüst, "A Unified Framework for Cohesion Measurement in Object-Oriented Systems," *Empirical Software Engineering (EMSE)*, vol. 3, no. 1, pp. 65–117, 1998. https://doi.org/10.1023/A:1009783721306

[276] L. C. Briand, J. W. Daly, and J. K. Wust, "A Unified Framework for Coupling Measurement in Object-Oriented Systems," *Transaction on Software Engineering (TSE)*, vol. 25, no. 1, pp. 91–121, 1999. https://doi.org/10.1109/32.748920

[277] S. Peldszus, D. Strüber, and J. Jürjens, "Model-Based Security Analysis of Feature-Oriented Software Product Lines," in *Proceedings of the 17th International Conference on Generative Programming: Concepts and Experiences (GPCE)*. Association for Computing Machinery (ACM), 2018, pp. 93–106. https://doi.org/10.1145/3278122.3278126

[278] K. Pohl, G. Boeckle, and F. van der Linden, *Software Product Line Engineering: Foundations, Principles, and Techniques*. Springer, 2005. https://doi.org/10.1007/3-540-28901-1

[279] S. Apel, D. S. Batory, C. Kästner, and G. Saake, *Feature-Oriented Software Product Lines—Concepts and Implementation*. Springer, 2013. https://doi.org/10.1007/978-3-642-37521-7

[280] P. Clements and L. Northrop, *Software Product Lines: Practices and Patterns*, ser. SEI Series in Software Engineering. Addison-Wesley, 2001.

[281] K. C. Kang, S. G. Cohen, J. A. Hess, W. E. Novak, and A. S. Peterson, "Feature-oriented Domain Analysis (FODA) Feasibility Study," CMU/SEI-90TR-21, Tech. Rep., 1990.

[282] K. Czarnecki, S. Helsen, and U. Eisenecker, "Staged Configuration Using Feature Models," in *Proceedings of the 3rd International Conference on Software Product Lines (SPLC)*, ser. Lecture Notes in Computer Science (LNCS), R. L. Nord, Ed., vol. 3154. Springer, 2004, pp. 266–283. https://doi.org/10.1007/978-3-540-28630-1_17

[283] D. Benavides, P. Trinidad, and A. Ruiz-Cortés, "Automated Reasoning on Feature Models," in *Proceedings of the 17th International Conference on Advanced Information Systems Engineering (CAiSE)*, ser. Lecture Notes in Computer Science (LNCS), O. Pastor and J. F. e Cunha, Eds., vol. 3520. Springer, 2005, pp. 491–503. https://doi.org/10.1007/11431855_34

[284] C. Kastner, T. Thum, G. Saake, J. Feigenspan, T. Leich, F. Wielgorz, and S. Apel, "FeatureIDE: A Tool Framework for Feature-Oriented Software Development," in *Proceedings of the 31st International Conference on Software Engineering (ICSE)*. IEEE Computer Society, 2009, pp. 611–614. https://doi.org/10.1109/ICSE.2009.5070568

[285] METOP GmbH, "FeatureIDE Website," 2020. [Online]. Available: http://www.featureide.com/

[286] K. Czarnecki and M. Antkiewicz, "Mapping Features to Models: A Template Approach Based on Superimposed Variants," in *Proceedings of the 4th International Conference on Generative Programming and Component Engineering (GPCE)*, ser. Lecture Notes in Computer Science (LNCS), R. Glück and M. Lowry, Eds., vol. 3676. Springer, 2005, pp. 422–437. https://doi.org/10.1007/11561347_28

[287] H. Cichos, S. Oster, M. Lochau, and A. Schürr, "Model-Based Coverage-Driven Test Suite Generation for Software Product Lines," in *Proceedings of the 14th International Conference on Model-driven Engineering Languages and Systems (MODELS)*, ser.

Lecture Notes in Computer Science (LNCS), J. Whittle, T. Clark, and T. Kühne, Eds. 6981: Springer, 2011, pp. 425–439. https://doi.org/10.1007/978-3-642-24485-8_31

[288] C. Kästner and S. Apel, "Virtual Separation of Concerns – A Second Chance for Preprocessors," *Journal of Object Technology (JOT)*, vol. 8, no. 6, pp. 59–78, 2009. https://doi.org/10.5381/jot.2009.8.6.c5

[289] P. T. Devanbu and S. Stubblebine, "Software Engineering for Security: A Roadmap," in *Proceedings of the Conference on the Future of Software Engineering*. Association for Computing Machinery (ACM), 2000, pp. 227–239. https://doi.org/10.1145/336512. 336559

[290] H. S. de Andrade, E. S. de Almeida, and I. Crnkovic, "Architectural Bad Smells in Software Product Lines: An Exploratory Study," in *Companion Volume of the Proceeding of the 11th Working Conference on Software Architecture (WICSA)*, ser. International Conference Proceeding Series (ICPS). Association for Computing Machinery (ACM), 2014, pp. 12:1–12:6. https://doi.org/10.1145/2578128.2578237

[291] C. Kästner, S. Apel, and G. Saake, "Type Checking Annotation-based Product Lines," *Transactions on Software Engineering and Methodology (TOSEM)*, vol. 21, no. 3, pp. 14:1–14:39, 2012. https://doi.org/10.1145/2211616.2211617

[292] "Mobilephoto." [Online]. Available: http://homepages.dcc.ufmg.br/~figueiredo/spl/ icse08/

[293] "Lampiro." [Online]. Available: https://github.com/pinturic/lampiro/tree/master/ lampiro

[294] L. Wozniak and P. Clements, "How Automotive Engineering is Taking Product Line Engineering to the Extreme," in *Proceedings of the 19th International Conference on Software Product Line (SPLC)*, ser. International Conference Proceeding Series (ICPS). Association for Computing Machinery (ACM), 2015, pp. 327–336. https:// doi.org/10.1145/2791060.2791071

[295] D. Reuling, J. Bürdek, S. Rotärmel, M. Lochau, and U. Kelter, "Fault-Based Product-Line Testing: Effective Sample Generation Based on Feature-Diagram Mutation," in *Proceedings of the 19th International Conference on Software Product Line (SPLC)*. Association for Computing Machinery (ACM), 2015, pp. 131–140. https://doi.org/10. 1145/2791060.2791074

[296] S. Ruland, L. Luthmann, J. Bürdek, S. Lity, T. Thüm, M. Lochau, and M. Ribeiro, "Measuring Effectiveness of Sample-Based Product-Line Testing," in *Proceedings of the 17th International Conference on Generative Programming: Concepts and Experiences (GPCE)*, vol. 53, no. 9. Association for Computing Machinery (ACM), 2018, pp. 119–133. https://doi.org/10.1145/3278122.3278130

[297] D. BrUMLey, P. Poosankam, D. Song, and J. Zheng, "Automatic Patch-based Exploit Generation is Possible: Techniques and Implications," in *Proceedings of the Symposium on Security and Privacy (SP)*, B. Werner, Ed. IEEE Computer Society, 2008, pp. 143–157. https://doi.org/10.1109/SP.2008.17

[298] A. Nappa, R. Johnson, L. Bilge, J. Caballero, and T. Dumitras, "The Attack of the Clones: A Study of the Impact of Shared Code on Vulnerability Patching," in *Proceedings of the Symposium on Security and Privacy (SP)*. IEEE Computer Society, 2015, pp. 692–708. https://doi.org/10.1109/SP.2015.48

[299] Adaptive Ltd., BoldSoft, Borland Software Corporation, Compuware Corporation, Dresden University of Technology, France Telecom, International Business Machines,

IONA, Kabira Technologies Inc., Kings College, Klasse Objecten, Open Canarias, SL, Oracle, Project Technology Inc., Rational Software Corporation, SAP AG, Softeam, Syntropy Ltd., Telelogic, Thales, University of Bremen, University of Kent, University of York, Willink Transformations Ltd, and Zeligsoft, Inc., "Object Constraint Language (OCL)," Object Management Group (OMG), OMG Standard formal/2014-02-03, 2014, version 2.4. [Online]. Available: http://www.omg.org/spec/OCL/2.4/

[300] K. Czarnecki and K. Pietroszek, "Verifying Feature-based Model Templates Against Well-formedness OCL Constraints," in *Proceedings of the 5th International Conference on Generative Programming and Component Engineering (GPCE)*, S. Jarzabek, D. Schmidt, and T. Veldhuizen, Eds. Association for Computing Machinery (ACM), 2006, pp. 211–220. https://doi.org/10.1145/1173706.1173738

[301] American Systems Corporation, PTC Inc., BAE SYSTEMS, The Boeing Company, Ceira Technologies, Deere & Company, Airbus, EmbeddedPlus Engineering, European Aeronautic Defence and Space Company N.V., Eurostep Group AB, Gentleware AG, I-Logix, Inc., International Business Machines, International Council on Systems Engineering, Israel Aircraft Industries, Lockheed Martin Corporation, Mentor Graphics, Motorola, Inc., National Aeronautics and Space Administration, No Magic, Inc., Northrop Grumman, Object Management Group, oose Innovative Informatik eG, PivotPoint Technology Corporation, Raytheon Company, Sparx Systems, Telelogic AB, and THALES, "System Modeling Language (SysML)," Object Management Group (OMG), OMG Standard formal/19-11-01, 2019, version 1.6. [Online]. Available: https://www.omg.org/spec/SysML

[302] C. P. Gomes, H. Kautz, A. Sabharwal, and B. Selman, "Satisfiability Solvers," *Foundations of Artificial Intelligence*, vol. 3, pp. 89–134, 2008.

[303] J. Jürjens and R. Rumm, "Model-based Security Analysis of the German Health Card Architecture," *Methods of Information in Medicine*, vol. 47, no. 5, pp. 409–416, 2008. https://doi.org/10.3414/ME9122

[304] J. Lloyd and J. Jürjens, "Security Analysis of a Biometric Authentication System using UMLsec and JML," in *Proceedings of the 12th International Conference on Model Driven Engineering Languages and Systems (MODELS)*, ser. Lecture Notes in Computer Science (LNCS), A. Schürr and B. Selic, Eds., vol. 5795. Springer, 2009, pp. 77–91. https://doi.org/10.1007/978-3-8348-9788-6/_9

[305] S. Peldszus, A. S. Ahmadian, M. Salnitri, J. Jürjens, M. Pavlidis, and H. Mouratidis, *Visual Privacy Management*. Springer, 2020, ch. Visual Privacy Management, pp. 77–108. https://doi.org/10.1007/978-3-030-59944-7_4

[306] M. Reininger, "End-to-End Security in a Reinsurance Company, Remote Access to the Company Network," Master's thesis, TU Munich, 2006.

[307] A. Capozucca, B. Cheng, G. Georg, N. Guelfi, P. Istoan, G. Mussbacher, A. Jensen, J.-M. Jézéquel, J. Kienzle, J. Klein *et al.*, "Requirements Definition Document for a Software Product Line of Car Crash Management Systems," Colorado State University, Tech. Rep. CS-11-105, 2011. [Online]. Available: https://www.cs.colostate.edu/TechReports/Reports/2011/tr11-105.pdf

[308] D. Strüber, T. Kehrer, T. Arendt, C. Pietsch, and D. Reuling, "Scalability of Model Transformations: Position Paper and Benchmark Set," in *Proceedings of the 4rd Workshop on Scalable Model Driven Engineering (BigMDE)*, ser. CEUR Workshop Proceedings, D. Kolovos, D. D. Ruscio, N. Matragkas, J. S. Cuadrado, I. Rath, and M. Tisi,

Eds., vol. 1652, 2016, pp. 21–30. [Online]. Available: http://ceur-ws.org/Vol-1652/paper3.pdf

[309] A. Hern and agencies, "Apple Removes Malicious Programs After First Major Attack on App Store," The Guardian online, 2015. [Online]. Available: https://www.theguardian.com/technology/2015/sep/21/apple-removes-malicious-programs-after-first-major-attack-on-app-store?CMP=share_btn_link

[310] D. Spaar and F. A. Scherschel, "Beemer, Open Thyself! – Security Vulnerabilities in BMW's ConnectedDrive," *c't – Magazin für Computertechnik*, vol. 5, pp. 86–89, 2015. [Online]. Available: https://heise.de/-2540957

[311] H. Bruneliere, E. Burger, J. Cabot, and M. Wimmer, "A Feature-based Survey of Model View Approaches," *Software & Systems Modeling (SoSyM)*, pp. 1–22, 2017. https://doi.org/10.1007/s10270-017-0622-9

[312] C. Kästner, S. Apel, and M. Kuhlemann, "Granularity in Software Product Lines," in *Proceedings of the 30th International Conference on Software Engineering (ICSE)*. Association for Computing Machinery (ACM), 2008, pp. 311–320. https://doi.org/10.1145/1368088.1368131

[313] D. Strüber, S. Peldszus, and J. Jürjens, "Taming Multi-Variability of Software Product Line Transformations," in *Proceedings of the 21st International Conference on Fundamental Approaches in Software Engineering (FASE)*, ser. Lecture Notes in Computer Science (LNCS), A. Russo and A. Schürr, Eds., vol. 10802. Springer, 2018, pp. 337–355. https://doi.org/10.1007/978-3-319-89363-1_19

[314] S. Schulze, T. Thüm, M. Kuhlemann, and G. Saake, "Variant-preserving Refactoring in Feature-oriented Software Product Lines," in *Proceedings of the 6th International Workshop on Variability Modeling of Software-intensive Systems (VAMOS)*, ser. International Conference Proceeding Series (ICPS). Association for Computing Machinery (ACM), 2012, pp. 73–81. https://doi.org/10.1145/2110147.2110156

[315] P. Borba, L. Teixeira, and R. Gheyi, "A Theory of Software Product Line Refinement," *Theoretical Computer Science*, vol. 455, pp. 2–30, 2012. https://doi.org/10.1016/j.tcs.2012.01.031

[316] S. Lity, M. Kowal, and I. Schaefer, "Higher-order Delta Modeling for Software Product Line Evolution," in *Proceedings of the 7th International Workshop on Feature-oriented Software (FOSD)*. Association for Computing Machinery (ACM), 2016, pp. 39–48. https://doi.org/10.1145/3001867.3001872

[317] R. Salay, M. Famelis, J. Rubin, A. D. Sandro, and M. Chechik, "Lifting Model Transformations to Product Lines," in *Proceedings of the 36th International Conference on Software Engineering (ICSE)*. Association for Computing Machinery (ACM), 2014, pp. 117–128. https://doi.org/10.1145/2568225.2568267

[318] D. Kolovos, L. Rose, N. Matragkas, R. Paige, E. Guerra, J. S. Cuadrado, J. De Lara, I. Ráth, D. Varró, M. Tisi, and J. Cabot, "A Research Roadmap towards Achieving Scalability in Model Driven Engineering," in *Proceedings of the Workshop on Scalability in Model Driven Engineering (BigMDE)*, D. D. Ruscio, D. S. Kolovos, and N. Matragkas, Eds. Association for Computing Machinery (ACM), 2013, pp. 1–10. https://doi.org/10.1145/2487766.2487768

[319] M. Sijtema, "Introducing Variability Rules in ATL for Managing Variability in MDE-based Product Lines," in *Proceedings of the 2nd Workshop on Model Transformation with ATL (MTATL)*, ser. CEUR Workshop Proceedings, M. D. D. Fabro, F. Jouault,

and I. Kurtev, Eds., vol. 711. CEUR-WS, 2010, pp. 39–49. [Online]. Available: http://ceur-ws.org/Vol-711/paper5.pdf

[320] A. Anjorin, K. Saller, M. Lochau, and A. Schürr, "Modularizing Triple Graph Grammars Using Rule Refinement," in *Proceedings of the 17th International Conference on Fundamental Approaches to Software Engineering (FASE)*, ser. Lecture Notes in Computer Science (LNCS), S. Gnesi and A. Rensink, Eds., vol. 8411. Springer, 2014, pp. 340–355. https://doi.org/10.1007/978-3-642-54804-8_24

[321] J. Hussein, L. Moreau *et al.*, "A Template-based Graph Transformation System for the PROV Data Model," in *Proceedings of the 7th International Workshop on Graph Computation Models (GCM)*, 2016.

[322] D. Strüber, "Model-Driven Engineering in the Large: Refactoring Techniques for Models and Model Transformation Systems," Ph.D. dissertation, Philipps-Universität Marburg, 2016.

[323] D. Strüber, J. Rubin, T. Arendt, M. Chechik, G. Taentzer, and J. Plöger, "Variability-based Model Transformation: Formal Foundation and Application," *Formal Aspects of Computing (FAOC)*, vol. 30, no. 1, pp. 133–162, 2018. https://doi.org/10.1007/s00165-017-0441-3

[324] C. Kästner, S. Apel, S. Trujillo, M. Kuhlemann, and D. Batory, "Language-independent Safe Decomposition of Legacy Applications into Features," University of Magdeburg, Tech. Rep., 2008.

[325] A. Di Sandro, R. Salay, M. Famelis, S. Kokaly, and M. Chechik, "MMINT: A Graphical Tool for Interactive Model Management," in *Proceedings of the Posters & Demonstrations at the Models Conference*, ser. CEUR Workshop Proceedings, V. Kulkarni and O. Badreddin, Eds., vol. 1554. CEUR-WS, 2015, pp. 16–19. [Online]. Available: http://ceur-ws.org/Vol-1554/PD_MoDELS_2015_paper_6.pdf

[326] D. Strüber and S. Schulz, "A Tool Environment for Managing Families of Model Transformation Rules," in *Proceedings of the International Conference on Graph Transformation (ICGT)*, ser. Lecture Notes in Computer Science (LNCS), R. Echahed and M. Minas, Eds., vol. 9761. Springer, 2016, pp. 89–101. https://doi.org/10.1007/978-3-319-40530-8_6

[327] J. Rubin and M. Chechik, "Combining Related Products into Product Lines," in *Proceedings of the International Conference on Fundamental Approaches to Software Engineering (FASE)*, ser. Lecture Notes in Computer Science (LNCS), J. de Lara and A. Zisman, Eds., vol. 7212. Springer, 2012, pp. 285–300. https://doi.org/10.1007/978-3-642-28872-2_20

[328] D. Strüber, J. Rubin, T. Arendt, M. Chechik, G. Taentzer, and J. Plöger, "RuleMerger: Automatic Construction of Variability-Based Model Transformation Rules," in *Proceedings of the 19th International Conference on Fundamental Approaches to Software Engineering (FASE)*, ser. Lecture Notes in Computer Science (LNCS), P. Stevens and A. Wąsowski, Eds., vol. 9633. Springer, 2016, pp. 122–140. https://doi.org/10.1007/978-3-662-49665-7_8

[329] K. Czarnecki and S. Helsen, "Feature-Based Survey of Model Transformation Approaches," *IBM Systems Journal*, vol. 45, no. 3, pp. 621–645, 2006. https://doi.org/10.1147/sj.453.0621

[330] E. Richa, E. Borde, and L. Pautet, "Translation of ATL to AGT and Application to a Code Generator for Simulink," *Software & Systems Modeling (SoSyM)*, vol. 18, pp. 321–344, 2017. https://doi.org/10.1007/s10270-017-0607-8

[331] I. Rychkova, M. Kirsch-Pinheiro, and B. L. Grand, "Context-Aware Agile Business Process Engine: Foundations and Architecture," in *Proceedings of the 14th Working Conference on Business Process Modeling, Development, and Support (BPMDS)*, ser. Lecture Notes in Business Information Processing (LNBIP), S. Nurcan, H. A. Proper, P. Soffer, J. Krogstie, R. Schmidt, and T. H. Bider, Eds., vol. 147. Springer, 2013, pp. 31–47. https://doi.org/10.1007/978-3-642-38484-4_4

[332] M. Chechik, M. Famelis, R. Salay, and D. Strüber, "Perspectives of Model Transformation Reuse," in *Proceedings of the 12th International Conference on Integrated Formal Methods (IFM)*, ser. Lecture Notes in Computer Science (LNCS), E. Ábrahám and M. Huisman, Eds., vol. 9681. Springer, 2016, pp. 28–44. https://doi.org/10.1007/978-3-319-33693-0_3

[333] A. Habel, R. Heckel, and G. Taentzer, "Graph Grammars with Negative Application Conditions," *Fundamenta Informaticae*, vol. 26, no. 3/4, pp. 287–313, 1996.

[334] T. Kehrer, U. Kelter, and G. Taentzer, "A Rule-based Approach to the Semantic Lifting of Model Differences in the Context of Model Versioning," in *Proceedings of the 26th International Conference of Automated Software Engineering (ASE)*. IEEE Computer Society, 2011, pp. 163–172. https://doi.org/10.1109/ASE.2011.6100050

[335] D. Strüber, J. Plöger, and V. Acretoaie, "Clone Detection for Graph-Based Model Transformation Languages," in *Proceedings of the 9th International Conference on Theory and Practice of Model Transformations (ICMT)*, ser. Lecture Notes in Computer Science (LNCS), P. V. Gorp and G. Engels, Eds., vol. 9765. Springer, 2016, pp. 191–206. https://doi.org/10.1007/978-3-319-42064-6_13

[336] E. Biermann, C. Ermel, and G. Taentzer, "Lifting Parallel Graph Transformation Concepts to Model Transformation Based on the Eclipse Modeling Framework," *Electronic Communications of the EASST*, vol. 26, 2010. https://doi.org/10.14279/tuj.eceasst.26.353

[337] D. Strüber, A. Anjorin, and T. Berger, "Variability Representations in Class Models: An Empirical Assessment," in *Proceedings of the 23rd International Conference on Model Driven Engineering Languages and Systems (MODELS)*. Association for Computing Machinery (ACM), 2020, pp. 240–251. https://doi.org/10.1145/3365438.3410935

[338] G. Perrouin, M. Amrani, M. Acher, B. Combemale, A. Legay, and P.-Y. Schobbens, "Featured Model Types: Towards Systematic Reuse in Modelling Language Engineering," in *Proceedings of the 8th International Workshop on Modeling in Software Engineering (MISE)*. Association for Computing Machinery (ACM), 2016, pp. 1–7. https://doi.org/10.1145/2896982.2896987

[339] D. Batory, "Feature-oriented Programming and the AHEAD Tool Suite," in *Proceedings of the International Conference on Software Engineering (ICSE)*. IEEE Computer Science, 2004, pp. 702–703. https://doi.org/10.1109/ICSE.2004.1317496

[340] S. Trujillo, D. Batory, and O. Diaz, "Feature Oriented Model Driven Development: A Case Study for Portlets," in *Proceedings of the International Conference on Software Engineering (ICSE)*. IEEE Computer Society, 2007, pp. 44–53. https://doi.org/10.1109/ICSE.2007.36

[341] L. Lambers, D. Strüber, G. Taentzer, K. Born, and J. Huebert, "Multi-granular Conflict and Dependency Analysis in Software Engineering Based on Graph Transformation," in *Proceedings of the 40th International Conference on Software Engineering (ICSE)*. Association for Computing Machinery (ACM), 2018, pp. 716–727. https://doi.org/10.1145/3180155.3180258

[342] P. Runeson and M. Höst, "Guidelines for Conducting and Reporting Case Study Research in Software Engineering," *Empirical Software Engineering (EMSE)*, vol. 14, no. 131, 2009. https://doi.org/10.1007/s10664-008-9102-8

[343] J. Bürger, S. Gärtner, T. Ruhroth, J. Zweihoff, J. Jürjens, and K. Schneider, "Restoring Security of Long-living Systems by Co-evolution," in *Proceedings of the 39th Annual Computer Software and Applications Conference (COMPSAC)*, vol. 2, 2015, pp. 153–158.

[344] T. A. Wagner and S. L. Graham, "Efficient and Flexible Incremental Parsing," *Transactions on Programming Languages and Systems (TOPLAS)*, vol. 20, no. 5, pp. 980–1013, 1998. https://doi.org/10.1145/293677.293678

[345] S. Winkler and J. von Pilgrim, "A Survey of Traceability in Requirements Engineering and Model-driven Development," *Software & Systems Modeling (SoSyM)*, vol. 9, pp. 529–565, 2010. https://doi.org/10.1007/s10270-009-0145-0

[346] C. Atkinson, D. Stoll, and P. Bostan, "Orthographic Software Modeling: A Practical Approach to View-based Development," in *Proceedings of the International Conference on Evaluation of Novel Approaches to Software Engineering (ENASE)*, ser. Communications in Computer and Information Science (CCIS), L. Maciaszek, C. González-Pérez, and S. Jablonski, Eds., vol. 69. Springer, 2009, pp. 206–219. https://doi.org/10.1007/978-3-642-14819-4_15

[347] M. E. Kramer, E. Burger, and M. Langhammer, "View-centric Engineering with Synchronized Heterogeneous Models," in *Proceedings of the 1st Workshop on View-based, Aspect-oriented and Orthographic Software Modelling (VAO)*. Association for Computing Machinery (ACM), 2013. https://doi.org/10.1145/2489861.2489864

[348] M. Konersmann, "Explicitly Integrated Architecture-an Approach for Integrating Software Architecture Model Information with Program Code," Ph.D. dissertation, University of Duisburg-Essen, 2018.

[349] J. Bezivin, F. Jouault, and P. Valduriez, "On the Need for Megamodels," in *Proceedings of the OOPSLA & GPCE Workshop Workshopon Best Practices for Model-driven Software Development*, 2004.

[350] J. McKinna and P. Stevens, "How to Regain Equilibrium without Losing your Balance? Scenarios for BX Deployment (Discussion Paper)," in *Proceedings of the 5th International Workshop on Bidirectional Transformations (BX)*, ser. CEUR Workshop Proceedings, A. Anjorin and J. Gibbons, Eds., vol. 1571. CEUR-WS, 2016, pp. 32–34. [Online]. Available: http://ceur-ws.org/Vol-1571/paper_12.pdf

[351] P. Stevens, "Connecting Software Build with Maintaining Consistency between Models: Towards Sound, Optimal, and Flexible Building from Megamodels," *Software and Systems Modeling (SoSyM)*, vol. 19, pp. 935–958, 2020. https://doi.org/10.1007/s10270-020-00788-4

[352] "Enterprise Architect." [Online]. Available: http://www.sparxsystems.de

[353] W. Fang, B. P. Miller, and J. A. Kupsch, "Automated Tracing and Visualization of Software Security Structure and Properties," in *Proceedings of the 9th International*

Symposium on Visualization for Cyber Security (VIZSEC), ser. International Conference Proceeding Series (ICPS). Association for Computing Machinery (ACM), 2012, pp. 9–16. https://doi.org/10.1145/2379690.2379692

[354] A. Nhlabatsi, Y. Yu, A. Zisman, T. Tun, N. Khan, A. Bandara, and B. Nuseibeh, "Managing Security Control Assumptions using Causal Traceability," in *Proceedings of the 8ᵗʰ International Symposium on Software and Systems Traceability (SST)*. IEEE Computer Society, 2015. https://doi.org/10.1109/SST.2015.14

[355] B. Dit, M. Revelle, M. Gethers, and D. Poshyvanyk, "Feature Location in Source Code: A Taxonomy and Survey," *Journal of Software: Evolution and Process*, vol. 25, no. 1, pp. 53–95, 2013. https://doi.org/10.1002/smr.567

[356] J. Rubin and M. Chechik, "A Survey of Feature Location Techniques," in *Domain Engineering: Product Lines, Conceptual Models, and Languages*, I. Reinhartz-Berger, A. Sturm, T. Clark, S. Cohen, and J. Bettin, Eds. Springer, 2013, pp. 29–58. https://doi.org/10.1007/978-3-642-36654-3_2

[357] W. Zhao, L. Zhang, Y. Liu, J. Sun, and F. Yang, "SNIAFL: Towards a Static Noninteractive Approach to Feature Location," *Transactions on Software Engineering and Methodology (TOSEM)*, vol. 15, no. 2, pp. 195–226, 2006. https://doi.org/10.1145/1131421.1131424

[358] D. Strüber, J. Rubin, G. Taentzer, and M. Chechik, "Splitting Models Using Information Retrieval and Model Crawling Techniques," in *Proceedings of the 17ᵗʰ International Conference on Fundamental Approaches to Software Engineering (FASE)*, ser. Lecture Notes in Computer Science (LNCS), S. Gnesi and A. Rensink, Eds., vol. 8411. Springer, 2014, pp. 47–62. https://doi.org/10.1007/978-3-642-54804-8_4

[359] J. Font, L. Arcega, Ø. Haugen, and C. Cetina, "Feature Location in Models through a Genetic Algorithm Driven by Information Retrieval Techniques," in *Proceedings of the 19ᵗʰ International Conference on Model-driven Engineering Languages and Systems (MODELS)*. Association for Computing Machinery (ACM), 2016, pp. 272–282. https://doi.org/10.1145/2976767.2976789

[360] K. Lano, D. Clark, and K. Androutsopoulos, "Safety and Security Analysis of Object-Oriented Models," in *Proceedings of the 21ˢᵗ International Conference on Computer Safety, Reliability and Security (SafeComp)*, ser. Lecture Notes in Computer Science (LNCS), S. Anderson, M. Felici, and S. Bologna, Eds., vol. 2434. Springer, 2002, pp. 82–93. https://doi.org/10.1007/3-540-45732-1_10

[361] P. H. Nguyen, M. Kramer, J. Klein, and Y. L. Traon, "An Extensive Systematic Review on the Model-Driven Development of Secure Systems," *Information and Software Technology (IST)*, vol. 68, pp. 62–81, 2015. https://doi.org/10.1016/j.infsof.2015.08.006

[362] J. Jürjens, "Secure Information Flow for Concurrent Processes," in *Proceedings of the 11ᵗʰ International Conference on Concurrency Theory (CONCUR)*, ser. Lecture Notes in Computer Science (LNCS), C. Palamidessi, Ed., vol. 1877. Springer, 2000, pp. 395–409. https://doi.org/10.1007/3-540-44618-4_29

[363] J. Jürjens, "Modelling Audit Security for Smart-Card Payment Schemes with UMLSec," in *Proceedings on the International Conference on Ict Systems Security and Privacy Protection – Trusted Information: The New Decade Challenge*, ser. IFIP International Federation for Information Processing (IFIPAICT), M. Dupuy and P. Paradi-

nas, Eds., vol. 65. Springer, 2001, pp. 93–107. https://doi.org/10.1007/0-306-46998-7_7

[364] A. S. Ahmadian, F. Coerschulte, and J. Jürjens, "Supporting the Security Certification and Privacy Level Agreements in the Context of Clouds," in *Proceedings of the 5th International Symposium on Business Modeling and Software Design (BMSD)*, ser. Lecture Notes in Business Information Processing (LNBIP), B. Shishkov, Ed., vol. 257. Springer, 2016, pp. 80–95. https://doi.org/10.1007/978-3-319-40512-4_5

[365] S. Ahmadian and J. Jürjens, "Supporting Model-based Privacy Analysis by Exploiting Privacy Level Agreements," in *Proceedings of the International Conference on Cloud Computing Technology and Science (CloudCom)*, R. Bilof, Ed. IEEE Computer Society, 2016, pp. 360–365. https://doi.org/10.1109/CloudCom.2016.0063

[366] A. S. Ahmadian, D. Strüber, V. Riediger, and J. Jürjens, "Model-based Privacy Analysis in Industrial Ecosystems," in *Proceedings of the 13th European Conference on Modelling Foundations and Applications (ECMFA)*, ser. Lecture Notes in Computer Science (LNCS), A. Anjorin and H. Espinoza, Eds., vol. 10376. Springer, 2017, pp. 215–231. https://doi.org/10.1007/978-3-319-61482-3_13

[367] A. S. Ahmadian, "Model-Based Privacy by Design," Ph.D. dissertation, University of Koblenz-Landau, 2020.

[368] Q. Ramadan, "Data protection assurance by design: Support for conflict detection, requirements traceability and fairness analysis," Ph.D. dissertation, University of Koblenz and Landau, 2020.

[369] Q. Ramadan, A. S. Ahmadian, J. Jürjens, S. Staab, and D. Strüber, "Explaining Algorithmic Decisions with respect to Fairness," in *Proceedings of the Multi-Conference on Software Engineering and Software Management (SE/SWM)*, S. Becker, I. Bogicevic, G. Herzwurm, and S. Wagner, Eds. Gesellschaft für Informatik e.V., 2019, pp. 161–162. https://doi.org/10.18420/se2019-50

[370] Q. Ramadan, A. S. Ahmadian, D. Strüber, J. Jürjens, and S. Staab, "Model-Based Discrimination Analysis: A Position Paper," in *Proceedings of the International Workshop on Software Fairness*. Association for Computing Machinery (ACM), 2018, p. 22–28. https://doi.org/10.1145/3194770.3194775

[371] I. Siveroni, A. Zisman, and G. Spanoudakis, "A UML-based Static Verification Framework for Security," *Requirements Engineering Journal (RE)*, vol. 15, no. 1, pp. 95–118, 2010. https://doi.org/10.1007/s00766-009-0091-y

[372] B. Katt, M. Gander, R. Breu, and M. Felderer, "Enhancing Model Driven Security through Pattern Refinement Techniques," in *Proceedings of the 10th International Symposium on Formal Methods for Components and Objects (FMCO)*, ser. Lecture Notes in Computer Science (LNCS), B. Beckert, F. Damiani, F. S. de Boer, and M. M. Bonsangue, Eds., vol. 7542. Springer, 2011, pp. 169–183. https://doi.org/10.1007/978-3-642-35887-6_9

[373] P. H. Nguyen, K. Yskout, T. Heyman, J. Klein, R. Scandariato, and Y. L. Traon, "SoSPa: A System of Security Design Patterns for Systematically Engineering Secure Systems," in *Proceedings of the 18th International Conference on Model-driven Engineering Languages and Systems (MODELS)*. IEEE Computer Society, 2015, pp. 246–255. https://doi.org/10.1109/MODELS.2015.7338255

[374] K. Yskout, R. Scandariato, and W. Joosen, "Do Security Patterns Really Help Designers?" in *Proceedings of the 37th International Conference on Software Engineering*

(ICSE). IEEE Computer Society, 2015, pp. 292–302. https://doi.org/10.1109/ICSE. 2015.49

[375] G. Georg, I. Ray, K. Anastasakis, B. Bordbar, M. Toahchoodee, and S. H. Houmb, "An Aspect-oriented Methodology for Designing Secure Applications," *Information and Software Technology (IST)*, vol. 51, no. 5, pp. 846–864, 2009. https://doi.org/10.1016/ j.infsof.2008.05.004

[376] C. L. Heitmeyer, M. Archer, E. I. Leonard, and J. McLean, "Applying Formal Methods to a Certifiably Secure Software System," *Transactions on Software Engineering (TSE)*, vol. 34, no. 1, pp. 82–98, 2008. https://doi.org/10.1109/TSE.2007.70772

[377] Q. Ramadan, M. Salnitri, D. Strüber, J. Jürjens, and P. Giorgini, "From Secure Business Process Modeling to Design-Level Security Verification," in *Proceedings of the 20th International Conference on Model-driven Engineering Languages and Systems (MODELS)*. IEEE Computer Society, 2017, pp. 123–133. https://doi.org/10.1109/ MODELS.2017.10

[378] M. Salnitri, F. Dalpiaz, and P. Giorgini, "Designing Secure Business Processes with SecBPMN," *Software & Systems Modeling (SoSyM)*, vol. 16, no. 3, pp. 737–757, 2017. https://doi.org/10.1007/s10270-015-0499-4

[379] P. H. Nguyen, G. Nain, J. Klein, T. Mouelhi, and Y. L. Traon, "Modularity and Dynamic Adaptation of Flexibly Secure Systems: Model-Driven Adaptive Delegation in Access Control Management," *Transactions on Aspect-Oriented Software Development (AOSD)*, vol. XI, pp. 109–144, 2014. https://doi.org/10.1007/978-3-642-55099- 7_4

[380] P. H. Nguyen, "Model-Driven Security With Modularity and Reusability for Engineering Secure Software Systems," Ph.D. dissertation, Université du Luxembourg, 2015.

[381] I. Schieferdecker, J. Grossmann, and M. Schneider, "Model-Based Security Testing," in *Proceedings of the 7th Workshop on Model-Based Testing (MBT)*, ser. Electronic Proceedings in Theoretical Computer Science (EPTCS), vol. 80. Open Publishing Association, 2012, pp. 1–12. https://doi.org/10.4204/EPTCS.80.1

[382] M. Abi-Antoun, D. Wang, and P. Torr, "Checking Threat Modeling Data Flow Diagrams for Implementation Conformance and Security," in *Proceedings of the 22nd International Conference of Automated Software Engineering (ASE)*. Association for Computing Machinery (ACM), 2007, pp. 393–396. https://doi.org/10.1145/1321631. 1321692

[383] S. M. Perez, J. García-Alfaro, F. Cuppens, N. Cuppens-Boulahia, and J. Cabot, "Model-Driven Extraction and Analysis of Network Security Policies," in *Proceedings of the International Conference on Model-driven Engineering Languages and Systems (MODELS)*, ser. Lecture Notes in Computer Science (LNCS), A. Moreira, B. Schätz, J. Gray, A. Vallecillo, and P. Clarke, Eds., vol. 8107. Springer, 2013, pp. 52–68. https:// doi.org/10.1007/978-3-642-41533-3_4

[384] S. Martínez, V. Cosentino, and J. Cabot, "Model-based Analysis of Java EE Web Security Configurations," in *Proceedings of the 8th International Workshop on Modeling in Software Engineering (MISE)*. Association for Computing Machinery (ACM), 2016, pp. 55–61. https://doi.org/10.1145/2896982.2896986

[385] M. Anisetti, C. A. Ardagna, and E. Damiani, "A Low-Cost Security Certification Scheme for Evolving Services," in *Proceedings of the 19th International Conference*

on *Web Services (ICWS)*, R. Bilof, Ed. IEEE Computer Society, 2012, pp. 122–129. https://doi.org/10.1109/ICWS.2012.53

[386] R. F. Paige, P. J. Brooke, and J. S. Ostroff, "Metamodel-based Model Conformance and Multiview Consistency Checking," *Transactions on Software Engineering and Methodology (TOSEM)*, vol. 16, no. 3, p. 11, 2007. https://doi.org/10.1145/1243987. 1243989

[387] Z. Diskin, Y. Xiong, and K. Czarnecki, "Specifying Overlaps of Heterogeneous Models for Global Consistency Checking," in *Proceedings of the International Conference on Model-driven Engineering Languages and Systems (MODELS)*, ser. Lecture Notes in Computer Science (LNCS), J. Dingel and A. Solberg, Eds., vol. 6627. Springer, 2010, pp. 165–179. https://doi.org/10.1007/978-3-642-21210-9_16

[388] H. König and Z. Diskin, "Efficient Consistency Checking of Interrelated Models," in *Proceedings of the 13th European Conference on Modelling Foundations and Applications (ECMFA)*, ser. Lecture Notes in Computer Science (LNCS), A. Anjorin and H. Espinoza, Eds., vol. 10376, 2017, pp. 161–178. https://doi.org/10.1007/978-3-319-61482-3_10

[389] A. Reder and A. Egyed, "Incremental Consistency Checking for Complex Design Rules and Larger Model Changes," in *Proceedings of the International Conference on Model-driven Engineering Languages and Systems (MODELS)*, 2012, pp. 202–218.

[390] F. Simon, F. Steinbruckner, and C. Lewerentz, "Metrics Based Refactoring," in *Proceedings 5th European Conference on Software Maintenance and Reengineering (CSMR)*. IEEE Computer Society, 2001, pp. 30–38. https://doi.org/10.1109/CSMR. 2001.914965

[391] M. Mäntylä, "Bad Smells in Software – A Taxonomy and an Empirical Study," Master's thesis, Helsinki University of Technology, 2003.

[392] M. J. Munro, "Product Metrics for Automatic Identification of Bad Smell Design Problems in Java Source-Code," in *Proceedings of the 11th International Software Metrics Symposium (METRICS)*. IEEE Computer Society, 2005, pp. 15–15. https://doi.org/10.1109/METRICS.2005.38

[393] S. Lee, S. Hwang, and S. Ryu, "All about Activity Injection: Threats, Semantics, and Detection," in *Proceedings of the 32nd International Conference on Automated Software Engineering (ASE)*. IEEE Computer Society, 2017, pp. 252–262. https://doi. org/10.1109/ASE.2017.8115638

[394] I. Ion, B. Dragovic, and B. Crispo, "Extending the Java Virtual Machine to Enforce Fine-Grained Security Policies in Mobile Devices," in *Proceedings of the 23rd Annual Computer Security Applications Conference (ACSAC)*. IEEE Computer Society, 2007, pp. 233–242. https://doi.org/10.1109/ACSAC.2007.36

[395] C.-A. Staicu, M. Pradel, and B. Livshits, "SYNODE Understanding and Automatically Preventing Injection Attacks on NODE.JS," *Proceedings of the Network and Distributed System Security Symposium (NDSS)*, 2018. https://doi.org/10.14722/ndss. 2018.23071

[396] S. Ognawala, M. Ochoa, A. Pretschner, and T. Limmer, "Macke: Compositional Analysis of Low-level Vulnerabilities with Symbolic Execution," in *Proceedings of the 31st International Conference on Automated Software Engineering (ASE)*. Association for Computing Machinery (ACM), 2016, pp. 780–785. https://doi.org/10.1145/2970276. 2970281

[397] T. W. Pratt, "A Hierarchical Graph Model of the Semantics of Programs," in *Proceedings of the American Federation of Information Processing Societies (AFIPS) Spring Joint Computer Conference (SJCC)*. Association for Computing Machinery (ACM), 1969, pp. 813–825. https://doi.org/10.1145/1476793.1476930

[398] B. Hoffmann, D. Janssens, and N. Van Eetvelde, "Cloning and Expanding Graph Transformation Rules for Refactoring," *Electronic Notes in Theoretical Computer Science (ENTCS)*, vol. 152, pp. 53–67, 2006. https://doi.org/10.1016/j.entcs.2006.01.014

[399] MelinaMongiovi, R. Gheyi, G. Soares, L. Teixeira, and P. Borba, "Making Refactoring Safer Through Impact Analysis," *Science of Computer Programming*, vol. 93, no. A, pp. 39–64, 2014. https://doi.org/10.1016/j.scico.2013.11.001

[400] S. Ghaith and M. Ó Cinnéide, "Improving Software Security using Search-based Refactoring," in *Proceedings of the 4th International Symposium Onsearch Based Software Engineering (SSBSE)*, ser. Lecture Notes in Computer Science (LNCS), G. Fraser and J. T. de Souza, Eds., vol. 7515. Springer, 2012, pp. 121–135. https://doi.org/10.1007/978-3-642-33119-0_10

[401] C. Abid, V. Alizadeh, M. Kessentini, M. Dhaouadi, and R. Kazman, "Prioritizing Refactorings for Security-critical Code," *Automated Software Engineering*, vol. 28, no. 4, 2021. https://doi.org/10.1007/s10515-021-00281-2

[402] T. Thüm, D. Batory, and C. Kästner, "Reasoning About Edits to Feature Models," in *Proceedings of the 31st International Conference on Software Engineering (ICSE)*. IEEE Computer Society, 2009, pp. 254–264. https://doi.org/10.1109/ICSE.2009.5070526

[403] J. Bürdek, T. Kehrer, M. Lochau, D. Reuling, U. Kelter, and A. Schürr, "Reasoning About Product-Line Evolution using Complex Feature Model Differences," *Automated Software Engineering*, vol. 23, no. 4, pp. 687–733, 2016. https://doi.org/10.1007/s10515-015-0185-3

[404] G. Taentzer, R. Salay, D. Strüber, and M. Chechik, "Transformations of Software Product Lines: A Generalizing Framework based on Category Theory," in *Proceedings of the 20th International Conference on Model-driven Engineering Languages and Systems (MODELS)*. IEEE Computer Society, 2017, pp. 101–111. https://doi.org/10.1109/MODELS.2017.22

[405] I. Schaefer, L. Bettini, V. Bono, F. Damiani, and N. Tanzarella, "Delta-oriented Programming of Software Product Lines," in *Proceedings of the International Conference on Software Product Lines (SPLC)*, ser. Lecture Notes in Computer Science (LNCS), J. Bosch and J. Lee, Eds., vol. 6287. Springer, 2010, pp. 77–91. https://doi.org/10.1007/978-3-642-15579-6_6

[406] F. Damiani, R. Hähnle, E. Kamburjan, and M. Lienhardt, "A Unified and Formal Programming Model for Deltas and Traits," in *Proceedings of the 20th International Conference on Fundamental Approaches to Software Engineering (FASE)*, ser. Lecture Notes in Computer Science (LNCS), M. Huisman and J. Rubin, Eds., vol. 10202, Springer. Springer, 2017, pp. 424–441. https://doi.org/10.1007/978-3-662-54494-5_25

[407] X. He, Z. Hu, and Y. Liu, "Towards Variability Management in Bidirectional Model Transformation," in *Proceedings of the 41st Annual Computer Software and Applications Conference (COMPSAC)*, vol. 1. IEEE Computer Society, 2017, pp. 224–233. https://doi.org/10.1109/COMPSAC.2017.252

[408] A. Rensink, "Compositionality in Graph Transformation," in *Proceedings of the International Colloquium on Automata, Languages and Programming (ICALP)*, ser. Lecture Notes in Computer Science (LNCS), S. Abramsky, C. Gavoille, C. Kirchner, F. Meyer auf der Heide, and P. G. Spirakis, Eds., vol. 6199. Springer, 2010, pp. 309–320. https://doi.org/10.1007/978-3-642-14162-1_26

[409] L. Sion, D. V. Landuyt, K. Yskout, and W. Joosen, "Towards Systematically Addressing Security Variability in Software Product Lines," in *Proceedings of the 20th International Systems and Software Product Line Conference (SPLC)*, ser. International Conference Proceeding Series (ICPS), H. Mei, R. Rabiser, B. Xie, C. Elsner, Y. Xie, J. Andersson, A. R. Cortés, K. Czarnecki, B. Selic, A. Wąsowski, X. Peng, J. Simmonds, J. Wei, T. Berger, N. Siegmund, L. Zhang, E. Bagheri, and Y. Xiong, Eds. Association for Computing Machinery (ACM), 2016, pp. 342–343. https://doi.org/10.1145/2934466.2966353

[410] V. Myllärniemi, M. Raatikainen, and T. Männistö, "Representing and Configuring Security Variability in Software Product Lines," in *Proceedings of the 11th International Conference on Quality of Software Architectures (QOSA)*. Association for Computing Machinery (ACM), 2015, pp. 1–10. https://doi.org/10.1145/2737182.2737183

[411] S. Nadi and S. Krüger, "Variability Modeling of Cryptographic Components: Clafer Experience Report," in *Proceedings of the 10th International Workshop on Variability Modelling of Software-intensive (VAMOS)*, ser. International Conference Proceeding Series (ICPS), I. Schaefer, V. Alves, and E. S. de Almeida, Eds. Association for Computing Machinery (ACM), 2016, pp. 105–112. https://doi.org/10.1145/2866614.2866629

[412] D. Mellado, E. Fernández-Medina, and M. Piattini, "Towards Security Requirements Management for Software Product Lines: A Security Domain Requirements Engineering Process," *Computer Standards & Interfaces*, vol. 30, no. 6, pp. 361–371, 2008. https://doi.org/10.1016/j.csi.2008.03.004

[413] D. Mellado, H. Mouratidis, and E. Fernández-Medina, "Secure Tropos Framework for Software Product Lines Requirements Engineering," *Computer Standards & Interfaces*, vol. 36, no. 4, pp. 711–722, 2014. https://doi.org/10.1016/j.csi.2013.12.006

[414] T. E. Fægri and S. O. Hallsteinsen, "A Software Product Line Reference Architecture for Security," in *Software Product Lines*, T. Käköla and J. C. Duenas, Eds. Springer, 2006, ch. Product Line Architecture, pp. 275–326. https://doi.org/10.1007/978-3-540-33253-4_8

[415] T. Thüm, S. Apel, C. Kästner, I. Schaefer, and G. Saake, "A Classification and Survey of Analysis Strategies for Software Product Lines," *ACM Computing Surveys*, vol. 47, no. 1, pp. 6:1–6:45, 2014. https://doi.org/10.1145/2580950

[416] M. F. Johansen, Ø. Haugen, F. Fleurey, A. G. Eldegard, and T. Syversen, "Generating Better Partial Covering Arrays by Modeling Weights on Sub-product Lines," in *Proceedings of the 15th International Conference on Model-driven Engineering Languages and Systems (MODELS)*, ser. Lecture Notes in Computer Science (LNCS), R. B. France, J. Kazmeier, R. Breu, and C. Atkinson, Eds., vol. 7590. Springer, 2012, pp. 269–284. https://doi.org/10.1007/978-3-642-33666-9_18

[417] S. Ali, T. Yue, L. C. Briand, and S. Walawege, "A Product Line Modeling and Configuration Methodology to Support Model-Based Testing: An Industrial Case Study," in *Proceedings of the 15th International Conference on Model-driven Engineering*

Languages and Systems (MODELS), ser. Lecture Notes in Computer Science (LNCS), R. B. France, J. Kazmeier, R. Breu, and C. Atkinson, Eds., vol. 7590, 2012, pp. 726–742. https://doi.org/10.1007/978-3-642-33666-9_46

[418] M. Lochau, S. Peldszus, M. Kowal, and I. Schaefer, "Model-based Testing," in *Formal Methods for Executable Software Models (SFM)*, ser. Lecture Notes in Computer Science (LNCS), M. Bernardo, F. Damiani, R. Hähnle, E. B. Johnsen, and I. Schaefer, Eds. Springer, 2014, vol. 8483, pp. 310–342. https://doi.org/10.1007/978-3-319-07317-0_8

[419] R. Lachmann, S. Beddig, S. Lity, S. Schulze, and I. Schaefer, "Risk-based Integration Testing of Software Product Lines," in *Proceedings of the 11th International Workshop on Variability Modelling of Software-intensive Systems (VAMOS)*, ser. International Conference Proceeding Series (ICPS). Association for Computing Machinery (ACM), 2017, pp. 52–59. https://doi.org/10.1145/3023956.3023958

[420] C. Kästner, P. G. Giarrusso, T. Rendel, S. Erdweg, K. Ostermann, and T. Berger, "Variability-aware Parsing in the Presence of Lexical Macros and Conditional Compilation," in *Proceedings of International Conference on Object Oriented Programming Systems Languages and Applications (OOPSLA)*, ser. SIGPLAN Notices, vol. 46, no. 10. Association for Computing Machinery (ACM), 2011, pp. 805–824. https://doi.org/10.1145/2048066.2048128

[421] A. Gruler, M. Leucker, and K. Scheidemann, "Modeling and Model Checking Software Product Lines," in *Proceedings of the International Conference on Formal Methods for Open Object-based Distributed Systems (FMOODS)*, ser. Lecture Notes in Computer Science (LNCS), G. Barthe and F. S. de Boer, Eds., vol. 5051. Springer, 2008, pp. 113–131. https://doi.org/10.1007/978-3-540-68863-1_8

[422] D. C. Schmidt, "Guest Editor's Introduction: Model-driven Engineering," *IEEE Computer*, vol. 39, no. 2, pp. 0025–31, 2006.

[423] B. Rumpe, *Agile Modeling with UML: Code Generation, Testing, Refactoring*. Springer, 2017.

[424] D. Bildhauer and J. Ebert, "Querying Software Abstraction Graphs," in *Working Session on Query Technologies and Applications for Program Comprehension (QTAPC)*, 2008.

[425] J. Ebert and D. Bildhauer, "Reverse Engineering Using Graph Queries," in *Graph Transformations and Model-driven Engineering: Essays Dedicated to Manfred Nagl on the Occasion of his 65th Birthday*, ser. Lecture Notes in Computer Science (LNCS), G. Engels, C. Lewerentz, W. Schäfer, A. Schürr, and B. Westfechtel, Eds. Springer, 2010, vol. 5765, ch. Software Architectures and Reengineering, pp. 335–362.

[426] S. Gärtner, T. Ruhroth, J. Bürger, K. Schneider, and J. Jürjens, "Maintaining Requirements for Long-living Software Systems by Incorporating Security Knowledge," in *Proceedings of the 22nd International Requirements Engineering Conference (RE)*. IEEE Computer Society, 2014, pp. 103–112. https://doi.org/10.1109/RE.2014.6912252

Printed in the United States
by Baker & Taylor Publisher Services